W9-BKM-511

Alfred, Lord Tennyson

IDYLLS OF THE KING

Edited by
J. M. GRAY

NEW HAVEN AND LONDON
YALE UNIVERSITY PRESS

First published in 1983 in the United Kingdom in a paperback edition by Penguin
Books Limited in the series Penguin English Poets. First published 1983 in the
United States of America by Yale University Press.

Introduction and notes copyright © 1983 by J. M. Gray
All rights reserved.
This book may not be reproduced, in whole or in part, in any form (beyond that
copying permitted by Sections 107 and 108 of the U.S. Copyright Law and except
by reviewers for the public press), without written permission from the publishers.

Printed in Great Britain

The English Poets; 16
Library of Congress catalog card number: 82-62851
ISBN 0-300-03059-2
ISBN 0-300-03060-6 (pbk.)

Contents

Table of Dates

Table of Dates

8

Table of Dates

Introduction

As the dates of 'The Lady of Shalott' (1832) and the autobiographical 'Merlin and the Gleam' (1889) show, Tennyson's poetry on Arthurian themes and subjects reflects a lifetime's interest in the legend. Midway through his poetic career is his major serial poem on Arthurian themes *Idylls of the King*, composed in two creative spells (1856–9, 1868–74). The first series, published in 1859, capitalized on the legend's popularity earlier created by the poet in 'Morte d'Arthur' (1842), which was itself to be incorporated in turn into the expanded Arthurian scheme in 1870. Running to well over ten thousand lines of blank verse, *Idylls of the King* is Tennyson's longest and most ambitious work. As early schemes and outlines suggest, the poet had set out almost from the first to treat the legend comprehensively. But to make a suitable poetic synthesis was to take maturity and time. It was not until 1856, when he was forty-seven, that Tennyson knew he was ready, and in 1859 he published the first set of four *Idylls* (later the longest of these was split, making a fifth) based on a very wide reading and assimilation of Arthurian sources and traditions. Of the first series (even then titled *Idylls of the King*) 40,000 copies were sold within a few weeks, and the poem was repeatedly reprinted. Apart from a dedication in 1862 the series was not immediately supplemented, despite its popularity. Tennyson delayed almost a decade, chiefly because of uncertainty as to how the crucial central episode of the Grail should be treated. The poet resolved these difficulties late in 1868, and composed 'The Holy Grail' in a ten-day blaze of inspiration. After this the rest of the poem rapidly took shape. Four more, including the 'Morte d'Arthur' (unchanged except for suitably framing lines to incorporate it into the whole), were published in December 1869 (dated 1870). The next few years saw the remaining three poems completed, and further important supplementation to two others, but Tennyson withheld publication of the last written, 'Balin and Balan', for another decade, until 1885. To the last Tennyson made small but significant supplementation.

Neither these additions and minor modifications nor the long period of supplementation is to be taken as uncertainty over the plan of the serial poem. Each episode is designed and executed to fulfil a separate segment of the whole. The dominant figure round which everything is grouped is Arthur. He is the essential connecting link to the whole series.

Introduction

There are few difficulties associated with editing the text of the *Idylls*. Two editions are of importance. The Eversley Edition is that authorized by Tennyson himself, and it has annotations supplied by the poet and by his elder son, Hallam (indicated by T. and H. T. respectively in the notes). This however has recently been superseded by the comprehensive edition edited by Christopher Ricks. I am greatly indebted to this, especially for identifying major passages of Malory and other Arthurian sources which Tennyson utilized for his poem.

Further Reading

Editions

Idylls of the King annotated by Alfred, Lord Tennyson, edited by Hallam, Lord Tennyson (the Eversley Edition), Macmillan, 1908, 1913.
The Poems of Tennyson edited by Christopher Ricks, Longman, 1969.
A Variorum Edition of Tennyson's 'Idylls of the King' edited by John Pfordresher, Columbia University Press, 1973.

Bibliographies and Reference Works

A. E. Baker, *A Concordance to the Poetical and Dramatic Works of Alfred, Lord Tennyson*, Routledge, 1914, reissued 1965 (inaccurate and incomplete but indispensable).

Nancie Campbell, *Tennyson in Lincoln, A Catalogue of the Collections in the Research Centre*, The Tennyson Society, Vol. I (1972), Vol. II (1973).

Recent material is listed in F. E. Faverty, ed. *The Victorian Poets: A Guide to Research*, Harvard, 1968, and in the annual bibliographies of studies in Victorian literature in the *MLA International Bibliography* and *Victorian Studies*.

Biography and Criticism

William R. Brashear, 'Tennyson's Tragic Vitalism: *Idylls of the King*', *Victorian Poetry* VI (1968), 29–49.

Jerome H. Buckley, *Tennyson: The Growth of a Poet*, Harvard University Press, 1960.

A. Dwight Culler, *The Poetry of Tennyson*, Yale University Press, 1977.

Martin Dodsworth, 'Patterns of Morbidity: Repetition in Tennyson's Poetry', *The Major Victorian Poets: Reconsiderations*, ed. Isobel Armstrong, Routledge & Kegan Paul, 1969.

J. Phillip Eggers, *King Arthur's Laureate*, New York University Press, 1971.

Edward Engelberg, 'The Beast Image in Tennyson's *Idylls of the King*,' *English Literary History* XXII (1955), 287–92.

D. F. Goslee, 'The Stages in Tennyson's Composition of "Balin and Balan"', *The Huntington Library Quarterly* XXXVIII (1975), 247–68.

Further Reading

J. M. Gray, 'A Study in Idyl: Tennyson's "The Coming of Arthur"',
Renaissance and Modern Studies XIV (1970), 111–50.

Tennyson's Doppelgänger: 'Balin and Balan', The Tennyson Society, Lincoln, 1971.

Thro' the Vision of the Night: A Study of Source, Evolution and Structure in Tennyson's 'Idylls of the King', Edinburgh University Press, McGill-Queen's University Press, 1980.

Donald S. Hair, 'Tennyson's *Idylls of the King*: Truth "In the Fashion of the Day"', *English Studies in Canada* II (1976), 288–98.

John Dixon Hunt, 'The Poetry of Distance: Tennyson's *Idylls of the King*', *Victorian Poetry*, ed. Malcolm Bradbury and David Palmer, Edward Arnold, 1972.

'"Story Painters and Picture Writers": Tennyson's *Idylls* and Victorian Painting', *Tennyson*, ed. D. J. Palmer, Bell, 1973.

E. D. H. Johnson, *The Alien Vision of Victorian Poetry*, Princeton University Press, 1952.

Fred Kaplan, 'Woven Paces and Waving Hands: Tennyson's Merlin as Fallen Artist', *Victorian Poetry* VII (1969), 285–98.

James R. Kincaid, 'Tennyson's "Gareth and Lynette"', *Texas Studies in Literature and Language* XIII (1972), 663–71.

Tennyson's Major Poems: The Comic and Ironic Patterns, Yale University Press, 1975.

Henry Kozicki, *Tennyson and Clio: History in the Major Poems*, Johns Hopkins University Press, 1979.

George P. Landow, 'Closing the Frame: Having Faith and Keeping Faith in Tennyson's "The Passing of Arthur"', *Bulletin of the John Rylands University Library* LVI (1974), 423–42.

Harold Littledale, *Essays on Lord Tennyson's 'Idylls of the King'*, Macmillan, 1893, repr. with appendix, 1907, 1912.

M. W. MacCallum, *Tennyson's 'Idylls of the King' and Arthurian Story from the XVIth Century*, Maclehose, 1894.

Joseph B. McCullough and Claude C. Brew, 'A Study of the Publication of Tennyson's *Idylls of the King*', *PBSA* LXV (1971), 156–69.

Kerry McSweeney, *Tennyson and Swinburne as Romantic Naturalists*, University of Toronto Press, 1981.

Robert Bernard Martin, *Tennyson: The Unquiet Heart*, Oxford University Press with Faber & Faber, 1980.

Herbert Marshall McLuhan, 'Tennyson and Picturesque Poetry' and 'Tennyson and the Romantic Epic', in J. Killham (ed.), *Critical Essays on the Poetry of Tennyson*, Routledge & Kegan Paul, 1960.

Howard Maynadier, *The Arthur of the English Poets*, Houghton Mifflin, 1907.

Further Reading

Walter Nash, 'The Poetics of Idyll', unpublished doctoral thesis, Nottingham, 1972.

'Tennyson: "The Epic" and the Old "Morte"', *Cambridge Quarterly* VI (1975), 326–49.

Robert Pattison, *Tennyson and Tradition*, Harvard University Press, 1979.

Valerie Pitt, *Tennyson Laureate*, Barrie & Rockliff, 1962.

Lawrence Poston, '"Pelleas and Ettarre": Tennyson's "Troilus"', *Victorian Poetry* IV (1966), 199–204.

F. E. L. Priestley, 'Tennyson's *Idylls*', in J. Killham (ed.), *Critical Essays on the Poetry of Tennyson*, Routledge & Kegan Paul, 1960.

Language and Structure in Tennyson's Poetry, Deutsch, 1973.

John R. Reed, *Perception and Design in Tennyson's 'Idylls of the King'*, Ohio University Press, 1970.

Christopher Ricks, *Tennyson*, Macmillan, 1972.

John D. Rosenberg, *The Fall of Camelot*, Harvard University Press, 1973.

Clyde de L. Ryals, *From the Great Deep: Essays on 'Idylls of the King'*, Ohio University Press, 1967.

W. David Shaw, *Tennyson's Style*, Cornell University Press, 1977.

E. W. Slinn, 'Deception and Artifice in "Idylls of the King"', *Victorian Poetry* XI (1973), 1–14.

Stanley J. Solomon, 'Tennyson's Paradoxical King', *Victorian Poetry* I (1963), 258–71.

David Staines, 'Tennyson's "The Holy Grail": The Tragedy of Percivale', *Modern Language Review* LXIX (1974), 745–56.

'The Prose Drafts of Tennyson's *Idylls of the King*', *Harvard Library Bulletin* XXII (1974), 280–308.

Sir Charles Tennyson, *Alfred Tennyson*, Macmillan, 1949.

Six Tennyson Essays, Cassell, 1954.

Hallam, Lord Tennyson, *Alfred Lord Tennyson: A Memoir*, 2 vols., Macmillan, 1897.

Kathleen Tillotson, 'Tennyson's Serial Poem', *Mid-Victorian Studies*, Athlone Press, 1965.

Paul Turner, *Tennyson*, Routledge & Kegan Paul, 1976.

R. B. Wilkenfeld, 'Tennyson's Camelot: The Kingdom of Folly', *University of Toronto Quarterly* XXXVII (1968), 281–94.

IDYLLS OF THE KING

Dedication

These to His Memory – since he held them dear,
Perchance as finding there unconsciously
Some image of himself – I dedicate,
I dedicate, I consecrate with tears –
These Idylls.   5

       And indeed He seems to me
Scarce other than my king's ideal knight,
'Who reverenced his conscience as his king;
Whose glory was, redressing human wrong;
Who spake no slander, no, nor listen'd to it;
Who loved one only and who clave to her –'   10
Her – over all whose realms to their last isle,
Commingled with the gloom of imminent war,
The shadow of His loss drew like eclipse,
Darkening the world. We have lost him: he is gone:
We know him now: all narrow jealousies   15
Are silent; and we see him as he moved,
How modest, kindly, all-accomplish'd, wise,
With what sublime repression of himself,
And in what limits, and how tenderly;
Not swaying to this faction or to that;   20
Not making his high place the lawless perch
Of wing'd ambitions, nor a vantage-ground
For pleasure; but thro' all this tract of years
Wearing the white flower of a blameless life,
Before a thousand peering littlenesses,   25
In that fierce light which beats upon a throne,
And blackens every blot: for where is he,
Who dares foreshadow for an only son
A lovelier life, a more unstain'd, than his?
Or how should England dreaming of *his* sons   30
Hope more for these than some inheritance

Of such a life, a heart, a mind as thine,
Thou noble Father of her Kings to be,
Laborious for her people and her poor –
35   Voice in the rich dawn of an ampler day –
Far-sighted summoner of War and Waste
To fruitful strifes and rivalries of peace –
Sweet nature gilded by the gracious gleam
Of letters, dear to Science, dear to Art,
40   Dear to thy land and ours, a Prince indeed,
Beyond all titles, and a household name,
Hereafter, thro' all times, Albert the Good.

    Break not, O woman's-heart, but still endure;
Break not, for thou art Royal, but endure,
45   Remembering all the beauty of that star
Which shone so close beside Thee that ye made
One light together, but has past and leaves
The Crown a lonely splendour.

                       May all love,
His love, unseen but felt, o'ershadow Thee,
50   The love of all Thy sons encompass Thee,
The love of all Thy daughters cherish Thee,
The love of all Thy people comfort Thee,
Till God's love set Thee at his side again!

The Coming of Arthur

Leodogran, the King of Cameliard,
Had one fair daughter, and none other child;
And she was fairest of all flesh on earth,
Guinevere, and in her his one delight.

  For many a petty king ere Arthur came   5
Ruled in this isle, and ever waging war
Each upon other, wasted all the land;
And still from time to time the heathen host
Swarm'd overseas, and harried what was left.
And so there grew great tracts of wilderness,   10
Wherein the beast was ever more and more,
But man was less and less, till Arthur came.
For first Aurelius lived and fought and died,
And after him King Uther fought and died,
But either fail'd to make the kingdom one.   15
And after these King Arthur for a space,
And thro' the puissance of his Table Round,   *NATIONAL UNITY*
Drew all their petty princedoms under him,
Their king and head, and made a realm, and reign'd.

  And thus the land of Cameliard was waste,   20
Thick with wet woods, and many a beast therein,
And none or few to scare or chase the beast;
So that wild dog, and wolf and boar and bear
Came night and day, and rooted in the fields,
And wallow'd in the gardens of the King.   25
And ever and anon the wolf would steal
The children and devour, but now and then,
Her own brood lost or dead, lent her fierce teat
To human sucklings; and the children, housed
In her foul den, there at their meat would growl,   30
And mock their foster-mother on four feet,

Till, straighten'd, they grew up to wolf-like men,
Worse than the wolves. And King Leodogran
Groan'd for the Roman legions here again,
35   And Cæsar's eagle: then his brother king,
Urien, assail'd him: last a heathen horde,
Reddening the sun with smoke and earth with blood,
And on the spike that split the mother's heart
Spitting the child, brake on him, till, amazed,
40   He knew not whither he should turn for aid.

But – for he heard of Arthur newly crown'd,
Tho' not without an uproar made by those
Who cried, 'He is not Uther's son' – the King
Sent to him, saying, 'Arise, and help us thou!
45   For here between the man and beast we die.'

And Arthur yet had done no deed of arms,
But heard the call, and came: and Guinevere
Stood by the castle walls to watch him pass;
But since he neither wore on helm or shield
50   The golden symbol of his kinglihood,
But rode a simple knight among his knights,
And many of these in richer arms than he,
She saw him not, or mark'd not, if she saw,
One among many, tho' his face was bare.
55   But Arthur, looking downward as he past,
Felt the light of her eyes into his life
Smite on the sudden, yet rode on, and pitch'd
His tents beside the forest. Then he drave
The heathen; after, slew the beast, and fell'd
60   The forest, letting in the sun, and made
Broad pathways for the hunter and the knight
And so return'd.

                    For while he linger'd there,
A doubt that ever smoulder'd in the hearts
Of those great Lords and Barons of his realm
65   Flash'd forth and into war: for most of these,
Colleaguing with a score of petty kings,
Made head against him, crying, 'Who is he

That he should rule us? who hath proven him
King Uther's son? for lo! we look at him,
And find nor face nor bearing, limbs nor voice,   70
Are like to those of Uther whom we knew.
This is the son of Gorloïs, not the King;
This is the son of Anton, not the King.'

   And Arthur, passing thence to battle, felt
Travail, and throes and agonies of the life,   75
Desiring to be join'd with Guinevere;
And thinking as he rode, 'Her father said
That there between the man and beast they die.
Shall I not lift her from this land of beasts
Up to my throne, and side by side with me?   80
What happiness to reign a lonely king,
Vext – O ye stars that shudder over me,
O earth that soundest hollow under me,
Vext with waste dreams? for saving I be join'd
To her that is the fairest under heaven,   85
I seem as nothing in the mighty world,
And cannot will my will, nor work my work
Wholly, nor make myself in mine own realm
Victor and lord. But were I join'd with her,
Then might we live together as one life,   90
And reigning with one will in everything
Have power on this dark land to lighten it,
And power on this dead world to make it live.'

   Thereafter – as he speaks who tells the tale –
When Arthur reach'd a field-of-battle bright   95
With pitch'd pavilions of his foe, the world
Was all so clear about him, that he saw
The smallest rock far on the faintest hill,
And even in high day the morning star.
So when the King had set his banner broad,   100
At once from either side, with trumpet-blast,
And shouts, and clarions shrilling unto blood,
The long-lanced battle let their horses run.
And now the Barons and the kings prevail'd,
And now the King, as here and there that war   105

Went swaying; but the Powers who walk the world
Made lightnings and great thunders over him,
And dazed all eyes, till Arthur by main might,
And mightier of his hands with every blow,
110 And leading all his knighthood threw the kings
Carádos, Urien, Cradlemont of Wales,
Claudias, and Clariance of Northumberland,
The King Brandagoras of Latangor,
With Anguisant of Erin, Morganore,
115 And Lot of Orkney. Then, before a voice
As dreadful as the shout of one who sees
To one who sins, and deems himself alone
And all the world asleep, they swerved and brake
Flying, and Arthur call'd to stay the brands
120 That hack'd among the flyers, 'Ho! they yield!'
So like a painted battle the war stood
Silenced, the living quiet as the dead,
And in the heart of Arthur joy was lord.
He laugh'd upon his warrior whom he loved
125 And honour'd most. 'Thou dost not doubt me King,
So well thine arm hath wrought for me to-day.'
'Sir and my liege,' he cried, 'the fire of God
Descends upon thee in the battle-field:
I know thee for my King!' Whereat the two,
130 For each had warded either in the fight,
Sware on the field of death a deathless love.
And Arthur said, 'Man's word is God in man:
Let chance what will, I trust thee to the death.'

Then quickly from the foughten field he sent
135 Ulfius, and Brastias, and Bedivere,
His new-made knights, to King Leodogran,
Saying, 'If I in aught have served thee well,
Give me thy daughter Guinevere to wife.'

Whom when he heard, Leodogran in heart
140 Debating – 'How should I that am a king,
However much he holp me at my need,
Give my one daughter saving to a king,
And a king's son?' – lifted his voice, and call'd

24

A hoary man, his chamberlain, to whom
He trusted all things, and of him required   145
His counsel: 'Knowest thou aught of Arthur's birth?'

Then spake the hoary chamberlain and said,
'Sir King, there be but two old men that know:
And each is twice as old as I; and one
Is Merlin, the wise man that ever served   150
King Uther thro' his magic art; and one
Is Merlin's master (so they call him) Bleys,
Who taught him magic; but the scholar ran
Before the master, and so far, that Bleys
Laid magic by, and sat him down, and wrote   155
All things and whatsoever Merlin did
In one great annal-book, where after-years
Will learn the secret of our Arthur's birth.'

To whom the King Leodogran replied,   160
'O friend, had I been holpen half as well
By this King Arthur as by thee to-day,
Then beast and man had had their share of me:
But summon here before us yet once more
Ulfius, and Brastias, and Bedivere.'

Then, when they came before him, the King said,   165
'I have seen the cuckoo chased by lesser fowl,
And reason in the chase: but wherefore now
Do these your lords stir up the heat of war,
Some calling Arthur born of Gorloïs,
Others of Anton? Tell me, ye yourselves,   170
Hold ye this Arthur for King Uther's son?'

And Ulfius and Brastias answer'd, 'Ay.'
Then Bedivere, the first of all his knights
Knighted by Arthur at his crowning, spake –
For bold in heart and act and word was he,   175
Whenever slander breathed against the King –

'Sir, there be many rumours on this head:
For there be those who hate him in their hearts,

Call him baseborn, and since his ways are sweet,
180 And theirs are bestial, hold him less than man:
And there be those who deem him more than man,
And dream he dropt from heaven: but my belief
In all this matter – so ye care to learn –
Sir, for ye know that in King Uther's time
185 The prince and warrior Gorloïs, he that held
Tintagil castle by the Cornish sea,
Was wedded with a winsome wife, Ygerne:
And daughters had she borne him, – one whereof,
Lot's wife, the Queen of Orkney, Bellicent,
190 Hath ever like a loyal sister cleaved
To Arthur, – but a son she had not borne.
And Uther cast upon her eyes of love:
But she, a stainless wife to Gorloïs,
So loathed the bright dishonour of his love,
195 That Gorloïs and King Uther went to war:
And overthrown was Gorloïs and slain.
Then Uther in his wrath and heat besieged
Ygerne within Tintagil, where her men,
Seeing the mighty swarm about their walls,
200 Left her and fled, and Uther enter'd in,
And there was none to call to but himself.
So, compass'd by the power of the King,
Enforced she was to wed him in her tears,
And with a shameful swiftness: afterward,
205 Not many moons, King Uther died himself,
Moaning and wailing for an heir to rule
After him, lest the realm should go to wrack.
And that same night, the night of the new year,
By reason of the bitterness and grief
210 That vext his mother, all before his time
Was Arthur born, and all as soon as born
Deliver'd at a secret postern-gate
To Merlin, to be holden far apart
Until his hour should come; because the lords
215 Of that fierce day were as the lords of this,
Wild beasts, and surely would have torn the child
Piecemeal among them, had they known; for each
But sought to rule for his own self and hand,

And many hated Uther for the sake
Of Gorloïs. Wherefore Merlin took the child,   220
And gave him to Sir Anton, an old knight
And ancient friend of Uther; and his wife
Nursed the young prince, and rear'd him with her own;
And no man knew. And ever since the lords
Have foughten like wild beasts among themselves,   225
So that the realm has gone to wrack: but now,
This year, when Merlin (for his hour had come)
Brought Arthur forth, and set him in the hall,
Proclaiming, 'Here is Uther's heir, your king,'
A hundred voices cried, 'Away with him!   230
No king of ours! a son of Gorloïs he,
Or else the child of Anton, and no king,
Or else baseborn.' Yet Merlin thro' his craft,
And while the people clamour'd for a king,
Had Arthur crown'd; but after, the great lords   235
Banded, and so brake out in open war.'

Then while the King debated with himself
If Arthur were the child of shamefulness,
Or born the son of Gorloïs, after death,
Or Uther's son, and born before his time,   240
Or whether there were truth in anything
Said by these three, there came to Cameliard,
With Gawain and young Modred, her two sons,
Lot's wife, the Queen of Orkney, Bellicent;
Whom as he could, not as he would, the King   245
Made feast for, saying, as they sat at meat,

'A doubtful throne is ice on summer seas.
Ye come from Arthur's court. Victor his men
Report him! Yea, but ye – think ye this king –
So many those that hate him, and so strong,   250
So few his knights, however brave they be –
Hath body enow to hold his foemen down?'

'O King,' she cried, 'and I will tell thee: few,
Few, but all brave, all of one mind with him;
For I was near him when the savage yells   255

Of Uther's peerage died, and Arthur sat
Crown'd on the daïs, and his warriors cried,
'Be thou the king, and we will work thy will
Who love thee.' Then the King in low deep tones,
260 And simple words of great authority,
Bound them by so strait vows to his own self,
That when they rose, knighted from kneeling, some
Were pale as at the passing of a ghost,
Some flush'd, and others dazed, as one who wakes
265 Half-blinded at the coming of a light.

'But when he spake and cheer'd his Table Round
With large, divine, and comfortable words,
Beyond my tongue to tell thee – I beheld
From eye to eye thro' all their Order flash
270 A momentary likeness of the King:
And ere it left their faces, thro' the cross
And those around it and the Crucified,
Down from the casement over Arthur, smote
Flame-colour, vert and azure, in three rays,
275 One falling upon each of three fair queens,
Who stood in silence near his throne, the friends
Of Arthur, gazing on him, tall, with bright
Sweet faces, who will help him at his need.

'And there I saw mage Merlin, whose vast wit
280 And hundred winters are but as the hands
Of loyal vassals toiling for their liege.

'And near him stood the Lady of the Lake,
Who knows a subtler magic than his own –
Clothed in white samite, mystic, wonderful.
285 She gave the King his huge cross-hilted sword,
Whereby to drive the heathen out: a mist
Of incense curl'd about her, and her face
Wellnigh was hidden in the minster gloom;
But there was heard among the holy hymns
290 A voice as of the waters, for she dwells
Down in a deep; calm, whatsoever storms

28

May shake the world, and when the surface rolls,
Hath power to walk the waters like our Lord.

'There likewise I beheld Excalibur
Before him at his crowning borne, the sword   295
That rose from out the bosom of the lake,
And Arthur row'd across and took it – rich
With jewels, elfin Urim, on the hilt,
Bewildering heart and eye – the blade so bright
That men are blinded by it – on one side,   300
Graven in the oldest tongue of all this world,
"Take me," but turn the blade and ye shall see,
And written in the speech ye speak yourself,
"Cast me away!" And sad was Arthur's face
Taking it, but old Merlin counsell'd him,   305
"Take thou and strike! the time to cast away
Is yet far-off." So this great brand the king
Took, and by this will beat his foemen down.'

TEMPTATIONS OF KINGSHIP

Thereat Leodogran rejoiced, but thought
To sift his doubtings to the last, and ask'd,   310
Fixing full eyes of question on her face,
'The swallow and the swift are near akin,
But thou art closer to this noble prince,
Being his own dear sister;' and she said,
'Daughter of Gorloïs and Ygerne am I;'   315
'And therefore Arthur's sister?' ask'd the King.
She answer'd, 'These be secret things,' and sign'd
To those two sons to pass, and let them be.
And Gawain went, and breaking into song
Sprang out, and follow'd by his flying hair   320
Ran like a colt, and leapt at all he saw:
But Modred laid his ear beside the doors,
And there half-heard; the same that afterward
Struck for the throne, and striking found his doom.

GAWAIN MODRED

And then the Queen made answer, 'What know I?   325
For dark my mother was in eyes and hair,
And dark in hair and eyes am I; and dark

Was Gorloïs, yea and dark was Uther too,
Wellnigh to blackness; but this King is fair
330 Beyond the race of Britons and of men.
Moreover, always in my mind I hear
A cry from out the dawning of my life,
A mother weeping, and I hear her say,
"O that ye had some brother, pretty one,
335 To guard thee on the rough ways of the world."'

'Ay,' said the King, 'and hear ye such a cry?
But when did Arthur chance upon thee first?'

'O King!' she cried, 'and I will tell thee true:
He found me first when yet a little maid:
340 Beaten I had been for a little fault
Whereof I was not guilty; and out I ran
And flung myself down on a bank of heath,
And hated this fair world and all therein,
And wept, and wish'd that I were dead; and he –
345 I know not whether of himself he came,
Or brought by Merlin, who, they say, can walk
Unseen at pleasure – he was at my side,
And spake sweet words, and comforted my heart,
And dried my tears, being a child with me.
350 And many a time he came, and evermore
As I grew greater grew with me; and sad
At times he seem'd, and sad with him was I,
Stern too at times, and then I loved him not,
But sweet again, and then I loved him well.
355 And now of late I see him less and less,
But those first days had golden hours for me,
For then I surely thought he would be king.

'But let me tell thee now another tale:
For Bleys, our Merlin's master, as they say,
360 Died but of late, and sent his cry to me,
To hear him speak before he left his life.
Shrunk like a fairy changeling lay the mage;
And when I enter'd told me that himself
And Merlin ever served about the King,

Uther, before he died; and on the night 365
When Uther in Tintagil past away
Moaning and wailing for an heir, the two
Left the still King, and passing forth to breathe,
Then from the castle gateway by the chasm
Descending thro' the dismal night – a night 370
In which the bounds of heaven and earth were lost –
Beheld, so high upon the dreary deeps
It seem'd in heaven, a ship, the shape thereof
A dragon wing'd, and all from stem to stern
Bright with a shining people on the decks, 375
And gone as soon as seen. And then the two
Dropt to the cove, and watch'd the great sea fall,
Wave after wave, each mightier than the last,
Till last, a ninth one, gathering half the deep
And full of voices, slowly rose and plunged 380
Roaring, and all the wave was in a flame:
And down the wave and in the flame was borne
A naked babe, and rode to Merlin's feet,
Who stoopt and caught the babe, and cried "The King!
Here is an heir for Uther!" And the fringe 385
Of that great breaker, sweeping up the strand,
Lash'd at the wizard as he spake the word,
And all at once all round him rose in fire,
So that the child and he were clothed in fire.
And presently thereafter follow'd calm, 390
Free sky and stars: "And this same child," he said,
"Is he who reigns; nor could I part in peace
Till this were told." And saying this the seer
Went thro' the strait and dreadful pass of death,
Not ever to be question'd any more 395
Save on the further side; but when I met
Merlin, and ask'd him if these things were truth –
The shining dragon and the naked child
Descending in the glory of the seas –
He laugh'd as is his wont, and answer'd me 400
In riddling triplets of old time, and said:

"'Rain, rain, and sun! a rainbow in the sky!
A young man will be wiser by and by;

31

An old man's wit may wander ere he die.

405   Rain, rain, and sun! a rainbow on the lea!
And truth is this to me, and that to thee;
And truth or clothed or naked let it be.

    Rain, sun, and rain! and the free blossom blows:
Sun, rain, and sun! and where is he who knows?
410 From the great deep to the great deep he goes.''

    'So Merlin riddling anger'd me; but thou
Fear not to give this King thine only child,
Guinevere: so great bards of him will sing
Hereafter; and dark sayings from of old
415 Ranging and ringing thro' the minds of men,
And echo'd by old folk beside their fires
For comfort after their wage-work is done,
Speak of the King; and Merlin in our time
Hath spoken also, not in jest, and sworn
420 Tho' men may wound him that he will not die,
But pass, again to come; and then or now
Utterly smite the heathen underfoot,
Till these and all men hail him for their king.'

    She spake and King Leodogran rejoiced,
425 But musing 'Shall I answer yea or nay?'
Doubted, and drowsed, nodded and slept, and saw,
Dreaming, a slope of land that ever grew,
Field after field, up to a height, the peak
Haze-hidden, and thereon a phantom king,
430 Now looming, and now lost; and on the slope
The sword rose, the hind fell, the herd was driven,
Fire glimpsed; and all the land from roof and rick,
In drifts of smoke before a rolling wind,
Stream'd to the peak, and mingled with the haze
435 And made it thicker; while the phantom king
Sent out at times a voice; and here or there
Stood one who pointed toward the voice, the rest
Slew on and burnt, crying, 'No king of ours,
No son of Uther, and no king of ours;'
440 Till with a wink his dream was changed, the haze
Descended, and the solid earth became

As nothing, but the King stood out in heaven,
Crown'd. And Leodogran awoke, and sent
Ulfius, and Brastias and Bedivere,
Back to the court of Arthur answering yea.   445

Then Arthur charged his warrior whom he loved
And honour'd most, Sir Lancelot, to ride forth
And bring the Queen; – and watch'd him from the
    gates:
And Lancelot past away among the flowers,
(For then was latter April) and return'd   450
Among the flowers, in May, with Guinevere.
To whom arrived, by Dubric the high saint,
Chief of the church in Britain, and before
The stateliest of her altar-shrines, the King
That morn was married, while in stainless white,   455
The fair beginners of a nobler time,
And glorying in their vows and him, his knights
Stood round him, and rejoicing in his joy.
Far shone the fields of May thro' open door,
The sacred altar blossom'd white with May,   460
The Sun of May descended on their King,
They gazed on all earth's beauty in their Queen,
Roll'd incense, and there past along the hymns
A voice as of the waters, while the two
Sware at the shrine of Christ a deathless love: 465
And Arthur said, 'Behold, thy doom is mine.
Let chance what will, I love thee to the death!'
To whom the Queen replied with drooping eyes,
'King and my lord, I love thee to the death!'
And holy Dubric spread his hands and spake,   470
'Reign ye, and live and love, and make the world
Other, and may thy Queen be one with thee,
And all this Order of thy Table Round
Fulfil the boundless purpose of their King!'

So Dubric said; but when they left the shrine   475
Great Lords from Rome before the portal stood,
In scornful stillness gazing as they past;
Then while they paced a city all on fire

33

With sun and cloth of gold, the trumpets blew,
480   And Arthur's knighthood sang before the King: –

'Blow trumpet, for the world is white with May;
Blow trumpet, the long night hath roll'd away!
Blow thro' the living world – "Let the King reign."

'Shall Rome or Heathen rule in Arthur's realm?
485   Flash brand and lance, fall battleaxe upon helm,
Fall battleaxe, and flash brand! Let the King reign.

'Strike for the King and live! his knights have heard
That God hath told the King a secret word.
Fall battleaxe, and flash brand! Let the King reign.

490   'Blow trumpet! he will lift us from the dust.
Blow trumpet! live the strength and die the lust!
Clang battleaxe, and clash brand! Let the King reign.

'Strike for the King and die! and if thou diest,
The King is King, and ever wills the highest.
495   Clang battleaxe, and clash brand! Let the King reign.

'Blow, for our Sun is mighty in his May!
Blow, for our Sun is mightier day by day!
Clang battleaxe, and clash brand! Let the King reign.

'The King will follow Christ, and we the King
500   In whom high God hath breathed a secret thing.
Fall battleaxe, and flash brand! Let the King reign.'

So sang the knighthood, moving to their hall.
There at the banquet those great Lords from Rome,
The slowly-fading mistress of the world,
505   Strode in, and claim'd their tribute as of yore.
But Arthur spake, 'Behold, for these have sworn
To wage my wars, and worship me their King;
The old order changeth, yielding place to new;
And we that fight for our fair father Christ,
510   Seeing that ye be grown too weak and old

34

To drive the heathen from your Roman wall,
No tribute will we pay:' so those great lords
Drew back in wrath, and Arthur strove with Rome.

And Arthur and his knighthood for a space
Were all one will, and thro' that strength the King   515
Drew in the petty princedoms under him,
Fought, and in twelve great battles overcame
The heathen hordes, and made a realm and reign'd.

[handwritten annotation: VARIATION ON L. 19]

[handwritten annotation: ONLY LINES ABOUT CAMELOT AS CAMELOT]

Need to free ourselves from allegory — but also true allegory... Gareth comes to mental maturity + sexual maturity

Gareth and Lynette

The last tall son of Lot and Bellicent,
And tallest, Gareth, in a showerful spring
Stared at the spate. A slender-shafted Pine
Lost footing, fell, and so was whirl'd away.
5 'How he went down,' said Gareth, 'as a false knight
Or evil king before my lance if lance
Were mine to use – O senseless cataract,
Bearing all down in thy precipitancy –
And yet thou art but swollen with cold snows
10 And mine is living blood: thou dost His will,
The Maker's, and not knowest, and I that know,
Have strength and wit, in my good mother's hall
Linger with vacillating obedience,
Prison'd, and kept and coax'd and whistled to –
15 Since the good mother holds me still a child!
Good mother is bad mother unto me!
A worse were better; yet no worse would I.
Heaven yield her for it, but in me put force
To weary her ears with one continuous prayer,
20 Until she let me fly discaged to sweep
In ever-highering eagle-circles up
To the great Sun of Glory, and thence swoop
Down upon all things base, and dash them dead,
A knight of Arthur, working out his will,
25 To cleanse the world. Why, Gawain, when he came
With Modred hither in the summertime,
Ask'd me to tilt with him, the proven knight.
Modred for want of worthier was the judge.
Then I so shook him in the saddle, he said,
30 "Thou hast half prevail'd against me," said so – he –
Tho' Modred biting his thin lips was mute,
For he is alway sullen: what care I?'

36

And Gareth went, and hovering round her chair
Ask'd, 'Mother, tho' ye count me still the child,
Sweet mother, do ye love the child?' She laugh'd,   35
'Thou art but a wild-goose to question it.'
'Then, mother, an ye love the child,' he said,
'Being a goose and rather tame than wild,
Hear the child's story.' 'Yea, my well-beloved,
An 'twere but of the goose and golden eggs.'   40

And Gareth answer'd her with kindling eyes,
'Nay, nay, good mother, but this egg of mine
Was finer gold than any goose can lay;
For this an Eagle, a royal Eagle, laid
Almost beyond eye-reach, on such a palm   45
As glitters gilded in thy Book of Hours.
And there was ever haunting round the palm
A lusty youth, but poor, who often saw
The splendour sparkling from aloft, and thought
"An I could climb and lay my hand upon it,   50
Then were I wealthier than a leash of kings."
But ever when he reach'd a hand to climb,
One, that had loved him from his childhood, caught
And stay'd him, "Climb not lest thou break thy neck,
I charge thee by my love," and so the boy,   55
Sweet mother, neither clomb, nor brake his neck,
But brake his very heart in pining for it,
And past away.'

        To whom the mother said,
'True love, sweet son, had risk'd himself and climb'd,
And handed down the golden treasure to him.'   60

And Gareth answer'd her with kindling eyes,
'Gold? said I gold? – ay then, why he, or she,
Or whosoe'er it was, or half the world
Had ventured – *had* the thing I spake of been
Mere gold – but this was all of that true steel,   65
Whereof they forged the brand Excalibur,
And lightnings play'd about it in the storm,

And all the little fowl were flurried at it,
And there were cries and clashings in the nest,
70   That sent him from his senses: let me go.'

Then Bellicent bemoan'd herself and said,
'Hast thou no pity upon my loneliness?
Lo, where thy father Lot beside the hearth
Lies like a log, and all but smoulder'd out!
75   For ever since when traitor to the King
He fought against him in the Barons' war,
And Arthur gave him back his territory,
His age hath slowly droopt, and now lies there
A yet-warm corpse, and yet unburiable,
80   No more; nor sees, nor hears, nor speaks, nor knows.
And both thy brethren are in Arthur's hall,
Albeit neither loved with that full love
I feel for thee, nor worthy such a love:
Stay therefore thou; red berries charm the bird,
85   And thee, mine innocent, the jousts, the wars,
Who never knewest finger-ache, nor pang
Of wrench'd or broken limb – an often chance
In those brain-stunning shocks, and tourney-falls,
Frights to my heart; but stay: follow the deer
90   By these tall firs and our fast-falling burns;
So make thy manhood mightier day by day;
Sweet is the chase: and I will seek thee out
Some comfortable bride and fair, to grace
Thy climbing life, and cherish my prone year,
95   Till falling into Lot's forgetfulness
I know not thee, myself, nor anything.
Stay, my best son! ye are yet more boy than man.'

Then Gareth, 'An ye hold me yet for child,
Hear yet once more the story of the child.
100   For, mother, there was once a King, like ours.
The prince his heir, when tall and marriageable,
Ask'd for a bride; and thereupon the King
Set two before him. One was fair, strong, arm'd –
But to be won by force – and many men
105   Desired her; one, good lack, no man desired.

And these were the conditions of the King:
That save he won the first by force, he needs
Must wed that other, whom no man desired,
A red-faced bride who knew herself so vile,
That evermore she long'd to hide herself,   110
Nor fronted man or woman, eye to eye –
Yea – some she cleaved to, but they died of her.
And one – they call'd her Fame; and one, – O Mother,
How can ye keep me tether'd to you – Shame.
Man am I grown, a man's work must I do.   115
Follow the deer? follow the Christ, the King,
Live pure, speak true, right wrong, follow the King –
Else, wherefore born?'

              To whom the mother said,
'Sweet son, for there be many who deem him not,
Or will not deem him, wholly proven King –   120
Albeit in mine own heart I knew him King,
When I was frequent with him in my youth,
And heard him Kingly speak, and doubted him
No more than he, himself; but felt him mine,
Of closest kin to me: yet – wilt thou leave   125
Thine easeful biding here, and risk thine all,
Life, limbs, for one that is not proven King?
Stay, till the cloud that settles round his birth
Hath lifted but a little. Stay, sweet son.'

And Gareth answer'd quickly, 'Not an hour,   130
So that ye yield me – I will walk thro' fire,
Mother, to gain it – your full leave to go.
Not proven, who swept the dust of ruin'd Rome
From off the threshold of the realm, and crush'd
The Idolaters, and made the people free?   135
Who should be King save him who makes us free?'

So when the Queen, who long had sought in vain
To break him from the intent to which he grew,
Found her son's will unwaveringly one,
She answer'd craftily, 'Will ye walk thro' fire?   140
Who walks thro' fire will hardly heed the smoke.

Ay, go then, an ye must: only one proof,
Before thou ask the King to make thee knight,
Of thine obedience and thy love to me,
Thy mother, – I demand.'

145   And Gareth cried,
'A hard one, or a hundred, so I go.
Nay – quick! the proof to prove me to the quick!'

But slowly spake the mother looking at him,
'Prince, thou shalt go disguised to Arthur's hall,
150   And hire thyself to serve for meats and drinks
Among the scullions and the kitchen-knaves,
And those that hand the dish across the bar.
Nor shalt thou tell thy name to anyone.
And thou shalt serve a twelvemonth and a day.'

155   For so the Queen believed that when her son
Beheld his only way to glory lead
Low down thro' villain kitchen-vassalage,
Her own true Gareth was too princely-proud
To pass thereby; so should he rest with her,
160   Closed in her castle from the sound of arms.

Silent awhile was Gareth, then replied,
'The thrall in person may be free in soul,
And I shall see the jousts. Thy son am I,
And since thou art my mother, must obey.
165   I therefore yield me freely to thy will;
For hence will I, disguised, and hire myself
To serve with scullions and with kitchen-knaves;
Nor tell my name to any – no, not the King.'

Gareth awhile linger'd. The mother's eye
170   Full of the wistful fear that he would go,
And turning toward him whereso'er he turn'd,
Perplext his outward purpose, till an hour,
When waken'd by the wind which with full voice
Swept bellowing thro' the darkness on to dawn,
175   He rose, and out of slumber calling two

That still had tended on him from his birth,
Before the wakeful mother heard him, went.

  The three were clad like tillers of the soil.
Southward they set their faces. The birds made
Melody on branch, and melody in mid air.   180
The damp hill-slopes were quicken'd into green,
And the live green had kindled into flowers,
For it was past the time of Easterday.

  So, when their feet were planted on the plain
That broaden'd toward the base of Camelot,   185
Far off they saw the silver-misty morn
Rolling her smoke about the Royal mount,
That rose between the forest and the field.
At times the summit of the high city flash'd;
At times the spires and turrets half-way down   190
Prick'd thro' the mist; at times the great gate shone
Only, that open'd on the field below:
Anon, the whole fair city had disappear'd.

  Then those who went with Gareth were amazed,
One crying, 'Let us go no further, lord.   195
Here is a city of Enchanters, built
By fairy Kings.' The second echo'd him,
'Lord, we have heard from our wise man at home
To Northward, that this King is not the King,
But only changeling out of Fairyland,   200
Who drave the heathen hence by sorcery
And Merlin's glamour.' Then the first again,
'Lord, there is no such city anywhere,
But all a vision.'

                Gareth answer'd them
With laughter, swearing he had glamour enow   205
In his own blood, his princedom, youth and hopes,
To plunge old Merlin in the Arabian sea;
So push'd them all unwilling toward the gate.
And there was no gate like it under heaven.
For barefoot on the keystone, which was lined   210

And rippled like an ever-fleeting wave,
The Lady of the Lake stood: all her dress
Wept from her sides as water flowing away;
But like the cross her great and goodly arms
215   Stretch'd under all the cornice and upheld:
And drops of water fell from either hand;
And down from one a sword was hung, from one
A censer, either worn with wind and storm;
And o'er her breast floated the sacred fish;
220   And in the space to left of her, and right,
Were Arthur's wars in weird devices done,
New things and old co-twisted, as if Time
Were nothing, so inveterately, that men
Were giddy gazing there; and over all
225   High on the top were those three Queens, the friends
Of Arthur, who should help him at his need.

Then those with Gareth for so long a space
Stared at the figures, that at last it seem'd
The dragon-boughts and elvish emblemings
230   Began to move, seethe, twine and curl: they call'd
To Gareth, 'Lord, the gateway is alive.'

And Gareth likewise on them fixt his eyes
So long, that ev'n to him they seem'd to move.
Out of the city a blast of music peal'd.
235   Back from the gate started the three, to whom
From out thereunder came an ancient man,
Long-bearded, saying, 'Who be ye, my sons?'

Then Gareth, 'We be tillers of the soil,
Who leaving share in furrow come to see
240   The glories of our King: but these, my men,
(Your city moved so weirdly in the mist)
Doubt if the King be King at all, or come
From Fairyland; and whether this be built
By magic, and by fairy Kings and Queens;
245   Or whether there be any city at all,
Or all a vision: and this music now
Hath scared them both, but tell thou these the truth.'

Then that old Seer made answer playing on him
And saying, 'Son, I have seen the good ship sail
Keel upward, and mast downward, in the heavens,   250
And solid turrets topsy-turvy in air:
And here is truth; but an it please thee not,
Take thou the truth as thou hast told it me.
For truly as thou sayest, a Fairy King
And Fairy Queens have built the city, son;   255
They came from out a sacred mountain-cleft
Toward the sunrise, each with harp in hand,
And built it to the music of their harps.
And, as thou sayest, it is enchanted, son,
For there is nothing in it as it seems   260
Saving the King; tho' some there be that hold
The King a shadow, and the city real:
Yet take thou heed of him, for, so thou pass
Beneath this archway, then wilt thou become
A thrall to his enchantments, for the King   265
Will bind thee by such vows, as is a shame
A man should not be bound by, yet the which
No man can keep; but, so thou dread to swear,
Pass not beneath this gateway, but abide
Without, among the cattle of the field.   270
For an ye heard a music, like enow
They are building still, seeing the city is built
To music, therefore never built at all,
And therefore built for ever.'

                              Gareth spake
Anger'd, 'Old Master, reverence thine own beard   275
That looks as white as utter truth, and seems
Wellnigh as long as thou art statured tall!
Why mockest thou the stranger that hath been
To thee fair-spoken?'

                       But the Seer replied,
'Know ye not then the Riddling of the Bards?   280
"Confusion, and illusion, and relation,
Elusion, and occasion, and evasion"?
I mock thee not but as thou mockest me,

And all that see thee, for thou art not who
285 Thou seemest, but I know thee who thou art.
And now thou goest up to mock the King,
Who cannot brook the shadow of any lie.'

Unmockingly the mocker ending here
290 Turn'd to the right, and past along the plain;
Whom Gareth looking after said, 'My men,
Our one white lie sits like a little ghost
Here on the threshold of our enterprise.
Let love be blamed for it, not she, nor I:
Well, we will make amends.'

        With all good cheer
295 He spake and laugh'd, then enter'd with his twain
Camelot, a city of shadowy palaces
And stately, rich in emblem and the work
Of ancient kings who did their days in stone;
Which Merlin's hand, the Mage at Arthur's court,
300 Knowing all arts, had touch'd, and everywhere
At Arthur's ordinance, tipt with lessening peak
And pinnacle, and had made it spire to heaven.
And ever and anon a knight would pass
Outward, or inward to the hall: his arms
305 Clash'd; and the sound was good to Gareth's ear.
And out of bower and casement shyly glanced
Eyes of pure women, wholesome stars of love;
And all about a healthful people stept
As in the presence of a gracious king.

310 Then into hall Gareth ascending heard
A voice, the voice of Arthur, and beheld
Far over heads in that long-vaulted hall
The splendour of the presence of the King
Throned, and delivering doom – and look'd no more –
315 But felt his young heart hammering in his ears,
And thought, 'For this half-shadow of a lie
The truthful King will doom me when I speak.'
Yet pressing on, tho' all in fear to find

44

Sir Gawain or Sir Modred, saw nor one
Nor other, but in all the listening eyes   320
Of those tall knights, that ranged about the throne,
Clear honour shining like the dewy star
Of dawn, and faith in their great King, with pure
Affection, and the light of victory,
And glory gain'd, and evermore to gain.   325

   Then came a widow crying to the King,
'A boon, Sir King! Thy father, Uther, reft
From my dead lord a field with violence:
For howsoe'er at first he proffer'd gold,
Yet, for the field was pleasant in our eyes,   330
We yielded not; and then he reft us of it
Perforce, and left us neither gold nor field.'

   Said Arthur, 'Whether would ye? gold or field?'
To whom the woman weeping, 'Nay, my lord,
The field was pleasant in my husband's eye.'   335

   And Arthur, 'Have thy pleasant field again,
And thrice the gold for Uther's use thereof,
According to the years. No boon is here,
But justice, so thy say be proven true.
Accursed, who from the wrongs his father did   340
Would shape himself a right!'

                  And while she past,
Came yet another widow crying to him,
'A boon, Sir King! Thine enemy, King, am I.
With thine own hand thou slewest my dear lord,
A knight of Uther in the Barons' war,   345
When Lot and many another rose and fought
Against thee, saying thou wert basely born.
I held with these, and loathe to ask thee aught.
Yet lo! my husband's brother had my son
Thrall'd in his castle, and hath starved him dead;   350
And standeth seized of that inheritance
Which thou that slewest the sire hast left the son.

45

So tho' I scarce can ask it thee for hate,
Grant me some knight to do the battle for me,
355   Kill the foul thief, and wreak me for my son.'

Then strode a good knight forward, crying to him,
'A boon, Sir King! I am her kinsman, I.
Give me to right her wrong, and slay the man.'

Then came Sir Kay, the seneschal, and cried,
360   'A boon, Sir King! ev'n that thou grant her none,
This railer, that hath mock'd thee in full hall –
None; or the wholesome boon of gyve and gag.'

But Arthur, 'We sit King, to help the wrong'd
Thro' all our realm. The woman loves her lord.
365   Peace to thee, woman, with thy loves and hates!
The kings of old had doom'd thee to the flames,
Aurelius Emrys would have scourged thee dead,
And Uther slit thy tongue: but get thee hence –
Lest that rough humour of the kings of old
370   Return upon me! Thou that art her kin,
Go likewise; lay him low and slay him not,
But bring him here, that I may judge the right,
According to the justice of the King:
Then, be he guilty, by that deathless King
375   Who lived and died for men, the man shall die.'

Then came in hall the messenger of Mark,
A name of evil savour in the land,
The Cornish king. In either hand he bore
What dazzled all, and shone far-off as shines
380   A field of charlock in the sudden sun
Between two showers, a cloth of palest gold,
Which down he laid before the throne, and knelt,
Delivering, that his lord, the vassal king,
Was ev'n upon his way to Camelot;
385   For having heard that Arthur of his grace
Had made his goodly cousin, Tristram, knight,
And, for himself was of the greater state,
Being a king, he trusted his liege-lord

Would yield him this large honour all the more;
So pray'd him well to accept this cloth of gold,   390
In token of true heart and feälty.

   Then Arthur cried to rend the cloth, to rend
In pieces, and so cast it on the hearth.
An oak-tree smoulder'd there. 'The goodly knight!   395
What! shall the shield of Mark stand among these?'
For, midway down the side of that long hall
A stately pile, – whereof along the front,
Some blazon'd, some but carven, and some blank,
There ran a treble range of stony shields, –   400
Rose, and high-arching overbrow'd the hearth.
And under every shield a knight was named:
For this was Arthur's custom in his hall;
When some good knight had done one noble deed,
His arms were carven only; but if twain   405
His arms were blazon'd also; but if none,
The shield was blank and bare without a sign
Saving the name beneath; and Gareth saw
The shield of Gawain blazon'd rich and bright,
And Modred's blank as death; and Arthur cried   410
To rend the cloth and cast it on the hearth.

   'More like are we to reave him of his crown
Than make him knight because men call him king.
The kings we found, ye know we stay'd their hands
From war among themselves, but left them kings;   415
Of whom were any bounteous, merciful,
Truth-speaking, brave, good livers, them we enroll'd
Among us, and they sit within our hall.
But Mark hath tarnish'd the great name of king,
As Mark would sully the low state of churl: 420
And, seeing he hath sent us cloth of gold,
Return, and meet, and hold him from our eyes,
Lest we should lap him up in cloth of lead,
Silenced for ever – craven – a man of plots,
Craft, poisonous counsels, wayside ambushings –
No fault of thine: let Kay the seneschal   425
Look to thy wants, and send thee satisfied –
Accursed, who strikes nor lets the hand be seen!'

47

And many another suppliant crying came
With noise of ravage wrought by beast and man,
430   And evermore a knight would ride away.

Last, Gareth leaning both hands heavily
Down on the shoulders of the twain, his men,
Approach'd between them toward the King, and ask'd,
'A boon, Sir King (his voice was all ashamed),
435   For see ye not how weak and hungerworn
I seem – leaning on these? grant me to serve
For meat and drink among thy kitchen-knaves
A twelvemonth and a day, nor seek my name.
Hereafter I will fight.'

                  To him the King,
440   'A goodly youth and worth a goodlier boon!
But so thou wilt no goodlier, then must Kay,
The master of the meats and drinks, be thine.'

He rose and past; then Kay, a man of mien
Wan-sallow as the plant that feels itself
Root-bitten by white lichen,

445   'Lo ye now!
This fellow hath broken from some Abbey, where,
God wot, he had not beef and brewis enow,
However that might chance! but an he work,
Like any pigeon will I cram his crop,
450   And sleeker shall he shine than any hog.'

Then Lancelot standing near, 'Sir Seneschal,
Sleuth-hound thou knowest, and gray, and all the hounds;
A horse thou knowest, a man thou dost not know:
Broad brows and fair, a fluent hair and fine,
455   High nose, a nostril large and fine, and hands
Large, fair and fine! – Some young lad's mystery –
But, or from sheepcot or king's hall, the boy
Is noble-natured. Treat him with all grace,
Lest he should come to shame thy judging of him.'

Then Kay, 'What murmurest thou of mystery?   460
Think ye this fellow will poison the King's dish?
Nay, for he spake too fool-like: mystery!
Tut, an the lad were noble, he had ask'd
For horse and armour: fair and fine, forsooth!
Sir Fine-face, Sir Fair-hands? but see thou to it   465
That thine own fineness, Lancelot, some fine day
Undo thee not – and leave my man to me.'

So Gareth all for glory underwent
The sooty yoke of kitchen-vassalage;
Ate with young lads his portion by the door,   470
And couch'd at night with grimy kitchen-knaves.
And Lancelot ever spake him pleasantly,
But Kay the seneschal, who loved him not,
Would hustle and harry him, and labour him
Beyond his comrade of the hearth, and set   475
To turn the broach, draw water, or hew wood,
Or grosser tasks; and Gareth bow'd himself
With all obedience to the King, and wrought
All kind of service with a noble ease
That graced the lowliest act in doing it.   480
And when the thralls had talk among themselves,
And one would praise the love that linkt the King
And Lancelot – how the King had saved his life
In battle twice, and Lancelot once the King's –
For Lancelot was the first in Tournament,   485
But Arthur mightiest on the battle-field –
Gareth was glad. Or if some other told,   MYSTERY
How once the wandering forester at dawn,   OF
Far over the blue tarns and hazy seas,   BIRTH
On Caer-Eryri's highest found the King,   INCREASES 490
A naked babe, of whom the Prophet spake,
'He passes to the Isle Avilion,
He passes and is heal'd and cannot die' –
Gareth was glad. But if their talk were foul,
Then would he whistle rapid as any lark,   495
Or carol some old roundelay, and so loud
That first they mock'd, but, after, reverenced him.

Or Gareth telling some prodigious tale
Of knights, who sliced a red life-bubbling way
500   Thro' twenty folds of twisted dragon, held
All in a gap-mouth'd circle his good mates
Lying or sitting round him, idle hands,
Charm'd; till Sir Kay, the seneschal, would come
Blustering upon them, like a sudden wind
505   Among dead leaves, and drive them all apart.
Or when the thralls had sport among themselves,
So there were any trial of mastery,
He, by two yards in casting bar or stone
Was counted best; and if there chanced a joust,
510   So that Sir Kay nodded him leave to go,
Would hurry thither, and when he saw the knights
Clash like the coming and retiring wave,
And the spear spring, and good horse reel, the boy
Was half beyond himself for ecstasy.

515   So for a month he wrought among the thralls;
But in the weeks that follow'd, the good Queen,
Repentant of the word she made him swear,
And saddening in her childless castle, sent,
Between the in-crescent and de-crescent moon,
520   Arms for her son, and loosed him from his vow.

This, Gareth hearing from a squire of Lot
With whom he used to play at tourney once,
When both were children, and in lonely haunts
Would scratch a ragged oval on the sand,
525   And each at either dash from either end –
Shame never made girl redder than Gareth joy.
He laugh'd; he sprang. 'Out of the smoke, at once
I leap from Satan's foot to Peter's knee –
These news be mine, none other's – nay, the King's –
530   Descend into the city:' whereon he sought
The King alone, and found, and told him all.

'I have stagger'd thy strong Gawain in a tilt
For pastime; yea, he said it: joust can I.
Make me thy knight – in secret! let my name

Be hidd'n, and give me the first quest, I spring   535
Like flame from ashes.'

                 Here the King's calm eye
Fell on, and check'd, and made him flush, and bow
Lowly, to kiss his hand, who answer'd him,
'Son, the good mother let me know thee here,
And sent her wish that I would yield thee thine.   540
Make thee my knight? my knights are sworn to vows
Of utter hardihood, utter gentleness,
And, loving, utter faithfulness in love,
And uttermost obedience to the King.'

Then Gareth, lightly springing from his knees,   545
'My King, for hardihood I can promise thee.
For uttermost obedience make demand
Of whom ye gave me to, the Seneschal,
No mellow master of the meats and drinks!
And as for love, God wot, I love not yet,   550
But love I shall, God willing.'

                 And the King –
'Make thee my knight in secret? yea, but he,
Our noblest brother, and our truest man,
And one with me in all, he needs must know.'

'Let Lancelot know, my King, let Lancelot know,   555
Thy noblest and thy truest!'

                 And the King –
'But wherefore would ye men should wonder at you?
Nay, rather for the sake of me, their King,
And the deed's sake my knighthood do the deed,
Than to be noised of.'

                 Merrily Gareth ask'd,   560
'Have I not earn'd my cake in baking of it?
Let be my name until I make my name!
My deeds will speak: it is but for a day.'
So with a kindly hand on Gareth's arm

565 Smiled the great King, and half-unwillingly
Loving his lusty youthhood yielded to him.
Then, after summoning Lancelot privily,
'I have given him the first quest: he is not proven.
Look therefore when he calls for this in hall,
570 Thou get to horse and follow him far away.
Cover the lions on thy shield, and see
Far as thou mayest, he be nor ta'en nor slain.'

Then that same day there past into the hall
A damsel of high lineage, and a brow
575 May-blossom, and a cheek of apple-blossom,
Hawk-eyes; and lightly was her slender nose
Tip-tilted like the petal of a flower;
She into hall past with her page and cried,

'O King, for thou hast driven the foe without,
580 See to the foe within! bridge, ford, beset
By bandits, everyone that owns a tower
The Lord for half a league. Why sit ye there?
Rest would I not, Sir King, an I were king,
Till ev'n the lonest hold were all as free
585 From cursed bloodshed, as thine altar-cloth
From that best blood it is a sin to spill.'

'Comfort thyself,' said Arthur, 'I nor mine
Rest: so my knighthood keep the vows they swore,
The wastest moorland of our realm shall be
590 Safe, damsel, as the centre of this hall.
What is thy name? thy need?'

'My name?' she said —
'Lynette my name; noble; my need, a knight
To combat for my sister, Lyonors,
A lady of high lineage, of great lands,
595 And comely, yea, and comelier than myself.
She lives in Castle Perilous: a river
Runs in three loops about her living-place;
And o'er it are three passings, and three knights
Defend the passings, brethren, and a fourth

And of that four the mightiest, holds her stay'd   600
In her own castle, and so besieges her
To break her will, and make her wed with him:
And but delays his purport till thou send
To do the battle with him, thy chief man
Sir Lancelot whom he trusts to overthrow,   605
Then wed, with glory: but she will not wed
Save whom she loveth, or a holy life.
Now therefore have I come for Lancelot.'

Then Arthur mindful of Sir Gareth ask'd,
'Damsel, ye know this Order lives to crush   610
All wrongers of the Realm. But say, these four,
Who be they? What the fashion of the men?'

'They be of foolish fashion, O Sir King,
The fashion of that old knight-errantry
Who ride abroad, and do but what they will;   615
Courteous or bestial from the moment, such
As have nor law nor king; and three of these
Proud in their fantasy call themselves the Day,
Morning-Star, and Noon-Sun, and Evening-Star,
Being strong fools; and never a whit more wise   620
The fourth, who alway rideth arm'd in black,
A huge man-beast of boundless savagery.
He names himself the Night and oftener Death,
And wears a helmet mounted with a skull,
And bears a skeleton figured on his arms,   625
To show that who may slay or scape the three,
Slain by himself, shall enter endless night.
And all these four be fools, but mighty men,
And therefore am I come for Lancelot.'

Hereat Sir Gareth call'd from where he rose,   630
A head with kindling eyes above the throng,
'A boon, Sir King – this quest!' then – for he mark'd
Kay near him groaning like a wounded bull –
'Yea, King, thou knowest thy kitchen-knave am I,
And mighty thro' thy meats and drinks am I,   635
And I can topple over a hundred such.

Thy promise, King,' and Arthur glancing at him,
Brought down a momentary brow. 'Rough, sudden,
And pardonable, worthy to be knight –
640   Go therefore,' and all hearers were amazed.

But on the damsel's forehead shame, pride, wrath
Slew the May-white: she lifted either arm,
'Fie on thee, King! I ask'd for thy chief knight,
And thou hast given me but a kitchen-knave.'
645   Then ere a man in hall could stay her, turn'd,
Fled down the lane of access to the King,
Took horse, descended the slope street, and past
The weird white gate, and paused without, beside
The field of tourney, murmuring 'kitchen-knave.'

650   Now two great entries open'd from the hall,
At one end one, that gave upon a range
Of level pavement where the King would pace
At sunrise, gazing over plain and wood;
And down from this a lordly stairway sloped
655   Till lost in blowing trees and tops of towers;
And out by this main doorway past the King.
But one was counter to the hearth, and rose
High that the highest-crested helm could ride
Therethro' nor graze: and by this entry fled
660   The damsel in her wrath, and on to this
Sir Gareth strode, and saw without the door
King Arthur's gift, the worth of half a town,
A warhorse of the best, and near it stood
The two that out of north had follow'd him:
665   This bare a maiden shield, a casque; that held
The horse, the spear; whereat Sir Gareth loosed
A cloak that dropt from collar-bone to heel,
A cloth of roughest web, and cast it down,
And from it like a fuel-smother'd fire,
670   That lookt half-dead, brake bright, and flash'd as those
Dull-coated things, that making slide apart
Their dusk wing-cases, all beneath there burns
A jewell'd harness, ere they pass and fly.

So Gareth ere he parted flash'd in arms.
Then as he donn'd the helm, and took the shield   675
And mounted horse and graspt a spear, of grain
Storm-strengthen'd on a windy site, and tipt
With trenchant steel, around him slowly prest
The people, while from out of kitchen came
The thralls in throng, and seeing who had work'd   680
Lustier than any, and whom they could but love,
Mounted in arms, threw up their caps and cried,
'God bless the King, and all his fellowship!'
And on thro' lanes of shouting Gareth rode
Down the slope street, and past without the gate.   685

    So Gareth past with joy; but as the cur
Pluckt from the cur he fights with, ere his cause
Be cool'd by fighting, follows, being named,
His owner, but remembers all, and growls
Remembering, so Sir Kay beside the door   690
Mutter'd in scorn of Gareth whom he used
To harry and hustle.

                        'Bound upon a quest
With horse and arms – the King hath past his time –
My scullion knave! Thralls to your work again,
For an your fire be low ye kindle mine!   695
Will there be dawn in West and eve in East?
Begone! – my knave! – belike and like enow
Some old head-blow not heeded in his youth
So shook his wits they wander in his prime –
Crazed! How the villain lifted up his voice,   700
Nor shamed to bawl himself a kitchen-knave.
Tut: he was tame and meek enow with me,
Till peacock'd up with Lancelot's noticing.
Well – I will after my loud knave, and learn
Whether he know me for his master yet.   705
Out of the smoke he came, and so my lance
Hold, by God's grace, he shall into the mire –
Thence, if the King awaken from his craze,
Into the smoke again.'

But Lancelot said,
710 'Kay, wherefore wilt thou go against the King,
For that did never he whereon ye rail,
But ever meekly served the King in thee?
Abide: take counsel; for this lad is great
And lusty, and knowing both of lance and sword.'
715 'Tut, tell not me,' said Kay, 'ye are overfine
To mar stout knaves with foolish courtesies:'
Then mounted, on thro' silent faces rode
Down the slope city, and out beyond the gate.

But by the field of tourney lingering yet
720 Mutter'd the damsel, 'Wherefore did the King
Scorn me? for, were Sir Lancelot lackt, at least
He might have yielded to me one of those
Who tilt for lady's love and glory here,
Rather than – O sweet heaven! O fie upon him –
His kitchen-knave.'

725   To whom Sir Gareth drew
(And there were none but few goodlier than he)
Shining in arms, 'Damsel, the quest is mine.
Lead, and I follow.' She thereat, as one
That smells a foul-flesh'd agaric in the holt,
730 And deems it carrion of some woodland thing,
Or shrew, or weasel, nipt her slender nose
With petulant thumb and finger, shrilling, 'Hence!
Avoid, thou smellest all of kitchen-grease.
And look who comes behind,' for there was Kay.
735 'Knowest thou not me? thy master? I am Kay.
We lack thee by the hearth.'

                    And Gareth to him,
'Master no more! too well I know thee, ay –
The most ungentle knight in Arthur's hall.'
'Have at thee then,' said Kay: they shock'd, and Kay
740 Fell shoulder-slipt, and Gareth cried again,
'Lead, and I follow,' and fast away she fled.

But after sod and shingle ceased to fly

Behind her, and the heart of her good horse
Was nigh to burst with violence of the beat,
Perforce she stay'd, and overtaken spoke.   745

'What doest thou, scullion, in my fellowship?
Deem'st thou that I accept thee aught the more
Or love thee better, that by some device
Full cowardly, or by mere unhappiness,
Thou hast overthrown and slain thy master – thou! –
Dish-washer and broach-turner, loon! – to me
Thou smellest all of kitchen as before.'   750

'Damsel,' Sir Gareth answer'd gently, 'say
Whate'er ye will, but whatsoe'er ye say,
I leave not till I finish this fair quest,   755
Or die therefore.'

                       'Ay, wilt thou finish it?
Sweet lord, how like a noble knight he talks!
The listening rogue hath caught the manner of it.
But, knave, anon thou shalt be met with, knave,
And then by such a one that thou for all   760
The kitchen brewis that was ever supt
Shalt not once dare to look him in the face.'

'I shall assay,' said Gareth with a smile
That madden'd her, and away she flash'd again
Down the long avenues of a boundless wood,   765
And Gareth following was again beknaved.

'Sir Kitchen-knave, I have miss'd the only way
Where Arthur's men are set along the wood;
The wood is nigh as full of thieves as leaves:
If both be slain, I am rid of thee; but yet,   770
Sir Scullion, canst thou use that spit of thine?
Fight, an thou canst: I have miss'd the only way.'

So till the dusk that follow'd evensong
Rode on the two, reviler and reviled;
Then after one long slope was mounted, saw,   775

Bowl-shaped, thro' tops of many thousand pines
A gloomy-gladed hollow slowly sink
To westward – in the deeps whereof a mere,
Round as the red eye of an Eagle-owl,
780 Under the half-dead sunset glared; and shouts
Ascended, and there brake a servingman
Flying from out of the black wood, and crying,
'They have bound my lord to cast him in the mere.'
Then Gareth, 'Bound am I to right the wrong'd,
785 But straitlier bound am I to bide with thee.'
And when the damsel spake contemptuously,
'Lead, and I follow,' Gareth cried again,
'Follow, I lead!' so down among the pines
He plunged; and there, blackshadow'd nigh the mere,
790 And mid-thigh-deep in bulrushes and reed,
Saw six tall men haling a seventh along,
A stone about his neck to drown him in it.
Three with good blows he quieted, but three
Fled thro' the pines; and Gareth loosed the stone
795 From off his neck, then in the mere beside
Tumbled it; oilily bubbled up the mere.
Last, Gareth loosed his bonds and on free feet
Set him, a stalwart Baron, Arthur's friend.

    'Well that ye came, or else these caitiff rogues
800 Had wreak'd themselves on me; good cause is theirs
To hate me, for my wont hath ever been
To catch my thief, and then like vermin here
Drown him, and with a stone about his neck;
And under this wan water many of them
805 Lie rotting, but at night let go the stone,
And rise, and flickering in a grimly light
Dance on the mere. Good now, ye have saved a life
Worth somewhat as the cleanser of this wood.
And fain would I reward thee worshipfully.
What guerdon will ye?'

810   Gareth sharply spake,
'None! for the deed's sake have I done the deed,
In uttermost obedience to the King.
But wilt thou yield this damsel harbourage?'

58

    Whereat the Baron saying, 'I well believe
You be of Arthur's Table,' a light laugh   815
Broke from Lynette, 'Ay, truly of a truth,
And in a sort, being Arthur's kitchen-knave! –
But deem not I accept thee aught the more,
Scullion, for running sharply with thy spit
Down on a rout of craven foresters.   820
A thresher with his flail had scatter'd them.
Nay – for thou smellest of the kitchen still.
But an this lord will yield us harbourage,
Well.'

    So she spake. A league beyond the wood,   825
All in a full-fair manor and a rich,
His towers where that day a feast had been
Held in high hall, and many a viand left,
And many a costly cate, received the three.
And there they placed a peacock in his pride   830
Before the damsel, and the Baron set
Gareth beside her, but at once she rose.

    'Meseems, that here is much discourtesy,
Setting this knave, Lord Baron, at my side.
Hear me – this morn I stood in Arthur's hall,
And pray'd the King would grant me Lancelot   835
To fight the brotherhood of Day and Night –
The last a monster unsubduable
Of any save of him for whom I call'd –
Suddenly bawls this frontless kitchen-knave,
"The quest is mine; thy kitchen-knave am I,   840
And mighty thro' thy meats and drinks am I."
Then Arthur all at once gone mad replies,
"Go therefore," and so gives the quest to him –
Him – here – a villain fitter to stick swine
Than ride abroad redressing women's wrong,   845
Or sit beside a noble gentlewoman.'

    Then half-ashamed and part-amazed, the lord
Now look'd at one and now at other, left
The damsel by the peacock in his pride,

850 And, seating Gareth at another board,
     Sat down beside him, ate and then began.

     'Friend, whether thou be kitchen-knave, or not,
     Or whether it be the maiden's fantasy,
     And whether she be mad, or else the King,
855 Or both or neither, or thyself be mad,
     I ask not: but thou strikest a strong stroke,
     For strong thou art and goodly therewithal,
     And saver of my life; and therefore now,
     For here be mighty men to joust with, weigh
860 Whether thou wilt not with thy damsel back
     To crave again Sir Lancelot of the King.
     Thy pardon; I but speak for thine avail,
     The saver of my life.'

                         And Gareth said,
     'Full pardon, but I follow up the quest,
865 Despite of Day and Night and Death and Hell.'

     So when, next morn, the lord whose life he saved
     Had, some brief space, convey'd them on their way
     And left them with God-speed, Sir Gareth spake,
     'Lead, and I follow.' Haughtily she replied,

870 'I fly no more: I allow thee for an hour.
     Lion and stoat have isled together, knave,
     In time of flood. Nay, furthermore, methinks
     Some ruth is mine for thee. Back wilt thou, fool?
     For hard by here is one will overthrow
875 And slay thee: then will I to court again,
     And shame the King for only yielding me
     My champion from the ashes of his hearth.'

     To whom Sir Gareth answer'd courteously,
     'Say thou thy say, and I will do my deed.
880 Allow me for mine hour, and thou wilt find
     My fortunes all as fair as hers who lay
     Among the ashes and wedded the King's son.'

Then to the shore of one of those long loops
Wherethro' the serpent river coil'd, they came.
Rough-thicketed were the banks and steep; the stream   885
Full, narrow; this a bridge of single arc
Took at a leap; and on the further side
Arose a silk pavilion, gay with gold
In streaks and rays, and all Lent-lily in hue,
Save that the dome was purple, and above,   890
Crimson, a slender banneret fluttering.
And therebefore the lawless warrior paced
Unarm'd, and calling, 'Damsel, is this he,
The champion thou hast brought from Arthur's hall?
For whom we let thee pass.' 'Nay, nay,' she said,   895
'Sir Morning-Star. The King in utter scorn
Of thee and thy much folly hath sent thee here
His kitchen-knave: and look thou to thyself:
See that he fall not on thee suddenly,
And slay thee unarm'd: he is not knight but knave.'   900

Then at his call, 'O daughters of the Dawn,
And servants of the Morning-Star, approach,
Arm me,' from out the silken curtain-folds
Bare-footed and bare-headed three fair girls
In gilt and rosy raiment came: their feet   905
In dewy grasses glisten'd; and the hair
All over glanced with dewdrop or with gem
Like sparkles in the stone Avanturine.
These arm'd him in blue arms, and gave a shield
Blue also, and thereon the morning star.   910
And Gareth silent gazed upon the knight,
Who stood a moment, ere his horse was brought,
Glorying; and in the stream beneath him, shone
Immingled with Heaven's azure waveringly,
The gay pavilion and the naked feet,   915
His arms, the rosy raiment, and the star.

Then she that watch'd him, 'Wherefore stare ye so?
Thou shakest in thy fear: there yet is time:
Flee down the valley before he get to horse.
Who will cry shame? Thou art not knight but knave.'   920

Said Gareth, 'Damsel, whether knave or knight,
Far liefer had I fight a score of times
Than hear thee so missay me and revile.
Fair words were best for him who fights for thee;
925 But truly foul are better, for they send
That strength of anger thro' mine arms, I know
That I shall overthrow him.'

                              And he that bore
The star, when mounted, cried from o'er the bridge,
'A kitchen-knave, and sent in scorn of me!
930 Such fight not I, but answer scorn with scorn.
For this were shame to do him further wrong
Than set him on his feet, and take his horse
And arms, and so return him to the King.
Come, therefore, leave thy lady lightly, knave.
935 Avoid: for it beseemeth not a knave
To ride with such a lady.'

                              'Dog, thou liest.
I spring from loftier lineage than thine own.'
He spake; and all at fiery speed the two
Shock'd on the central bridge, and either spear
940 Bent but not brake, and either knight at once,
Hurl'd as a stone from out of a catapult
Beyond his horse's crupper and the bridge,
Fell, as if dead; but quickly rose and drew,
And Gareth lash'd so fiercely with his brand
945 He drave his enemy backward down the bridge,
The damsel crying, 'Well-stricken, kitchen-knave!'
Till Gareth's shield was cloven; but one stroke
Laid him that clove it grovelling on the ground.

Then cried the fall'n, 'Take not my life: I yield.'
950 And Gareth, 'So this damsel ask it of me
Good – I accord it easily as a grace.'
She reddening, 'Insolent scullion: I of thee?
I bound to thee for any favour ask'd!'
'Then shall he die.' And Gareth there unlaced
955 His helmet as to slay him, but she shriek'd,

'Be not so hardy, scullion, as to slay
One nobler than thyself.' 'Damsel, thy charge
Is an abounding pleasure to me. Knight,
Thy life is thine at her command. Arise
And quickly pass to Arthur's hall, and say   960
His kitchen-knave hath sent thee. See thou crave
His pardon for thy breaking of his laws.
Myself, when I return, will plead for thee.
Thy shield is mine – farewell; and, damsel, thou,
Lead, and I follow.'

              And fast away she fled.   965
Then when he came upon her, spake, 'Methought,
Knave, when I watch'd thee striking on the bridge
The savour of thy kitchen came upon me
A little faintlier: but the wind hath changed:
I scent it twenty-fold.' And then she sang,   970
'"O morning star" (not that tall felon there
Whom thou by sorcery or unhappiness
Or some device, hast foully overthrown),
"O morning star that smilest in the blue,
O star, my morning dream hath proven true,   975
Smile sweetly, thou! my love hath smiled on me."

 'But thou begone, take counsel, and away,
For hard by here is one that guards a ford –
The second brother in their fool's parable –
Will pay thee all thy wages, and to boot.   980
Care not for shame: thou art not knight but knave.'

 To whom Sir Gareth answer'd, laughingly,
'Parables? Hear a parable of the knave.
When I was kitchen-knave among the rest
Fierce was the hearth, and one of my co-mates   985
Own'd a rough dog, to whom he cast his coat,
"Guard it," and there was none to meddle with it.
And such a coat art thou, and thee the King
Gave me to guard, and such a dog am I,
To worry, and not to flee – and – knight or knave –   990
The knave that doth thee service as full knight

63

Is all as good, meseems, as any knight
Toward thy sister's freeing.'

'Ay, Sir Knave!
Ay, knave, because thou strikest as a knight,
995   Being but knave, I hate thee all the more.'

'Fair damsel, you should worship me the more,
That, being but knave, I throw thine enemies.'

'Ay, ay,' she said, 'but thou shalt meet thy match.'

So when they touch'd the second river-loop,
1000   Huge on a huge red horse, and all in mail
Burnish'd to blinding, shone the Noonday Sun
Beyond a raging shallow. As if the flower,
That blows a globe of after arrowlets,
Ten thousand-fold had grown, flash'd the fierce shield,
1005   All sun; and Gareth's eyes had flying blots
Before them when he turn'd from watching him.
He from beyond the roaring shallow roar'd,
'What doest thou, brother, in my marches here?'
And she athwart the shallow shrill'd again,
1010   'Here is a kitchen-knave from Arthur's hall
Hath overthrown thy brother, and hath his arms.'
'Ugh!' cried the Sun, and vizoring up a red
And cipher face of rounded foolishness,
Push'd horse across the foamings of the ford,
1015   Whom Gareth met midstream: no room was there
For lance or tourney-skill: four strokes they struck
With sword, and these were mighty; the new knight
Had fear he might be shamed; but as the Sun
Heaved up a ponderous arm to strike the fifth,
1020   The hoof of his horse slipt in the stream, the stream
Descended, and the Sun was wash'd away.

Then Gareth laid his lance athwart the ford;
So drew him home; but he that fought no more,
As being all bone-batter'd on the rock,
1025   Yielded; and Gareth sent him to the King.

'Myself when I return will plead for thee.'
'Lead, and I follow.' Quietly she led.
'Hath not the good wind, damsel, changed again?'
'Nay, not a point: nor art thou victor here.
There lies a ridge of slate across the ford;   1030
His horse thereon stumbled – ay, for I saw it.

'"O Sun" (not this strong fool whom thou, Sir Knave,
Hast overthrown thro' mere unhappiness),
"O Sun, that wakenest all to bliss or pain,
O moon, that layest all to sleep again,
Shine sweetly: twice my love hath smiled on me."   1035

'What knowest thou of lovesong or of love?
Nay, nay, God wot, so thou wert nobly born,
Thou hast a pleasant presence. Yea, perchance, –

'"O dewy flowers that open to the sun,   1040
O dewy flowers that close when day is done,
Blow sweetly: twice my love hath smiled on me."

'What knowest thou of flowers, except, belike,
To garnish meats with? hath not our good King
Who lent me thee, the flower of kitchendom,   1045
A foolish love for flowers? what stick ye round
The pasty? wherewithal deck the boar's head?
Flowers? nay, the boar hath rosemaries and bay.

'"O birds, that warble to the morning sky,
O birds that warble as the day goes by,   1050
Sing sweetly: twice my love hath smiled on me."

'What knowest thou of birds, lark, mavis, merle,
Linnet? what dream ye when they utter forth
May-music growing with the growing light,
Their sweet sun-worship? these be for the snare   1055
(So runs thy fancy) these be for the spit,
Larding and basting. See thou have not now
Larded thy last, except thou turn and fly.
There stands the third fool of their allegory.'

1060   For there beyond a bridge of treble bow,
All in a rose-red from the west, and all
Naked it seem'd, and glowing in the broad
Deep-dimpled current underneath, the knight,
That named himself the Star of Evening, stood.

1065   And Gareth, 'Wherefore waits the madman there
Naked in open dayshine?' 'Nay,' she cried,
'Not naked, only wrapt in harden'd skins
That fit him like his own; and so ye cleave
His armour off him, these will turn the blade.'

1070   Then the third brother shouted o'er the bridge,
'O brother-star, why shine ye here so low?
Thy ward is higher up: but have ye slain
The damsel's champion?' and the damsel cried,

'No star of thine, but shot from Arthur's heaven
1075 With all disaster unto thine and thee!
For both thy younger brethren have gone down
Before this youth; and so wilt thou, Sir Star;
Art thou not old?'

                'Old, damsel, old and hard,
Old, with the might and breath of twenty boys.'
1080 Said Gareth, 'Old, and over-bold in brag!
But that same strength which threw the Morning Star
Can throw the Evening.'

             Then that other blew
A hard and deadly note upon the horn.
'Approach and arm me!' With slow steps from out
1085 An old storm-beaten, russet, many-stain'd
Pavilion, forth a grizzled damsel came,
And arm'd him in old arms, and brought a helm
With but a drying evergreen for crest,
And gave a shield whereon the Star of Even
1090 Half-tarnish'd and half-bright, his emblem, shone.
But when it glitter'd o'er the saddle-bow,
They madly hurl'd together on the bridge;

And Gareth overthrew him, lighted, drew,
There met him drawn, and overthrew him again,
But up like fire he started: and as oft   1095
As Gareth brought him grovelling on his knees,
So many a time he vaulted up again;
Till Gareth panted hard, and his great heart,
Foredooming all his trouble was in vain,
Labour'd within him, for he seem'd as one   1100
That all in later, sadder age begins
To war against ill uses of a life,
But these from all his life arise, and cry,
'Thou hast made us lords, and canst not put us down!'
He half despairs; so Gareth seem'd to strike   1105
Vainly, the damsel clamouring all the while,
'Well done, knave-knight, well stricken, O good
          knight-knave –
O knave, as noble as any of all the knights –
Shame me not, shame me not. I have prophesied –
Strike, thou art worthy of the Table Round –   1110
His arms are old, he trusts the harden'd skin –
Strike – strike – the wind will never change again.'
And Gareth hearing ever stronglier smote,
And hew'd great pieces of his armour off him,
But lash'd in vain against the harden'd skin,   1115
And could not wholly bring him under, more
Than loud Southwesterns, rolling ridge on ridge,
The buoy that rides at sea, and dips and springs
For ever; till at length Sir Gareth's brand
Clash'd his, and brake it utterly to the hilt.   1120
'I have thee now;' but forth that other sprang,
And, all unknightlike, writhed his wiry arms
Around him, till he felt, despite his mail,
Strangled, but straining ev'n his uttermost
Cast, and so hurl'd him headlong o'er the bridge   1125
Down to the river, sink or swim; and cried,
'Lead, and I follow.'

              But the damsel said,
'I lead no longer; ride thou at my side;
Thou art the kingliest of all kitchen-knaves.

1130 '"O trefoil, sparkling on the rainy plain,
O rainbow with three colours after rain,
Shine sweetly: thrice my love hath smiled on me."

'Sir, – and, good faith, I fain had added – Knight,
But that I heard thee call thyself a knave, –
1135 Shamed am I that I so rebuked, reviled,
Missaid thee; noble I am; and thought the King
Scorn'd me and mine; and now thy pardon, friend,
For thou hast ever answer'd courteously,
And wholly bold thou art, and meek withal
1140 As any of Arthur's best, but, being knave,
Hast mazed my wit: I marvel what thou art.'

'Damsel,' he said, 'you be not all to blame,
Saving that you mistrusted our good King
Would handle scorn, or yield you, asking, one
1145 Not fit to cope your quest. You said your say;
Mine answer was my deed. Good sooth! I hold
He scarce is knight, yea but half-man, nor meet
To fight for gentle damsel, he, who lets
His heart be stirr'd with any foolish heat
1150 At any gentle damsel's waywardness.
Shamed? care not! thy foul sayings fought for me:
And seeing now thy words are fair, methinks
There rides no knight, not Lancelot, his great self,
Hath force to quell me.'

                              Nigh upon that hour
1155 When the lone hern forgets his melancholy,
Lets down his other leg, and stretching, dreams
Of goodly supper in the distant pool,
Then turn'd the noble damsel smiling at him,
And told him of a cavern hard at hand,
1160 Where bread and baken meats and good red wine
Of Southland, which the Lady Lyonors
Had sent her coming champion, waited him.

Anon they past a narrow comb wherein
Were slabs of rock with figures, knights on horse

Sculptured, and deckt in slowly-waning hues.   1165
'Sir Knave, my knight, a hermit once was here,
Whose holy hand hath fashion'd on the rock
The war of Time against the soul of man.
And yon four fools have suck'd their allegory
From these damp walls, and taken but the form.   1170
Know ye not these?' and Gareth lookt and read –
In letters like to those the vexillary
Hath left crag-carven o'er the streaming Gelt –
'PHOSPHORUS,' then 'MERIDIES' – 'HESPERUS' –
'NOX' – 'MORS,' beneath five figures, armèd men,   1175
Slab after slab, their faces forward all,
And running down the Soul, a Shape that fled
With broken wings, torn raiment and loose hair,
For help and shelter to the hermit's cave.
'Follow the faces, and we find it. Look,   1180
Who comes behind?'

          For one – delay'd at first
Thro' helping back the dislocated Kay
To Camelot, then by what thereafter chanced,
The damsel's headlong error thro' the wood –
Sir Lancelot, having swum the river-loops –   1185
His blue shield-lions cover'd – softly drew
Behind the twain, and when he saw the star
Gleam, on Sir Gareth's turning to him, cried,
'Stay, felon knight, I avenge me for my friend.'
And Gareth crying prick'd against the cry;   1190
But when they closed – in a moment – at one touch
Of that skill'd spear, the wonder of the world –
Went sliding down so easily, and fell,
That when he found the grass within his hands
He laugh'd; the laughter jarr'd upon Lynette: 1195
Harshly she ask'd him, 'Shamed and overthrown,
And tumbled back into the kitchen-knave,
Why laugh ye? that ye blew your boast in vain?'

'Nay, noble damsel, but that I, the son
Of old King Lot and good Queen Bellicent,   1200
And victor of the bridges and the ford,

And knight of Arthur, here lie thrown by whom
I know not, all thro' mere unhappiness –
Device and sorcery and unhappiness –
Out, sword; we are thrown!' And Lancelot answer'd,
1205   'Prince,
O Gareth – thro' the mere unhappiness
Of one who came to help thee, not to harm,
Lancelot, and all as glad to find thee whole,
As on the day when Arthur knighted him.'

1210   Then Gareth, 'Thou – Lancelot! – thine the hand
That threw me? An some chance to mar the boast
Thy brethren of thee make – which could not chance –
Had sent thee down before a lesser spear,
Shamed had I been, and sad – O Lancelot – thou!'

1215   Whereat the maiden, petulant, 'Lancelot,
Why came ye not, when call'd? and wherefore now
Come ye, not call'd? I gloried in my knave,
Who being still rebuked, would answer still
Courteous as any knight – but now, if knight,
1220 The marvel dies, and leaves me fool'd and trick'd,
And only wondering wherefore play'd upon:
And doubtful whether I and mine be scorn'd.
Where should be truth if not in Arthur's hall,
In Arthur's presence? Knight, knave, prince and fool,
I hate thee and for ever.'

1225   And Lancelot said,
'Blessèd be thou, Sir Gareth! knight art thou
To the King's best wish. O damsel, be you wise
To call him shamed, who is but overthrown?
Thrown have I been, nor once, but many a time.
1230 Victor from vanquish'd issues at the last,
And overthrower from being overthrown.
With sword we have not striven; and thy good horse
And thou are weary; yet not less I felt
Thy manhood thro' that wearied lance of thine.
1235 Well hast thou done; for all the stream is freed,
And thou hast wreak'd his justice on his foes,

70

And when reviled, hast answer'd graciously,
And makest merry when overthrown. Prince, Knight,
Hail, Knight and Prince, and of our Table Round!'

And then when turning to Lynette he told   1240
The tale of Gareth, petulantly she said,
'Ay well – ay well – for worse than being fool'd
Of others, is to fool one's self. A cave,
Sir Lancelot, is hard by, with meats and drinks
And forage for the horse, and flint for fire.   1245
But all about it flies a honeysuckle.
Seek, till we find.' And when they sought and found,
Sir Gareth drank and ate, and all his life
Past into sleep; on whom the maiden gazed.
'Sound sleep be thine! sound cause to sleep hast thou.   1250
Wake lusty! Seem I not as tender to him
As any mother? Ay, but such a one
As all day long hath rated at her child,
And vext his day, but blesses him asleep –
Good lord, how sweetly smells the honeysuckle   1255
In the hush'd night, as if the world were one
Of utter peace, and love, and gentleness!
O Lancelot, Lancelot' – and she clapt her hands –
'Full merry am I to find my goodly knave
Is knight and noble. See now, sworn have I,   1260
Else yon black felon had not let me pass,
To bring thee back to do the battle with him.
Thus an thou goest, he will fight thee first;
Who doubts thee victor? so will my knight-knave
Miss the full flower of this accomplishment.'   1265

Said Lancelot, 'Peradventure he, you name,
May know my shield. Let Gareth, an he will,
Change his for mine, and take my charger, fresh,
Not to be spurr'd, loving the battle as well
As he that rides him.' 'Lancelot-like,' she said,   1270
'Courteous in this, Lord Lancelot, as in all.'

And Gareth, wakening, fiercely clutch'd the shield;
'Ramp ye lance-splintering lions, on whom all spears

71

Are rotten sticks! ye seem agape to roar!
1275 Yea, ramp and roar at leaving of your lord! –
Care not, good beasts, so well I care for you.
O noble Lancelot, from my hold on these
Streams virtue – fire – thro' one that will not shame
Even the shadow of Lancelot under shield.
Hence: let us go.'

1280   Silent the silent field
They traversed. Arthur's harp tho' summer-wan,
In counter motion to the clouds, allured
The glance of Gareth dreaming on his liege.
A star shot: 'Lo,' said Gareth, 'the foe falls!'
1285 An owl whoopt: 'Hark the victor pealing there!'
Suddenly she that rode upon his left
Clung to the shield that Lancelot lent him, crying,
'Yield, yield him this again: 'tis he must fight:
I curse the tongue that all thro' yesterday
1290 Reviled thee, and hath wrought on Lancelot now
To lend thee horse and shield: wonders ye have done;
Miracles ye cannot: here is glory enow
In having flung the three: I see thee maim'd,
Mangled: I swear thou canst not fling the fourth.'

1295 'And wherefore, damsel? tell me all ye know.
You cannot scare me; nor rough face, or voice,
Brute bulk of limb, or boundless savagery
Appal me from the quest.'

                               'Nay, Prince,' she cried,
'God wot, I never look'd upon the face,
1300 Seeing he never rides abroad by day;
But watch'd him have I like a phantom pass
Chilling the night: nor have I heard the voice.
Always he made his mouthpiece of a page
Who came and went, and still reported him
1305 As closing in himself the strength of ten,
And when his anger tare him, massacring
Man, woman, lad and girl – yea, the soft babe!
Some hold that he hath swallow'd infant flesh,

72

Monster! O Prince, I went for Lancelot first,
The quest is Lancelot's: give him back the shield.'   1310

    Said Gareth laughing, 'An he fight for this,
Belike he wins it as the better man:
Thus – and not else!'

                      But Lancelot on him urged
All the devisings of their chivalry
When one might meet a mightier than himself;   1315
How best to manage horse, lance, sword and shield,
And so fill up the gap where force might fail
With skill and fineness. Instant were his words.

    Then Gareth, 'Here be rules. I know but one –
To dash against mine enemy and to win.   1320
Yet have I watch'd thee victor in the joust,
And seen thy way.' 'Heaven help thee,' sigh'd Lynette.

    Then for a space, and under cloud that grew
To thunder-gloom palling all stars, they rode
In converse till she made her palfrey halt,   1325
Lifted an arm, and softly whisper'd, 'There.'
And all the three were silent seeing, pitch'd
Beside the Castle Perilous on flat field,
A huge pavilion like a mountain peak
Sunder the glooming crimson on the marge,   1330
Black, with black banner, and a long black horn
Beside it hanging; which Sir Gareth graspt,
And so, before the two could hinder him,
Sent all his heart and breath thro' all the horn.
Echo'd the walls; a light twinkled; anon   1335
Came lights and lights, and once again he blew;
Whereon were hollow tramplings up and down
And muffled voices heard, and shadows past;
Till high above him, circled with her maids,
The Lady Lyonors at a window stood,   1340
Beautiful among lights, and waving to him
White hands, and courtesy; but when the Prince
Three times had blown – after long hush – at last –

73

The huge pavilion slowly yielded up,
1345   Thro' those black foldings, that which housed therein.
High on a nightblack horse, in nightblack arms,
With white breast-bone, and barren ribs of Death,
And crown'd with fleshless laughter – some ten steps –
In the half-light – thro' the dim dawn – advanced
1350   The monster, and then paused, and spake no word.

But Gareth spake and all indignantly,
'Fool, for thou hast, men say, the strength of ten,
Canst thou not trust the limbs thy God hath given,
But must, to make the terror of thee more,
1355   Trick thyself out in ghastly imageries
Of that which Life hath done with, and the clod,
Less dull than thou, will hide with mantling flowers
As if for pity?' But he spake no word;
Which set the horror higher: a maiden swoon'd;
1360   The Lady Lyonors wrung her hands and wept,
As doom'd to be the bride of Night and Death;
Sir Gareth's head prickled beneath his helm;
And ev'n Sir Lancelot thro' his warm blood felt
Ice strike, and all that mark'd him were aghast.

1365   At once Sir Lancelot's charger fiercely neigh'd,
And Death's dark war-horse bounded forward with him.
Then those that did not blink the terror, saw
That Death was cast to ground, and slowly rose.
But with one stroke Sir Gareth split the skull.
1370   Half fell to right and half to left and lay.
Then with a stronger buffet he clove the helm
As throughly as the skull; and out from this
Issued the bright face of a blooming boy
Fresh as a flower new-born, and crying, 'Knight,
1375   Slay me not: my three brethren bad me do it,
To make a horror all about the house,
And stay the world from Lady Lyonors.
They never dream'd the passes would be past.'
Answer'd Sir Gareth graciously to one
1380   Not many a moon his younger, 'My fair child,
What madness made thee challenge the chief knight

[handwritten margin note: THIS THING THAT IS DEATH IS REALLY YOUTH – J.W.]

Of Arthur's hall?' 'Fair Sir, they bad me do it.
They hate the King, and Lancelot, the King's friend,
They hoped to slay him somewhere on the stream,
They never dream'd the passes could be past.'   1385

Then sprang the happier day from underground;
And Lady Lyonors and her house, with dance
And revel and song, made merry over Death,
As being after all their foolish fears
And horrors only proven a blooming boy.   1390
So large mirth lived and Gareth won the quest.

And he that told the tale in older times
Says that Sir Gareth wedded Lyonors,
But he, that told it later, says Lynette.

The Marriage of Geraint

The brave Geraint, a knight of Arthur's court,
A tributary prince of Devon, one
Of that great Order of the Table Round,
Had married Enid, Yniol's only child,
And loved her, as he loved the light of Heaven.
And as the light of Heaven varies, now
At sunrise, now at sunset, now by night
With moon and trembling stars, so loved Geraint
To make her beauty vary day by day,
In crimsons and in purples and in gems.
And Enid, but to please her husband's eye,
Who first had found and loved her in a state
Of broken fortunes, daily fronted him
In some fresh splendour; and the Queen herself,
Grateful to Prince Geraint for service done,
Loved her, and often with her own white hands
Array'd and deck'd her, as the loveliest,
Next after her own self, in all the court.
And Enid loved the Queen, and with true heart
Adored her, as the stateliest and the best
And loveliest of all women upon earth.
And seeing them so tender and so close,
Long in their common love rejoiced Geraint.
But when a rumour rose about the Queen,
Touching her guilty love for Lancelot,
Tho' yet there lived no proof, nor yet was heard
The world's loud whisper breaking into storm,
Not less Geraint believed it; and there fell
A horror on him, lest his gentle wife,
Thro' that great tenderness for Guinevere,
Had suffer'd, or should suffer any taint
In nature: wherefore going to the King,
He made this pretext, that his princedom lay

Close on the borders of a territory,
Wherein were bandit earls, and caitiff knights,   35
Assassins, and all flyers from the hand
Of Justice, and whatever loathes a law:
And therefore, till the King himself should please
To cleanse this common sewer of all his realm,
He craved a fair permission to depart,   40
And there defend his marches; and the King
Mused for a little on his plea, but, last,
Allowing it, the Prince and Enid rode,
And fifty knights rode with them, to the shores
Of Severn, and they past to their own land;   45
Where, thinking, that if ever yet was wife
True to her lord, mine shall be so to me,
He compass'd her with sweet observances
And worship, never leaving her, and grew
Forgetful of his promise to the King,   50
Forgetful of the falcon and the hunt,
Forgetful of the tilt and tournament,
Forgetful of his glory and his name,
Forgetful of his princedom and its cares.
And this forgetfulness was hateful to her.   55
And by and by the people, when they met
In twos and threes, or fuller companies,
Began to scoff and jeer and babble of him
As of a prince whose manhood was all gone,
And molten down in mere uxoriousness.   60
And this she gather'd from the people's eyes:
This too the women who attired her head,
To please her, dwelling on his boundless love,
Told Enid, and they sadden'd her the more:
And day by day she thought to tell Geraint,   65
But could not out of bashful delicacy;
While he that watch'd her sadden, was the more
Suspicious that her nature had a taint.

At last, it chanced that on a summer morn
(They sleeping each by either) the new sun   70
Beat thro' the blindless casement of the room,
And heated the strong warrior in his dreams;

Who, moving, cast the coverlet aside,
And bared the knotted column of his throat,
75   The massive square of his heroic breast,
And arms on which the standing muscle sloped,
As slopes a wild brook o'er a little stone,
Running too vehemently to break upon it.
And Enid woke and sat beside the couch,
80   Admiring him, and thought within herself,
Was ever man so grandly made as he?
Then, like a shadow, past the people's talk
And accusation of uxoriousness
Across her mind, and bowing over him,
85   Low to her own heart piteously she said:

'O noble breast and all-puissant arms,
Am I the cause, I the poor cause that men
Reproach you, saying all your force is gone?
I *am* the cause, because I dare not speak
90   And tell him what I think and what they say.
And yet I hate that he should linger here;
I cannot love my lord and not his name.
Far liefer had I gird his harness on him,
And ride with him to battle and stand by,
95   And watch his mightful hand striking great blows
At caitiffs and at wrongers of the world.
Far better were I laid in the dark earth,
Not hearing any more his noble voice,
Not to be folded more in these dear arms,
100   And darken'd from the high light in his eyes,
Than that my lord thro' me should suffer shame.
Am I so bold, and could I so stand by,
And see my dear lord wounded in the strife,
Or maybe pierced to death before mine eyes,
105   And yet not dare to tell him what I think,
And how men slur him, saying all his force
Is melted into mere effeminacy?
O me, I fear that I am no true wife.'

Half inwardly, half audibly she spoke,
110   And the strong passion in her made her weep

True tears upon his broad and naked breast,
And these awoke him, and by great mischance
He heard but fragments of her later words,
And that she fear'd she was not a true wife.
And then he thought, 'In spite of all my care,   115
For all my pains, poor man, for all my pains,
She is not faithful to me, and I see her
Weeping for some gay knight in Arthur's hall.'
Then tho' he loved and reverenced her too much
To dream she could be guilty of foul act,   120
Right thro' his manful breast darted the pang
That makes a man, in the sweet face of her
Whom he loves most, lonely and miserable.
At this he hurl'd his huge limbs out of bed,
And shook his drowsy squire awake and cried,   125
'My charger and her palfrey;' then to her,
'I will ride forth into the wilderness;
For tho' it seems my spurs are yet to win,
I have not fall'n so low as some would wish.
And thou, put on thy worst and meanest dress   130
And ride with me.' And Enid ask'd, amazed,
'If Enid errs, let Enid learn her fault.'
But he, 'I charge thee, ask not, but obey.'
Then she bethought her of a faded silk,
A faded mantle and a faded veil,   135
And moving toward a cedarn cabinet,
Wherein she kept them folded reverently
With sprigs of summer laid between the folds,
She took them, and array'd herself therein,
Remembering when first he came on her   140
Drest in that dress, and how he loved her in it,
And all her foolish fears about the dress,
And all his journey to her, as himself
Had told her, and their coming to the court.

For Arthur on the Whitsuntide before   145
Held court at old Caerleon upon Usk.
There on a day, he sitting high in hall,
Before him came a forester of Dean,

Wet from the woods, with notice of a hart
150 Taller than all his fellows, milky-white,
First seen that day: these things he told the King.
Then the good King gave order to let blow
His horns for hunting on the morrow morn.
And when the Queen petition'd for his leave
155 To see the hunt, allow'd it easily.
So with the morning all the court were gone.
But Guinevere lay late into the morn,
Lost in sweet dreams, and dreaming of her love
For Lancelot, and forgetful of the hunt;
160 But rose at last, a single maiden with her,
Took horse, and forded Usk, and gain'd the wood;
There, on a little knoll beside it, stay'd
Waiting to hear the hounds; but heard instead
A sudden sound of hoofs, for Prince Geraint,
165 Late also, wearing neither hunting-dress
Nor weapon, save a golden-hilted brand,
Came quickly flashing thro' the shallow ford
Behind them, and so gallop'd up the knoll.
A purple scarf, at either end whereof
170 There swung an apple of the purest gold,
Sway'd round about him, as he gallop'd up
To join them, glancing like a dragon-fly
In summer suit and silks of holiday.
Low bow'd the tributary Prince, and she,
175 Sweetly and statelily, and with all grace
Of womanhood and queenhood, answer'd him:
'Late, late, Sir Prince,' she said, 'later than we!'
'Yea, noble Queen,' he answer'd, 'and so late
That I but come like you to see the hunt,
180 Not join it.' 'Therefore wait with me,' she said;
'For on this little knoll, if anywhere,
There is good chance that we shall hear the hounds:
Here often they break covert at our feet.'

And while they listen'd for the distant hunt,
185 And chiefly for the baying of Cavall,
King Arthur's hound of deepest mouth, there rode
Full slowly by a knight, lady, and dwarf;

Whereof the dwarf lagg'd latest, and the knight
Had vizor up, and show'd a youthful face,
Imperious, and of haughtiest lineaments.   190
And Guinevere, not mindful of his face
In the King's hall, desired his name, and sent
Her maiden to demand it of the dwarf;
Who being vicious, old and irritable,
And doubling all his master's vice of pride,   195
Made answer sharply that she should not know.
'Then will I ask it of himself,' she said.
'Nay, by my faith, thou shalt not,' cried the dwarf;
'Thou art not worthy ev'n to speak of him;'
And when she put her horse toward the knight,   200
Struck at her with his whip, and she return'd
Indignant to the Queen; whereat Geraint
Exclaiming, 'Surely I will learn the name,'
Made sharply to the dwarf, and ask'd it of him,
Who answer'd as before; and when the Prince   205
Had put his horse in motion toward the knight,
Struck at him with his whip, and cut his cheek.
The Prince's blood spirted upon the scarf,
Dyeing it; and his quick, instinctive hand
Caught at the hilt, as to abolish him: 210
But he, from his exceeding manfulness
And pure nobility of temperament,
Wroth to be wroth at such a worm, refrain'd
From ev'n a word, and so returning said:

'I will avenge this insult, noble Queen,   215
Done in your maiden's person to yourself:
And I will track this vermin to their earths:
For tho' I ride unarm'd, I do not doubt
To find, at some place I shall come at, arms
On loan, or else for pledge; and, being found,   220
Then will I fight him, and will break his pride,
And on the third day will again be here,
So that I be not fall'n in fight. Farewell.'

'Farewell, fair Prince,' answer'd the stately Queen.
'Be prosperous in this journey, as in all;   225

And may you light on all things that you love,
And live to wed with her whom first you love:
But ere you wed with any, bring your bride,
And I, were she the daughter of a king,
230   Yea, tho' she were a beggar from the hedge,
Will clothe her for her bridals like the sun.'

And Prince Geraint, now thinking that he heard
The noble hart at bay, now the far horn,
A little vext at losing of the hunt,
235   A little at the vile occasion, rode,
By ups and downs, thro' many a grassy glade
And valley, with fixt eye following the three.
At last they issued from the world of wood,
And climb'd upon a fair and even ridge,
240   And show'd themselves against the sky, and sank.
And thither came Geraint, and underneath
Beheld the long street of a little town
In a long valley, on one side whereof,
White from the mason's hand, a fortress rose;
245   And on one side a castle in decay,
Beyond a bridge that spann'd a dry ravine:
And out of town and valley came a noise
As of a broad brook o'er a shingly bed
Brawling, or like a clamour of the rooks
250   At distance, ere they settle for the night.

And onward to the fortress rode the three,
And enter'd, and were lost behind the walls.
'So,' thought Geraint, 'I have track'd him to his earth.'
And down the long street riding wearily,
255   Found every hostel full, and everywhere
Was hammer laid to hoof, and the hot hiss
And bustling whistle of the youth who scour'd
His master's armour; and of such a one
He ask'd, 'What means the tumult in the town?'
260   Who told him, scouring still, 'The sparrow-hawk!'
Then riding close behind an ancient churl,
Who, smitten by the dusty sloping beam,
Went sweating underneath a sack of corn,

Ask'd yet once more what meant the hubbub here?
Who answer'd gruffly, 'Ugh! the sparrow-hawk.'   265
Then riding further past an armourer's,
Who, with back turn'd, and bow'd above his work,
Sat riveting a helmet on his knee,
He put the self-same query, but the man
Not turning round, nor looking at him, said: 270
'Friend, he that labours for the sparrow-hawk
Has little time for idle questioners.'
Whereat Geraint flash'd into sudden spleen:
'A thousand pips eat up your sparrow-hawk!
Tits, wrens, and all wing'd nothings peck him dead!   275
Ye think the rustic cackle of your bourg
The murmur of the world! What is it to me?
O wretched set of sparrows, one and all,
Who pipe of nothing but of sparrow-hawks!
Speak, if ye be not like the rest, hawk-mad,   280
Where can I get me harbourage for the night?
And arms, arms, arms to fight my enemy? Speak!'
Whereat the armourer turning all amazed
And seeing one so gay in purple silks,
Came forward with the helmet yet in hand   285
And answer'd, 'Pardon me, O stranger knight;
We hold a tourney here to-morrow morn,
And there is scantly time for half the work.
Arms? truth! I know not: all are wanted here.
Harbourage? truth, good truth, I know not, save,   290
It may be, at Earl Yniol's, o'er the bridge
Yonder.' He spoke and fell to work again.

Then rode Geraint, a little spleenful yet,
Across the bridge that spann'd the dry ravine.
There musing sat the hoary-headed Earl,   295
(His dress a suit of fray'd magnificence,
Once fit for feasts of ceremony) and said:
'Whither, fair son?' to whom Geraint replied,
'O friend, I seek a harbourage for the night.'
Then Yniol, 'Enter therefore and partake   300
The slender entertainment of a house
Once rich, now poor, but ever open-door'd.'

'Thanks, venerable friend,' replied Geraint;
'So that ye do not serve me sparrow-hawks
305   For supper, I will enter, I will eat
With all the passion of a twelve hours' fast.'
Then sigh'd and smiled the hoary-headed Earl,
And answer'd, 'Graver cause than yours is mine
To curse this hedgerow thief, the sparrow-hawk:
310   But in, go in; for save yourself desire it,
We will not touch upon him ev'n in jest.'

Then rode Geraint into the castle court,
His charger trampling many a prickly star
Of sprouted thistle on the broken stones.
315   He look'd and saw that all was ruinous.
Here stood a shatter'd archway plumed with fern;
And here had fàll'n a great part of a tower,
Whole, like a crag that tumbles from the cliff,
And like a crag was gay with wilding flowers:
320   And high above a piece of turret stair,
Worn by the feet that now were silent, wound
Bare to the sun, and monstrous ivy-stems
Claspt the gray walls with hairy-fibred arms,
And suck'd the joining of the stones, and look'd
325   A knot, beneath, of snakes, aloft, a grove.

And while he waited in the castle court,
The voice of Enid, Yniol's daughter, rang
Clear thro' the open casement of the hall,
Singing; and as the sweet voice of a bird,
330   Heard by the lander in a lonely isle,
Moves him to think what kind of bird it is
That sings so delicately clear, and make
Conjecture of the plumage and the form;
So the sweet voice of Enid moved Geraint;
335   And made him like a man abroad at morn
When first the liquid note beloved of men
Comes flying over many a windy wave
To Britain, and in April suddenly
Breaks from a coppice gemm'd with green and red,
340   And he suspends his converse with a friend,

Or it may be the labour of his hands,
To think or say, 'There is the nightingale;'
So fared it with Geraint, who thought and said,
'Here, by God's grace, is the one voice for me.'

It chanced the song that Enid sang was one   345
Of Fortune and her wheel, and Enid sang:

'Turn, Fortune, turn thy wheel and lower the proud;
Turn thy wild wheel thro' sunshine, storm, and cloud;
Thy wheel and thee we neither love nor hate.

'Turn, Fortune, turn thy wheel with smile or frown;   350
With that wild wheel we go not up or down;
Our hoard is little, but our hearts are great.

'Smile and we smile, the lords of many lands;
Frown and we smile, the lords of our own hands;
For man is man and master of his fate.   355

'Turn, turn thy wheel above the staring crowd;
Thy wheel and thou are shadows in the cloud;
Thy wheel and thee we neither love nor hate.'

'Hark, by the bird's song ye may learn the nest,'
Said Yniol; 'enter quickly.' Entering then,   360
Right o'er a mount of newly-fallen stones,
The dusky-rafter'd many-cobweb'd hall,
He found an ancient dame in dim brocade;
And near her, like a blossom vermeil-white,
That lightly breaks a faded flower-sheath,   365
Moved the fair Enid, all in faded silk,
Her daughter. In a moment thought Geraint,
'Here by God's rood is the one maid for me.'
But none spake word except the hoary Earl:
'Enid, the good knight's horse stands in the court;   370
Take him to stall, and give him corn, and then
Go to the town and buy us flesh and wine;
And we will make us merry as we may.
Our hoard is little, but our hearts are great.'

375　He spake: the Prince, as Enid past him, fain
　　To follow, strode a stride, but Yniol caught
　　His purple scarf, and held, and said, 'Forbear!
　　Rest! the good house, tho' ruin'd, O my son,
　　Endures not that her guest should serve himself.'
380　And reverencing the custom of the house
　　Geraint, from utter courtesy, forbore.

　　So Enid took his charger to the stall;
　　And after went her way across the bridge,
　　And reach'd the town, and while the Prince and Earl
385　Yet spoke together, came again with one,
　　A youth, that following with a costrel bore
　　The means of goodly welcome, flesh and wine.
　　And Enid brought sweet cakes to make them cheer,
　　And in her veil enfolded, manchet bread.
390　And then, because their hall must also serve
　　For kitchen, boil'd the flesh, and spread the board,
　　And stood behind, and waited on the three.
　　And seeing her so sweet and serviceable,
　　Geraint had longing in him evermore
395　To stoop and kiss the tender little thumb,
　　That crost the trencher as she laid it down:
　　But after all had eaten, then Geraint,
　　For now the wine made summer in his veins,
　　Let his eye rove in following, or rest
400　On Enid at her lowly handmaid-work,
　　Now here, now there, about the dusky hall;
　　Then suddenly addrest the hoary Earl:

　　'Fair Host and Earl, I pray your courtesy;
　　This sparrow-hawk, what is he? tell me of him.
405　His name? but no, good faith, I will not have it:
　　For if he be the knight whom late I saw
　　Ride into that new fortress by your town,
　　White from the mason's hand, then have I sworn
　　From his own lips to have it – I am Geraint
410　Of Devon – for this morning when the Queen
　　Sent her own maiden to demand the name,
　　His dwarf, a vicious under-shapen thing,

Struck at her with his whip, and she return'd
Indignant to the Queen; and then I swore
That I would track this caitiff to his hold,   415
And fight and break his pride, and have it of him.
And all unarm'd I rode, and thought to find
Arms in your town, where all the men are mad;
They take the rustic murmur of their bourg
For the great wave that echoes round the world;   420
They would not hear me speak: but if ye know
Where I can light on arms, or if yourself
Should have them, tell me, seeing I have sworn
That I will break his pride and learn his name,
Avenging this great insult done the Queen.'   425

Then cried Earl Yniol, 'Art thou he indeed,
Geraint, a name far-sounded among men
For noble deeds? and truly I, when first
I saw you moving by me on the bridge,
Felt ye were somewhat, yea, and by your state   430
And presence might have guess'd you one of those
That eat in Arthur's hall at Camelot.
Nor speak I now from foolish flattery;
For this dear child hath often heard me praise
Your feats of arms, and often when I paused   435
Hath ask'd again, and ever loved to hear;
So grateful is the noise of noble deeds
To noble hearts who see but acts of wrong:
O never yet had woman such a pair
Of suitors as this maiden; first Limours,   440
A creature wholly given to brawls and wine,
Drunk even when he woo'd; and be he dead
I know not, but he past to the wild land.
The second was your foe, the sparrow-hawk,
My curse, my nephew – I will not let his name   445
Slip from my lips if I can help it – he,
When I that knew him fierce and turbulent
Refused her to him, then his pride awoke;
And since the proud man often is the mean,
He sow'd a slander in the common ear,   450
Affirming that his father left him gold,

And in my charge, which was not render'd to him;
Bribed with large promises the men who served
About my person, the more easily
455   Because my means were somewhat broken into
Thro' open doors and hospitality;
Raised my own town against me in the night
Before my Enid's birthday, sack'd my house;
From mine own earldom foully ousted me;
460   Built that new fort to overawe my friends,
For truly there are those who love me yet;
And keeps me in this ruinous castle here,
Where doubtless he would put me soon to death,
But that his pride too much despises me:
465   And I myself sometimes despise myself;
For I have let men be, and have their way;
Am much too gentle, have not used my power:
Nor know I whether I be very base
Or very manful, whether very wise
470   Or very foolish; only this I know,
That whatsoever evil happen to me,
I seem to suffer nothing heart or limb,
But can endure it all most patiently.'

'Well said, true heart,' replied Geraint, 'but arms,
475   That if the sparrow-hawk, this nephew, fight
In next day's tourney I may break his pride.'

And Yniol answer'd, 'Arms, indeed, but old
And rusty, old and rusty, Prince Geraint,
Are mine, and therefore at thine asking, thine.
480   But in this tournament can no man tilt,
Except the lady he loves best be there.
Two forks are fixt into the meadow ground,
And over these is placed a silver wand,
And over that a golden sparrow-hawk,
485   The prize of beauty for the fairest there.
And this, what knight soever be in field
Lays claim to for the lady at his side,
And tilts with my good nephew thereupon,
Who being apt at arms and big of bone

Has ever won it for the lady with him,   490
And toppling over all antagonism
Has earn'd himself the name of sparrow-hawk.
But thou, that hast no lady, canst not fight.'

To whom Geraint with eyes all bright replied,
Leaning a little toward him, 'Thy leave!   495
Let *me* lay lance in rest, O noble host,
For this dear child, because I never saw,
Tho' having seen all beauties of our time,
Nor can see elsewhere, anything so fair.
And if I fall her name will yet remain   500
Untarnish'd as before; but if I live,
So aid me Heaven when at mine uttermost,
As I will make her truly my true wife.'

Then, howsoever patient, Yniol's heart
Danced in his bosom, seeing better days.   505
And looking round he saw not Enid there,
(Who hearing her own name had stol'n away)
But that old dame, to whom full tenderly
And fondling all her hand in his he said,
'Mother, a maiden is a tender thing,   510
And best by her that bore her understood.
Go thou to rest, but ere thou go to rest.
Tell her, and prove her heart toward the Prince.'

So spake the kindly-hearted Earl, and she
With frequent smile and nod departing found,   515
Half disarray'd as to her rest, the girl;
Whom first she kiss'd on either cheek, and then
On either shining shoulder laid a hand,
And kept her off and gazed upon her face,
And told her all their converse in the hall,   520
Proving her heart: but never light and shade
Coursed one another more on open ground
Beneath a troubled heaven, than red and pale
Across the face of Enid hearing her;
While slowly falling as a scale that falls,   525
When weight is added only grain by grain,

Sank her sweet head upon her gentle breast;
Nor did she lift an eye nor speak a word,
Rapt in the fear and in the wonder of it;
530 So moving without answer to her rest
She found no rest, and ever fail'd to draw
The quiet night into her blood, but lay
Contemplating her own unworthiness;
And when the pale and bloodless east began
535 To quicken to the sun, arose, and raised
Her mother too, and hand in hand they moved
Down to the meadow where the jousts were held,
And waited there for Yniol and Geraint.

And thither came the twain, and when Geraint
540 Beheld her first in field, awaiting him,
He felt, were she the prize of bodily force,
Himself beyond the rest pushing could move
The chair of Idris. Yniol's rusted arms
Were on his princely person, but thro' these
545 Princelike his bearing shone; and errant knights
And ladies came, and by and by the town
Flow'd in, and settling circled all the lists.
And there they fixt the forks into the ground,
And over these they placed the silver wand,
550 And over that the golden sparrow-hawk.
Then Yniol's nephew, after trumpet blown,
Spake to the lady with him and proclaim'd,
'Advance and take, as fairest of the fair,
What I these two years past have won for thee,
555 The prize of beauty.' Loudly spake the Prince,
'Forbear: there is a worthier,' and the knight
With some surprise and thrice as much disdain
Turn'd, and beheld the four, and all his face
Glow'd like the heart of a great fire at Yule,
560 So burnt he was with passion, crying out,
'Do battle for it then,' no more; and thrice
They clash'd together, and thrice they brake their spears.
Then each, dishorsed and drawing, lash'd at each
So often and with such blows, that all the crowd
565 Wonder'd, and now and then from distant walls

There came a clapping as of phantom hands.
So twice they fought, and twice they breathed, and still
The dew of their great labour, and the blood
Of their strong bodies, flowing, drain'd their force.
But either's force was match'd till Yniol's cry,   570
'Remember that great insult done the Queen,'
Increased Geraint's, who heaved his blade aloft,
And crack'd the helmet thro', and bit the bone,
And fell'd him, and set foot upon his breast,
And said, 'Thy name?' To whom the fallen man   575
Made answer, groaning, 'Edyrn, son of Nudd!
Ashamed am I that I should tell it thee.
My pride is broken: men have seen my fall.'
'Then, Edyrn, son of Nudd,' replied Geraint,
'These two things shalt thou do, or else thou diest.   580
First, thou thyself, with damsel and with dwarf,
Shalt ride to Arthur's court, and coming there,
Crave pardon for that insult done the Queen,
And shalt abide her judgment on it; next,
Thou shalt give back their earldom to thy kin.   585
These two things shalt thou do, or thou shalt die.'
And Edyrn answer'd, 'These things will I do,
For I have never yet been overthrown,
And thou hast overthrown me, and my pride
Is broken down, for Enid sees my fall!'   590
And rising up, he rode to Arthur's court,
And there the Queen forgave him easily.
And being young, he changed and came to loathe
His crime of traitor, slowly drew himself
Bright from his old dark life, and fell at last   595
In the great battle fighting for the King.

But when the third day from the hunting-morn
Made a low splendour in the world, and wings
Moved in her ivy, Enid, for she lay
With her fair head in the dim-yellow light,   600
Among the dancing shadows of the birds,
Woke and bethought her of her promise given
No later than last eve to Prince Geraint –
So bent he seem'd on going the third day,

605 He would not leave her, till her promise given –
To ride with him this morning to the court,
And there be made known to the stately Queen,
And there be wedded with all ceremony.
At this she cast her eyes upon her dress,
610 And thought it never yet had look'd so mean,
For as a leaf in mid-November is
To what it was in mid-October, seem'd
The dress that now she look'd on to the dress
She look'd on ere the coming of Geraint.
615 And still she look'd, and still the terror grew
Of that strange bright and dreadful thing, a court,
All staring at her in her faded silk:
And softly to her own sweet heart she said:

'This noble prince who won our earldom back,
620 So splendid in his acts and his attire,
Sweet heaven, how much I shall discredit him!
Would he could tarry with us here awhile,
But being so beholden to the Prince,
It were but little grace in any of us,
625 Bent as he seem'd on going this third day,
To seek a second favour at his hands.
Yet if he could but tarry a day or two,
Myself would work eye dim, and finger lame,
Far liefer than so much discredit him.'

630 And Enid fell in longing for a dress
All branch'd and flower'd with gold, a costly gift
Of her good mother, given her on the night
Before her birthday, three sad years ago,
That night of fire, when Edyrn sack'd their house,
635 And scatter'd all they had to all the winds:
For while the mother show'd it, and the two
Were turning and admiring it, the work
To both appear'd so costly, rose a cry
That Edyrn's men were on them, and they fled
640 With little save the jewels they had on,
Which being sold and sold had bought them bread:
And Edyrn's men had caught them in their flight,

And placed them in this ruin; and she wish'd
The Prince had found her in her ancient home;
Then let her fancy flit across the past,   645
And roam the goodly places that she knew;
And last bethought her how she used to watch,
Near that old home, a pool of golden carp;
And one was patch'd and blurr'd and lustreless
Among his burnish'd brethren of the pool;   650
And half asleep she made comparison
Of that and these to her own faded self
And the gay court, and fell asleep again;
And dreamt herself was such a faded form
Among her burnish'd sisters of the pool;   655
But this was in the garden of a king;
And tho' she lay dark in the pool, she knew
That all was bright; that all about were birds
Of sunny plume in gilded trellis-work;
That all the turf was rich in plots that look'd   660
Each like a garnet or a turkis in it;
And lords and ladies of the high court went
In silver tissue talking things of state;
And children of the King in cloth of gold
Glanced at the doors or gambol'd down the walks;   665
And while she thought 'They will not see me,' came
A stately queen whose name was Guinevere,
And all the children in their cloth of gold
Ran to her, crying, 'If we have fish at all
Let them be gold; and charge the gardeners now   670
To pick the faded creature from the pool,
And cast it on the mixen that it die.'
And therewithal one came and seized on her,
And Enid started waking, with her heart
All overshadow'd by the foolish dream,   675
And lo! it was her mother grasping her
To get her well awake; and in her hand
A suit of bright apparel, which she laid
Flat on the couch, and spoke exultingly:

    'See here, my child, how fresh the colours look,   680
How fast they hold, like colours of a shell

That keeps the wear and polish of the wave.
Why not? It never yet was worn, I trow:
Look on it, child, and tell me if ye know it.'

685   And Enid look'd, but all confused at first,
      Could scarce divide it from her foolish dream:
      Then suddenly she knew it and rejoiced,
      And answer'd, 'Yea, I know it; your good gift,
      So sadly lost on that unhappy night;

690   Your own good gift!' 'Yea, surely,' said the dame,
      'And gladly given again this happy morn.
      For when the jousts were ended yesterday,
      Went Yniol thro' the town, and everywhere
      He found the sack and plunder of our house

695   All scatter'd thro' the houses of the town;
      And gave command that all which once was ours
      Should now be ours again: and yester-eve,
      While ye were talking sweetly with your Prince,
      Came one· with this and laid it in my hand,

700   For love or fear, or seeking favour of us,
      Because we have our earldom back again.
      And yester-eve I would not tell you of it,
      But kept it for a sweet surprise at morn.
      Yea, truly is it not a sweet surprise?

705   For I myself unwillingly have worn
      My faded suit, as you, my child, have yours,
      And howsoever patient, Yniol his.
      Ah, dear, he took me from a goodly house,
      With store of rich apparel, sumptuous fare,

710   And page, and maid, and squire, and seneschal,
      And pastime both of hawk and hound, and all
      That appertains to noble maintenance.
      Yea, and he brought me to a goodly house;
      But since our fortune swerved from sun to shade,

715   And all thro' that young traitor, cruel need
      Constrain'd us, but a better time has come;
      So clothe yourself in this, that better fits
      Our mended fortunes and a Prince's bride:
      For tho' ye won the prize of fairest fair,

720   And tho' I heard him call you fairest fair,

94

Let never maiden think, however fair,
She is not fairer in new clothes than old.
And should some great court-lady say, the Prince
Hath pick'd a ragged-robin from the hedge,
And like a madman brought her to the court, 725
Then were ye shamed, and, worse, might shame the Prince
To whom we are beholden; but I know,
When my dear child is set forth at her best,
That neither court nor country, tho' they sought
Thro' all the provinces like those of old 730
That lighted on Queen Esther, has her match.'

Here ceased the kindly mother out of breath;
And Enid listen'd brightening as she lay;
Then, as the white and glittering star of morn
Parts from a bank of snow, and by and by 735
Slips into golden cloud, the maiden rose,
And left her maiden couch, and robed herself,
Help'd by the mother's careful hand and eye,
Without a mirror, in the gorgeous gown;
Who, after, turn'd her daughter round, and said, 740
She never yet had seen her half so fair;
And call'd her like that maiden in the tale,
Whom Gwydion made by glamour out of flowers,
And sweeter than the bride of Cassivelaun,
Flur, for whose love the Roman Cæsar first 745
Invaded Britain, 'But we beat him back,
As this great Prince invaded us, and we,
Not beat him back, but welcomed him with joy.
And I can scarcely ride with you to court,
For old am I, and rough the ways and wild; 750
But Yniol goes, and I full oft shall dream
I see my princess as I see her now,
Clothed with my gift, and gay among the gay.'

But while the women thus rejoiced, Geraint
Woke where he slept in the high hall, and call'd 755
For Enid, and when Yniol made report
Of that good mother making Enid gay
In such apparel as might well beseem

95

His princess, or indeed the stately Queen,
760 He answer'd: 'Earl, entreat her by my love,
Albeit I give no reason but my wish,
That she ride with me in her faded silk.'
Yniol with that hard message went; it fell
Like flaws in summer laying lusty corn:
765 For Enid, all abash'd she knew not why,
Dared not to glance at her good mother's face,
But silently, in all obedience,
Her mother silent too, nor helping her,
Laid from her limbs the costly-broider'd gift,
770 And robed them in her ancient suit again,
And so descended. Never man rejoiced
More than Geraint to greet her thus attired;
And glancing all at once as keenly at her
As careful robins eye the delver's toil,
775 Made her cheek burn and either eyelid fall,
But rested with her sweet face satisfied;
Then seeing cloud upon the mother's brow,
Her by both hands he caught, and sweetly said,

'O my new mother, be not wroth or grieved
780 At thy new son, for my petition to her.
When late I left Caerleon, our great Queen,
In words whose echo lasts, they were so sweet,
Made promise, that whatever bride I brought,
Herself would clothe her like the sun in Heaven.
785 Thereafter, when I reach'd this ruin'd hall,
Beholding one so bright in dark estate,
I vow'd that could I gain her, our fair Queen,
No hand but hers, should make your Enid burst
Sunlike from cloud – and likewise thought perhaps,
790 That service done so graciously would bind
The two together; fain I would the two
Should love each other: how can Enid find
A nobler friend? Another thought was mine;
I came among you here so suddenly,
795 That tho' her gentle presence at the lists
Might well have served for proof that I was loved,
I doubted whether daughter's tenderness,

Or easy nature, might not let itself
Be moulded by your wishes for her weal;
Or whether some false sense in her own self   800
Of my contrasting brightness, overbore
Her fancy dwelling in this dusky hall;
And such a sense might make her long for court
And all its perilous glories: and I thought,
That could I someway prove such force in her   805
Link'd with such love for me, that at a word
(No reason given her) she could cast aside
A splendour dear to women, new to her,
And therefore dearer; or if not so new,
Yet therefore tenfold dearer by the power   810
Of intermitted usage; then I felt
That I could rest, a rock in ebbs and flows,
Fixt on her faith. Now, therefore, I do rest,
A prophet certain of my prophecy,
That never shadow of mistrust can cross   815
Between us. Grant me pardon for my thoughts:
And for my strange petition I will make
Amends hereafter by some gaudy-day,
When your fair child shall wear your costly gift
Beside your own warm hearth, with, on her knees,   820
Who knows? another gift of the high God,
Which, maybe, shall have learn'd to lisp you thanks.'

He spoke: the mother smiled, but half in tears,
Then brought a mantle down and wrapt her in it,
And claspt and kiss'd her, and they rode away.   825

Now thrice that morning Guinevere had climb'd
The giant tower, from whose high crest, they say,
Men saw the goodly hills of Somerset,
And white sails flying on the yellow sea;
But not to goodly hill or yellow sea   830
Look'd the fair Queen, but up the vale of Usk,
By the flat meadow, till she saw them come;
And then descending met them at the gates,
Embraced her with all welcome as a friend,
And did her honour as the Prince's bride,   835

And clothed her for her bridals like the sun;
And all that week was old Caerleon gay,
For by the hands of Dubric, the high saint,
They twain were wedded with all ceremony.

840   And this was on the last year's Whitsuntide.
But Enid ever kept the faded silk,
Remembering how first he came on her,
Drest in that dress, and how he loved her in it.
And all her foolish fears about the dress,
845   And all his journey toward her, as himself
Had told her, and their coming to the court.

And now this morning when he said to her,
'Put on your worst and meanest dress,' she found
And took it, and array'd herself therein.

Geraint and Enid

O purblind race of miserable men,
How many among us at this very hour
Do forge a life-long trouble for ourselves,
By taking true for false, or false for true;
Here, thro' the feeble twilight of this world   5
Groping, how many, until we pass and reach
That other, where we see as we are seen!

So fared it with Geraint, who issuing forth
That morning, when they both had got to horse,
Perhaps because he loved her passionately,   10
And felt that tempest brooding round his heart,
Which, if he spoke at all, would break perforce
Upon a head so dear in thunder, said:
'Not at my side. I charge thee ride before,
Ever a good way on before; and this   15
I charge thee, on thy duty as a wife,
Whatever happens, not to speak to me,
No, not a word!' and Enid was aghast;
And forth they rode, but scarce three paces on,
When crying out, 'Effeminate as I am,   20
I will not fight my way with gilded arms,
All shall be iron;' he loosed a mighty purse,
Hung at his belt, and hurl'd it toward the squire.
So the last sight that Enid had of home
Was all the marble threshold flashing, strown   25
With gold and scatter'd coinage, and the squire
Chafing his shoulder: then he cried again,
'To the wilds!' and Enid leading down the tracks
Thro' which he bad her lead him on, they past
The marches, and by bandit-haunted holds,   30
Gray swamps and pools, waste places of the hern,
And wildernesses, perilous paths, they rode:

Round was their pace at first, but slacken'd soon:
A stranger meeting them had surely thought
35   They rode so slowly and they look'd so pale,
That each had suffer'd some exceeding wrong.
For he was ever saying to himself,
'O I that wasted time to tend upon her,
To compass her with sweet observances,
40   To dress her beautifully and keep her true' –
And there he broke the sentence in his heart
Abruptly, as a man upon his tongue
May break it, when his passion masters him.
And she was ever praying the sweet heavens
45   To save her dear lord whole from any wound.
And ever in her mind she cast about
For that unnoticed failing in herself,
Which made him look so cloudy and so cold;
Till the great plover's human whistle amazed
50   Her heart, and glancing round the waste she fear'd
In every wavering brake an ambuscade.
Then thought again, 'If there be such in me,
I might amend it by the grace of Heaven,
If he would only speak and tell me of it.'

55   But when the fourth part of the day was gone,
Then Enid was aware of three tall knights
On horseback, wholly arm'd, behind a rock
In shadow, waiting for them, caitiffs all;
And heard one crying to his fellow, 'Look,
60   Here comes a laggard hanging down his head,
Who seems no bolder than a beaten hound;
Come, we will slay him and will have his horse
And armour, and his damsel shall be ours.'

Then Enid ponder'd in her heart, and said:
65   'I will go back a little to my lord,
And I will tell him all their caitiff talk;
For, be he wroth even to slaying me,
Far liefer by his dear hand had I die,
Than that my lord should suffer loss or shame.'

Then she went back some paces of return,　　　　70
Met his full frown timidly firm, and said;
'My lord, I saw three bandits by the rock
Waiting to fall on you, and heard them boast
That they would slay you, and possess your horse
And armour, and your damsel should be theirs.'　　75

He made a wrathful answer: 'Did I wish
Your warning or your silence? one command
I laid upon you, not to speak to me,
And thus ye keep it! Well then, look – for now,
Whether ye wish me victory or defeat,　　　　80
Long for my life, or hunger for my death,
Yourself shall see my vigour is not lost.'

Then Enid waited pale and sorrowful,
And down upon him bare the bandit three.
And at the midmost charging, Prince Geraint　　85
Drave the long spear a cubit thro' his breast
And out beyond; and then against his brace
Of comrades, each of whom had broken on him
A lance that splinter'd like an icicle,
Swung from his brand a windy buffet out　　　90
Once, twice, to right, to left, and stunn'd the twain
Or slew them, and dismounting like a man
That skins the wild beast after slaying him,
Stript from the three dead wolves of woman born
The three gay suits of armour which they wore,　　95
And let the bodies lie, but bound the suits
Of armour on their horses, each on each,
And tied the bridle-reins of all the three
Together, and said to her, 'Drive them on
Before you;' and she drove them thro' the waste.　　100

He follow'd nearer: ruth began to work
Against his anger in him, while he watch'd
The being he loved best in all the world,
With difficulty in mild obedience
Driving them on: he fain had spoken to her,　　105

And loosed in words of sudden fire the wrath
And smoulder'd wrong that burnt him all within;
But evermore it seem'd an easier thing
At once without remorse to strike her dead,
110 Than to cry 'Halt,' and to her own bright face
Accuse her of the least immodesty:
And thus tongue-tied, it made him wroth the more
That she *could* speak whom his own ear had heard
Call herself false: and suffering thus he made
115 Minutes an age: but in scarce longer time
Than at Caerleon the full-tided Usk,
Before he turn to fall seaward again,
Pauses, did Enid, keeping watch, behold
In the first shallow shade of a deep wood,
120 Before a gloom of stubborn-shafted oaks,
Three other horsemen waiting, wholly arm'd,
Whereof one seem'd far larger than her lord,
And shook her pulses, crying, 'Look, a prize!
Three horses and three goodly suits of arms,
125 And all in charge of whom? a girl: set on.'
'Nay,' said the second, 'yonder comes a knight.'
The third, 'A craven; how he hangs his head.'
The giant answer'd merrily, 'Yea, but one?
Wait here, and when he passes fall upon him.'

130 And Enid ponder'd in her heart and said,
'I will abide the coming of my lord,
And I will tell him all their villainy.
My lord is weary with the fight before,
And they will fall upon him unawares.
135 I needs must disobey him for his good;
How should I dare obey him to his harm?
Needs must I speak, and tho' he kill me for it,
I save a life dearer to me than mine.'

And she abode his coming, and said to him
140 With timid firmness, 'Have I leave to speak?'
He said, 'Ye take it, speaking,' and she spoke.

'There lurk three villains yonder in the wood,
And each of them is wholly arm'd, and one
Is larger-limb'd than you are, and they say
That they will fall upon you while ye pass.'   145

To which he flung a wrathful answer back:
'And if there were an hundred in the wood,
And every man were larger-limb'd than I,
And all at once should sally out upon me,
I swear it would not ruffle me so much   150
As you that not obey me. Stand aside,
And if I fall, cleave to the better man.'

And Enid stood aside to wait the event,
Not dare to watch the combat, only breathe
Short fits of prayer, at every stroke a breath.   155
And he, she dreaded most, bare down upon him.
Aim'd at the helm, his lance err'd; but Geraint's,
A little in the late encounter strain'd,
Struck thro' the bulky bandit's corselet home,
And then brake short, and down his enemy roll'd,   160
And there lay still; as he that tells the tale
Saw once a great piece of a promontory,
That had a sapling growing on it, slide
From the long shore-cliff's windy walls to the beach,
And there lie still, and yet the sapling grew: 165
So lay the man transfixt. His craven pair
Of comrades making slowlier at the Prince,
When now they saw their bulwark fallen, stood;
On whom the victor, to confound them more,
Spurr'd with his terrible war-cry; for as one,   170
That listens near a torrent mountain-brook,
All thro' the crash of the near cataract hears
The drumming thunder of the huger fall
At distance, were the soldiers wont to hear
His voice in battle, and be kindled by it,   175
And foemen scared, like that false pair who turn'd
Flying, but, overtaken, died the death
Themselves had wrought on many an innocent.

Thereon Geraint, dismounting, pick'd the lance
180 That pleased him best, and drew from those dead wolves
Their three gay suits of armour, each from each,
And bound them on their horses, each on each,
And tied the bridle-reins of all the three
Together, and said to her, 'Drive them on
185 Before you,' and she drove them thro' the wood.

He follow'd nearer still: the pain she had
To keep them in the wild ways of the wood,
Two sets of three laden with jingling arms,
Together, served a little to disedge
190 The sharpness of that pain about her heart:
And they themselves, like creatures gently born
But into bad hands fall'n, and now so long
By bandits groom'd, prick'd their light ears, and felt
Her low firm voice and tender government.

195 So thro' the green gloom of the wood they past,
And issuing under open heavens beheld
A little town with towers, upon a rock,
And close beneath, a meadow gemlike chased
In the brown wild, and mowers mowing in it:
200 And down a rocky pathway from the place
There came a fair-hair'd youth, that in his hand
Bare victual for the mowers: and Geraint
Had ruth again on Enid looking pale:
Then, moving downward to the meadow ground,
205 He, when the fair-hair'd youth came by him, said,
'Friend, let her eat; the damsel is so faint.'
'Yea, willingly,' replied the youth; 'and thou,
My lord, eat also, tho' the fare is coarse,
And only meet for mowers;' then set down
210 His basket, and dismounting on the sward
They let the horses graze, and ate themselves.
And Enid took a little delicately,
Less having stomach for it than desire
To close with her lord's pleasure; but Geraint
215 Ate all the mowers' victual unawares,
And when he found all empty, was amazed;

And 'Boy,' said he, 'I have eaten all, but take
A horse and arms for guerdon; choose the best.'
He, reddening in extremity of delight,
'My lord, you overpay me fifty-fold.'   220
'Ye will be all the wealthier,' cried the Prince.
'I take it as free gift, then,' said the boy,
'Not guerdon; for myself can easily,
While your good damsel rests, return, and fetch
Fresh victual for these mowers of our Earl;   225
For these are his, and all the field is his,
And I myself am his; and I will tell him
How great a man thou art: he loves to know
When men of mark are in his territory:
And he will have thee to his palace here,   230
And serve thee costlier than with mowers' fare.'

Then said Geraint, 'I wish no better fare:
I never ate with angrier appetite
Than when I left your mowers dinnerless.
And into no Earl's palace will I go.   235
I know, God knows, too much of palaces!
And if he want me, let him come to me.
But hire us some fair chamber for the night.
And stalling for the horses, and return
With victual for these men, and let us know.'   240

'Yea, my kind lord,' said the glad youth, and went,
Held his head high, and thought himself a knight,
And up the rocky pathway disappear'd,
Leading the horse, and they were left alone.

But when the Prince had brought his errant eyes   245
Home from the rock, sideways he let them glance
At Enid, where she droopt: his own false doom,
That shadow of mistrust should never cross
Betwixt them, came upon him, and he sigh'd;
Then with another humorous ruth remark'd   250
The lusty mowers labouring dinnerless,
And watch'd the sun blaze on the turning scythe,
And after nodded sleepily in the heat.

But she, remembering her old ruin'd hall,
255 And all the windy clamour of the daws
About her hollow turret, pluck'd the grass
There growing longest by the meadow's edge,
And into many a listless annulet,
Now over, now beneath her marriage ring,
260 Wove and unwove it, till the boy return'd
And told them of a chamber, and they went;
Where, after saying to her, 'If ye will,
Call for the woman of the house,' to which
She answer'd, 'Thanks, my lord;' the two remain'd
265 Apart by all the chamber's width, and mute
As creatures voiceless thro' the fault of birth,
Or two wild men supporters of a shield,
Painted, who stare at open space, nor glance
The one at other, parted by the shield.

270 On a sudden, many a voice along the street,
And heel against the pavement echoing, burst
Their drowse; and either started while the door,
Push'd from without, drave backward to the wall,
And midmost of a rout of roisterers,
275 Femininely fair and dissolutely pale,
Her suitor in old years before Geraint,
Enter'd, the wild lord of the place, Limours.
He moving up with pliant courtliness,
Greeted Geraint full face, but stealthily,
280 In the mid-warmth of welcome and graspt hand,
Found Enid with the corner of his eye,
And knew her sitting sad and solitary.
Then cried Geraint for wine and goodly cheer
To feed the sudden guest, and sumptuously
285 According to his fashion, bad the host
Call in what men soever were his friends,
And feast with these in honour of their Earl;
'And care not for the cost; the cost is mine.'

And wine and food were brought, and Earl Limours
290 Drank till he jested with all ease, and told
Free tales, and took the word and play'd upon it,

And made it of two colours; for his talk,
When wine and free companions kindled him,
Was wont to glance and sparkle like a gem
Of fifty facets; thus he moved the Prince   295
To laughter and his comrades to applause.
Then, when the Prince was merry, ask'd Limours,
'Your leave, my lord, to cross the room, and speak
To your good damsel there who sits apart,
And seems so lonely?' 'My free leave,' he said;   300
'Get her to speak: she doth not speak to me.'
Then rose Limours, and looking at his feet,
Like him who tries the bridge he fears may fail,
Crost and came near, lifted adoring eyes,
Bow'd at her side and utter'd whisperingly: 305

   'Enid, the pilot star of my lone life,
Enid, my early and my only love,
Enid, the loss of whom hath turn'd me wild –
What chance is this? how is it I see you here?
Ye are in my power at last, are in my power.   310
Yet fear me not: I call mine own self wild,
But keep a touch of sweet civility
Here in the heart of waste and wilderness.
I thought, but that your father came between,
In former days you saw me favourably.   315
And if it were so do not keep it back:
Make me a little happier: let me know it:
Owe you me nothing for a life half-lost?
Yea, yea, the whole dear debt of all you are.
And, Enid, you and he, I see with joy,   320
Ye sit apart, you do not speak to him,
You come with no attendance, page or maid,
To serve you – doth he love you as of old?
For, call it lovers' quarrels, yet I know
Tho' men may bicker with the things they love,   325
They would not make them laughable in all eyes,
Not while they loved them; and your wretched dress,
A wretched insult on you, dumbly speaks
Your story, that this man loves you no more.
Your beauty is no beauty to him now: 330

A cómmon chance – right well I know it – pall'd –
For I know men: nor will ye win him back,
For the man's love once gone never returns.
But here is one who loves you as of old;
335 With more exceeding passion than of old:
Good, speak the word: my followers ring him round:
He sits unarm'd; I hold a finger up;
They understand: nay; I do not mean blood:
Nor need ye look so scared at what I say:
340 My malice is no deeper than a moat,
No stronger than a wall: there is the keep;
He shall not cross us more; speak but the word:
Or speak it not; but then by Him that made me
The one true lover whom you ever own'd,
345 I will make use of all the power I have.
O pardon me! the madness of that hour,
When first I parted from thee, moves me yet.'

At this the tender sound of his own voice
And sweet self-pity, or the fancy of it,
350 Made his eye moist; but Enid fear'd his eyes,
Moist as they were, wine-heated from the feast;
And answer'd with such craft as women use,
Guilty or guiltless, to stave off a chance
That breaks upon them perilously, and said:

355 'Earl, if you love me as in former years,
And do not practise on me, come with morn,
And snatch me from him as by violence;
Leave me to-night: I am weary to the death.'

Low at leave-taking, with his brandish'd plume
360 Brushing his instep, bow'd the all-amorous Earl,
And the stout Prince bad him a loud good-night.
He moving homeward babbled to his men,
How Enid never loved a man but him,
Nor cared a broken egg-shell for her lord.

365 But Enid left alone with Prince Geraint,
Debating his command of silence given,

And that she now perforce must violate it,
Held commune with herself, and while she held
He fell asleep, and Enid had no heart
To wake him, but hung o'er him, wholly pleased   370
To find him yet unwounded after fight,
And hear him breathing low and equally.
Anon she rose, and stepping lightly, heap'd
The pieces of his armour in one place,
All to be there against a sudden need;   375
Then dozed awhile herself, but overtoil'd
By that day's grief and travel, evermore
Seem'd catching at a rootless thorn, and then
Went slipping down horrible precipices,
And strongly striking out her limbs awoke;   380
Then thought she heard the wild Earl at the door,
With all his rout of random followers,
Sound on a dreadful trumpet, summoning her;
Which was the red cock shouting to the light,
As the gray dawn stole o'er the dewy world,   385
And glimmer'd on his armour in the room.
And once again she rose to look at it,
But touch'd it unawares: jangling, the casque
Fell, and he started up and stared at her.
Then breaking his command of silence given,   390
She told him all that Earl Limours had said,
Except the passage that he loved her not;
Nor left untold the craft herself had used;
But ended with apology so sweet,
Low-spoken, and of so few words, and seem'd   395
So justified by that necessity,
That tho' he thought 'was it for him she wept
In Devon?' he but gave a wrathful groan,
Saying, 'Your sweet faces make good fellows fools
And traitors. Call the host and bid him bring   400
Charger and palfrey.' So she glided out
Among the heavy breathings of the house,
And like a household Spirit at the walls
Beat, till she woke the sleepers, and return'd:
Then tending her rough lord, tho' all unask'd,   405
In silence, did him service as a squire;

Till issuing arm'd he found the host and cried,
'Thy reckoning, friend?' and ere he learnt it, 'Take
Five horses and their armours;' and the host
410 Suddenly honest, answer'd in amaze,
'My lord, I scarce have spent the worth of one!'
'Ye will be all the wealthier,' said the Prince,
And then to Enid, 'Forward! and to-day
I charge you, Enid, more especially,
415 What thing soever ye may hear, or see,
Or fancy (tho' I count it of small use
To charge you) that ye speak not but obey.'

And Enid answer'd, 'Yea, my lord, I know
Your wish, and would obey; but riding first,
420 I hear the violent threats you do not hear,
I see the danger which you cannot see:
Then not to give you warning, that seems hard;
Almost beyond me: yet I would obey.'

'Yea so,' said he, 'do it: be not too wise;
425 Seeing that ye are wedded to a man,
Not all mismated with a yawning clown,
But one with arms to guard his head and yours,
With eyes to find you out however far,
And ears to hear you even in his dreams.'

430 With that he turn'd and look'd as keenly at her
As careful robins eye the delver's toil;
And that within her, which a wanton fool,
Or hasty judger would have call'd her guilt,
Made her cheek burn and either eyelid fall.
435 And Geraint look'd and was not satisfied.

Then forward by a way which, beaten broad,
Led from the territory of false Limours
To the waste earldom of another earl,
Doorm, whom his shaking vassals call'd the Bull,
440 Went Enid with her sullen follower on.
Once she look'd back, and when she saw him ride
More near by many a rood than yestermorn,

It wellnigh made her cheerful; till Geraint
Waving an angry hand as who should say
'Ye watch me,' sadden'd all her heart again.   445
But while the sun yet beat a dewy blade,
The sound of many a heavily-galloping hoof
Smote on her ear, and turning round she saw
Dust, and the points of lances bicker in it.
Then not to disobey her lord's behest,   450
And yet to give him warning, for he rode
As if he heard not, moving back she held
Her finger up, and pointed to the dust.
At which the warrior in his obstinacy,
Because she kept the letter of his word,   455
Was in a manner pleased, and turning, stood.
And in the moment after, wild Limours,
Borne on a black horse, like a thunder-cloud
Whose skirts are loosen'd by the breaking storm,
Half ridden off with by the thing he rode,   460
And all in passion uttering a dry shriek,
Dash'd on Geraint, who closed with him, and bore
Down by the length of lance and arm beyond
The crupper, and so left him stunn'd or dead,
And overthrew the next that follow'd him,   465
And blindly rush'd on all the rout behind.
But at the flash and motion of the man
They vanish'd panic-stricken, like a shoal
Of darting fish, that on a summer morn
Adown the crystal dykes at Camelot   470
Come slipping o'er their shadows on the sand,
But if a man who stands upon the brink
But lift a shining hand against the sun,
There is not left the twinkle of a fin
Betwixt the cressy islets white in flower;   475
So, scared but at the motion of the man,
Fled all the boon companions of the Earl,
And left him lying in the public way;
So vanish friendships only made in wine.

Then like a stormy sunlight smiled Geraint,   480
Who saw the chargers of the two that fell

Start from their fallen lords, and wildly fly,
Mixt with the flyers. 'Horse and man,' he said,
'All of one mind and all right-honest friends!
485   Not a hoof left: and I methinks till now
Was honest – paid with horses and with arms;
I cannot steal or plunder, no nor beg:
And so what say ye, shall we strip him there
Your lover? has your palfrey heart enough
490   To bear his armour? shall we fast, or dine?
No? – then do thou, being right honest, pray
That we may meet the horsemen of Earl Doorm,
I too would still be honest.' Thus he said:
And sadly gazing on her bridle-reins,
495   And answering not one word, she led the way.

But as a man to whom a dreadful loss
Falls in a far land and he knows it not,
But coming back he learns it, and the loss
So pains him that he sickens nigh to death;
500   So fared it with Geraint, who being prick'd
In combat with the follower of Limours,
Bled underneath his armour secretly,
And so rode on, nor told his gentle wife
What ail'd him, hardly knowing it himself,
505   Till his eye darken'd and his helmet wagg'd;
And at a sudden swerving of the road,
Tho' happily down on a bank of grass,
The Prince, without a word, from his horse fell.

And Enid heard the clashing of his fall,
510   Suddenly came, and at his side all pale
Dismounting, loosed the fastenings of his arms,
Nor let her true hand falter, nor blue eye
Moisten, till she had lighted on his wound,
And tearing off her veil of faded silk
515   Had bared her forehead to the blistering sun,
And swathed the hurt that drain'd her dear lord's life.
Then after all was done that hand could do,
She rested, and her desolation came
Upon her, and she wept beside the way.

And many past, but none regarded her,   520
For in that realm of lawless turbulence,
A woman weeping for her murder'd mate
Was cared as much for as a summer shower:
One took him for a victim of Earl Doorm,
Nor dared to waste a perilous pity on him: 525
Another hurrying past, a man-at-arms,
Rode on a mission to the bandit Earl;
Half whistling and half singing a coarse song,
He drove the dust against her veilless eyes:
Another, flying from the wrath of Doorm   530
Before an ever-fancied arrow, made
The long way smoke beneath him in his fear;
At which her palfrey whinnying lifted heel,
And scour'd into the coppices and was lost,
While the great charger stood, grieved like a man.   535

But at the point of noon the huge Earl Doorm,
Broad-faced with under-fringe of russet beard,
Bound on a foray, rolling eyes of prey,
Came riding with a hundred lances up;
But ere he came, like one that hails a ship,   540
Cried out with a big voice, 'What, is he dead?'
'No, no, not dead!' she answer'd in all haste.
'Would some of your kind people take him up,
And bear him hence out of this cruel sun?
Most sure am I, quite sure, he is not dead.'   545

Then said Earl Doorm: 'Well, if he be not dead,
Why wail ye for him thus? ye seem a child.
And be he dead, I count you for a fool;
Your wailing will not quicken him: dead or not,
Ye mar a comely face with idiot tears.   550
Yet, since the face *is* comely – some of you,
Here, take him up, and bear him to our hall:
An if he live, we will have him of our band;
And if he die, why earth has earth enough
To hide him. See ye take the charger too,   555
A noble one.'

He spake, and past away,
But left two brawny spearmen, who advanced,
Each growling like a dog, when his good bone
Seems to be pluck'd at by the village boys
560   Who love to vex him eating, and he fears
To lose his bone, and lays his foot upon it,
Gnawing and growling: so the ruffians growl'd,
Fearing to lose, and all for a dead man,
Their chance of booty from the morning's raid,
565   Yet raised and laid him on a litter-bier,
Such as they brought upon their forays out
For those that might be wounded; laid him on it
All in the hollow of his shield, and took
And bore him to the naked hall of Doorm,
570   (His gentle charger following him unled)
And cast him and the bier in which he lay
Down on an oaken settle in the hall,
And then departed, hot in haste to join
Their luckier mates, but growling as before,
575   And cursing their lost time, and the dead man,
And their own Earl, and their own souls, and her.
They might as well have blest her: she was deaf
To blessing or to cursing save from one.

So for long hours sat Enid by her lord,
580   There in the naked hall, propping his head,
And chafing his pale hands, and calling to him.
Till at the last he waken'd from his swoon,
And found his own dear bride propping his head,
And chafing his faint hands, and calling to him;
585   And felt the warm tears falling on his face;
And said to his own heart, 'She weeps for me:'
And yet lay still, and feign'd himself as dead,
That he might prove her to the uttermost,
And say to his own heart, 'She weeps for me.'

590   But in the falling afternoon return'd
The huge Earl Doorm with plunder to the hall.
His lusty spearmen follow'd him with noise:
Each hurling down a heap of things that rang

Against the pavement, cast his lance aside,
And doff'd his helm: and then there flutter'd in,   595
Half-bold, half-frighted, with dilated eyes,
A tribe of women, dress'd in many hues,
And mingled with the spearmen: and Earl Doorm
Struck with a knife's haft hard against the board,
And call'd for flesh and wine to feed his spears.   600
And men brought in whole hogs and quarter beeves,
And all the hall was dim with steam of flesh:
And none spake word, but all sat down at once,
And ate with tumult in the naked hall,
Feeding like horses when you hear them feed;   605
Till Enid shrank far back into herself,
To shun the wild ways of the lawless tribe.
But when Earl Doorm had eaten all he would,
He roll'd his eyes about the hall, and found
A damsel drooping in a corner of it.   610
Then he remember'd her, and how she wept;
And out of her there came a power upon him;
And rising on the sudden he said, 'Eat!
I never yet beheld a thing so pale.
God's curse, it makes me mad to see you weep.   615
Eat! Look yourself. Good luck had your good man,
For were I dead who is it would weep for me?
Sweet lady, never since I first drew breath
Have I beheld a lily like yourself.
And so there lived some colour in your cheek,   620
There is not one among my gentlewomen
Were fit to wear your slipper for a glove.
But listen to me, and by me be ruled,
And I will do the thing I have not done,
For ye shall share my earldom with me, girl,   625
And we will live like two birds in one nest,
And I will fetch you forage from all fields,
For I compel all creatures to my will.'

He spoke: the brawny spearman let his cheek
Bulge with the unswallow'd piece, and turning stared;   630
While some, whose souls the old serpent long had drawn
Down, as the worm draws in the wither'd leaf

And makes it earth, hiss'd each at other's ear
What shall not be recorded – women they,
635 Women, or what had been those gracious things,
But now desired the humbling of their best,
Yea, would have help'd him to it: and all at once
They hated her, who took no thought of them,
But answer'd in low voice, her meek head yet
640 Drooping, 'I pray you of your courtesy,
He being as he is, to let me be.'

She spake so low he hardly heard her speak,
But like a mighty patron, satisfied
With what himself had done so graciously,
645 Assumed that she had thank'd him, adding, 'Yea,
Eat and be glad, for I account you mine.'

She answer'd meekly, 'How should I be glad
Henceforth in all the world at anything,
Until my lord arise and look upon me?'

650 Here the huge Earl cried out upon her talk,
As all but empty heart and weariness
And sickly nothing; suddenly seized on her,
And bare her by main violence to the board,
And thrust the dish before her, crying, 'Eat.'

655 'No, no,' said Enid, vext, 'I will not eat
Till yonder man upon the bier arise,
And eat with me.' 'Drink, then,' he answer'd. 'Here!'
(And fill'd a horn with wine and held it to her,)
'Lo! I, myself, when flush'd with fight, or hot,
660 God's curse, with anger – often I myself,
Before I well have drunken, scarce can eat:
Drink therefore and the wine will change your will.'

'Not so,' she cried, 'by Heaven, I will not drink
Till my dear lord arise and bid me do it,
665 And drink with me; and if he rise no more,
I will not look at wine until I die.'

At this he turn'd all red and paced his hall,
Now gnaw'd his under, now his upper lip,
And coming up close to her, said at last:
'Girl, for I see ye scorn my courtesies,   670
Take warning: yonder man is surely dead;
And I compel all creatures to my will.
Not eat nor drink? And wherefore wail for one,
Who put your beauty to this flout and scorn
By dressing it in rags? Amazed am I,   675
Beholding how ye butt against my wish,
That I forbear you thus: cross me no more.
At least put off to please me this poor gown,
This silken rag, this beggar-woman's weed:
I love that beauty should go beautifully: 680
For see ye not my gentlewomen here,
How gay, how suited to the house of one
Who loves that beauty should go beautifully?
Rise therefore; robe yourself in this: obey.'

He spoke, and one among his gentlewomen   685
Display'd a splendid silk of foreign loom,
Where like a shoaling sea the lovely blue
Play'd into green, and thicker down the front
With jewels than the sward with drops of dew,
When all night long a cloud clings to the hill,   690
And with the dawn ascending lets the day
Strike where it clung: so thickly shone the gems.

But Enid answer'd, harder to be moved
Than hardest tyrants in their day of power,
With life-long injuries burning unavenged,   695
And now their hour has come; and Enid said:

'In this poor gown my dear lord found me first,
And loved me serving in my father's hall:
In this poor gown I rode with him to court,
And there the Queen array'd me like the sun: 700
In this poor gown he bad me clothe myself,
When now we rode upon this fatal quest

Of honour, where no honour can be gain'd:
And this poor gown I will not cast aside
705   Until himself arise a living man,
And bid me cast it. I have griefs enough:
Pray you be gentle, pray you let me be:
I never loved, can never love but him:
Yea, God, I pray you of your gentleness,
710   He being as he is, to let me be.'

Then strode the brute Earl up and down his hall,
And took his russet beard between his teeth;
Last, coming up quite close, and in his mood
Crying, 'I count it of no more avail,
715   Dame, to be gentle than ungentle with you;
Take my salute,' unknightly with flat hand,
However lightly, smote her on the cheek.

Then Enid, in her utter helplessness,
And since she thought, 'He had not dared to do it,
720   Except he surely knew my lord was dead,'
Sent forth a sudden sharp and bitter cry,
As of a wild thing taken in the trap,
Which sees the trapper coming thro' the wood.

This heard Geraint, and grasping at his sword,
725   (It lay beside him in the hollow shield),
Made but a single bound, and with a sweep of it
Shore thro' the swarthy neck, and like a ball
The russet-bearded head roll'd on the floor.
So died Earl Doorm by him he counted dead.
730   And all the men and women in the hall
Rose when they saw the dead man rise, and fled
Yelling as from a spectre, and the two
Were left alone together, and he said:

'Enid, I have used you worse than that dead man;
735   Done you more wrong: we both have undergone
That trouble which has left me thrice your own:
Henceforward I will rather die than doubt.
And here I lay this penance on myself,

Not, tho' mine own ears heard you yestermorn –
You thought me sleeping; but I heard you say,   740
I heard you say, that you were no true wife:
I swear I will not ask your meaning in it:
I do believe yourself against yourself,
And will henceforward rather die than doubt.'

And Enid could not say one tender word,   745
She felt so blunt and stupid at the heart:
She only pray'd him, 'Fly, they will return
And slay you; fly, your charger is without,
My palfrey lost.' 'Then, Enid, shall you ride
Behind me.' 'Yea,' said Enid, 'let us go.'   750
And moving out they found the stately horse,
Who now no more a vassal to the thief,
But free to stretch his limbs in lawful fight,
Neigh'd with all gladness as they came, and stoop'd
With a low whinny toward the pair: and she   755
Kiss'd the white star upon his noble front,
Glad also; then Geraint upon the horse
Mounted, and reach'd a hand, and on his foot
She set her own and climb'd; he turn'd his face
And kiss'd her climbing, and she cast her arms   760
About him, and at once they rode away.

And never yet, since high in Paradise
O'er the four rivers the first roses blew,
Came purer pleasure unto mortal kind
Than lived thro' her, who in that perilous hour   765
Put hand to hand beneath her husband's heart,
And felt him hers again: she did not weep,
But o'er her meek eyes came a happy mist
Like that which kept the heart of Eden green
Before the useful trouble of the rain: 770
Yet not so misty were her meek blue eyes
As not to see before them on the path,
Right in the gateway of the bandit hold,
A knight of Arthur's court, who laid his lance
In rest, and made as if to fall upon him.   775
Then, fearing for his hurt and loss of blood,

She, with her mind all full of what had chanced,
Shriek'd to the stranger 'Slay not a dead man!'
'The voice of Enid,' said the knight; but she,
780 Beholding it was Edyrn son of Nudd,
Was moved so much the more, and shriek'd again,
'O cousin, slay not him who gave you life.'
And Edyrn moving frankly forward spake:
'My lord Geraint, I greet you with all love;
785 I took you for a bandit knight of Doorm;
And fear not, Enid, I should fall upon him,
Who love you, Prince, with something of the love
Wherewith we love the Heaven that chastens us.
For once, when I was up so high in pride
790 That I was halfway down the slope to Hell,
By overthrowing me you threw me higher.
Now, made a knight of Arthur's Table Round
And since I knew this Earl, when I myself
Was half a bandit in my lawless hour,
795 I come the mouthpiece of our King to Doorm
(The King is close behind me) bidding him
Disband himself, and scatter all his powers,
Submit, and hear the judgment of the King.'

'He hears the judgment of the King of kings,'
800 Cried the wan Prince; and 'and lo, the powers of Doorm
Are scatter'd,' and he pointed to the field,
Where, huddled here and there on mound and knoll,
Were men and women staring and aghast,
While some yet fled; and then he plainlier told
805 How the huge Earl lay slain within his hall.
But when the knight besought him, 'Follow me,
Prince, to the camp, and in the King's own ear
Speak what has chanced; ye surely have endured
Strange chances here alone;' that other flush'd
810 And hung his head, and halted in reply,
Fearing the mild face of the blameless King,
And after madness acted question ask'd:
Till Edyrn crying, 'If ye will not go
To Arthur, then will Arthur come to you,'
815 'Enough,' he said, 'I follow,' and they went.

But Enid in their going had two fears,
One from the bandit scatter'd in the field,
And one from Edyrn. Every now and then,
When Edyrn rein'd his charger at her side,
She shrank a little. In a hollow land,   820
From which old fires have broken, men may fear
Fresh fire and ruin. He, perceiving, said:

'Fair and dear cousin, you that most had cause
To fear me, fear no longer, I am changed.
Yourself were first the blameless cause to make   825
My nature's prideful sparkle in the blood
Break into furious flame; being repulsed
By Yniol and yourself, I schemed and wrought
Until I overturn'd him; then set up
(With one main purpose ever at my heart)   830
My haughty jousts, and took a paramour;
Did her mock-honour as the fairest fair,
And, toppling over all antagonism,
So wax'd in pride, that I believed myself
Unconquerable, for I was wellnigh mad: 835
And, but for my main purpose in these jousts,
I should have slain your father, seized yourself.
I lived in hope that sometime you would come
To these my lists with him whom best you loved;
And there, poor cousin, with your meek blue eyes,   840
The truest eyes that ever answer'd Heaven,
Behold me overturn and trample on him.
Then, had you cried, or knelt, or pray'd to me,
I should not less have kill'd him. And you came, –
But once you came, – and with your own true eyes   845
Beheld the man you loved (I speak as one
Speaks of a service done him) overthrow
My proud self, and my purpose three years old,
And set his foot upon me, and give me life.
There was I broken down; there was I saved: 850
Tho' thence I rode all-shamed, hating the life
He gave me, meaning to be rid of it.
And all the penance the Queen laid upon me
Was but to rest awhile within her court;

855 Where first as sullen as a beast new-caged,
And waiting to be treated like a wolf,
Because I knew my deeds were known, I found,
Instead of scornful pity or pure scorn,
Such fine reserve and noble reticence,
860 Manners so kind, yet stately, such a grace
Of tenderest courtesy, that I began
To glance behind me at my former life,
And find that it had been the wolf's indeed:
And oft I talk'd with Dubric, the high saint,
865 Who, with mild heat of holy oratory,
Subdued me somewhat to that gentleness,
Which, when it weds with manhood, makes a man.
And you were often there about the Queen,
But saw me not, or mark'd not if you saw;
870 Nor did I care or dare to speak with you,
But kept myself aloof till I was changed;
And fear not, cousin; I am changed indeed.'

He spoke, and Enid easily believed,
Like simple noble natures, credulous
875 Of what they long for, good in friend or foe,
There most in those who most have done them ill.
And when they reach'd the camp the King himself
Advanced to greet them, and beholding her
Tho' pale, yet happy, ask'd her not a word,
880 But went apart with Edyrn, whom he held
In converse for a little, and return'd,
And, gravely smiling, lifted her from horse,
And kiss'd her with all pureness, brother-like,
And show'd an empty tent allotted her,
885 And glancing for a minute, till he saw her
Pass into it, turn'd to the Prince, and said:

'Prince, when of late ye pray'd me for my leave
To move to your own land, and there defend
Your marches, I was prick'd with some reproof,
890 As one that let foul wrong stagnate and be,
By having look'd too much thro' alien eyes,
And wrought too long with delegated hands,

Not used mine own: but now behold me come
To cleanse this common sewer of all my realm,
With Edyrn and with others: have ye look'd   895
At Edyrn? have ye seen how nobly changed?
This work of his is great and wonderful.
His very face with change of heart is changed.
The world will not believe a man repents:
And this wise world of ours is mainly right.   900
Full seldom doth a man repent, or use
Both grace and will to pick the vicious quitch
Of blood and custom wholly out of him,
And make all clean, and plant himself afresh.
Edyrn has done it, weeding all his heart   905
As I will weed this land before I go.
I, therefore, made him of our Table Round,
Not rashly, but have proved him everyway
One of our noblest, our most valorous,
Sanest and most obedient: and indeed   910
This work of Edyrn wrought upon himself
After a life of violence, seems to me
A thousand-fold more great and wonderful
Than if some knight of mine, risking his life,
My subject with my subjects under him,   915
Should make an onslaught single on a realm
Of robbers, tho' he slew them one by one,
And were himself nigh wounded to the death.'

So spake the King; low bow'd the Prince, and felt
His work was neither great nor wonderful,   920
And past to Enid's tent; and thither came
The King's own leech to look into his hurt;
And Enid tended on him there; and there
Her constant motion round him, and the breath
Of her sweet tendance hovering over him,   925
Fill'd all the genial courses of his blood
With deeper and with ever deeper love,
As the south-west that blowing Bala lake
Fills all the sacred Dee. So past the days.

But while Geraint lay healing of his hurt,   930

The blameless King went forth and cast his eyes
On each of all whom Uther left in charge
Long since, to guard the justice of the King:
He look'd and found them wanting; and as now
935 Men weed the white horse on the Berkshire hills
To keep him bright and clean as heretofore,
He rooted out the slothful officer
Or guilty, which for bribe had wink'd at wrong,
And in their chairs set up a stronger race
940 With hearts and hands, and sent a thousand men
To till the wastes, and moving everywhere
Clear'd the dark places and let in the law,
And broke the bandit holds and cleansed the land.

Then, when Geraint was whole again, they past
945 With Arthur to Caerleon upon Usk.
There the great Queen once more embraced her friend,
And clothed her in apparel like the day.
And tho' Geraint could never take again
That comfort from their converse which he took
950 Before the Queen's fair name was breathed upon,
He rested well content that all was well.
Thence after tarrying for a space they rode,
And fifty knights rode with them to the shores
Of Severn, and they past to their own land.
955 And there he kept the justice of the King
So vigorously yet mildly, that all hearts
Applauded, and the spiteful whisper died:
And being ever foremost in the chase,
And victor at the tilt and tournament,
960 They call'd him the great Prince and man of men.
But Enid, whom her ladies loved to call
Enid the Fair, a grateful people named
Enid the Good; and in their halls arose
The cry of children, Enids and Geraints
965 Of times to be; nor did he doubt her more,
But rested in her fealty, till he crown'd
A happy life with a fair death, and fell
Against the heathen of the Northern Sea
In battle, fighting for the blameless King.

NARRATIVE
DEVICE OF
DOUBLING

FREUD- THE UNCANNY-
THE DOUBLENESS

Balin and Balan

Pellam the King, who held and lost with Lot
In that first war, and had his realm restored
But render'd tributary, fail'd of late
To send his tribute; wherefore Arthur call'd
His treasurer, one of many years, and spake,   5
'Go thou with him and him and bring it to us,
Lest we should set one truer on his throne.
Man's word is God in man.'

                His Baron said
'We go but harken: there be two strange knights   10
Who sit near Camelot at a fountain side,
A mile beneath the forest, challenging
And overthrowing every knight who comes.
Wilt thou I undertake them as we pass,
And send them to thee?'

                Arthur laugh'd upon him.
'Old friend, too old to be so young, depart,   15
Delay not thou for ought, but let them sit,
Until they find a lustier than themselves.'

So these departed. Early, one fair dawn,
The light-wing'd spirit of his youth return'd
On Arthur's heart; he arm'd himself and went,   20
So coming to the fountain-side beheld
Balin and Balan sitting statuelike,
Brethren, to right and left the spring, that down,
From underneath a plume of lady-fern,
Sang, and the sand danced at the bottom of it.   25
And on the right of Balin Balin's horse
Was fast beside an alder, on the left
Of Balan Balan's near a poplartree.

'Fair Sirs,' said Arthur, 'wherefore sit ye here?'
30 Balin and Balan answer'd 'For the sake
Of glory; we be mightier men than all
In Arthur's court; that also have we proved;
For whatsoever knight against us came
Or I or he have easily overthrown.'

35 'I too,' said Arthur, 'am of Arthur's hall,
But rather proven in his Paynim wars
Than famous jousts; but see, or proven or not,
Whether me likewise ye can overthrow.'
And Arthur lightly smote the brethren down,
40 And lightly so return'd, and no man knew.

Then Balin rose, and Balan, and beside
The carolling water set themselves again,
And spake no word until the shadow turn'd;
When from the fringe of coppice round them burst
45 A spangled pursuivant, and crying 'Sirs,
Rise, follow! ye be sent for by the King,'
They follow'd; whom when Arthur seeing ask'd
'Tell me your names; why sat ye by the well?'
Balin the stillness of a minute broke
50 Saying 'An unmelodious name to thee,
Balin, "the Savage" – that addition thine –
My brother and my better, this man here,
Balan. I smote upon the naked skull
A thrall of thine in open hall, my hand
55 Was gauntleted, half slew him; for I heard
He had spoken evil of me; thy just wrath
Sent me a three-years' exile from thine eyes.
I have not lived my life delightsomely:
For I that did that violence to thy thrall,
60 Had often wrought some fury on myself,
Saving for Balan: those three kingless years
Have past – were wormwood-bitter to me. King,
Methought that if we sat beside the well,
And hurl'd to ground what knight soever spurr'd
65 Against us, thou would'st take me gladlier back,
And make, as ten-times worthier to be thine
Than twenty Balins, Balan knight. I have said.'

No so – not all. A man of thine to-day
Abash'd us both, and brake my boast. Thy will?'
Said Arthur 'Thou hast ever spoken truth;   70
Thy too fierce manhood would not let thee lie.
Rise, my true knight. As children learn, be thou
Wiser for falling! walk with me, and move
To music with thine Order and the King.
Thy chair, a grief to all the brethren, stands   75
Vacant, but thou retake it, mine again!'

    Thereafter, when Sir Balin enter'd hall,
The Lost one Found was greeted as in Heaven
With joy that blazed itself in woodland wealth
Of leaf, and gayest garlandage of flowers,   80
Along the walls and down the board; they sat,
And cup clash'd cup; they drank and some one sang,
Sweet-voiced, a song of welcome, whereupon
Their common shout in chorus, mounting, made
Those banners of twelve battles overhead   85
Stir, as they stirr'd of old, when Arthur's host
Proclaim'd him Victor, and the day was won.

    Then Balan added to their Order lived
A wealthier life than heretofore with these
And Balin, till their embassage return'd.   90

    'Sir King' they brought report 'we hardly found,
So bush'd about it is with gloom, the hall
Of him to whom ye sent us, Pellam, once
A Christless foe of thine as ever dash'd
Horse against horse; but seeing that thy realm   95
Hath prosper'd in the name of Christ, the King
Took, as in rival heat, to holy things;
And finds himself descended from the Saint
Arimathæan Joseph; him who first
Brought the great faith to Britain over seas;   100
He boasts his life as purer than thine own;
Eats scarce enow to keep his pulse abeat;
Hath push'd aside his faithful wife, nor lets
Or dame or damsel enter at his gates

105   Lest he should be polluted. This gray King
       Show'd us a shrine wherein were wonders – yea –
       Rich arks with priceless bones of martyrdom,
       Thorns of the crown and shivers of the cross,
       And therewithal (for thus he told us) brought
110   By holy Joseph hither, that same spear
       Wherewith the Roman pierced the side of Christ.
       He much amazed us; after, when we sought
       The tribute, answer'd "I have quite foregone
       All matters of this world: Garlon, mine heir,
115   Of him demand it," which this Garlon gave
       With much ado, railing at thine and thee.

     'But when we left, in those deep woods we found
       A knight of thine spear-stricken from behind,
       Dead, whom we buried; more than one of us
120   Cried out on Garlon, but a woodman there
       Reported of some demon in the woods
       Was once a man, who driven by evil tongues
       From all his fellows, lived alone, and came
       To learn black magic, and to hate his kind
125   With such a hate, that when he died, his soul
       Became a Fiend, which, as the man in life
       Was wounded by blind tongues he saw not whence,
       Strikes from behind. This woodman show'd the cave
       From which he sallies, and wherein he dwelt.
130   We saw the hoof-print of a horse, no more.'

     Then Arthur, 'Let who goes before me, see
       He do not fall behind me: foully slain
       And villainously! who will hunt for me
       This demon of the woods?' Said Balan, 'I'!
135   So claim'd the quest and rode away, but first,
       Embracing Balin, 'Good my brother, hear!
       Let not thy moods prevail, when I am gone
       Who used to lay them! hold them outer fiends,
       Who leap at thee to tear thee; shake them aside,
140   Dreams ruling when wit sleeps! yea, but to dream
       That any of these would wrong thee, wrongs thyself.
       Witness their flowery welcome. Bound are they

To speak no evil. Truly save for fears,
My fears for thee, so rich a fellowship
Would make me wholly blest: thou one of them,   145
Be one indeed: consider them, and all
Their bearing in their common bond of love,
No more of hatred than in Heaven itself,
No more of jealousy than in Paradise.'

    So Balan warn'd, and went; Balin remain'd: 150
Who – for but three brief moons had glanced away
From being knighted till he smote the thrall,
And faded from the presence into years
Of exile – now would strictlier set himself
To learn what Arthur meant by courtesy,   155
Manhood, and knighthood; wherefore hover'd round
Lancelot, but when he mark'd his high sweet smile
In passing, and a transitory word
Make knight or churl or child or damsel seem
From being smiled at happier in themselves –   160
Sigh'd, as a boy lame-born beneath a height,
That glooms his valley, sighs to see the peak
Sun-flush'd, or touch at night the northern star;
For one from out his village lately climb'd
And brought report of azure lands and fair,   165
Far seen to left and right; and he himself
Hath hardly scaled with help a hundred feet
Up from the base: so Balin marvelling oft
How far beyond him Lancelot seem'd to move,
Groan'd, and at times would mutter, 'These be gifts,   170
Born with the blood, not learnable, divine,
Beyond *my* reach. Well had I foughten – well –
In those fierce wars, struck hard – and had I crown'd
With my slain self the heaps of whom I slew –
So – better! – But this worship of the Queen,   175
That honour too wherein she holds him – this,
This was the sunshine that hath given the man
A growth, a name that branches o'er the rest,
And strength against all odds, and what the King
So prizes – overprizes – gentleness.   180
Her likewise would I worship an I might.

I never can be close with her, as he
That brought her hither. Shall I pray the King
To let me bear some token of his Queen
185   Whereon to gaze, remembering her – forget
My heats and violences? live afresh?
What, if the Queen disdain'd to grant it! nay
Being so stately-gentle, would she make
My darkness blackness? and with how sweet grace
190   She greeted my return! Bold will I be –
Some goodly cognizance of Guinevere,
In lieu of this rough beast upon my shield,
Langued gules, and tooth'd with grinning savagery.'

    And Arthur, when Sir Balin sought him, said
195   'What wilt thou bear?' Balin was bold, and ask'd
To bear her own crown-royal upon shield,
Whereat she smiled and turn'd her to the King,
Who answer'd 'Thou shalt put the crown to use.
The crown is but the shadow of the King,
200   And this a shadow's shadow, let him have it,
So this will help him of his violences!'
'No shadow' said Sir Balin 'O my Queen,
But light to me! no shadow, O my King,
But golden earnest of a gentler life!'

205   So Balin bare the crown, and all the knights
Approved him, and the Queen, and all the world
Made music, and he felt his being move
In music with his Order, and the King.

    The nightingale, full-toned in middle May,
210   Hath ever and anon a note so thin
It seems another voice in other groves;
Thus, after some quick burst of sudden wrath,
The music in him seem'd to change, and grow
Faint and far-off.

              And once he saw the thrall
215   His passion half had gauntleted to death,

That causer of his banishment and shame,
Smile at him, as he deem'd, presumptuously:
His arm half rose to strike again, but fell:
The memory of that cognizance on shield
Weighted it down, but in himself he moan'd: 220

'Too high this mount of Camelot for me:
These high-set courtesies are not for me.
Shall I not rather prove the worse for these?
Fierier and stormier from restraining, break
Into some madness ev'n before the Queen?'   225

Thus, as a hearth lit in a mountain home,
And glancing on the window, when the gloom
Of twilight deepens round it, seems a flame
That rages in the woodland far below,
So when his moods were darken'd, court and King   230
And all the kindly warmth of Arthur's hall
Shadow'd an angry distance: yet he strove
To learn the graces of their Table, fought
Hard with himself, and seem'd at length in peace.

Then chanced, one morning, that Sir Balin sat   235
Close-bower'd in that garden nigh the hall.
A walk of roses ran from door to door;
A walk of lilies crost it to the bower:
And down that range of roses the great Queen
Came with slow steps, the morning on her face;   240
And all in shadow from the counter door
Sir Lancelot as to meet her, then at once,
As if he saw not, glanced aside, and paced
The long white walk of lilies toward the bower.
Follow'd the Queen; Sir Balin heard her 'Prince,   245
Art thou so little loyal to thy Queen,
As pass without good morrow to thy Queen?'
To whom Sir Lancelot with his eyes on earth,
'Fain would I still be loyal to the Queen.'
'Yea so' she said 'but so to pass me by –   250
So loyal scarce is loyal to thyself,
Whom all men rate the king of courtesy.
Let be: ye stand, fair lord, as in a dream.'

Then Lancelot with his hand among the flowers
255 'Yea – for a dream. Last night methought I saw
That maiden Saint who stands with lily in hand
In yonder shrine. All round her prest the dark,
And all the light upon her silver face
Flow'd from the spiritual lily that she held.
260 Lo! these her emblems drew mine eyes – away:
For see, how perfect-pure! As light a flush
As hardly tints the blossom of the quince
Would mar their charm of stainless maidenhood.'

'Sweeter to me' she said 'this garden rose
265 Deep-hued and many-folded! sweeter still
The wild-wood hyacinth and the bloom of May.
Prince, we have ridd'n before among the flowers
In those fair days – not all as cool as these,
Tho' season-earlier. Art thou sad? or sick?
270 Our noble King will send thee his own leech –
Sick? or for any matter anger'd at me?'

Then Lancelot lifted his large eyes; they dwelt
Deep-tranced on hers, and could not fall: her hue
Changed at his gaze: so turning side by side
275 They past, and Balin started from his bower.

'Queen? subject? but I see not what I see.
Damsel and lover? hear not what I hear.
My father hath begotten me in his wrath.
I suffer from the things before me, know,
280 Learn nothing; am not worthy to be knight;
A churl, a clown!' and in him gloom on gloom
Deepen'd: he sharply caught his lance and shield,
Nor stay'd to crave permission of the King,
But, mad for strange adventure, dash'd away.

285 He took the selfsame track as Balan, saw
The fountain where they sat together, sigh'd
'Was I not better there with him?' and rode
The skyless woods, but under open blue
Came on the hoarhead woodman at a bough

Wearily hewing. 'Churl, thine axe!' he cried,   290
Descended, and disjointed it at a blow:
To whom the woodman utter'd wonderingly
'Lord, thou couldst lay the Devil of these woods
If arm of flesh could lay him.' Balin cried
'Him, or the viler devil who plays his part,   295
To lay that devil would lay the Devil in me.'
'Nay' said the churl, 'our devil is a truth,
I saw the flash of him but yestereven.
And some *do* say that our Sir Garlon too
Hath learn'd black magic, and to ride unseen.   300
Look to the cave.' But Balin answer'd him
'Old fabler, these be fancies of the churl,
Look to thy woodcraft,' and so leaving him,
Now with slack rein and careless of himself,
Now with dug spur and raving at himself,   305
Now with droopt brow down the long glades he rode;
So mark'd not on his right a cavern-chasm
Yawn over darkness, where, nor far within,
The whole day died, but, dying, gleam'd on rocks
Roof-pendent, sharp; and others from the floor,   310
Tusklike, arising, made that mouth of night
Whereout the Demon issued up from Hell.
He mark'd not this, but blind and deaf to all
Save that chain'd rage, which ever yelpt within,
Past eastward from the falling sun. At once   315
He felt the hollow-beaten mosses thud
And tremble, and then the shadow of a spear,
Shot from behind him, ran along the ground.
Sideways he started from the path, and saw,
With pointed lance as if to pierce, a shape,   320
A light of armour by him flash, and pass
And vanish in the woods; and follow'd this,
But all so blind in rage that unawares
He burst his lance against a forest bough,
Dishorsed himself, and rose again, and fled   325
Far, till the castle of a King, the hall
Of Pellam, lichen-bearded, grayly draped
With streaming grass, appear'd, low-built but strong;
The ruinous donjon as a knoll of moss,

330 The battlement overtopt with ivytods,
A home of bats, in every tower an owl.

Then spake the men of Pellam crying 'Lord,
Why wear ye this crown-royal upon shield?'
Said Balin 'For the fairest and the best
335 Of ladies living gave me this to bear.'
So stall'd his horse, and strode across the court,
But found the greetings both of knight and King
Faint in the low dark hall of banquet: leaves
Laid their green faces flat against the panes,
340 Sprays grated, and the canker'd boughs without
Whined in the wood; for all was hush'd within,
Till when at feast Sir Garlon likewise ask'd
'Why wear ye that crown-royal?' Balin said
'The Queen we worship, Lancelot, I, and all,
345 As fairest, best and purest, granted me
To bear it!' Such a sound (for Arthur's knights
Were hated strangers in the hall) as makes
The white swan-mother, sitting, when she hears
A strange knee rustle thro' her secret reeds,
350 Made Garlon, hissing; then he sourly smiled.
'Fairest I grant her: I have seen; but best,
Best, purest? *thou* from Arthur's hall, and yet
So simple! hast thou eyes, or if, are these
So far besotted that they fail to see
355 This fair wife-worship cloaks a secret shame?
Truly, ye men of Arthur be but babes.'

A goblet on the board by Balin, boss'd
With holy Joseph's legend, on his right
Stood, all of massiest bronze: one side had sea
360 And ship and sail and angels blowing on it:
And one was rough with wattling, and the walls
Of that low church he built at Glastonbury.
This Balin graspt, but while in act to hurl,
Thro' memory of that token on the shield
365 Relax'd his hold: 'I will be gentle' he thought
'And passing gentle' caught his hand away
Then fiercely to Sir Garlon 'Eyes have I

That saw to-day the shadow of a spear,
Shot from behind me, run along the ground;
Eyes too that long have watch'd how Lancelot draws   370
From homage to the best and purest, might,
Name, manhood, and a grace, but scantly thine,
Who, sitting in thine own hall, canst endure
To mouth so huge a foulness – to thy guest,
Me, me of Arthur's Table. Felon talk!   375
Let be! no more!'

          But not the less by night
The scorn of Garlon, poisoning all his rest,
Stung him in dreams. At length, and dim thro' leaves
Blinkt the white morn, sprays grated, and old boughs
Whined in the wood. He rose, descended, met   380
The scorner in the castle court, and fain,
For hate and loathing, would have past him by;
But when Sir Garlon utter'd mocking-wise;
'What, wear ye still that same crown-scandalous?'
His countenance blacken'd, and his forehead veins   385
Bloated, and branch'd; and tearing out of sheath
The brand, Sir Balin with a fiery 'Ha!
So thou be shadow, here I make thee ghost,'
Hard upon helm smote him, and the blade flew
Splintering in six, and clinkt upon the stones.   390
Then Garlon, reeling slowly backward, fell,
And Balin by the banneret of his helm
Dragg'd him, and struck, but from the castle a cry
Sounded across the court, and – men-at-arms,
A score with pointed lances, making at him –   395
He dash'd the pummel at the foremost face,
Beneath a low door dipt, and made his feet
Wings thro' a glimmering gallery, till he mark'd
The portal of King Pellam's chapel wide
And inward to the wall; he stept behind;   400
Thence in a moment heard them pass like wolves
Howling; but while he stared about the shrine,
In which he scarce could spy the Christ for Saints,
Beheld before a golden altar lie
The longest lance his eyes had ever seen,   405

Point-painted red; and seizing thereupon
Push'd thro' an open casement down, lean'd on it,
Leapt in a semicircle, and lit on earth;
Then hand at ear, and harkening from what side
410 The blindfold rummage buried in the walls
Might echo, ran the counter path, and found
His charger, mounted on him and away.
An arrow whizz'd to the right, one to the left,
One overhead; and Pellam's feeble cry
415 'Stay, stay him! he defileth heavenly things
With earthly uses' – made him quickly dive
Beneath the boughs, and race thro' many a mile
Of dense and open, till his goodly horse,
Arising wearily at a fallen oak,
420 Stumbled headlong, and cast him face to ground.

Half-wroth he had not ended, but all glad,
Knightlike, to find his charger yet unlamed,
Sir Balin drew the shield from off his neck,
Stared at the priceless cognizance, and thought
425 'I have shamed thee so that now thou shamest me,
Thee will I bear no more,' high on a branch
Hung it, and turn'd aside into the woods,
And there in gloom cast himself all along,
Moaning 'My violences, my violences!'

430 But now the wholesome music of the wood
Was dumb'd by one from out the hall of Mark,
A damsel-errant, warbling, as she rode
The woodland alleys, Vivien, with her Squire.

'The fire of Heaven has kill'd the barren cold,
435 And kindled all the plain and all the wold.
The new leaf ever pushes off the old.
The fire of Heaven is not the flame of Hell.

'Old priest, who mumble worship in your quire –
Old monk and nun, ye scorn the world's desire,
440 Yet in your frosty cells ye feel the fire!
The fire of Heaven is not the flame of Hell.

'The fire of Heaven is on the dusty ways.
The wayside blossoms open to the blaze.
The whole wood-world is one full peal of praise.
The fire of Heaven is not the flame of Hell.   445

'The fire of Heaven is lord of all things good,
And starve not thou this fire within thy blood,
But follow Vivien thro' the fiery flood!
The fire of Heaven is not the flame of Hell!'

Then turning to her Squire 'This fire of Heaven,   450
This old sun-worship, boy, will rise again,
And beat the cross to earth, and break the King
And all his Table.'

             Then they reach'd a glade,
Where under one long lane of cloudless air
Before another wood, the royal crown   455
Sparkled, and swaying upon a restless elm
Drew the vague glance of Vivien, and her Squire;
Amazed were these; 'Lo there' she cried – 'a crown –
Borne by some high lord-prince of Arthur's hall,
And there a horse! the rider? where is he?   460
See, yonder lies one dead within the wood.
Not dead; he stirs! – but sleeping. I will speak.
Hail, royal knight, we break on thy sweet rest,
Not, doubtless, all unearn'd by noble deeds.
But bounden art thou, if from Arthur's hall,   465
To help the weak. Behold, I fly from shame,
A lustful King, who sought to win my love
Thro' evil ways: the knight, with whom I rode,
Hath suffer'd misadventure, and my squire
Hath in him small defence; but thou, Sir Prince,   470
Wilt surely guide me to the warrior King,
Arthur the blameless, pure as any maid,
To get me shelter for my maidenhood.
I charge thee by that crown upon thy shield,
And by the great Queen's name, arise and hence.'   475

And Balin rose, 'Thither no more! nor Prince
Nor knight am I, but one that hath defamed

The cognizance she gave me: here I dwell
Savage among the savage woods, here die –
480   Die: let the wolves' black maws ensepulchre
Their brother beast, whose anger was his lord.
O me, that such a name as Guinevere's,
Which our high Lancelot hath so lifted up,
And been thereby uplifted, should thro' me,
485   My violence, and my villainy, come to shame.'

    Thereat she suddenly laugh'd and shrill, anon
Sigh'd all as suddenly. Said Balin to her
'Is this thy courtesy – to mock me, ha?
Hence, for I will not with thee.' Again she sigh'd
490   'Pardon, sweet lord! we maidens often laugh
When sick at heart, when rather we should weep.
I knew thee wrong'd. I brake upon thy rest,
And now full loth am I to break thy dream,
But thou art man, and canst abide a truth,
495   Tho' bitter. Hither, boy – and mark me well.
Dost thou remember at Caerleon once –
A year ago – nay, then I love thee not –
Ay, thou rememberest well – one summer dawn –
By the great tower – Caerleon upon Usk –
500   Nay, truly we were hidden: this fair lord,
The flower of all their vestal knighthood, knelt
In amorous homage – knelt – what else? – O ay
Knelt, and drew down from out his night-black hair
And mumbled that white hand whose ring'd caress
505   Had wander'd from her own King's golden head,
And lost itself in darkness, till she cried –
I thought the great tower would crash down on both –
"Rise, my sweet King, and kiss me on the lips,
Thou art my King." This lad, whose lightest word
510   Is mere white truth in simple nakedness,
Saw them embrace: he reddens, cannot speak,
So bashful, he! but all the maiden Saints,
The deathless mother-maidenhood of Heaven
Cry out upon her. Up then, ride with me!
515   Talk not of shame! thou canst not, an thou would'st,
Do these more shame than these have done themselves.'

She lied with ease; but horror-stricken he,
Remembering that dark bower at Camelot,
Breathed in a dismal whisper 'It is truth.'

Sunnily she smiled 'And even in this lone wood,   520
Sweet lord, ye do right well to whisper this.
Fools prate, and perish traitors. Woods have tongues,
As walls have ears: but thou shalt go with me,
And we will speak at first exceeding low.
Meet is it the good King be not deceived.   525
See now, I set thee high on vantage ground,
From whence to watch the time, and eagle-like
Stoop at thy will on Lancelot and the Queen.'

She ceased; his evil spirit upon him leapt,
He ground his teeth together, sprang with a yell,   530
Tore from the branch, and cast on earth, the shield,
Drove his mail'd heel athwart the royal crown,
Stampt all into defacement, hurl'd it from him
Among the forest weeds, and cursed the tale,
The told-of, and the teller.

                              That weird yell,   535
Unearthlier than all shriek of bird or beast,
Thrill'd thro' the woods; and Balan lurking there
(His quest was unaccomplish'd) heard and thought
'The scream of that Wood-devil I came to quell!'
Then nearing 'Lo! he hath slain some brother-knight,   540
And tramples on the goodly shield to show
His loathing of our Order and the Queen.
My quest, meseems, is here. Or devil or man
Guard thou thine head.' Sir Balin spake not word,
But snatch'd a sudden buckler from the Squire,   545
And vaulted on his horse, and so they crash'd
In onset, and King Pellam's holy spear,
Reputed to be red with sinless blood,
Redden'd at once with sinful, for the point
Across the maiden shield of Balan prick'd   550
The hauberk to the flesh; and Balin's horse
Was wearied to the death, and, when they clash'd,

Rolling back upon Balin, crush'd the man
Inward, and either fell, and swoon'd away.

555   Then to her Squire mutter'd the damsel 'Fools!
This fellow hath wrought some foulness with his Queen:
Else never had he borne her crown, nor raved
And thus foam'd over at a rival name:
But thou, Sir Chick, that scarce hast broken shell,
560 Art yet half-yolk, not even come to down –
Who never sawest Caerleon upon Usk –
And yet hast often pleaded for my love –
See what I see, be thou where I have been,
Or else Sir Chick – dismount and loose their casques
565 I fain would know what manner of men they be.'
And when the Squire had loosed them, 'Goodly! – look!
They might have cropt the myriad flower of May,
And butt each other here, like brainless bulls,
Dead for one heifer!'

                Then the gentle Squire
570 'I hold them happy, so they died for love:
And, Vivien, tho' ye beat me like your dog,
I too could die, as now I live, for thee.'

    'Live on, Sir Boy,' she cried. 'I better prize
The living dog than the dead lion: away!
575 I cannot brook to gaze upon the dead.'
Then leapt her palfrey o'er the fallen oak,
And bounding forward 'Leave them to the wolves.'

    But when their foreheads felt the cooling air,
Balin first woke, and seeing that true face,
580 Familiar up from cradle-time, so wan,
Crawl'd slowly with low moans to where he lay,
And on his dying brother cast himself
Dying; and *he* lifted faint eyes; he felt
One near him; all at once they found the world,
585 Staring wild-wide; then with a childlike wail,
And drawing down the dim disastrous brow
That o'er him hung, he kiss'd it, moan'd and spake;

'O Balin, Balin, I that fain had died
To save thy life, have brought thee to thy death.
Why had ye not the shield I knew? and why   590
Trampled ye thus on that which bare the Crown?'

Then Balin told him brokenly, and in gasps,
All that had chanced, and Balan moan'd again.

'Brother, I dwelt a day in Pellam's hall:
This Garlon mock'd me, but I heeded not.   595
And one said "Eat in peace! a liar is he,
And hates thee for the tribute!" this good knight
Told me, that twice a wanton damsel came,
And sought for Garlon at the castle-gates,
Whom Pellam drove away with holy heat.   600
I well believe this damsel, and the one
Who stood beside thee even now, the same.
"She dwells among the woods" he said "and meets
And dallies with him in the Mouth of Hell."
Foul are their lives; foul are their lips; they lied.   605
Pure as our own true Mother is our Queen.'

'O brother' answer'd Balin 'woe is me!
My madness all thy life has been thy doom,
Thy curse, and darken'd all thy day; and now
The night has come. I scarce can see thee now.   610
Goodnight! for we shall never bid again
Goodmorrow – Dark my doom was here, and dark
It will be there. I see thee now no more.
I would not mine again should darken thine,
Goodnight, true brother.'

     Balan answer'd low   615
'Goodnight, true brother here! goodmorrow there!
We two were born together, and we die
Together by one doom:' and while he spoke
Closed his death-drowsing eyes, and slept the sleep
With Balin, either lock'd in either's arm.   620

Merlin and Vivien

A storm was coming, but the winds were still,
And in the wild woods of Broceliande,
Before an oak, so hollow, huge and old
It look'd a tower of ivied masonwork,
5   At Merlin's feet the wily Vivien lay.

For he that always bare in bitter grudge
The slights of Arthur and his Table, Mark
 The Cornish King, had heard a wandering voice,
A minstrel of Caerleon by strong storm
10 Blown into shelter at Tintagil, say
That out of naked knightlike purity
Sir Lancelot worshipt no unmarried girl
But the great Queen herself, fought in her name,
Sware by her – vows like theirs, that high in heaven
15 Love most, but neither marry, nor are given
In marriage, angels of our Lord's report.

He ceased, and then – for Vivien sweetly said
(She sat beside the banquet nearest Mark),
'And is the fair example follow'd, Sir,
20 In Arthur's household?' – answer'd innocently:

'Ay, by some few – ay, truly – youths that hold
It more beseems the perfect virgin knight
To worship woman as true wife beyond
All hopes of gaining, than as maiden girl.
25 They place their pride in Lancelot and the Queen.
So passionate for an utter purity
Beyond the limit of their bond, are these,
For Arthur bound them not to singleness.
Brave hearts and clean! and yet – God guide them – young.'

Then Mark was half in heart to hurl his cup   30
Straight at the speaker, but forbore: he rose
To leave the hall, and, Vivien following him,
Turn'd to her: 'Here are snakes within the grass;
And you methinks, O Vivien, save ye fear
The monkish manhood, and the mask of pure   35
Worn by this court, can stir them till they sting.'

And Vivien answer'd, smiling scornfully,
'Why fear? because that foster'd at *thy* court
I savour of thy – virtues? fear them? no.
As Love, if Love be perfect, casts out fear,   40
So Hate, if Hate be perfect, casts out fear.
My father died in battle against the King,
My mother on his corpse in open field;
She bore me there, for born from death was I
Among the dead and sown upon the wind –   45
And then on thee! and shown the truth betimes,
That old true filth, and bottom of the well,
Where Truth is hidden. Gracious lessons thine
And maxims of the mud! "This Arthur pure!
Great Nature thro' the flesh herself hath made   50
Gives him the lie! There is no being pure,
My cherub; saith not Holy Writ the same?" –
If I were Arthur, I would have thy blood.
Thy blessing, stainless King! I bring thee back,
When I have ferreted out their burrowings,   55
The hearts of all this Order in mine hand –
Ay – so that fate and craft and folly close,
Perchance, one curl of Arthur's golden beard.
To me this narrow grizzled fork of thine
Is cleaner-fashion'd – Well, I loved thee first,   60
That warps the wit.'

                Loud laugh'd the graceless Mark
But Vivien, into Camelot stealing, lodged
Low in the city, and on a festal day
When Guinevere was crossing the great hall
Cast herself down, knelt to the Queen, and wail'd.   65

'Why kneel ye there? What evil have ye wrought?
Rise!' and the damsel bidden rise arose
And stood with folded hands and downward eyes
Of glancing corner, and all meekly said,
70 'None wrought, but suffer'd much, an orphan maid!
My father died in battle for thy King,
My mother on his corpse – in open field,
The sad sea-sounding wastes of Lyonnesse –
Poor wretch – no friend! – and now by Mark the King
75 For that small charm of feature mine, pursued –
If any such be mine – I fly to thee.
Save, save me thou – Woman of women – thine
The wreath of beauty, thine the crown of power,
Be thine the balm of pity, O Heaven's own white
80 Earth-angel, stainless bride of stainless King –
Help, for he follows! take me to thyself!
O yield me shelter for mine innocency
Among thy maidens!'

                    Here her slow sweet eyes
85 Fear-tremulous, but humbly hopeful, rose
Fixt on her hearer's, while the Queen who stood
All glittering like May sunshine on May leaves
In green and gold, and plumed with green replied,
'Peace, child! of overpraise and overblame
90 We choose the last. Our noble Arthur, him
Ye scarce can overpraise, will hear and know.
Nay – we believe all evil of thy Mark –
Well, we shall test thee farther; but this hour
We ride a-hawking with Sir Lancelot.
95 He hath given us a fair falcon which he train'd;
We go to prove it. Bide ye here the while.'

She past; and Vivien murmur'd after 'Go!
I bide the while.' Then thro' the portal-arch
Peering askance, and muttering broken-wise,
As one that labours with an evil dream,
100 Beheld the Queen and Lancelot get to horse.

'Is that the Lancelot! goodly – ay, but gaunt:
Courteous – amends for gauntness – takes her hand –

That glance of theirs, but for the street, had been
A clinging kiss – how hand lingers in hand!
Let go at last! – they ride away – to hawk   105
For waterfowl. Royaller game is mine.
For such a supersensual sensual bond
As that gray cricket chirpt of at our hearth –
Touch flax with flame – a glance will serve – the liars!
Ah little rat that borest in the dyke   110
Thy hole by night to let the boundless deep
Down upon far-off cities while they dance –
Or dream – of thee they dream'd not – nor of me
These – ay, but each of either: ride, and dream
The mortal dream that never yet was mine –   115
Ride, ride and dream until ye wake – to me!
Then, narrow court and lubber King, farewell!
For Lancelot will be gracious to the rat,
And our wise Queen, if knowing that I know,
Will hate, loathe, fear – but honour me the more.'   120

    Yet while they rode together down the plain,
Their talk was all of training, terms of art,
Diet and seeling, jesses, leash and lure.
'She is too noble' he said 'to check at pies,
Nor will she rake: there is no baseness in her.'   125
Here when the Queen demanded as by chance
'Know ye the stranger woman?' 'Let her be,'
Said Lancelot and unhooded casting off
The goodly falcon free; she tower'd; her bells,
Tone under tone, shrill'd; and they lifted up   130
Their eager faces, wondering at the strength,
Boldness and royal knighthood of the bird
Who pounced her quarry and slew it. Many a time
As once – of old – among the flowers – they rode.

    But Vivien half-forgotten of the Queen   135
Among her damsels broidering sat, heard, watch'd
And whisper'd: thro' the peaceful court she crept
And whisper'd: then as Arthur in the highest
Leaven'd the world, so Vivien in the lowest,
Arriving at a time of golden rest,   140

And sowing one ill hint from ear to ear,
While all the heathen lay at Arthur's feet,
And no quest came, but all was joust and play,
Leaven'd his hall. They heard and let her be.

145   Thereafter as an enemy that has left
Death in the living waters, and withdrawn,
The wily Vivien stole from Arthur's court.

She hated all the knights, and heard in thought
Their lavish comment when her name was named.
150   For once, when Arthur walking all alone,
Vext at a rumour issued from herself
Of some corruption crept among his knights,
Had met her, Vivien, being greeted fair,
Would fain have wrought upon his cloudy mood
155   With reverent eyes mock-loyal, shaken voice,
And flutter'd adoration, and at last
With dark sweet hints of some who prized him more
Than who should prize him most; at which the King
Had gazed upon her blankly and gone by:
160   But one had watch'd, and had not held his peace:
It made the laughter of an afternoon
That Vivien should attempt the blameless King
And after that, she set herself to gain
Him, the most famous man of all those times,
165   Merlin, who knew the range of all their arts,
Had built the King his havens, ships, and halls,
Was also Bard, and knew the starry heavens;
The people call'd him Wizard; whom at first
She play'd about with slight and sprightly talk,
170   And vivid smiles, and faintly-venom'd points
Of slander, glancing here and grazing there;
And yielding to his kindlier moods, the Seer
Would watch her at her petulance, and play,
Ev'n when they seem'd unloveable, and laugh
175   As those that watch a kitten; thus he grew
Tolerant of what he half disdain'd, and she,
Perceiving that she was but half disdain'd,
Began to break her sports with graver fits,

Turn red or pale, would often when they met
Sigh fully, or all-silent gaze upon him   180
With such a fixt devotion, that the old man,
Tho' doubtful, felt the flattery, and at times
Would flatter his own wish in age for love,
And half believe her true: for thus at times
He waver'd; but that other clung to him,   185
Fixt in her will, and so the seasons went.

Then fell on Merlin a great melancholy;
He walk'd with dreams and darkness, and he found
A doom that ever poised itself to fall,
An ever-moaning battle in the mist,   190
World-war of dying flesh against the life,
Death in all life and lying in all love,
The meanest having power upon the highest,
And the high purpose broken by the worm.

So leaving Arthur's court he gain'd the beach;   195
There found a little boat, and stept into it;
And Vivien follow'd, but he mark'd her not.
She took the helm and he the sail; the boat
Drave with a sudden wind across the deeps,
And touching Breton sands, they disembark'd.   200
And then she follow'd Merlin all the way,
Ev'n to the wild woods of Broceliande.
For Merlin once had told her of a charm,
The which if any wrought on anyone
With woven paces and with waving arms,   205
The man so wrought on ever seem'd to lie
Closed in the four walls of a hollow tower,
From which was no escape for evermore;
And none could find that man for evermore,
Nor could he see but him who wrought the charm   210
Coming and going, and he lay as dead
And lost to life and use and name and fame.
And Vivien ever sought to work the charm
Upon the great Enchanter of the Time,
As fancying that her glory would be great   215
According to his greatness whom she quench'd.

There lay she all her length and kiss'd his feet,
As if in deepest reverence and in love.
A twist of gold was round her hair; a robe
220   Of samite without price, that more exprest
Than hid her, clung about her lissome limbs,
In colour like the satin-shining palm
On sallows in the windy gleams of March:
And while she kiss'd them, crying, 'Trample me,
225   Dear feet, that I have follow'd thro' the world,
And I will pay you worship; tread me down
And I will kiss you for it;' he was mute:
So dark a forethought roll'd about his brain,
As on a dull day in an Ocean cave
230   The blind wave feeling round his long sea-hall
In silence: wherefore, when she lifted up
A face of sad appeal, and spake and said,
'O Merlin, do ye love me?' and again,
'O Merlin, do ye love me?' and once more,
235   'Great Master, do ye love me?' he was mute.
And lissome Vivien, holding by his heel,
Writhed toward him, slided up his knee and sat,
Behind his ankle twined her hollow feet
Together, curved an arm about his neck,
240   Clung like a snake; and letting her left hand
Droop from his mighty shoulder, as a leaf,
Made with her right a comb of pearl to part
The lists of such a beard as youth gone out
Had left in ashes: then he spoke and said,
245   Not looking at her, 'Who are wise in love
Love most, say least,' and Vivien answer'd quick,
'I saw the little elf-god eyeless once
In Arthur's arras hall at Camelot:
But neither eyes nor tongue – O stupid child!
250   Yet you are wise who say it; let me think
Silence is wisdom: I am silent then,
And ask no kiss;' then adding all at once,
'And lo, I clothe myself with wisdom,' drew
The vast and shaggy mantle of his beard
255   Across her neck and bosom to her knee,
And call'd herself a gilded summer fly

Caught in a great old tyrant spider's web,
Who meant to eat her up in that wild wood
Without one word. So Vivien call'd herself,
But rather seem'd a lovely baleful star   260
Veil'd in gray vapour; till he sadly smiled:
'To what request for what strange boon,' he said,
'Are these your pretty tricks and fooleries,
O Vivien, the preamble? yet my thanks,
For these have broken up my melancholy.'   265

        And Vivien answer'd smiling saucily,
'What, O my Master, have ye found your voice?
I bid the stranger welcome. Thanks at last!
But yesterday you never open'd lip,
Except indeed to drink: no cup had we: 270
In mine own lady palms I cull'd the spring
That gather'd trickling dropwise from the cleft,
And made a pretty cup of both my hands
And offer'd you it kneeling: then you drank
And knew no more, nor gave me one poor word;   275
O no more thanks than might a goat have given
With no more sign of reverence than a beard.
And when we halted at that other well,
And I was faint to swooning, and you lay
Foot-gilt with all the blossom-dust of those   280
Deep meadows we had traversed, did you know
That Vivien bathed your feet before her own?
And yet no thanks: and all thro' this wild wood
And all this morning when I fondled you:
Boon, ay, there was a boon, one not so strange –   285
How had I wrong'd you? surely ye are wise,
But such a silence is more wise than kind.'

        And Merlin lock'd his hand in hers and said:
'O did ye never lie upon the shore,
And watch the curl'd white of the coming wave   290
Glass'd in the slippery sand before it breaks?
Ev'n such a wave, but not so pleasurable,
Dark in the glass of some presageful mood,
Had I for three days seen, ready to fall.

295 And then I rose and fled from Arthur's court
To break the mood. You follow'd me unask'd;
And when I look'd, and saw you following still,
My mind involved yourself the nearest thing
In that mind-mist: for shall I tell you truth?
300 You seem'd that wave about to break upon me
And sweep me from my hold upon the world,
My use and name and fame. Your pardon, child.
Your pretty sports have brighten'd all again.
And ask your boon, for boon I owe you thrice,
305 Once for wrong done you by confusion, next
For thanks it seems till now neglected, last
For these your dainty gambols: wherefore ask;
And take this boon so strange and not so strange.'

And Vivien answer'd smiling mournfully:
310 'O not so strange as my long asking it,
Not yet so strange as you yourself are strange,
Nor half so strange as that dark mood of yours.
I ever fear'd ye were not wholly mine;
And see, yourself have own'd ye did me wrong.
315 The people call you prophet: let it be:
But not of those that can expound themselves.
Take Vivien for expounder; she will call
That three-days-long presageful gloom of yours
No presage, but the same mistrustful mood
320 That makes you seem less noble than yourself,
Whenever I have ask'd this very boon,
Now ask'd again: for see you not, dear love,
That such a mood as that, which lately gloom'd
Your fancy when ye saw me following you,
325 Must make me fear still more you are not mine,
Must make me yearn still more to prove you mine,
And make me wish still more to learn this charm
Of woven paces and of waving hands,
As proof of trust. O Merlin, teach it me.
330 The charm so taught will charm us both to rest.
For, grant me some slight power upon your fate,
I, feeling that you felt me worthy trust,
Should rest and let you rest, knowing you mine.

And therefore be as great as ye are named,
Not muffled round with selfish reticence.   335
How hard you look and how denyingly!
O, if you think this wickedness in me,
That I should prove it on you unawares,
That makes me passing wrathful; then our bond
Had best be loosed for ever: but think or not,   340
By Heaven that hears I tell you the clean truth,
As clean as blood of babes, as white as milk:
O Merlin, may this earth, if ever I,
If these unwitty wandering wits of mine,
Ev'n in the jumbled rubbish of a dream,   345
Have tript on such conjectural treachery –
May this hard earth cleave to the Nadir hell
Down, down, and close again, and nip me flat,
If I be such a traitress. Yield my boon,
Till which I scarce can yield you all I am;   350
And grant my re-reiterated wish,
The great proof of your love: because I think,
However wise, ye hardly know me yet.'

    And Merlin loosed his hand from hers and said,
'I never was less wise, however wise,   355
Too curious Vivien, tho' you talk of trust,
Than when I told you first of such a charm.
Yea, if ye talk of trust I tell you this,
Too much I trusted when I told you that,
And stirr'd this vice in you which ruin'd man   360
Thro' woman the first hour; for howsoe'er
In children a great curiousness be well,
Who have to learn themselves and all the world,
In you, that are no child, for still I find
Your face is practised when I spell the lines,   365
I call it, – well, I will not call it vice:
But since you name yourself the summer fly,
I well could wish a cobweb for the gnat,
That settles, beaten back, and beaten back
Settles, till one could yield for weariness: 370
But since I will not yield to give you power
Upon my life and use and name and fame,

Why will ye never ask some other boon?
Yea, by God's rood, I trusted you too much.'

375 And Vivien, like the tenderest-hearted maid
That ever bided tryst at village stile,
Made answer, either eyelid wet with tears:
'Nay, Master, be not wrathful with your maid;
Caress her: let her feel herself forgiven
380 Who feels no heart to ask another boon.
I think ye hardly know the tender rhyme
Of "trust me not at all or all in all."
I heard the great Sir Lancelot sing it once,
And it shall answer for me. Listen to it.

385 "In Love, if Love be Love, if Love be ours,
Faith and unfaith can ne'er be equal powers:
Unfaith in aught is want of faith in all.

"It is the little rift within the lute,
That by and by will make the music mute,
390 And ever widening slowly silence all.

"The little rift within the lover's lute
Or little pitted speck in garner'd fruit,
That rotting inward slowly moulders all.

395 "It is not worth the keeping: let it go:
But shall it? answer, darling, answer, no.
And trust me not at all or all in all."

O Master, do ye love my tender rhyme?'

And Merlin look'd and half believed her true,
So tender was her voice, so fair her face,
400 So sweetly gleam'd her eyes behind her tears
Like sunlight on the plain behind a shower:
And yet he answer'd half indignantly:

'Far other was the song that once I heard
By this huge oak, sung nearly where we sit:

For here we met, some ten or twelve of us,   405
To chase a creature that was current then
In these wild woods, the hart with golden horns.
It was the time when first the question rose
About the founding of a Table Round,
That was to be, for love of God and men   410
And noble deeds, the flower of all the world.
And each incited each to noble deeds.
And while we waited, one, the youngest of us,
We could not keep him silent, out he flash'd,
And into such a song, such fire for fame,   415
Such trumpet-blowings in it, coming down
To such a stern and iron-clashing close,
That when he stopt we long'd to hurl together,
And should have done it; but the beauteous beast
Scared by the noise upstarted at our feet,   420
And like a silver shadow slipt away
Thro' the dim land; and all day long we rode
Thro' the dim land against a rushing wind,
That glorious roundel echoing in our ears,
And chased the flashes of his golden horns   425
Until they vanish'd by the fairy well
That laughs at iron – as our warriors did –
Where children cast their pins and nails, and cry,
"Laugh, little well!" but touch it with a sword,
It buzzes fiercely round the point; and there   430
We lost him: such a noble song was that.
But, Vivien, when you sang me that sweet rhyme,
I felt as tho' you knew this cursèd charm,
Were proving it on me, and that I lay
And felt them slowly ebbing, name and fame.'   435

And Vivien answer'd smiling mournfully:
'O mine have ebb'd away for evermore,
And all thro' following you to this wild wood,
Because I saw you sad, to comfort you.
Lo now, what hearts have men! they never mount   440
As high as woman in her selfless mood.
And touching fame, howe'er ye scorn my song,
Take one verse more – the lady speaks it – this:

'"My name, once mine, now thine, is closelier mine,
445 For fame, could fame be mine, that fame were thine,
And shame, could shame be thine, that shame were
    mine.
So trust me not at all or all in all."

'Says she not well? and there is more – this rhyme
Is like the fair pearl-necklace of the Queen,
450 That burst in dancing, and the pearls were spilt;
Some lost, some stolen, some as relics kept.
But nevermore the same two sister pearls
Ran down the silken thread to kiss each other
On her white neck – so is it with this rhyme:
455 It lives dispersedly in many hands,
And every minstrel sings it differently;
Yet is there one true line, the pearl of pearls:
"Man dreams of Fame while woman wakes to love."
Yea! Love, tho' Love were of the grossest, carves
460 A portion from the solid present, eats
And uses, careless of the rest; but Fame,
The Fame that follows death is nothing to us;
And what is Fame in life but half-disfame,
And counterchanged with darkness? ye yourself
465 Know well that Envy calls you Devil's son,
And since ye seem the Master of all Art,
They fain would make you Master of all vice.'

And Merlin lock'd his hand in hers and said,
'I once was looking for a magic weed,
470 And found a fair young squire who sat alone,
Had carved himself a knightly shield of wood,
And then was painting on it fancied arms,
Azure, an Eagle rising or, the Sun
In dexter chief; the scroll "I follow fame."
475 And speaking not, but leaning over him,
I took his brush and blotted out the bird,
And made a Gardener putting in a graff,
With this for motto, "Rather use than fame."
You should have seen him blush; but afterwards
480 He made a stalwart knight. O Vivien,

For you, methinks you think you love me well;
For me, I love you somewhat; rest: and Love
Should have some rest and pleasure in himself,
Not ever be too curious for a boon,
Too prurient for a proof against the grain   485
Of him ye say ye love: but Fame with men,
Being but ampler means to serve mankind,
Should have small rest or pleasure in herself,
But work as vassal to the larger love,
That dwarfs the petty love of one to one.   490
Use gave me Fame at first, and Fame again
Increasing gave me use. Lo, there my boon!
What other? for men sought to prove me vile,
Because I fain had given them greater wits:
And then did Envy call me Devil's son: 495
The sick weak beast seeking to help herself
By striking at her better, miss'd, and brought
Her own claw back, and wounded her own heart.
Sweet were the days when I was all unknown,
But when my name was lifted up, the storm   500
Brake on the mountain and I cared not for it.
Right well know I that Fame is half-disfame,
Yet needs must work my work. That other fame,
To one at least, who hath not children, vague,
The cackle of the unborn about the grave,   505
I cared not for it: a single misty star,
Which is the second in a line of stars
That seem a sword beneath a belt of three,
I never gazed upon it but I dreamt
Of some vast charm concluded in that star   510
To make fame nothing. Wherefore, if I fear,
Giving you power upon me thro' this charm,
That you might play me falsely, having power,
However well ye think ye love me now
(As sons of kings loving in pupilage   515
Have turn'd to tyrants when they came to power)
I rather dread the loss of use than fame;
If you – and not so much from wickedness,
As some wild turn of anger, or a mood
Of overstrain'd affection, it may be,   520

To keep me all to your own self, – or else
A sudden spurt of woman's jealousy, –
Should try this charm on whom ye say ye love.'

And Vivien answer'd smiling as in wrath:
525 'Have I not sworn? I am not trusted. Good!
Well, hide it, hide it; I shall find it out;
And being found take heed of Vivien.
A woman and not trusted, doubtless I
Might feel some sudden turn of anger born
530 Of your misfaith; and your fine epithet
Is accurate too, for this full love of mine
Without the full heart back may merit well
Your term of overstrain'd. So used as I,
My daily wonder is, I love at all.
535 And as to woman's jealousy, O why not?
O to what end, except a jealous one,
And one to make me jealous if I love,
Was this fair charm invented by yourself?
I well believe that all about this world
540 Ye cage a buxom captive here and there,
Closed in the four walls of a hollow tower
From which is no escape for evermore.'

Then the great Master merrily answer'd her:
'Full many a love in loving youth was mine;
545 I needed then no charm to keep them mine
But youth and love; and that full heart of yours
Whereof ye prattle, may now assure you mine;
So live uncharm'd. For those who wrought it first,
The wrist is parted from the hand that waved,
550 The feet unmortised from their ankle-bones
Who paced it, ages back: but will ye hear
The legend as in guerdon for your rhyme?

'There lived a king in the most Eastern East,
Less old than I, yet older, for my blood
555 Hath earnest in it of far springs to be.
A tawny pirate anchor'd in his port,
Whose bark had plunder'd twenty nameless isles;

And passing one, at the high peep of dawn,
He saw two cities in a thousand boats
All fighting for a woman on the sea.   560
And pushing his black craft among them all,
He lightly scatter'd theirs and brought her off,
With loss of half his people arrow-slain;
A maid so smooth, so white, so wonderful,
They said a light came from her when she moved: 565
And since the pirate would not yield her up,
The King impaled him for his piracy;
Then made her Queen: but those isle-nurtured eyes
Waged such unwilling tho' successful war
On all the youth, they sicken'd; councils thinn'd,   570
And armies waned, for magnet-like she drew
The rustiest iron of old fighters' hearts;
And beasts themselves would worship; camels knelt
Unbidden, and the brutes of mountain back
That carry kings in castles, bow'd black knees   575
Of homage, ringing with their serpent hands,
To make her smile, her golden ankle-bells.
What wonder, being jealous, that he sent
His horns of proclamation out thro' all
The hundred under-kingdoms that he sway'd   580
To find a wizard who might teach the King
Some charm, which being wrought upon the Queen
Might keep her all his own: to such a one
He promised more than ever king has given,
A league of mountain full of golden mines,   585
A province with a hundred miles of coast,
A palace and a princess, all for him:
But on all those who tried and fail'd, the King
Pronounced a dismal sentence, meaning by it
To keep the list low and pretenders back,   590
Or like a king, not to be trifled with –
Their heads should moulder on the city gates.
And many tried and fail'd, because the charm
Of nature in her overbore their own:
And many a wizard brow bleach'd on the walls: 595
And many weeks a troop of carrion crows
Hung like a cloud above the gateway towers.'

And Vivien breaking in upon him, said:
'I sit and gather honey; yet, methinks,
600 Thy tongue has tript a little: ask thyself.
The lady never made *unwilling* war
With those fine eyes: she had her pleasure in it,
And made her good man jealous with good cause.
And lived there neither dame nor damsel then
605 Wroth at a lover's loss? were all as tame,
I mean, as noble, as their Queen was fair?
Not one to flirt a venom at her eyes,
Or pinch a murderous dust into her drink,
Or make her paler with a poison'd rose?
610 Well, those were not our days: but did they find
A wizard? Tell me, was he like to thee?'

She ceased, and made her lithe arm round his neck
Tighten, and then drew back, and let her eyes
Speak for her, glowing on him, like a bride's
615 On her new lord, her own, the first of men.

He answer'd laughing, 'Nay, not like to me.
At last they found – his foragers for charms –
A little glassy-headed hairless man,
Who lived alone in a great wild on grass;
620 Read but one book, and ever reading grew
So grated down and filed away with thought,
So lean his eyes were monstrous; while the skin
Clung but to crate and basket, ribs and spine.
And since he kept his mind on one sole aim,
625 Nor ever touch'd fierce wine, nor tasted flesh,
Nor own'd a sensual wish, to him the wall
That sunders ghosts and shadow-casting men
Became a crystal, and he saw them thro' it,
And heard their voices talk behind the wall,
630 And learnt their elemental secrets, powers
And forces; often o'er the sun's bright eye
Drew the vast eyelid of an inky cloud,
And lash'd it at the base with slanting storm;
Or in the noon of mist and driving rain,
635 When the lake whiten'd and the pinewood roar'd,

And the cairn'd mountain was a shadow, sunn'd
The world to peace again: here was the man.
And so by force they dragg'd him to the King.
And then he taught the King to charm the Queen
In such-wise, that no man could see her more,   640
Nor saw she save the King, who wrought the charm,
Coming and going, and she lay as dead,
And lost all use of life: but when the King
Made proffer of the league of golden mines,
The province with a hundred miles of coast,   645
The palace and the princess, that old man
Went back to his old wild, and lived on grass,
And vanish'd, and his book came down to me.'

    And Vivien answer'd smiling saucily:
'Ye have the book: the charm is written in it: 650
Good: take my counsel: let me know it at once:
For keep it like a puzzle chest in chest,
With each chest lock'd and padlock'd thirty-fold,
And whelm all this beneath as vast a mound
As after furious battle turfs the slain   655
On some wild down above the windy deep,
I yet should strike upon a sudden means
To dig, pick, open, find and read the charm:
Then, if I tried it, who should blame me then?'

    And smiling as a master smiles at one   660
That is not of his school, nor any school
But that where blind and naked Ignorance
Delivers brawling judgments, unashamed,
On all things all day long, he answer'd her:

    'Thou read the book, my pretty Vivien!   665
O ay, it is but twenty pages long,
But every page having an ample marge,
And every marge enclosing in the midst
A square of text that looks a little blot,
The text no larger than the limbs of fleas;   670
And every square of text an awful charm,
Writ in a language that has long gone by.

So long, that mountains have arisen since
With cities on their flanks – thou read the book!
675 And every margin scribbled, crost, and cramm'd
With comment, densest condensation, hard
To mind and eye; but the long sleepless nights
Of my long life have made it easy to me.
And none can read the text, not even I;
680 And none can read the comment but myself;
And in the comment did I find the charm.
O, the results are simple; a mere child
Might use it to the harm of anyone,
And never could undo it: ask no more:
685 For tho' you should not prove it upon me,
But keep that oath ye sware, ye might, perchance,
Assay it on some one of the Table Round,
And all because ye dream they babble of you.'

And Vivien, frowning in true anger, said:
690 'What dare the full-fed liars say of me?
They ride abroad redressing human wrongs!
They sit with knife in meat and wine in horn!
They bound to holy vows of chastity!
Were I not woman, I could tell a tale.
695 But you are man, you well can understand
The shame that cannot be explain'd for shame.
Not one of all the drove should touch me: swine!'

Then answer'd Merlin careless of her words:
'You breathe but accusation vast and vague,
700 Spleen-born, I think, and proofless. If ye know,
Set up the charge ye know, to stand or fall!'

And Vivien answer'd frowning wrathfully:
'O ay, what say ye to Sir Valence, him
Whose kinsman left him watcher o'er his wife
705 And two fair babes, and went to distant lands;
Was one year gone, and on returning found
Not two but three? there lay the reckling, one
But one hour old! What said the happy sire?
A seven-month's babe had been a truer gift.
710 Those twelve sweet moons confused his fatherhood.'

Then answer'd Merlin, 'Nay, I know the tale.
Sir Valence wedded with an outland dame:
Some cause had kept him sunder'd from his wife:
One child they had: it lived with her: she died:
His kinsman travelling on his own affair   715
Was charged by Valence to bring home the child.
He brought, not found it therefore: take the truth.'

'O ay,' said Vivien, 'overtrue a tale.
What say ye then to sweet Sir Sagramore,
That ardent man? "to pluck the flower in season,"   720
So says the song, "I trow it is no treason."
O Master, shall we call him overquick
To crop his own sweet rose before the hour?'

And Merlin answer'd, 'Overquick art thou
To catch a loathly plume fall'n from the wing   725
Of that foul bird of rapine whose whole prey
Is man's good name: he never wrong'd his bride.
I know the tale. An angry gust of wind
Puff'd out his torch among the myriad-room'd
And many-corridor'd complexities   730
Of Arthur's palace: then he found a door,
And darkling felt the sculptured ornament
That wreathen round it made it seem his own;
And wearied out made for the couch and slept,
A stainless man beside a stainless maid;   735
And either slept, nor knew of other there;
Till the high dawn piercing the royal rose
In Arthur's casement glimmer'd chastely down,
Blushing upon them blushing, and at once
He rose without a word and parted from her: 740
But when the thing was blazed about the court,
The brute world howling forced them into bonds,
And as it chanced they are happy, being pure.'

'O ay,' said Vivien, 'that were likely too.
What say ye then to fair Sir Percivale   745
And of the horrid foulness that he wrought,
The saintly youth, the spotless lamb of Christ,

Or some black wether of St Satan's fold.
What, in the precincts of the chapel-yard,
750   Among the knightly brasses of the graves,
And by the cold Hic Jacets of the dead!'

And Merlin answer'd careless of her charge,
'A sober man is Percivale and pure;
But once in life was fluster'd with new wine,
755   Then paced for coolness in the chapel-yard;
Where one of Satan's shepherdesses caught
And meant to stamp him with her master's mark;
And that he sinn'd is not believable;
For, look upon his face! – but if he sinn'd,
760   The sin that practice burns into the blood,
And not the one dark hour which brings remorse,
Will brand us, after, of whose fold we be:
Or else were he, the holy king, whose hymns
Are chanted in the minster, worse than all.
765   But is your spleen froth'd out, or have ye more?'

And Vivien answer'd frowning yet in wrath:
'O ay; what say ye to Sir Lancelot, friend
Traitor or true? that commerce with the Queen,
I ask you, is it clamour'd by the child,
770   Or whisper'd in the corner? do ye know it?'

To which he answer'd sadly, 'Yea, I know it.
Sir Lancelot went ambassador, at first,
To fetch her, and she watch'd him from her walls.
A rumour runs, she took him for the King,
775   So fixt her fancy on him: let them be.
But have ye no one word of loyal praise
For Arthur, blameless King and stainless man?'

She answer'd with a low and chuckling laugh:
'Man! is he man at all, who knows and winks?
780   Sees what his fair bride is and does, and winks?
By which the good King means to blind himself,
And blinds himself and all the Table Round
To all the foulness that they work. Myself

Could call him (were it not for womanhood)
The pretty, popular name such manhood earns,   785
Could call him the main cause of all their crime;
Yea, were he not crown'd King, coward, and fool.'

    Then Merlin to his own heart, loathing, said:
'O true and tender! O my liege and King!
O selfless man and stainless gentleman,   790
Who wouldst against thine own eye-witness fain
Have all men true and leal, all women pure;
How, in the mouths of base interpreters,
From over-fineness not intelligible
To things with every sense as false and foul   795
As the poach'd filth that floods the middle street,
Is thy white blamelessness accounted blame!'

    But Vivien, deeming Merlin overborne
By instance, recommenced, and let her tongue
Rage like a fire among the noblest names,   800
Polluting, and imputing her whole self,
Defaming and defacing, till she left
Not even Lancelot brave, nor Galahad clean.

    Her words had issue other than she will'd.
He dragg'd his eyebrow bushes down, and made   805
A snowy penthouse for his hollow eyes,
And mutter'd in himself, 'Tell *her* the charm!
So, if she had it, would she rail on me
To snare the next, and if she have it not
So will she rail. What did the wanton say?   810
"Not mount as high;" we scarce can sink as low:
For men at most differ as Heaven and earth,
But women, worst and best, as Heaven and Hell.
I know the Table Round, my friends of old;
All brave, and many generous, and some chaste.   815
She cloaks the scar of some repulse with lies;
I well believe she tempted them and fail'd,
Being so bitter: for fine plots may fail,
Tho' harlots paint their talk as well as face
With colours of the heart that are not theirs.   820

163

I will not let her know: nine tithes of times
Face-flatterer and backbiter are the same.
And they, sweet soul, that most impute a crime
Are pronest to it, and impute themselves,
825   Wanting the mental range; or low desire
Not to feel lowest makes them level all;
Yea, they would pare the mountain to the plain,
To leave an equal baseness; and in this
Are harlots like the crowd, that if they find
830   Some stain or blemish in a name of note,
Not grieving that their greatest are so small,
Inflate themselves with some insane delight,
And judge all nature from her feet of clay,
Without the will to lift their eyes, and see
835   Her godlike head crown'd with spiritual fire,
And touching other worlds. I am weary of her.'

He spoke in words part heard, in whispers part,
Half-suffocated in the hoary fell
And many-winter'd fleece of throat and chin.
840   But Vivien, gathering somewhat of his mood,
And hearing 'harlot' mutter'd twice or thrice,
Leapt from her session on his lap, and stood
Stiff as a viper frozen; loathsome sight,
How from the rosy lips of life and love,
845   Flash'd the bare-grinning skeleton of death!
White was her cheek; sharp breaths of anger puff'd
Her fairy nostril out; her hand half-clench'd
Went faltering sideways downward to her belt,
And feeling; had she found a dagger there
850   (For in a wink the false love turns to hate)
She would have stabb'd him; but she found it not:
His eye was calm, and suddenly she took
To bitter weeping like a beaten child,
A long, long weeping, not consolable.
855   Then her false voice made way, broken with sobs:

'O crueller than was ever told in tale,
Or sung in song! O vainly lavish'd love!
O cruel, there was nothing wild or strange,

Or seeming shameful – for what shame in love,
So love be true, and not as yours is – nothing   860
Poor Vivien had not done to win his trust
Who call'd her what he call'd her – all her crime,
All – all – the wish to prove him wholly hers.'

She mused a little, and then clapt her hands
Together with a wailing shriek, and said: 865
'Stabb'd through the heart's affections to the heart!
Seethed like the kid in its own mother's milk!
Kill'd with a word worse than a life of blows!
I thought that he was gentle, being great:
O God, that I had loved a smaller man!   870
I should have found in him a greater heart.
O, I, that flattering my true passion, saw
The knights, the court, the King, dark in your light,
Who loved to make men darker than they are,
Because of that high pleasure which I had   875
To seat you sole upon my pedestal
Of worship – I am answer'd, and henceforth
The course of life that seem'd so flowery to me
With you for guide and master, only you,
Becomes the sea-cliff pathway broken short,   880
And ending in a ruin – nothing left,
But into some low cave to crawl, and there,
If the wolf spare me, weep my life away,
Kill'd with inutterable unkindliness.'

She paused, she turn'd away, she hung her head,   885
The snake of gold slid from her hair, the braid
Slipt and uncoil'd itself, she wept afresh,
And the dark wood grew darker toward the storm
In silence, while his anger slowly died
Within him, till he let his wisdom go   890
For ease of heart, and half believed her true:
Call'd her to shelter in the hollow oak,
'Come from the storm,' and having no reply,
Gazed at the heaving shoulder, and the face
Hand-hidden, as for utmost grief or shame;   895
Then thrice essay'd, by tenderest-touching terms,

To sleek her ruffled peace of mind, in vain.
At last she let herself be conquer'd by him,
And as the cageling newly flown returns,
900 The seeming-injured simple-hearted thing
Came to her old perch back, and settled there.
There while she sat, half-falling from his knees,
Half-nestled at his heart, and since he saw
The slow tear creep from her closed eyelid yet,
905 About her, more in kindness than in love,
The gentle wizard cast a shielding arm.
But she dislink'd herself at once and rose,
Her arms upon her breast across, and stood,
A virtuous gentlewoman deeply wrong'd,
910 Upright and flush'd before him: then she said:

'There must be now no passages of love
Betwixt us twain henceforward evermore;
Since, if I be what I am grossly call'd,
What should be granted which your own gross heart
915 Would reckon worth the taking? I will go.
In truth, but one thing now – better have died
Thrice than have ask'd it once – could make me stay –
That proof of trust – so often ask'd in vain!
How justly, after that vile term of yours,
920 I find with grief! I might believe you then,
Who knows? once more. Lo! what was once to me
Mere matter of the fancy, now hath grown
The vast necessity of heart and life.
Farewell; think gently of me, for I fear
925 My fate or folly, passing gayer youth
For one so old, must be to love thee still.
But ere I leave thee let me swear once more
That if I schemed against thy peace in this,
May yon just heaven, that darkens o'er me, send
930 One flash, that, missing all things else, may make
My scheming brain a cinder, if I lie.'

Scarce had she ceased, when out of heaven a bolt
(For now the storm was close above them) struck,
Furrowing a giant oak, and javelining

With darted spikes and splinters of the wood 935
The dark earth round. He raised his eyes and saw
The tree that shone white-listed thro' the gloom.
But Vivien, fearing heaven had heard her oath,
And dazzled by the livid-flickering fork,
And deafen'd with the stammering cracks and claps 940
That follow'd, flying back and crying out,
'O Merlin, tho' you do not love me, save,
Yet save me!' clung to him and hugg'd him close;
And call'd him dear protector in her fright,
Nor yet forgot her practice in her fright, 945
But wrought upon his mood and hugg'd him close.
The pale blood of the wizard at her touch
Took gayer colours, like an opal warm'd.
She blamed herself for telling hearsay tales:
She shook from fear, and for her fault she wept 950
Of petulancy; she call'd him lord and liege,
Her seer, her bard, her silver star of eve,
Her God, her Merlin, the one passionate love
Of her whole life; and ever overhead
Bellow'd the tempest, and the rotten branch 955
Snapt in the rushing of the river-rain
Above them; and in change of glare and gloom
Her eyes and neck glittering went and came;
Till now the storm, its burst of passion spent,
Moaning and calling out of other lands, 960
Had left the ravaged woodland yet once more
To peace; and what should not have been had been,
For Merlin, overtalk'd and overworn,
Had yielded, told her all the charm, and slept.

Then, in one moment, she put forth the charm 965
Of woven paces and of waving hands,
And in the hollow oak he lay as dead,
And lost to life and use and name and fame.

Then crying 'I have made his glory mine,'
And shrieking out 'O fool!' the harlot leapt 970
Adown the forest, and the thicket closed
Behind her, and the forest echo'd 'fool.'

Lancelot and Elaine

Elaine the fair, Elaine the loveable,
Elaine, the lily maid of Astolat,
High in her chamber up a tower to the east
Guarded the sacred shield of Lancelot;
5   Which first she placed where morning's earliest ray
Might strike it, and awake her with the gleam;
Then fearing rust or soilure fashion'd for it
A case of silk, and braided thereupon
All the devices blazon'd on the shield
10   In their own tinct, and added, of her wit,
A border fantasy of branch and flower,
And yellow-throated nestling in the nest.
Nor rested thus content, but day by day,
Leaving her household and good father, climb'd
15   That eastern tower, and entering barr'd her door,
Stript off the case, and read the naked shield,
Now guess'd a hidden meaning in his arms,
Now made a pretty history to herself
Of every dint a sword had beaten in it,
20   And every scratch a lance had made upon it,
Conjecturing when and where: this cut is fresh;
That ten years back; this dealt him at Caerlyle;
That at Caerleon; this at Camelot:
And ah God's mercy, what a stroke was there!
25   And here a thrust that might have kill'd, but God
Broke the strong lance, and roll'd his enemy down,
And saved him: so she lived in fantasy.

How came the lily maid by that good shield
Of Lancelot, she that knew not ev'n his name?
30   He left it with her, when he rode to tilt
For the great diamond in the diamond jousts,

GLIMMER OF
ELAINE AS
MOTHER

168

Lancelot and Elaine

Which Arthur had ordain'd, and by that name
Had named them, since a diamond was the prize.

For Arthur, long before they crown'd him King,
Roving the trackless realms of Lyonnesse, 35
Had found a glen, gray boulder and black tarn.
A horror lived about the tarn, and clave
Like its own mists to all the mountain side:
For here two brothers, one a king, had met
And fought together; but their names were lost; 40
And each had slain his brother at a blow;
And down they fell and made the glen abhorr'd:
And there they lay till all their bones were bleach'd,
And lichen'd into colour with the crags:
And he, that once was king, had on a crown 45
Of diamonds, one in front, and four aside.
And Arthur came, and labouring up the pass,
All in a misty moonshine, unawares
Had trodden that crown'd skeleton, and the skull
Brake from the nape, and from the skull the crown 50
Roll'd into light, and turning on its rims
Fled like a glittering rivulet to the tarn:
And down the shingly scaur he plunged, and caught,
And set it on his head, and in his heart
Heard murmurs, 'Lo, thou likewise shalt be King.' 55

Thereafter, when a King, he had the gems
Pluck'd from the crown, and show'd them to his knights,
Saying, 'These jewels, whereupon I chanced
Divinely, are the kingdom's, not the King's –
For public use: henceforward let there be, 60
Once every year, a joust for one of these:
For so by nine years' proof we needs must learn
Which is our mightiest, and ourselves shall grow
In use of arms and manhood, till we drive
The heathen, who, some say, shall rule the land 65
Hereafter, which God hinder.' Thus he spoke:
And eight years past, eight jousts had been, and still
Had Lancelot won the diamond of the year,
With purpose to present them to the Queen,

169

70 When all were won; but meaning all at once
     To snare her royal fancy with a boon
     Worth half her realm, had never spoken word.

     Now for the central diamond and the last
     And largest, Arthur, holding then his court
75   Hard on the river nigh the place which now
     Is this world's hugest, let proclaim a joust
     At Camelot, and when the time drew nigh
     Spake (for she had been sick) to Guinevere,
     'Are you so sick, my Queen, you cannot move
80   To these fair jousts?' 'Yea, lord,' she said, 'ye know it.'
     'Then will ye miss,' he answer'd, 'the great deeds
     Of Lancelot, and his prowess in the lists,
     A sight ye love to look on.' And the Queen
     Lifted her eyes, and they dwelt languidly
85   On Lancelot, where he stood beside the King.
     He thinking that he read her meaning there,
     'Stay with me, I am sick; my love is more
     Than many diamonds,' yielded; and a heart
     Love-loyal to the least wish of the Queen
90   (However much he yearn'd to make complete
     The tale of diamonds for his destined boon)
     Urged him to speak against the truth, and say,
     'Sir King, mine ancient wound is hardly whole,
     And lets me from the saddle;' and the King
95   Glanced first at him, then her, and went his way.
     No sooner gone than suddenly she began:

     'To blame, my lord Sir Lancelot, much to blame!
     Why go ye not to these fair jousts? the knights
     Are half of them our enemies, and the crowd
100 Will murmur, "Lo the shameless ones, who take
     Their pastime now the trustful King is gone!"'
     Then Lancelot vext at having lied in vain:
     'Are ye so wise? ye were not once so wise,
     My Queen, that summer, when ye loved me first.
105 Then of the crowd ye took no more account
     Than of the myriad cricket of the mead,
     When its own voice clings to each blade of grass,

And every voice is nothing. As to knights,
Them surely can I silence with all ease.
But now my loyal worship is allow'd   110
Of all men: many a bard, without offence,
Has link'd our names together in his lay,
Lancelot, the flower of bravery, Guinevere,
The pearl of beauty: and our knights at feast
Have pledged us in this union, while the King   115
Would listen smiling. How then? is there more?
Has Arthur spoken aught? or would yourself,
Now weary of my service and devoir,
Henceforth be truer to your faultless lord?'

   She broke into a little scornful laugh: 120
'Arthur, my lord, Arthur, the faultless King,
That passionate perfection, my good lord –
But who can gaze upon the Sun in heaven?
He never spake word of reproach to me,
He never had a glimpse of mine untruth,   125
He cares not for me: only here to-day
There gleam'd a vague suspicion in his eyes:
Some meddling rogue has tamper'd with him – else
Rapt in this fancy of his Table Round,
And swearing men to vows impossible,   130
To make them like himself: but, friend, to me
He is all fault who hath no fault at all:
For who loves me must have a touch of earth;
The low sun makes the colour: I am yours,
Not Arthur's, as ye know, save by the bond.   135
And therefore hear my words: go to the jousts:
The tiny-trumpeting gnat can break our dream
When sweetest; and the vermin voices here
May buzz so loud – we scorn them, but they sting.'

   Then answer'd Lancelot, the chief of knights: 140
'And with what face, after my pretext made,
Shall I appear, O Queen, at Camelot, I
Before a King who honours his own word,
As if it were his God's?'

171

                          'Yea,' said the Queen,

145   'A moral child without the craft to rule,
Else had he not lost me: but listen to me,
If I must find you wit: we hear it said
That men go down before your spear at a touch,
But knowing you are Lancelot; your great name,
150   This conquers: hide it therefore; go unknown:
Win! by this kiss you will: and our true King
Will then allow your pretext, O my knight,
As all for glory; for to speak him true,
Ye know right well, how meek soe'er he seem,
155   No keener hunter after glory breathes.
He loves it in his knights more than himself:
They prove to him his work: win and return.'

      Then got Sir Lancelot suddenly to horse,
Wroth at himself. Not willing to be known,
160   He left the barren-beaten thoroughfare,
Chose the green path that show'd the rarer foot,
And there among the solitary downs,
Full often lost in fancy, lost his way;
Till as he traced a faintly-shadow'd track,
165   That all in loops and links among the dales
Ran to the Castle of Astolat, he saw
Fired from the west, far on a hill, the towers.
Thither he made, and blew the gateway horn.
Then came an old, dumb, myriad-wrinkled man,
170   Who let him into lodging and disarm'd.
And Lancelot marvell'd at the wordless man;
And issuing found the Lord of Astolat
With two strong sons, Sir Torre and Sir Lavaine,
Moving to meet him in the castle court;
175   And close behind them stept the lily maid
Elaine, his daughter: mother of the house
There was not: some light jest among them rose
With laughter dying down as the great knight
Approach'd them: then the Lord of Astolat:
180   'Whence comest thou, my guest, and by what name
Livest between the lips? for by thy state
And presence I might guess thee chief of those,

After the King, who eat in Arthur's halls.
Him have I seen: the rest, his Table Round,
Known as they are, to me they are unknown.'   185

    Then answer'd Lancelot, the chief of knights:
'Known am I, and of Arthur's hall, and known,
What I by mere mischance have brought, my shield.
But since I go to joust as one unknown
At Camelot for the diamond, ask me not,   190
Hereafter ye shall know me – and the shield –
I pray you lend me one, if such you have,
Blank, or at least with some device not mine.'

    Then said the Lord of Astolat, 'Here is Torre's:
Hurt in his first tilt was my son, Sir Torre.   195
And so, God wot, his shield is blank enough.
His ye can have.' Then added plain Sir Torre,
'Yea, since I cannot use it, ye may have it.'
Here laugh'd the father saying, 'Fie, Sir Churl,
Is that an answer for a noble knight?   200
Allow him! but Lavaine, my younger here,
He is so full of lustihood, he will ride,
Joust for it, and win, and bring it in an hour,
And set it in this damsel's golden hair,
To make her thrice as wilful as before.'   205

    'Nay, father, nay good father, shame me not
Before this noble knight,' said young Lavaine,
'For nothing. Surely I but play'd on Torre:
He seem'd so sullen, vext he could not go:
A jest, no more! for, knight, the maiden dreamt   210
That some one put this diamond in her hand,
And that it was too slippery to be held,
And slipt and fell into some pool or stream,
The castle-well, belike; and then I said
That *if* I went and *if* I fought and won it   215
(But all was jest and joke among ourselves)
Then must she keep it safelier. All was jest.
But, father, give me leave, an if he will,
To ride to Camelot with this noble knight:

220   Win shall I not, but do my best to win:
      Young as I am, yet would I do my best.'

      'So ye will grace me,' answer'd Lancelot,
      Smiling a moment, 'with your fellowship
      O'er these waste downs whereon I lost myself,
225   Then were I glad of you as guide and friend:
      And you shall win this diamond, – as I hear
      It is a fair large diamond, – if ye may,
      And yield it to this maiden, if ye will.'
      'A fair large diamond,' added plain Sir Torre,
230   'Such be for queens, and not for simple maids.'
      Then she, who held her eyes upon the ground,
      Elaine, and heard her name so tost about,
      Flush'd slightly at the slight disparagement
      Before the stranger knight, who, looking at her,
235   Full courtly, yet not falsely, thus return'd:
      'If what is fair be but for what is fair,
      And only queens are to be counted so,
      Rash were my judgment then, who deem this maid
      Might wear as fair a jewel as is on earth,
240   Not violating the bond of like to like.'

      He spoke and ceased: the lily maid Elaine,
      Won by the mellow voice before she look'd,
      Lifted her eyes, and read his lineaments.
      The great and guilty love he bare the Queen,
245   In battle with the love he bare his lord,
      Had marr'd his face, and mark'd it ere his time.
      Another sinning on such heights with one,
      The flower of all the west and all the world,
      Had been the sleeker for it: but in him
250   His mood was often like a fiend, and rose
      And drove him into wastes and solitudes
      For agony, who was yet a living soul.
      Marr'd as he was, he seem'd the goodliest man
      That ever among ladies ate in hall,
255   And noblest, when she lifted up her eyes.
      However marr'd, of more than twice her years,
      Seam'd with an ancient swordcut on the cheek,

And bruised and bronzed, she lifted up her eyes
And loved him, with that love which was her doom.

Then the great knight, the darling of the court,   260
Loved of the loveliest, into that rude hall
Stept with all grace, and not with half disdain
Hid under grace, as in a smaller time,
But kindly man moving among his kind:
Whom they with meats and vintage of their best   265
And talk and minstrel melody entertain'd.
And much they ask'd of court and Table Round,
And ever well and readily answer'd he:
But Lancelot, when they glanced at Guinevere,
Suddenly speaking of the wordless man,   270
Heard from the Baron that, ten years before,
The heathen caught and reft him of his tongue.
'He learnt and warn'd me of their fierce design
Against my house, and him they caught and maim'd;
But I, my sons, and little daughter fled   275
From bonds or death, and dwelt among the woods
By the great river in a boatman's hut.
Dull days were those, till our good Arthur broke
The Pagan yet once more on Badon hill.'

'O there, great lord, doubtless,' Lavaine said, rapt   280
By all the sweet and sudden passion of youth
Toward greatness in its elder, 'you have fought.
O tell us – for we live apart – you know
Of Arthur's glorious wars.' And Lancelot spoke
And answer'd him at full, as having been   285
With Arthur in the fight which all day long
Rang by the white mouth of the violent Glem;
And in the four loud battles by the shore
Of Duglas; that on Bassa; then the war
That thunder'd in and out the gloomy skirts   290
Of Celidon the forest; and again
By castle Gurnion, where the glorious King
Had on his cuirass worn our Lady's Head,
Carved of one emerald center'd in a sun
Of silver rays, that lighten'd as he breathed;   295

And at Caerleon had he help'd his lord,
When the strong neighings of the wild white Horse
Set every gilded parapet shuddering;
And up in Agned-Cathregonion too,
300 And down the waste sand-shores of Trath Treroit,
Where many a heathen fell; 'and on the mount
Of Badon I myself beheld the King
Charge at the head of all his Table Round,
And all his legions crying Christ and him,
305 And break them; and I saw him, after, stand
High on a heap of slain, from spur to plume
Red as the rising sun with heathen blood,
And seeing me, with a great voice he cried,
'They are broken, they are broken!' for the King,
310 However mild he seems at home, nor cares
For triumph in our mimic wars, the jousts –
For if his own knight cast him down, he laughs
Saying, his knights are better men than he –
Yet in this heathen war the fire of God
315 Fills him: I never saw his like: there lives
No greater leader.'

            While he utter'd this,
Low to her own heart said the lily maid,
'Save your great self, fair lord;' and when he fell
From talk of war to traits of pleasantry –
320 Being mirthful he, but in a stately kind –
She still took note that when the living smile
Died from his lips, across him came a cloud
Of melancholy severe, from which again,
Whenever in her hovering to and fro
325 The lily maid had striven to make him cheer,
There brake a sudden-beaming tenderness
Of manners and of nature: and she thought
That all was nature, all, perchance, for her.
And all night long his face before her lived,
330 As when a painter, poring on a face,
Divinely thro' all hindrance finds the man
Behind it, and so paints him that his face,
The shape and colour of a mind and life,

Lives for his children, ever at its best
And fullest; so the face before her lived,   335
Dark-splendid, speaking in the silence, full
Of noble things, and held her from her sleep.
Till rathe she rose, half-cheated in the thought
She needs must bid farewell to sweet Lavaine.
First as in fear, step after step, she stole   340
Down the long tower-stairs, hesitating:
Anon, she heard Sir Lancelot cry in the court,
'This shield, my friend, where is it?' and Lavaine
Past inward, as she came from out the tower.
There to his proud horse Lancelot turn'd, and smooth'd   345
The glossy shoulder, humming to himself.
Half-envious of the flattering hand, she drew
Nearer and stood. He look'd, and more amazed
Than if seven men had set upon him, saw
The maiden standing in the dewy light.   350
He had not dream'd she was so beautiful.
Then came on him a sort of sacred fear,
For silent, tho' he greeted her, she stood
Rapt on his face as if it were a God's.
Suddenly flash'd on her a wild desire,   355
That he should wear her favour at the tilt.
She braved a riotous heart in asking for it.
'Fair lord, whose name I know not – noble it is,
I well believe, the noblest – will you wear
My favour at this tourney?' 'Nay,' said he,   360
'Fair lady, since I never yet have worn
Favour of any lady in the lists.
Such is my wont, as those, who know me, know.'
'Yea, so,' she answer'd; 'then in wearing mine
Needs must be lesser likelihood, noble lord,   365
That those who know should know you.' And he turn'd
Her counsel up and down within his mind,
And found it true, and answer'd, 'True, my child.
Well, I will wear it: fetch it out to me:
What is it?' and she told him 'A red sleeve   370
Broider'd with pearls,' and brought it: then he bound
Her token on his helmet, with a smile
Saying, 'I never yet have done so much

For any maiden living,' and the blood
375 Sprang to her face and fill'd her with delight;
But left her all the paler, when Lavaine
Returning brought the yet-unblazon'd shield,
His brother's; which he gave to Lancelot,
Who parted with his own to fair Elaine:
380 'Do me this grace, my child, to have my shield
In keeping till I come.' 'A grace to me,'
She answer'd, 'twice to-day. I am your squire!'
Whereat Lavaine said, laughing, 'Lily maid,
For fear our people call you lily maid
385 In earnest, let me bring your colour back;
Once, twice, and thrice: now get you hence to bed:'
So kiss'd her, and Sir Lancelot his own hand,
And thus they moved away: she stay'd a minute,
Then made a sudden step to the gate, and there –
390 Her bright hair blown about the serious face
Yet rosy-kindled with her brother's kiss –
Paused by the gateway, standing near the shield
In silence, while she watch'd their arms far-off
Sparkle, until they dipt below the downs.
395 Then to her tower she climb'd, and took the shield,
There kept it, and so lived in fantasy.

Meanwhile the new companions past away
Far o'er the long backs of the bushless downs,
To where Sir Lancelot knew there lived a knight
400 Not far from Camelot, now for forty years
A hermit, who had pray'd, labour'd and pray'd,
And ever labouring had scoop'd himself
In the white rock a chapel and a hall
On massive columns, like a shorecliff cave,
405 And cells and chambers: all were fair and dry;
The green light from the meadows underneath
Struck up and lived along the milky roofs;
And in the meadows tremulous aspen-trees
And poplars made a noise of falling showers.
410 And thither wending there that night they bode.

But when the next day broke from underground,

And shot red fire and shadows thro' the cave,
They rose, heard mass, broke fast, and rode away:
Then Lancelot saying, 'Hear, but hold my name
Hidden, you ride with Lancelot of the Lake,'   415
Abash'd Lavaine, whose instant reverence,
Dearer to true young hearts than their own praise,
But left him leave to stammer, 'Is it indeed?'
And after muttering 'The great Lancelot,'
At last he got his breath and answer'd, 'One,   420
One have I seen – that other, our liege lord,
The dread Pendragon, Britain's King of kings,
Of whom the people talk mysteriously,
He will be there – then were I stricken blind
That minute, I might say that I had seen.'   425

So spake Lavaine, and when they reach'd the lists
By Camelot in the meadow, let his eyes
Run thro' the peopled gallery which half round
Lay like a rainbow fall'n upon the grass,
Until they found the clear-faced King, who sat   430
Robed in red samite, easily to be known,
Since to his crown the golden dragon clung,
And down his robe the dragon writhed in gold,
And from the carven-work behind him crept
Two dragons gilded, sloping down to make   435
Arms for his chair, while all the rest of them
Thro' knots and loops and folds innumerable
Fled ever thro' the woodwork, till they found
The new design wherein they lost themselves,
Yet with all ease, so tender was the work: 440
And, in the costly canopy o'er him set,
Blazed the last diamond of the nameless king.

Then Lancelot answer'd young Lavaine and said,
'Me you call great: mine is the firmer seat,
The truer lance: but there is many a youth   445
Now crescent, who will come to all I am
And overcome it; and in me there dwells
No greatness, save it be some far-off touch
Of greatness to know well I am not great:

450 There is the man.' And Lavaine gaped upon him
As on a thing miraculous, and anon
The trumpets blew; and then did either side,
They that assail'd, and they that held the lists,
Set lance in rest, strike spur, suddenly move,
455 Meet in the midst, and there so furiously
Shock, that a man far-off might well perceive,
If any man that day were left afield,
The hard earth shake, and a low thunder of arms.
And Lancelot bode a little, till he saw
460 Which were the weaker; then he hurl'd into it
Against the stronger: little need to speak
Of Lancelot in his glory! King, duke, earl,
Count, baron – whom he smote, he overthrew.

But in the field were Lancelot's kith and kin,
465 Ranged with the Table Round that held the lists,
Strong men, and wrathful that a stranger knight
Should do and almost overdo the deeds
Of Lancelot; and one said to the other, 'Lo!
What is he? I do not mean the force alone –
470 The grace and versatility of the man!
Is it not Lancelot?' 'When has Lancelot worn
Favour of any lady in the lists?
Not such his wont, as we, that know him, know.'
'How then? who then?' a fury seized them all,
475 A fiery family passion for the name
Of Lancelot, and a glory one with theirs.
They couch'd their spears and prick'd their steeds, and thus,
Their plumes driv'n backward by the wind they made
In moving, all together down upon him
480 Bare, as a wild wave in the wide North-sea,
Green-glimmering toward the summit, bears, with all
Its stormy crests that smoke against the skies,
Down on a bark, and overbears the bark,
And him that helms it, so they overbore
485 Sir Lancelot and his charger, and a spear
Down-glancing lamed the charger, and a spear
Prick'd sharply his own cuirass, and the head
Pierced thro' his side, and there snapt, and remain'd.

Then Sir Lavaine did well and worshipfully;
He bore a knight of old repute to the earth,   490
And brought his horse to Lancelot where he lay.
He up the side, sweating with agony, got,
But thought to do while he might yet endure,
And being lustily holpen by the rest,
His party, – tho' it seem'd half-miracle   495
To those he fought with, – drave his kith and kin,
And all the Table Round that held the lists,
Back to the barrier; then the trumpets blew
Proclaiming his the prize, who wore the sleeve
Of scarlet, and the pearls; and all the knights,   500
His party, cried 'Advance and take thy prize
The diamond;' but he answer'd, 'Diamond me
No diamonds! for God's love, a little air!
Prize me no prizes, for my prize is death!
Hence will I, and I charge you, follow me not.'   505

He spoke, and vanish'd suddenly from the field
With young Lavaine into the poplar grove.
There from his charger down he slid, and sat,
Gasping to Sir Lavaine, 'Draw the lance-head:'
'Ah my sweet lord Sir Lancelot,' said Lavaine,   510
'I dread me, if I draw it, you will die.'
But he, 'I die already with it: draw –
Draw,' – and Lavaine drew, and Sir Lancelot gave
A marvellous great shriek and ghastly groan,
And half his blood burst forth, and down he sank   515
For the pure pain, and wholly swoon'd away.
Then came the hermit out and bare him in,
There stanch'd his wound; and there, in daily doubt
Whether to live or die, for many a week
Hid from the wide world's rumour by the grove   520
Of poplars with their noise of falling showers,
And ever-tremulous aspen-trees, he lay.

But on that day when Lancelot fled the lists,
His party, knights of utmost North and West,
Lords of waste marches, kings of desolate isles,   525
Came round their great Pendragon, saying to him,

'Lo, Sire, our knight, thro' whom we won the day,
Hath gone sore wounded, and hath left his prize
Untaken, crying that his prize is death.'

530   'Heaven hinder,' said the King, 'that such an one,
So great a knight as we have seen to-day –
He seem'd to me another Lancelot –
Yea, twenty times I thought him Lancelot –
He must not pass uncared for. Wherefore, rise,

535   O Gawain, and ride forth and find the knight.
Wounded and wearied needs must he be near.
I charge you that you get at once to horse.
And, knights and kings, there breathes not one of you
Will deem this prize of ours is rashly given:

540   His prowess was too wondrous. We will do him
No customary honour: since the knight
Came not to us, of us to claim the prize,
Ourselves will send it after. Rise and take
This diamond, and deliver it, and return,

545   And bring us where he is, and how he fares,
And cease not from your quest until ye find.'

So saying, from the carven flower above,
To which it made a restless heart, he took,
And gave, the diamond: then from where he sat

550   At Arthur's right, with smiling face arose,
With smiling face and frowning heart, a Prince
In the mid might and flourish of his May,
Gawain, surnamed The Courteous, fair and strong,
And after Lancelot, Tristram, and Geraint

555   And Gareth, a good knight, but therewithal
Sir Modred's brother, and the child of Lot,
Nor often loyal to his word, and now
Wroth that the King's command to sally forth
In quest of whom he knew not, made him leave

560   The banquet, and concourse of knights and kings.

So all in wrath he got to horse and went;
While Arthur to the banquet, dark in mood,
Past, thinking 'Is it Lancelot who hath come
Despite the wound he spake of, all for gain

Of glory, and hath added wound to wound,   565
And ridd'n away to die?' So fear'd the King,
And, after two days' tarriance there, return'd.
Then when he saw the Queen, embracing ask'd,
'Love, are you yet so sick?' 'Nay, lord,' she said.
'And where is Lancelot?' Then the Queen amazed,   570
'Was he not with you? won he not your prize?'
'Nay, but one like him.' 'Why that like was he.'
And when the King demanded how she knew,
Said, 'Lord, no sooner had ye parted from us,
Than Lancelot told me of a common talk   575
That men went down before his spear at a touch,
But knowing he was Lancelot; his great name
Conquer'd; and therefore would he hide his name
From all men, ev'n the King, and to this end
Had made the pretext of a hindering wound,   580
That he might joust unknown of all, and learn
If his old prowess were in aught decay'd;
And added, "Our true Arthur, when he learns,
Will well allow my pretext, as for gain
Of purer glory."'

            Then replied the King: 585
'Far lovelier in our Lancelot had it been,
In lieu of idly dallying with the truth,
To have trusted me as he hath trusted thee.
Surely his King and most familiar friend
Might well have kept his secret. True, indeed,   590
Albeit I know my knights fantastical,
So fine a fear in our large Lancelot
Must needs have moved my laughter: now remains
But little cause for laughter: his own kin –
Ill news, my Queen, for all who love him, this! –   595
His kith and kin, not knowing, set upon him;
So that he went sore wounded from the field:
Yet good news too: for goodly hopes are mine
That Lancelot is no more a lonely heart.
He wore, against his wont, upon his helm   600
A sleeve of scarlet, broider'd with great pearls,
Some gentle maiden's gift.'

'Yea, lord,' she said,
'Thy hopes are mine,' and saying that, she choked,
And sharply turn'd about to hide her face,
605 Past to her chamber, and there flung herself
Down on the great King's couch, and writhed upon it,
And clench'd her fingers till they bit the palm,
And shriek'd out 'Traitor' to the unhearing wall,
Then flash'd into wild tears, and rose again,
610 And moved about her palace, proud and pale.

Gawain the while thro' all the region round
Rode with his diamond, wearied of the quest,
Touch'd at all points, except the poplar grove,
And came at last, tho' late, to Astolat:
615 Whom glittering in enamell'd arms the maid
Glanced at, and cried, 'What news from Camelot, lord?
What of the knight with the red sleeve?' 'He won.'
'I knew it,' she said. 'But parted from the jousts
Hurt in the side,' whereat she caught her breath;
620 Thro' her own side she felt the sharp lance go;
Thereon she smote her hand: wellnigh she swoon'd:
And, while he gazed wonderingly at her, came
The Lord of Astolat out, to whom the Prince
Reported who he was, and on what quest
625 Sent, that he bore the prize and could not find
The victor, but had ridd'n a random round
To seek him, and had wearied of the search.
To whom the Lord of Astolat, 'Bide with us,
And ride no more at random, noble Prince!
630 Here was the knight, and here he left a shield;
This will he send or come for: furthermore
Our son is with him; we shall hear anon,
Needs must we hear.' To this the courteous Prince
Accorded with his wonted courtesy,
635 Courtesy with a touch of traitor in it,
And stay'd; and cast his eyes on fair Elaine:
Where could be found face daintier? then her shape
From forehead down to foot, perfect – again
From foot to forehead exquisitely turn'd:
640 'Well – if I bide, lo! this wild flower for me!'

And oft they met among the garden yews,
And there he set himself to play upon her
With sallying wit, free flashes from a height
Above her, graces of the court, and songs,
Sighs, and slow smiles, and golden eloquence   645
And amorous adulation, till the maid
Rebell'd against it, saying to him, 'Prince,
O loyal nephew of our noble King,
Why ask you not to see the shield he left,
Whence you might learn his name? Why slight your King,   650
And lose the quest he sent you on, and prove
No surer than our falcon yesterday,
Who lost the hern we slipt her at, and went
To all the winds?' 'Nay, by mine head,' said he,
'I lose it, as we lose the lark in heaven,   655
O damsel, in the light of your blue eyes;
But an ye will it let me see the shield.'
And when the shield was brought, and Gawain saw
Sir Lancelot's azure lions, crown'd with gold,
Ramp in the field, he smote his thigh, and mock'd: 660
'Right was the King! our Lancelot! that true man!'
'And right was I,' she answer'd merrily, 'I,
Who dream'd my knight the greatest knight of all.'
'And if *I* dream'd,' said Gawain, 'that you love
This greatest knight, your pardon! lo, ye know it!   665
Speak therefore: shall I waste myself in vain?'
Full simple was her answer, 'What know I?
My brethren have been all my fellowship;
And I, when often they have talk'd of love,
Wish'd it had been my mother, for they talk'd,   670
Meseem'd, of what they knew not; so myself—
I know not if I know what true love is,
But if I know, then, if I love not him,
I know there is none other I can love.'
'Yea, by God's death,' said he, 'ye love him well,   675
But would not, knew ye what all others know,
And whom he loves.' 'So be it,' cried Elaine,
And lifted her fair face and moved away:
But he pursued her, calling, 'Stay a little!
One golden minute's grace! he wore your sleeve: 680

185

Would he break faith with one I may not name?
Must our true man change like a leaf at last?
Nay – like enow: why then, far be it from me
To cross our mighty Lancelot in his loves!
685 And, damsel, for I deem you know full well
Where your great knight is hidden, let me leave
My quest with you; the diamond also: here!
For if you love, it will be sweet to give it;
And if he love, it will be sweet to have it
690 From your own hand; and whether he love or not,
A diamond is a diamond. Fare you well
A thousand times! – a thousand times farewell!
Yet, if he love, and his love hold, we two
May meet at court hereafter: there, I think,
695 So ye will learn the courtesies of the court,
We two shall know each other.'

                      Then he gave,
And slightly kiss'd the hand to which he gave,
The diamond, and all wearied of the quest
Leapt on his horse, and carolling as he went
700 A true-love ballad, lightly rode away.

Thence to the court he past; there told the King
What the King knew, 'Sir Lancelot is the knight.'
And added, 'Sire, my liege, so much I learnt;
But fail'd to find him, tho' I rode all round
705 The region: but I lighted on the maid
Whose sleeve he wore; she loves him; and to her,
Deeming our courtesy is the truest law,
I gave the diamond; she will render it;
For by mine head she knows his hiding-place.'

710 The seldom-frowning King frown'd, and replied,
'Too courteous truly! ye shall go no more
On quest of mine, seeing that ye forget
Obedience is the courtesy due to kings.'

He spake and parted. Wroth, but all in awe,
715 For twenty strokes of the blood, without a word,

Linger'd that other, staring after him;
Then shook his hair, strode off, and buzz'd abroad
About the maid of Astolat, and her love.
All ears were prick'd at once, all tongues were loosed:
'The maid of Astolat loves Sir Lancelot,   720
Sir Lancelot loves the maid of Astolat.'
Some read the King's face, some the Queen's, and all
Had marvel what the maid might be, but most
Predoom'd her as unworthy. One old dame
Came suddenly on the Queen with the sharp news.   725
She, that had heard the noise of it before,
But sorrowing Lancelot should have stoop'd so low,
Marr'd her friend's aim with pale tranquillity.
So ran the tale like fire about the court,
Fire in dry stubble a nine-days' wonder flared: 730
Till ev'n the knights at banquet twice or thrice
Forgot to drink to Lancelot and the Queen,
And pledging Lancelot and the lily maid
Smiled at each other, while the Queen, who sat
With lips severely placid, felt the knot   735
Climb in her throat, and with her feet unseen
Crush'd the wild passion out against the floor
Beneath the banquet, where the meats became
As wormwood, and she hated all who pledged.

   But far away the maid in Astolat,   740
Her guiltless rival, she that ever kept
The one-day-seen Sir Lancelot in her heart,
Crept to her father, while he mused alone,
Sat on his knee, stroked his gray face and said,
'Father, you call me wilful, and the fault   745
Is yours who let me have my will, and now,
Sweet father, will you let me lose my wits?'
'Nay,' said he, 'surely.' 'Wherefore, let me hence,'
She answer'd, 'and find out our dear Lavaine.'
'Ye will not lose your wits for dear Lavaine: 750
Bide,' answer'd he: 'we needs must hear anon
Of him, and of that other.' 'Ay,' she said,
'And of that other, for I needs must hence
And find that other, wheresoe'er he be,

755 And with mine own hand give his diamond to him,
Lest I be found as faithless in the quest
As yon proud Prince who left the quest to me.
Sweet father, I behold him in my dreams
Gaunt as it were the skeleton of himself,
760 Death-pale, for lack of gentle maiden's aid.
The gentler-born the maiden, the more bound,
My father, to be sweet and serviceable
To noble knights in sickness, as ye know
When these have worn their tokens: let me hence
765 I pray you.' Then her father nodding said,
'Ay, ay, the diamond: wit ye well, my child,
Right fain were I to learn this knight were whole,
Being our greatest: yea, and you must give it –
And sure I think this fruit is hung too high
770 For any mouth to gape for save a queen's –
Nay, I mean nothing: so then, get you gone,
Being so very wilful you must go.'

Lightly, her suit allow'd, she slipt away,
And while she made her ready for her ride,
775 Her father's latest word humm'd in her ear,
'Being so very wilful you must go,'
And changed itself and echo'd in her heart,
'Being so very wilful you must die.'
But she was happy enough and shook it off,
780 As we shake off the bee that buzzes at us;
And in her heart she answer'd it and said,
'What matter, so I help him back to life?'
Then far away with good Sir Torre for guide
Rode o'er the long backs of the bushless downs
785 To Camelot, and before the city-gates
Came on her brother with a happy face
Making a roan horse caper and curvet
For pleasure all about a field of flowers:
Whom when she saw, 'Lavaine,' she cried, 'Lavaine,
790 How fares my lord Sir Lancelot?' He amazed,
'Torre and Elaine! why here? Sir Lancelot!
How know ye my lord's name is Lancelot?'
But when the maid had told him all her tale,

Then turn'd Sir Torre, and being in his moods
Left them, and under the strange-statued gate,   795
Where Arthur's wars were render'd mystically,
Past up the still rich city to his kin,
His own far blood, which dwelt at Camelot;
And her, Lavaine across the poplar grove
Led to the caves: there first she saw the casque   800
Of Lancelot on the wall: her scarlet sleeve,
Tho' carved and cut, and half the pearls away,
Stream'd from it still; and in her heart she laugh'd,
Because he had not loosed it from his helm,
But meant once more perchance to tourney in it.   805
And when they gain'd the cell wherein he slept,
His battle-writhen arms and mighty hands
Lay naked on the wolfskin, and a dream
Of dragging down his enemy made them move.
Then she that saw him lying unsleek, unshorn,   810
Gaunt as it were the skeleton of himself,
Utter'd a little tender dolorous cry.
The sound not wonted in a place so still
Woke the sick knight, and while he roll'd his eyes
Yet blank from sleep, she started to him, saying,   815
'Your prize the diamond sent you by the King:'
His eyes glisten'd: she fancied 'Is it for me?'
And when the maid had told him all the tale
Of King and Prince, the diamond sent, the quest
Assign'd to her not worthy of it, she knelt   820
Full lowly by the corners of his bed,
And laid the diamond in his open hand.
Her face was near, and as we kiss the child
That does the task assign'd, he kiss'd her face.
At once she slipt like water to the floor.   825
'Alas,' he said, 'your ride hath wearied you.
Rest must you have.' 'No rest for me,' she said;
'Nay, for near you, fair lord, I am at rest.'
What might she mean by that? his large black eyes,
Yet larger thro' his leanness, dwelt upon her,   830
Till all her heart's sad secret blazed itself
In the heart's colours on her simple face;
And Lancelot look'd and was perplext in mind,

And being weak in body said no more;
835 But did not love the colour; woman's love,
Save one, he not regarded, and so turn'd
Sighing, and feign'd a sleep until he slept.

Then rose Elaine and glided thro' the fields,
And past beneath the weirdly-sculptured gates
840 Far up the dim rich city to her kin;
There bode the night: but woke with dawn, and past
Down thro' the dim rich city to the fields,
Thence to the cave: so day by day she past
In either twilight ghost-like to and fro
845 Gliding, and every day she tended him,
And likewise many a night: and Lancelot
Would, tho' he call'd his wound a little hurt
Whereof he should be quickly whole, at times
Brain-feverous in his heat and agony, seem
850 Uncourteous, even he: but the meek maid
Sweetly forbore him ever, being to him
Meeker than any child to a rough nurse,
Milder than any mother to a sick child,
And never woman yet, since man's first fall,
855 Did kindlier unto man, but her deep love
Upbore her; till the hermit, skill'd in all
The simples and the science of that time,
Told him that her fine care had saved his life.
And the sick man forgot her simple blush,
860 Would call her friend and sister, sweet Elaine,
Would listen for her coming and regret
Her parting step, and held her tenderly,
And loved her with all love except the love
Of man and woman when they love their best,
865 Closest and sweetest, and had died the death
In any knightly fashion for her sake.
And peradventure had he seen her first
She might have made this and that other world
Another world for the sick man; but now
870 The shackles of an old love straiten'd him,
His honour rooted in dishonour stood,
And faith unfaithful kept him falsely true.

Yet the great knight in his mid-sickness made
Full many a holy vow and pure resolve.
These, as but born of sickness, could not live: 875
For when the blood ran lustier in him again,
Full often the bright image of one face,
Making a treacherous quiet in his heart,
Dispersed his resolution like a cloud.
Then if the maiden, while that ghostly grace   880
Beam'd on his fancy, spoke, he answer'd not,
Or short and coldly, and she knew right well
What the rough sickness meant, but what this meant
She knew not, and the sorrow dimm'd her sight,
And drave her ere her time across the fields   885
Far into the rich city, where alone
She murmur'd, 'Vain, in vain: it cannot be.
He will not love me: how then? must I die?'
Then as a little helpless innocent bird,
That has but one plain passage of few notes,   890
Will sing the simple passage o'er and o'er
For all an April morning, till the ear
Wearies to hear it, so the simple maid
Went half the night repeating, 'Must I die?'
And now to right she turn'd, and now to left,   895
And found no ease in turning or in rest;
And 'Him or death,' she mutter'd, 'death or him,'
Again and like a burthen, 'Him or death.'

But when Sir Lancelot's deadly hurt was whole,
To Astolat returning rode the three.   900
There morn by morn, arraying her sweet self
In that wherein she deem'd she look'd her best,
She came before Sir Lancelot, for she thought
'If I be loved, these are my festal robes,
If not, the victim's flowers before he fall.'   905
And Lancelot ever prest upon the maid
That she should ask some goodly gift of him
For her own self or hers; 'and do not shun
To speak the wish most near to your true heart;
Such service have ye done me, that I make   910
My will of yours, and Prince and Lord am I

In mine own land, and what I will I can.'
Then like a ghost she lifted up her face,
But like a ghost without the power to speak.
915 And Lancelot saw that she withheld her wish,
And bode among them yet a little space
Till he should learn it; and one morn it chanced
He found her in among the garden yews,
And said, 'Delay no longer, speak your wish,
920 Seeing I go to-day:' then out she brake:
'Going? and we shall never see you more.
And I must die for want of one bold word.'
'Speak: that I live to hear,' he said, 'is yours.'
Then suddenly and passionately she spoke:
925 'I have gone mad. I love you: let me die.'
'Ah, sister,' answer'd Lancelot, 'what is this?'
And innocently extending her white arms,
'Your love,' she said, 'your love – to be your wife.'
And Lancelot answer'd, 'Had I chosen to wed,
930 I had been wedded earlier, sweet Elaine:
But now there never will be wife of mine.'
'No, no,' she cried, 'I care not to be wife,
But to be with you still, to see your face,
To serve you, and to follow you thro' the world.'
935 And Lancelot answer'd, 'Nay, the world, the world,
All ear and eye, with such a stupid heart
To interpret ear and eye, and such a tongue
To blare its own interpretation – nay,
Full ill then should I quit your brother's love,
940 And your good father's kindness.' And she said,
'Not to be with you, not to see your face –
Alas for me then, my good days are done.'
'Nay, noble maid,' he answer'd, 'ten times nay!
This is not love: but love's first flash in youth,
945 Most common: yea, I know it of mine own self:
And you yourself will smile at your own self
Hereafter, when you yield your flower of life
To one more fitly yours, not thrice your age:
And then will I, for true you are and sweet
950 Beyond mine old belief in womanhood,
More specially should your good knight be poor,

Endow you with broad land and territory
Even to the half my realm beyond the seas,
So that would make you happy: furthermore,
Ev'n to the death, as tho' ye were my blood,   955
In all your quarrels will I be your knight.
This will I do, dear damsel, for your sake,
And more than this I cannot.'

                While he spoke
She neither blush'd nor shook, but deathly-pale
Stood grasping what was nearest, then replied: 960
'Of all this will I nothing;' and so fell,
And thus they bore her swooning to her tower.

Then spake, to whom thro' those black walls of yew
Their talk had pierced, her father: 'Ay, a flash,
I fear me, that will strike my blossom dead.   965
Too courteous are ye, fair Lord Lancelot.
I pray you, use some rough discourtesy
To blunt or break her passion.'

                Lancelot said,
'That were against me: what I can I will;'
And there that day remain'd, and toward even   970
Sent for his shield: full meekly rose the maid,
Stript off the case, and gave the naked shield;
Then, when she heard his horse upon the stones,
Unclasping flung the casement back, and look'd
Down on his helm, from which her sleeve had gone.   975
And Lancelot knew the little clinking sound;
And she by tact of love was well aware
That Lancelot knew that she was looking at him.
And yet he glanced not up, nor waved his hand,
Nor bad farewell, but sadly rode away.   980
This was the one discourtesy that he used.

So in her tower alone the maiden sat:
His very shield was gone; only the case,
Her own poor work, her empty labour, left.
But still she heard him, still his picture form'd   985

And grew between her and the pictured wall.
Then came her father, saying in low tones,
'Have comfort,' whom she greeted quietly.
Then came her brethren saying, 'Peace to thee,
990   Sweet sister,' whom she answer'd with all calm.
But when they left her to herself again,
Death, like a friend's voice from a distant field
Approaching thro' the darkness, call'd; the owls
Wailing had power upon her, and she mixt
995   Her fancies with the sallow-rifted glooms
Of evening, and the moanings of the wind.

And in those days she made a little song,
And call'd her song 'The Song of Love and Death,'
And sang it: sweetly could she make and sing.

1000   'Sweet is true love tho' given in vain, in vain;
And sweet is death who puts an end to pain:
I know not which is sweeter, no, not I.

'Love, art thou sweet? then bitter death must be:
1005   Love, thou art bitter; sweet is death to me.
O Love, if death be sweeter, let me die.

'Sweet love, that seems not made to fade away,
Sweet death, that seems to make us loveless clay,
I know not which is sweeter, no, not I.

'I fain would follow love, if that could be;
1010   I needs must follow death, who calls for me;
Call and I follow, I follow! let me die.'

High with the last line scaled her voice, and this,
All in a fiery dawning wild with wind
That shook her tower, the brothers heard, and thought
1015   With shuddering, 'Hark the Phantom of the house
That ever shrieks before a death,' and call'd
The father, and all three in hurry and fear
Ran to her, and lo! the blood-red light of dawn
Flared on her face, she shrilling, 'Let me die!'

As when we dwell upon a word we know,   1020
Repeating, till the word we know so well
Becomes a wonder, and we know not why,
So dwelt the father on her face, and thought
'Is this Elaine?' till back the maiden fell,
Then gave a languid hand to each, and lay,   1025
Speaking a still good-morrow with her eyes.
At last she said, 'Sweet brothers, yesternight
I seem'd a curious little maid again,
As happy as when we dwelt among the woods,
And when ye used to take me with the flood   1030
Up the great river in the boatman's boat.
Only ye would not pass beyond the cape
That has the poplar on it: there ye fixt
Your limit, oft returning with the tide.
And yet I cried because ye would not pass   1035
Beyond it, and far up the shining flood
Until we found the palace of the King.
And yet ye would not; but this night I dream'd
That I was all alone upon the flood,
And then I said, "Now shall I have my will:"   1040
And there I woke, but still the wish remain'd.
So let me hence that I may pass at last
Beyond the poplar and far up the flood,
Until I find the palace of the King.
There will I enter in among them all,   1045
And no man there will dare to mock at me;
But there the fine Gawain will wonder at me,
And there the great Sir Lancelot muse at me;
Gawain, who bad a thousand farewells to me,
Lancelot, who coldly went, nor bad me one: 1050
And there the King will know me and my love,
And there the Queen herself will pity me,
And all the gentle court will welcome me,
And after my long voyage I shall rest!'

'Peace,' said her father, 'O my child, ye seem   1055
Light-headed, for what force is yours to go
So far, being sick? and wherefore would ye look
On this proud fellow again, who scorns us all?'

Then the rough Torre began to heave and move,
1060   And bluster into stormy sobs and say,
'I never loved him: an I meet with him,
I care not howsoever great he be,
Then will I strike at him and strike him down,
Give me good fortune, I will strike him dead,
1065   For this discomfort he hath done the house.'

To whom the gentle sister made reply,
'Fret not yourself, dear brother, nor be wroth,
Seeing it is no more Sir Lancelot's fault
Not to love me, than it is mine to love
1070   Him of all men who seems to me the highest.'

'Highest?' the father answer'd, echoing 'highest?'
(He meant to break the passion in her) 'nay,
Daughter, I know not what you call the highest;
But this I know, for all the people know it,
1075   He loves the Queen, and in an open shame:
And she returns his love in open shame;
If this be high, what is it to be low?'

Then spake the lily maid of Astolat:
'Sweet father, all too faint and sick am I
1080   For anger: these are slanders: never yet
Was noble man but made ignoble talk.
He makes no friend who never made a foe.
But now it is my glory to have loved
One peerless, without stain: so let me pass,
1085   My father, howsoe'er I seem to you,
Not all unhappy, having loved God's best
And greatest, tho' my love had no return:
Yet, seeing you desire your child to live,
Thanks, but you work against your own desire;
1090   For if I could believe the things you say
I should but die the sooner; wherefore cease,
Sweet father, and bid call the ghostly man
Hither, and let me shrive me clean, and die.'

So when the ghostly man had come and gone,
1095   She with a face, bright as for sin forgiven,

Besought Lavaine to write as she devised
A letter, word for word; and when he ask'd
'Is it for Lancelot, is it for my dear lord?
Then will I bear it gladly;' she replied,
'For Lancelot and the Queen and all the world,   1100
But I myself must bear it.' Then he wrote
The letter she devised; which being writ
And folded, 'O sweet father, tender and true,
Deny me not,' she said – 'ye never yet
Denied my fancies – this, however strange,   1105
My latest: lay the letter in my hand
A little ere I die, and close the hand
Upon it; I shall guard it even in death.
And when the heat is gone from out my heart,
Then take the little bed on which I died   1110
For Lancelot's love, and deck it like the Queen's
For richness, and me also like the Queen
In all I have of rich, and lay me on it.
And let there be prepared a chariot-bier
To take me to the river, and a barge   1115
Be ready on the river, clothed in black.
I go in state to court, to meet the Queen.
There surely I shall speak for mine own self,
And none of you can speak for me so well.
And therefore let our dumb old man alone   1120
Go with me, he can steer and row, and he
Will guide me to that palace, to the doors.'

She ceased: her father promised; whereupon
She grew so cheerful that they deem'd her death
Was rather in the fantasy than the blood.   1125
But ten slow mornings past, and on the eleventh
Her father laid the letter in her hand,
And closed the hand upon it, and she died.
So that day there was dole in Astolat.

But when the next sun brake from underground,   1130
Then, those two brethren slowly with bent brows
Accompanying, the sad chariot-bier
Past like a shadow thro' the field, that shone

197

Full-summer, to that stream whereon the barge,
1135   Pall'd all its length in blackest samite, lay.
There sat the lifelong creature of the house,
Loyal, the dumb old servitor, on deck,
Winking his eyes, and twisted all his face.
So those two brethren from the chariot took
1140   And on the black decks laid her in her bed,
Set in her hand a lily, o'er her hung
The silken case with braided blazonings,
And kiss'd her quiet brows, and saying to her
'Sister, farewell for ever,' and again
1145   'Farewell, sweet sister,' parted all in tears.
Then rose the dumb old servitor, and the dead,
Oar'd by the dumb, went upward with the flood –
In her right hand the lily, in her left
The letter – all her bright hair streaming down –
1150   And all the coverlid was cloth of gold
Drawn to her waist, and she herself in white
All but her face, and that clear-featured face
Was lovely, for she did not seem as dead,
But fast asleep, and lay as tho' she smiled.

1155   That day Sir Lancelot at the palace craved
Audience of Guinevere, to give at last
The price of half a realm, his costly gift,
Hard-won and hardly won with bruise and blow
With deaths of others, and almost his own,
1160   The nine-years-fought-for diamonds: for he saw
One of her house, and sent him to the Queen
Bearing his wish, whereto the Queen agreed
With such and so unmoved a majesty
She might have seem'd her statue, but that he,
1165   Low-drooping till he wellnigh kiss'd her feet
For loyal awe, saw with a sidelong eye
The shadow of some piece of pointed lace,
In the Queen's shadow, vibrate on the walls,
And parted, laughing in his courtly heart.

1170   All in an oriel on the summer side,
Vine-clad, of Arthur's palace toward the stream,

They met, and Lancelot kneeling utter'd, 'Queen,
Lady, my liege, in whom I have my joy,
Take, what I had not won except for you,
These jewels, and make me happy, making them   1175
An armlet for the roundest arm on earth,
Or necklace for a neck to which the swan's
Is tawnier than her cygnet's: these are words:
Your beauty is your beauty, and I sin
In speaking, yet O grant my worship of it   1180
Words, as we grant grief tears. Such sin in words
Perchance, we both can pardon: but, my Queen,
I hear of rumours flying thro' your court.
Our bond, as not the bond of man and wife,
Should have in it an absoluter trust   1185
To make up that defect: let rumours be:
When did not rumours fly? these, as I trust
That you trust me in your own nobleness,
I may not well believe that you believe.'

While thus he spoke, half turn'd away, the Queen   1190
Brake from the vast oriel-embowering vine
Leaf after leaf, and tore, and cast them off,
Till all the place whereon she stood was green;
Then, when he ceased, in one cold passive hand
Received at once and laid aside the gems   1195
There on a table near her, and replied:

'It may be, I am quicker of belief
Than you believe me, Lancelot of the Lake.
Our bond is not the bond of man and wife.
This good is in it, whatsoe'er of ill,   1200
It can be broken easier. I for you
This many a year have done despite and wrong
To one whom ever in my heart of hearts
I did acknowledge nobler. What are these?
Diamonds for me! they had been thrice their worth   1205
Being your gift, had you not lost your own.
To loyal hearts the value of all gifts
Must vary as the giver's. Not for me!
For her! for your new fancy. Only this

1210 Grant me, I pray you: have your joys apart.
I doubt not that however changed, you keep
So much of what is graceful: and myself
Would shun to break those bounds of courtesy
In which as Arthur's Queen I move and rule:
1215 So cannot speak my mind. An end to this!
A strange one! yet I take it with Amen.
So pray you, add my diamonds to her pearls;
Deck her with these; tell her, she shines me down:
An armlet for an arm to which the Queen's
1220 Is haggard, or a necklace for a neck
O as much fairer – as a faith once fair
Was richer than these diamonds – hers not mine –
Nay, by the mother of our Lord himself,
Or hers or mine, mine now to work my will –
1225 She shall not have them.'

Saying which she seized,
And, thro' the casement standing wide for heat,
Flung them, and down they flash'd, and smote the
        stream.
Then from the smitten surface flash'd, as it were,
Diamonds to meet them, and they past away.
1230 Then while Sir Lancelot leant, in half disdain
At love, life, all things, on the window ledge,
Close underneath his eyes, and right across
Where these had fallen, slowly past the barge
Whereon the lily maid of Astolat
1235 Lay smiling, like a star in blackest night.

But the wild Queen, who saw not, burst away
To weep and wail in secret; and the barge,
On to the palace-doorway sliding, paused.
There two stood arm'd, and kept the door; to whom,
1240 All up the marble stair, tier over tier,
Were added mouths that gaped, and eyes that ask'd
'What is it?' but that oarsman's haggard face,
As hard and still as is the face that men
Shape to their fancy's eye from broken rocks

On some cliff-side, appall'd them, and they said,⁣   1245
'He is enchanted, cannot speak – and she,
Look how she sleeps – the Fairy Queen, so fair!
Yea, but how pale! what are they? flesh and blood?
Or come to take the King to Fairyland?
For some do hold our Arthur cannot die,   1250
But that he passes into Fairyland.'

While thus they babbled of the King, the King
Came girt with knights: then turn'd the tongueless man
From the half-face to the full eye, and rose
And pointed to the damsel, and the doors.   1255
So Arthur bad the meek Sir Percivale
And pure Sir Galahad to uplift the maid;
And reverently they bore her into hall.
Then came the fine Gawain and wonder'd at her,
And Lancelot later came and mused at her,   1260
And last the Queen herself, and pitied her:
But Arthur spied the letter in her hand,
Stoopt, took, brake seal, and read it; this was all:

'Most noble lord, Sir Lancelot of the Lake,
I, sometime call'd the maid of Astolat,   1265
Come, for you left me taking no farewell,
Hither, to take my last farewell of you.
I loved you, and my love had no return,
And therefore my true love has been my death.
And therefore to our Lady Guinevere,   1270
And to all other ladies, I make moan:
Pray for my soul, and yield me burial.
Pray for my soul thou too, Sir Lancelot,
As thou art a knight peerless.'

⁣   Thus he read;
And ever in the reading, lords and dames   1275
Wept, looking often from his face who read
To hers which lay so silent, and at times,
So touch'd were they, half-thinking that her lips,
Who had devised the letter, moved again.

1280
Then freely spoke Sir Lancelot to them all:
'My lord liege Arthur, and all ye that hear,
Know that for this most gentle maiden's death
Right heavy am I; for good she was and true,
But loved me with a love beyond all love
1285
In women, whomsoever I have known.
Yet to be loved makes not to love again;
Not at my years, however it hold in youth.
I swear by truth and knighthood that I gave
No cause, not willingly, for such a love:
1290
To this I call my friends in testimony,
Her brethren, and her father, who himself
Besought me to be plain and blunt, and use,
To break her passion, some discourtesy
Against my nature: what I could, I did.
1295
I left her and I bad her no farewell;
Tho', had I dreamt the damsel would have died,
I might have put my wits to some rough use,
And help'd her from herself.'

                    Then said the Queen
(Sea was her wrath, yet working after storm)
1300
'Ye might at least have done her so much grace,
Fair lord, as would have help'd her from her death.'
He raised his head, their eyes met and hers fell,
He adding,

                 'Queen, she would not be content
Save that I wedded her, which could not be.
1305
Then might she follow me thro' the world, she ask'd;
It could not be.   I told her that her love
Was but the flash of youth, would darken down
To rise hereafter in a stiller flame
Toward one more worthy of her – then would I,
1310
More specially were he, she wedded, poor,
Estate them with large land and territory
In mine own realm beyond the narrow seas,
To keep them in all joyance: more than this
I could not; this she would not, and she died.'

He pausing, Arthur answer'd, 'O my knight,   1315
It will be to thy worship, as my knight,
And mine, as head of all our Table Round,
To see that she be buried worshipfully.'

So toward that shrine which then in all the realm
Was richest, Arthur leading, slowly went   1320
The marshall'd Order of their Table Round,
And Lancelot sad beyond his wont, to see
The maiden buried, not as one unknown,
Nor meanly, but with gorgeous obsequies,
And mass, and rolling music, like a queen.   1325
And when the knights had laid her comely head
Low in the dust of half-forgotten kings,
Then Arthur spake among them, 'Let her tomb
Be costly, and her image thereupon,
And let the shield of Lancelot at her feet   1330
Be carven, and her lily in her hand.
And let the story of her dolorous voyage
For all true hearts be blazon'd on her tomb
In letters gold and azure!' which was wrought
Thereafter; but when now the lords and dames   1335
And people, from the high door streaming, brake
Disorderly, as homeward each, the Queen,
Who mark'd Sir Lancelot where he moved apart,
Drew near, and sigh'd in passing, 'Lancelot,
Forgive me; mine was jealousy in love.'   1340
He answer'd with his eyes upon the ground,
'That is love's curse; pass on, my Queen, forgiven.'
But Arthur, who beheld his cloudy brows,
Approach'd him, and with full affection said,

'Lancelot, my Lancelot, thou in whom I have   1345
Most joy and most affiance, for I know
What thou hast been in battle by my side,
And many a time have watch'd thee at the tilt
Strike down the lusty and long practised knight,
And let the younger and unskill'd go by   1350
To win his honour and to make his name,

And loved thy courtesies and thee, a man
Made to be loved; but now I would to God,
Seeing the homeless trouble in thine eyes,
1355 Thou couldst have loved this maiden, shaped, it seems,
By God for thee alone, and from her face,
If one may judge the living by the dead,
Delicately pure and marvellously fair,
Who might have brought thee, now a lonely man
1360 Wifeless and heirless, noble issue, sons
Born to the glory of thy name and fame,
My knight, the great Sir Lancelot of the Lake.'

Then answer'd Lancelot, 'Fair she was, my King,
Pure, as you ever wish your knights to be.
1365 To doubt her fairness were to want an eye,
To doubt her pureness were to want a heart –
Yea, to be loved, if what is worthy love
Could bind him, but free love will not be bound.'

'Free love, so bound, were freëst,' said the King.
1370 'Let love be free; free love is for the best:
And, after heaven, on our dull side of death,
What should be best, if not so pure a love
Clothed in so pure a loveliness? yet thee
She fail'd to bind, tho' being, as I think,
1375 Unbound as yet, and gentle, as I know.'

And Lancelot answer'd nothing, but he went,
And at the inrunning of a little brook
Sat by the river in a cove, and watch'd
The high reed wave, and lifted up his eyes
1380 And saw the barge that brought her moving down,
Far-off, a blot upon the stream, and said
Low in himself, 'Ah simple heart and sweet,
Ye loved me, damsel, surely with a love
Far tenderer than my Queen's. Pray for thy soul?
1385 Ay, that will I. Farewell too – now at last –
Farewell, fair lily. "Jealousy in love?"
Not rather dead love's harsh heir, jealous pride?
Queen, if I grant the jealousy as of love,

204

May not your crescent fear for name and fame
Speak, as it waxes, of a love that wanes?　　　　　1390
Why did the King dwell on my name to me?
Mine own name shames me, seeming a reproach,
Lancelot, whom the Lady of the Lake
Caught from his mother's arms – the wondrous one
Who passes thro' the vision of the night –　　　　1395
She chanted snatches of mysterious hymns
Heard on the winding waters, eve and morn
She kiss'd me saying, "Thou art fair, my child,
As a king's son," and often in her arms
She bare me, pacing on the dusky mere.　　　　　1400
Would she had drown'd me in it, where'er it be!
For what am I? what profits me my name
Of greatest knight? I fought for it, and have it:
Pleasure to have it, none; to lose it, pain;
Now grown a part of me: but what use in it?　　　1405
To make men worse by making my sin known?
Or sin seem less, the sinner seeming great?
Alas for Arthur's greatest knight, a man
Not after Arthur's heart! I needs must break
These bonds that so defame me: not without　　　1410
She wills it: would I, if she will'd it? nay,
Who knows? but if I would not, then may God,
I pray him, send a sudden Angel down
To seize me by the hair and bear me far,
And fling me deep in that forgotten mere,　　　　1415
Among the tumbled fragments of the hills.'

　　So groan'd Sir Lancelot in remorseful pain,
Now knowing he should die a holy man.

The Holy Grail

From noiseful arms, and acts of prowess done
In tournament or tilt, Sir Percivale,
Whom Arthur and his knighthood call'd The Pure,
Had pass'd into the silent life of prayer,
5   Praise, fast, and alms; and leaving for the cowl
The helmet in an abbey far away
From Camelot, there, and not long after, died.

And one, a fellow-monk among the rest,
Ambrosius, loved him much beyond the rest,
10   And honour'd him, and wrought into his heart
A way by love that waken'd love within,
To answer that which came: and as they sat
Beneath a world-old yew-tree, darkening half
The cloisters, on a gustful April morn
15   That puff'd the swaying branches into smoke
Above them, ere the summer when he died,
The monk Ambrosius question'd Percivale:

'O brother, I have seen this yew-tree smoke,
Spring after spring, for half a hundred years:
20   For never have I known the world without,
Nor ever stray'd beyond the pale: but thee,
When first thou camest – such a courtesy
Spake thro' the limbs and in the voice – I knew
For one of those who eat in Arthur's hall;
25   For good ye are and bad, and like to coins,
Some true, some light, but every one of you
Stamp'd with the image of the King; and now
Tell me, what drove thee from the Table Round,
My brother? was it earthly passion crost?'

30   'Nay,' said the knight; 'for no such passion mine.

But the sweet vision of the Holy Grail
Drove me from all vainglories, rivalries,
And earthly heats that spring and sparkle out
Among us in the jousts, while women watch
Who wins, who falls; and waste the spiritual strength 35
Within us, better offer'd up to Heaven.'

To whom the monk: 'The Holy Grail! – I trust
We are green in Heaven's eyes; but here too much
We moulder – as to things without I mean –
Yet one of your own knights, a guest of ours, 40
Told us of this in our refectory,
But spake with such a sadness and so low
We heard not half of what he said. What is it?
The phantom of a cup that comes and goes?'

'Nay, monk! what phantom?' answer'd Percivale. 45
'The cup, the cup itself, from which our Lord
Drank at the last sad supper with his own.
This, from the blessèd land of Aromat –
After the day of darkness, when the dead
Went wandering o'er Moriah – the good saint 50
Arimathæan Joseph, journeying brought
To Glastonbury, where the winter thorn
Blossoms at Christmas, mindful of our Lord.
And there awhile it bode; and if a man
Could touch or see it, he was heal'd at once, 55
By faith, of all his ills. But then the times
Grew to such evil that the holy cup
Was caught away to Heaven, and disappear'd.'

To whom the monk: 'From our old books I know
That Joseph came of old to Glastonbury, 60
And there the heathen Prince, Arviragus,
Gave him an isle of marsh whereon to build;
And there he built with wattles from the marsh
A little lonely church in days of yore,
For so they say, these books of ours, but seem 65
Mute of this miracle, far as I have read.
But who first saw the holy thing to-day?'

'A woman,' answer'd Percivale, 'a nun,
And one no further off in blood from me
70 Than sister; and if ever holy maid
With knees of adoration wore the stone,
A holy maid; tho' never maiden glow'd,
But that was in her earlier maidenhood,
With such a fervent flame of human love,
75 Which being rudely blunted, glanced and shot
Only to holy things; to prayer and praise
She gave herself, to fast and alms.   And yet
Nun as she was, the scandal of the Court,
Sin against Arthur and the Table Round,
80 And the strange sound of an adulterous race,
Across the iron grating of her cell
Beat, and she pray'd and fasted all the more.

'And he to whom she told her sins, or what
Her all but utter whiteness held for sin,
85 A man wellnigh a hundred winters old,
Spake often with her of the Holy Grail,
A legend handed down thro' five or six,
And each of these a hundred winters old,
From our Lord's time. And when King Arthur made
90 His Table Round, and all men's hearts became
Clean for a season, surely he had thought
That now the Holy Grail would come again;
But sin broke out. Ah, Christ, that it would come,
And heal the world of all their wickedness!
95 "O Father!" ask'd the maiden, "might it come
To me by prayer and fasting?" "Nay," said he,
"I know not, for thy heart is pure as snow."
And so she pray'd and fasted, till the sun
Shone, and the wind blew, thro' her, and I thought
100 She might have risen and floated when I saw her.

'For on a day she sent to speak with me.
And when she came to speak, behold her eyes
Beyond my knowing of them, beautiful,
Beyond all knowing of them, wonderful,
105 Beautiful in the light of holiness.

And "O my brother Percivale," she said,
"Sweet brother, I have seen the Holy Grail:
For, waked at dead of night, I heard a sound
As of a silver horn from o'er the hills
Blown, and I thought, 'It is not Arthur's use 110
To hunt by moonlight;' and the slender sound
As from a distance beyond distance grew
Coming upon me – O never harp nor horn,
Nor aught we blow with breath, or touch with hand,
Was like that music as it came; and then 115
Stream'd thro' my cell a cold and silver beam,
And down the long beam stole the Holy Grail,
Rose-red with beatings in it, as if alive,
Till all the white walls of my cell were dyed
With rosy colours leaping on the wall; 120
And then the music faded, and the Grail
Past, and the beam decay'd, and from the walls
The rosy quiverings died into the night.
So now the Holy Thing is here again
Among us, brother, fast thou too and pray, 125
And tell thy brother knights to fast and pray,
That so perchance the vision may be seen
By thee and those, and all the world be heal'd."

'Then leaving the pale nun, I spake of this
To all men; and myself fasted and pray'd 130
Always, and many among us many a week
Fasted and pray'd even to the uttermost,
Expectant of the wonder that would be.

'And one there was among us, ever moved
Among us in white armour, Galahad. 135
"God make thee good as thou art beautiful,"
Said Arthur, when he dubb'd him knight; and none,
In so young youth, was ever made a knight
Till Galahad; and this Galahad, when he heard
My sister's vision, fill'd me with amaze; 140
His eyes became so like her own, they seem'd
Hers, and himself her brother more than I.

'Sister or brother none had he; but some
Call'd him a son of Lancelot, and some said
145   Begotten by enchantment – chatterers they,
Like birds of passage piping up and down,
That gape for flies – we know not whence they come;
For when was Lancelot wanderingly lewd?

'But she, the wan sweet maiden, shore away
150   Clean from her forehead all that wealth of hair
Which made a silken mat-work for her feet;
And out of this she plaited broad and long
A strong sword-belt, and wove with silver thread
And crimson in the belt a strange device,
155   A crimson grail within a silver beam;
And saw the bright boy-knight, and bound it on him,
Saying, "My knight, my love, my knight of heaven,
O thou, my love, whose love is one with mine,
I, maiden, round thee, maiden, bind my belt.
160   Go forth, for thou shalt see what I have seen,
And break thro' all, till one will crown thee king
Far in the spiritual city:" and as she spake
She sent the deathless passion in her eyes
Thro' him, and made him hers, and laid her mind
165   On him, and he believed in her belief.

'Then came a year of miracle: O brother,
In our great hall there stood a vacant chair,
Fashion'd by Merlin ere he past away,
And carven with strange figures; and in and out
170   The figures, like a serpent, ran a scroll
Of letters in a tongue no man could read.
And Merlin call'd it "The Siege perilous,"
Perilous for good and ill; "for there," he said,
"No man could sit but he should lose himself:"
175   And once by misadvertence Merlin sat
In his own chair, and so was lost; but he,
Galahad, when he heard of Merlin's doom,
Cried, "If I lose myself, I save myself!"

'Then on a summer night it came to pass,

While the great banquet lay along the hall,   180
That Galahad would sit down in Merlin's chair.

'And all at once, as there we sat, we heard
A cracking and a riving of the roofs,
And rending, and a blast, and overhead
Thunder, and in the thunder was a cry.   185
And in the blast there smote along the hall
A beam of light seven times more clear than day:
And down the long beam stole the Holy Grail
All over cover'd with a luminous cloud,
And none might see who bare it, and it past.   190
But every knight beheld his fellow's face
As in a glory, and all the knights arose,
And staring each at other like dumb men
Stood, till I found a voice and sware a vow

'I sware a vow before them all, that I,   195
Because I had not seen the Grail, would ride
A twelvemonth and a day in quest of it,
Until I found and saw it, as the nun
My sister saw it; and Galahad sware the vow,
And good Sir Bors, our Lancelot's cousin, sware,   200
And Lancelot sware, and many among the knights,
And Gawain sware, and louder than the rest.'

Then spake the monk Ambrosius, asking him,
'What said the King? Did Arthur take the vow?'

'Nay, for my lord,' said Percivale, 'the King,   205
Was not in hall: for early that same day,
Scaped thro' a cavern from a bandit hold,
An outraged maiden sprang into the hall
Crying on help: for all her shining hair
Was smear'd with earth, and either milky arm   210
Red-rent with hooks of bramble, and all she wore
Torn as a sail that leaves the rope is torn
In tempest: so the King arose and went
To smoke the scandalous hive of those wild bees
That made such honey in his realm. Howbeit   215

Some little of this marvel he too saw,
Returning o'er the plain that then began
To darken under Camelot; whence the King
Look'd up, calling aloud, "Lo, there! the roofs
220 Of our great hall are roll'd in thunder-smoke!
Pray Heaven, they be not smitten by the bolt."
For dear to Arthur was that hall of ours,
As having there so oft with all his knights
Feasted, and as the stateliest under heaven.

225 'O brother, had you known our mighty hall,
Which Merlin built for Arthur long ago!
For all the sacred mount of Camelot,
And all the dim rich city, roof by roof,
Tower after tower, spire beyond spire,
230 By grove, and garden-lawn, and rushing brook,
Climbs to the mighty hall that Merlin built.
And four great zones of sculpture, set betwixt
With many a mystic symbol, gird the hall:
And in the lowest beasts are slaying men,
235 And in the second men are slaying beasts,
And on the third are warriors, perfect men,
And on the fourth are men with growing wings,
And over all one statue in the mould
Of Arthur, made by Merlin, with a crown,
240 And peak'd wings pointed to the Northern Star.
And eastward fronts the statue, and the crown
And both the wings are made of gold, and flame
At sunrise till the people in far fields,
Wasted so often by the heathen hordes,
245 Behold it, crying, "We have still a King."

'And, brother, had you known our hall within,
Broader and higher than any in all the lands!
Where twelve great windows blazon Arthur's wars,
And all the light that falls upon the board
250 Streams thro' the twelve great battles of our King.
Nay, one there is, and at the eastern end,
Wealthy with wandering lines of mount and mere,
Where Arthur finds the brand Excalibur.

And also one to the west, and counter to it,
And blank: and who shall blazon it? when and how? –   255
O there, perchance, when all our wars are done,
The brand Excalibur will be cast away.

'So to this hall full quickly rode the King,
In horror lest the work by Merlin wrought,
Dreamlike, should on the sudden vanish, wrapt   260
In unremorseful folds of rolling fire.
And in he rode, and up I glanced, and saw
The golden dragon sparkling over all:
And many of those who burnt the hold, their arms
Hack'd, and their foreheads grimed with smoke,
        and sear'd,   265
Follow'd, and in among bright faces, ours,
Full of the vision, prest: and then the King
Spake to me, being nearest, "Percivale."
(Because the hall was all in tumult – some
Vowing, and some protesting), "what is this?"   270

'O brother, when I told him what had chanced,
My sister's vision, and the rest, his face
Darken'd, as I have seen it more than once,
When some brave deed seem'd to be done in vain,   275
Darken; and "Woe is me, my knights," he cried,
"Had I been here, ye had not sworn the vow."
Bold was mine answer, "Had thyself been here,
My King, thou wouldst have sworn." "Yea, yea," said he,
"Art thou so bold and hast not seen the Grail?"

'"Nay, lord, I heard the sound, I saw the light,   280
But since I did not see the Holy Thing,
I sware a vow to follow it till I saw."

'Then when he ask'd us, knight by knight, if any
Had seen it, all their answers were as one:
"Nay, lord, and therefore have we sworn our vows."   285

'"Lo now," said Arthur, "have ye seen a cloud?
What go ye into the wilderness to see?"

'Then Galahad on the sudden, and in a voice
Shrilling along the hall to Arthur, call'd,
290 "But I, Sir Arthur, saw the Holy Grail,
I saw the Holy Grail and heard a cry –
'O Galahad, and O Galahad, follow me.'"

'"Ah, Galahad, Galahad," said the King, "for such
As thou art is the vision, not for these.
295 Thy holy nun and thou have seen a sign –
Holier is none, my Percivale, than she –
A sign to maim this Order which I made.
But ye, that follow but the leader's bell"
(Brother, the King was hard upon his knights)
300 "Taliessin is our fullest throat of song,
And one hath sung and all the dumb will sing.
Lancelot is Lancelot, and hath overborne
Five knights at once, and every younger knight,
Unproven, holds himself as Lancelot,
305 Till overborne by one, he learns – and ye,
What are ye? Galahads? – no, nor Percivales"
(For thus it pleased the King to range me close
After Sir Galahad); "nay," said he, "but men
With strength and will to right the wrong'd, of power
310 To lay the sudden heads of violence flat,
Knights that in twelve great battles splash'd and dyed
The strong White Horse in his own heathen blood –
But one hath seen, and all the blind will see.
Go, since your vows are sacred, being made:
315 Yet – for ye know the cries of all my realm
Pass thro' this hall – how often, O my knights,
Your places being vacant at my side,
This chance of noble deeds will come and go
Unchallenged, while ye follow wandering fires
320 Lost in the quagmire! Many of you, yea most,
Return no more: ye think I show myself
Too dark a prophet: come now, let us meet
The morrow morn once more in one full field
Of gracious pastime, that once more the King,
325 Before ye leave him for this Quest, may count

The yet-unbroken strength of all his knights,
Rejoicing in that Order which he made."

'So when the sun broke next from under ground,
All the great table of our Arthur closed
And clash'd in such a tourney and so full,   330
So many lances broken – never yet
Had Camelot seen the like, since Arthur came;
And I myself and Galahad, for a strength
Was in us from the vision, overthrew
So many knights that all the people cried,   335
And almost burst the barriers in their heat,
Shouting, "Sir Galahad and Sir Percivale!"

'But when the next day brake from under ground –
O brother, had you known our Camelot,
Built by old kings, age after age, so old   340
The King himself had fears that it would fall,
So strange, and rich, and dim; for where the roofs
Totter'd toward each other in the sky,
Met foreheads all along the street of those
Who watch'd us pass; and lower, and where the long   345
Rich galleries, lady-laden, weigh'd the necks
Of dragons clinging to the crazy walls,
Thicker than drops from thunder, showers of flowers
Fell as we past; and men and boys astride
On wyvern, lion, dragon, griffin, swan,   350
At all the corners, named us each by name,
Calling "God speed!" but in the ways below
The knights and ladies wept, and rich and poor
Wept, and the King himself could hardly speak
For grief, and all in middle street the Queen,   355
Who rode by Lancelot, wail'd and shriek'd aloud,
"This madness has come on us for our sins."
So to the Gate of the three Queens we came,
Where Arthur's wars are render'd mystically,
And thence departed every one his way.   360

'And I was lifted up in heart, and thought

Of all my late-shown prowess in the lists,
How my strong lance had beaten down the knights,
So many and famous names; and never yet
365 Had heaven appear'd so blue, nor earth so green,
For all my blood danced in me, and I knew
That I should light upon the Holy Grail.

'Thereafter, the dark warning of our King,
That most of us would follow wandering fires,
370 Came like a driving gloom across my mind.
Then every evil word I had spoken once,
And every evil thought I had thought of old,
And every evil deed I ever did,
Awoke and cried, "This Quest is not for thee."
375 And lifting up mine eyes, I found myself
Alone, and in a land of sand and thorns,
And I was thirsty even unto death;
And I, too, cried, "This Quest is not for thee."

'And on I rode, and when I thought my thirst
380 Would slay me, saw deep lawns, and then a brook,
With one sharp rapid, where the crisping white
Play'd ever back upon the sloping wave,
And took both ear and eye; and o'er the brook
Were apple-trees, and apples by the brook
385 Fallen, and on the lawns. "I will rest here,"
I said, "I am not worthy of the Quest;"
But even while I drank the brook, and ate
The goodly apples, all these things at once
Fell into dust, and I was left alone,
390 And thirsting, in a land of sand and thorns.

'And then behold a woman at a door
Spinning; and fair the house whereby she sat,
And kind the woman's eyes and innocent,
And all her bearing gracious; and she rose
395 Opening her arms to meet me, as who should say,
"Rest here;" but when I touch'd her, lo! she, too,
Fell into dust and nothing, and the house
Became no better than a broken shed,

And in it a dead babe; and also this
Fell into dust, and I was left alone.   400

    'And on I rode, and greater was my thirst.
Then flash'd a yellow gleam across the world,
And where it smote the plowshare in the field,
The plowman left his plowing, and fell down
Before it; where it glitter'd on her pail,   405
The milkmaid left her milking, and fell down
Before it, and I knew not why, but thought
"The sun is rising," tho' the sun had risen.
Then was I ware of one that on me moved
In golden armour with a crown of gold   410
About a casque all jewels; and his horse
In golden armour jewell'd everywhere:
And on the splendour came, flashing me blind;
And seem'd to me the Lord of all the world,
Being so huge. But when I thought he meant   415
To crush me, moving on me, lo! he, too,
Open'd his arms to embrace me as he came,
And up I went and touch'd him, and he, too,
Fell into dust, and I was left alone
And wearying in a land of sand and thorns.   420

    'And I rode on and found a mighty hill,
And on the top, a city wall'd: the spires
Prick'd with incredible pinnacles into heaven.
And by the gateway stirr'd a crowd; and these
Cried to me climbing, "Welcome, Percivale!   425
Thou mightiest and thou purest among men!"
And glad was I and clomb, but found at top
No man, nor any voice. And thence I past
Far thro' a ruinous city, and I saw
That man had once dwelt there; but there I found   430
Only one man of an exceeding age.
"Where is that goodly company," said I,
"That so cried out upon me?" and he had
Scarce any voice to answer, and yet gasp'd,
"Whence and what art thou?" and even as he spoke   435
Fell into dust, and disappear'd, and I

217

Was left alone once more, and cried in grief,
"Lo, if I find the Holy Grail itself
And touch it, it will crumble into dust."

440 'And thence I dropt into a lowly vale,
Low as the hill was high, and where the vale
Was lowest, found a chapel, and thereby
A holy hermit in a hermitage,
To whom I told my phantoms, and he said:

445 '"O son, thou hast not true humility,
The highest virtue, mother of them all;
For when the Lord of all things made Himself
Naked of glory for His mortal change,
'Take thou my robe,' she said, 'for all is thine,'
450 And all her form shone forth with sudden light
So that the angels were amazed, and she
Follow'd Him down, and like a flying star
Led on the gray-hair'd wisdom of the east;
But her thou hast not known: for what is this
455 Thou thoughtest of thy prowess and thy sins?
Thou hast not lost thyself to save thyself
As Galahad." When the hermit made an end,
In silver armour suddenly Galahad shone
Before us, and against the chapel door
460 Laid lance, and enter'd, and we knelt in prayer.
And there the hermit slaked my burning thirst,
And at the sacring of the mass I saw
The holy elements alone; but he,
"Saw ye no more? I, Galahad, saw the Grail,
465 The Holy Grail, descend upon the shrine:
I saw the fiery face as of a child
That smote itself into the bread, and went;
And hither am I come; and never yet
Hath what thy sister taught me first to see,
470 This Holy Thing, fail'd from my side, nor come
Cover'd, but moving with me night and day,
Fainter by day, but always in the night
Blood-red, and sliding down the blacken'd marsh
Blood-red, and on the naked mountain top

Blood-red, and in the sleeping mere below 475
Blood-red. And in the strength of this I rode,
Shattering all evil customs everywhere,
And past thro' Pagan realms, and made them mine,
And clash'd with Pagan hordes, and bore them down,
And broke thro' all, and in the strength of this 480
Come victor. But my time is hard at hand,
And hence I go; and one will crown me king
Far in the spiritual city; and come thou, too,
For thou shalt see the vision when I go."

'While thus he spake, his eye, dwelling on mine, 485
Drew me, with power upon me, till I grew
One with him, to believe as he believed.
Then, when the day began to wane, we went.

'There rose a hill that none but man could climb,
Scarr'd with a hundred wintry water-courses – 490
Storm at the top, and when we gain'd it, storm
Round us and death; for every moment glanced
His silver arms and gloom'd: so quick and thick
The lightnings here and there to left and right
Struck, till the dry old trunks about us, dead, 495
Yea, rotten with a hundred years of death,
Sprang into fire: and at the base we found
On either hand, as far as eye could see,
A great black swamp and of an evil smell,
Part black, part whiten'd with the bones of men, 500
Not to be crost, save that some ancient king
Had built a way, where, link'd with many a bridge,
A thousand piers ran into the great Sea.
And Galahad fled along them bridge by bridge,
And every bridge as quickly as he crost 505
Sprang into fire and vanish'd, tho' I yearn'd
To follow; and thrice above him all the heavens
Open'd and blazed with thunder such as seem'd
Shoutings of all the sons of God: and first
At once I saw him far on the great Sea, 510
In silver-shining armour starry-clear;
And o'er his head the Holy Vessel hung

Clothed in white samite or a luminous cloud.
And with exceeding swiftness ran the boat,
515 If boat it were – I saw not whence it came.
And when the heavens open'd and blazed again
Roaring, I saw him like a silver star –
And had he set the sail, or had the boat
Become a living creature clad with wings?
520 And o'er his head the Holy Vessel hung
Redder than any rose, a joy to me,
For now I knew the veil had been withdrawn.
Then in a moment when they blazed again
Opening, I saw the least of little stars
525 Down on the waste, and straight beyond the star
I saw the spiritual city and all her spires
And gateways in a glory like one pearl –
No larger, tho' the goal of all the saints –
Strike from the sea; and from the star there shot
530 A rose-red sparkle to the city, and there
Dwelt, and I knew it was the Holy Grail,
Which never eyes on earth again shall see.
Then fell the floods of heaven drowning the deep.
And how my feet recrost the deathful ridge
535 No memory in me lives; but that I touch'd
The chapel-doors at dawn I know; and thence
Taking my war-horse from the holy man,
Glad that no phantom vext me more, return'd
To whence I came, the gate of Arthur's wars.'

540 'O brother,' ask'd Ambrosius, – 'for in sooth
These ancient books – and they would win thee – teem,
Only I find not there this Holy Grail,
With miracles and marvels like to these,
Not all unlike; which oftentime I read,
545 Who read but on my breviary with ease,
Till my head swims; and then go forth and pass
Down to the little thorpe that lies so close,
And almost plaster'd like a martin's nest
To these old walls – and mingle with our folk;
550 And knowing every honest face of theirs
As well as ever shepherd knew his sheep,

And every homely secret in their hearts,
Delight myself with gossip and old wives,
And ills and aches, and teethings, lyings-in,
And mirthful sayings, children of the place,   555
That have no meaning half a league away:
Or lulling random squabbles when they rise,
Chafferings and chatterings at the market-cross,
Rejoice, small man, in this small world of mine,
Yea, even in their hens and in their eggs –   560
O brother, saving this Sir Galahad,
Came ye on none but phantoms in your quest,
No man, no woman?'

             Then Sir Percivale:
'All men, to one so bound by such a vow,
And women were as phantoms. O, my brother,   565
Why wilt thou shame me to confess to thee
How far I falter'd from my quest and vow?
For after I had lain so many nights,
A bedmate of the snail and eft and snake,
In grass and burdock, I was changed to wan   570
And meagre, and the vision had not come;
And then I chanced upon a goodly town
With one great dwelling in the middle of it;
Thither I made, and there was I disarm'd
By maidens each as fair as any flower: 575
But when they led me into hall, behold,
The Princess of that castle was the one,
Brother, and that one only, who had ever
Made my heart leap; for when I moved of old
A slender page about her father's hall,   580
And she a slender maiden, all my heart
Went after her with longing: yet we twain
Had never kiss'd a kiss, or vow'd a vow.
And now I came upon her once again,
And one had wedded her, and he was dead,   585
And all his land and wealth and state were hers.
And while I tarried, every day she set
A banquet richer than the day before
By me; for all her longing and her will

590 Was toward me as of old; till one fair morn,
I walking to and fro beside a stream
That flash'd across her orchard underneath
Her castle-walls, she stole upon my walk,
And calling me the greatest of all knights,
595 Embraced me, and so kiss'd me the first time,
And gave herself and all her wealth to me.
Then I remember'd Arthur's warning word,
That most of us would follow wandering fires,
And the Quest faded in my heart. Anon,
600 The heads of all her people drew to me,
With supplication both of knees and tongue:
"We have heard of thee: thou art our greatest knight, –
Our Lady says it, and we well believe:
Wed thou our Lady, and rule over us,
605 And thou shalt be as Arthur in our land."
O me, my brother! but one night my vow
Burnt me within, so that I rose and fled,
But wail'd and wept, and hated mine own self,
And ev'n the Holy Quest, and all but her;
610 Then after I was join'd with Galahad
Cared not for her, nor anything upon earth.'

Then said the monk, 'Poor men, when yule is cold,
Must be content to sit by little fires.
And this am I, so that ye care for me
615 Ever so little; yea, and blest be Heaven
That brought thee here to this poor house of ours
Where all the brethren are so hard, to warm
My cold heart with a friend: but O the pity
To find thine own first love once more – to hold,
620 Hold her a wealthy bride within thine arms,
Or all but hold, and then – cast her aside,
Foregoing all her sweetness, like a weed.
For we that want the warmth of double life,
We that are plagued with dreams of something sweet
625 Beyond all sweetness in a life so rich, –
Ah, blessèd Lord, I speak too earthlywise
Seeing I never stray'd beyond the cell,
But live like an old badger in his earth,

With earth about him everywhere, despite
All fast and penance. Saw ye none beside,   630
None of your knights?'

           'Yea so,' said Percivale:
'One night my pathway swerving east, I saw
The pelican on the casque of our Sir Bors
All in the middle of the rising moon:
And toward him spurr'd, and hail'd him, and he me,   635
And each made joy of either; then he ask'd,
"Where is he? hast thou seen him – Lancelot? – Once,"
Said good Sir Bors, "he dash'd across me – mad,
And maddening what he rode: and when I cried,
'Ridest thou then so hotly on a quest   640
So holy,' Lancelot shouted, 'Stay me not!
I have been the sluggard, and I ride apace,
For now there is a lion in the way.'
So vanish'd."

           'Then Sir Bors had ridden on
Softly, and sorrowing for our Lancelot,   645
Because his former madness, once the talk
And scandal of our table, had return'd;
For Lancelot's kith and kin so worship him
That ill to him is ill to them; to Bors
Beyond the rest: he well had been content   650
Not to have seen, so Lancelot might have seen,
The Holy Cup of healing; and, indeed,
Being so clouded with his grief and love,
Small heart was his after the Holy Quest:
If God would send the vision, well: if not,   655
The Quest and he were in the hands of Heaven.

'And then, with small adventure met, Sir Bors
Rode to the lonest tract of all the realm,
And found a people there among their crags,
Our race and blood, a remnant that were left   660
Paynim amid their circles, and the stones
They pitch up straight to heaven: and their wise men
Were strong in that old magic which can trace

The wandering of the stars, and scoff'd at him
665 And this high Quest as at a simple thing:
Told him he follow'd – almost Arthur's words –
A mocking fire: "what other fire than he,
Whereby the blood beats, and the blossom blows,
And the sea rolls, and all the world is warm'd?"
670 And when his answer chafed them, the rough crowd,
Hearing he had a difference with their priests,
Seized him, and bound and plunged him into a cell
Of great piled stones; and lying bounden there
In darkness thro' innumerable hours
675 He heard the hollow-ringing heaven sweep
Over him till by miracle – what else? –
Heavy as it was, a great stone slipt and fell,
Such as no wind could move: and thro' the gap
Glimmer'd the streaming scud: then came a night
680 Still as the day was loud; and thro' the gap
The seven clear stars of Arthur's Table Round –
For, brother, so one night, because they roll
Thro' such a round in heaven, we named the stars,
Rejoicing in ourselves and in our King –
685 And these, like bright eyes of familiar friends,
In on him shone: "And then to me, to me,"
Said good Sir Bors, "beyond all hopes of mine,
Who scarce had pray'd or ask'd it for myself –
Across the seven clear stars – O grace to me –
690 In colour like the fingers of a hand
Before a burning taper, the sweet Grail
Glided and past, and close upon it peal'd
A sharp quick thunder." Afterwards, a maid,
Who kept our holy faith among her kin
695 In secret, entering, loosed and let him go.'

To whom the monk: 'And I remember now
That pelican on the casque: Sir Bors it was
Who spake so low and sadly at our board;
And mighty reverent at our grace was he:
700 A square-set man and honest; and his eyes,
An out-door sign of all the warmth within,

Smiled with his lips – a smile beneath a cloud,
But heaven had meant it for a sunny one:
Ay, ay, Sir Bors, who else? But when ye reach'd
The city, found ye all your knights return'd,   705
Or was there sooth in Arthur's prophecy,
Tell me, and what said each, and what the King?'

Then answer'd Percivale: 'And that can I,
Brother, and truly; since the living words
Of so great men as Lancelot and our King   710
Pass not from door to door and out again,
But sit within the house. O, when we reach'd
The city, our horses stumbling as they trode
On heaps of ruin, hornless unicorns,
Crack'd basilisks, and splinter'd cockatrices,   715
And shatter'd talbots, which had left the stones
Raw, that they fell from, brought us to the hall.

'And there sat Arthur on the daïs-throne,
And those that had gone out upon the Quest,
Wasted and worn, and but a tithe of them,   720
And those that had not, stood before the King,
Who, when he saw me, rose, and bad me hail,
Saying, "A welfare in thine eye reproves
Our fear of some disastrous chance for thee
On hill, or plain, at sea, or flooding ford.   725
So fierce a gale made havoc here of late
Among the strange devices of our kings;
Yea, shook this newer, stronger hall of ours,
And from the statue Merlin moulded for us
Half-wrench'd a golden wing; but now – the Quest,   730
This vision – hast thou seen the Holy Cup,
That Joseph brought of old to Glastonbury?"

'So when I told him all thyself hast heard,
Ambrosius, and my fresh but fixt resolve
To pass away into the quiet life,   735
He answer'd not, but, sharply turning, ask'd
Of Gawain, "Gawain, was this Quest for thee?"

'"Nay, lord," said Gawain, "not for such as I.
Therefore I communed with a saintly man,
740 Who made me sure the Quest was not for me;
For I was much awearied of the Quest:
But found a silk pavilion in a field,
And merry maidens in it; and then this gale
Tore my pavilion from the tenting-pin,
745 And blew my merry maidens all about
With all discomfort; yea, and but for this,
My twelvemonth and a day were pleasant to me."

'He ceased; and Arthur turn'd to whom at first
He saw not, for Sir Bors, on entering, push'd
750 Athwart the throng to Lancelot, caught his hand,
Held it, and there, half-hidden by him, stood,
Until the King espied him, saying to him,
"Hail, Bors! if ever loyal man and true
Could see it, thou hast seen the Grail;" and Bors,
755 "Ask me not, for I may not speak of it:
I saw it;" and the tears were in his eyes.

'Then there remain'd but Lancelot, for the rest
Spake but of sundry perils in the storm;
Perhaps, like him of Cana in Holy Writ,
760 Our Arthur kept his best until the last;
"Thou, too, my Lancelot," ask'd the King, "my friend,
Our mightiest, hath this Quest avail'd for thee?"

'"Our mightiest!" answer'd Lancelot, with a groan;
"O King!" – and when he paused, methought I spied
765 A dying fire of madness in his eyes –
"O King, my friend, if friend of thine I be,
Happier are those that welter in their sin,
Swine in the mud, that cannot see for slime,
Slime of the ditch: but in me lived a sin
770 So strange, of such a kind, that all of pure,
Noble, and knightly in me twined and clung
Round that one sin, until the wholesome flower
And poisonous grew together, each as each,

Not to be pluck'd asunder; and when thy knights
Sware, I sware with them only in the hope   775
That could I touch or see the Holy Grail
They might be pluck'd asunder. Then I spake
To one most holy saint, who wept and said,
That save they could be pluck'd asunder, all
My quest were but in vain; to whom I vow'd   780
That I would work according as he will'd.
And forth I went, and while I yearn'd and strove
To tear the twain asunder in my heart,
My madness came upon me as of old,
And whipt me into waste fields far away;   785
There was I beaten down by little men,
Mean knights, to whom the moving of my sword
And shadow of my spear had been enow
To scare them from me once; and then I came
All in my folly to the naked shore,   790
Wide flats, where nothing but coarse grasses grew:
But such a blast, my King, began to blow,
So loud a blast along the shore and sea,
Ye could not hear the waters for the blast,
Tho' heapt in mounds and ridges all the sea   795
Drove like a cataract, and all the sand
Swept like a river, and the clouded heavens
Were shaken with the motion and the sound.
And blackening in the sea-foam sway'd a boat,
Half-swallow'd in it, anchor'd with a chain;   800
And in my madness to myself I said,
'I will embark and I will lose myself,
And in the great sea wash away my sin.'
I burst the chain, I sprang into the boat.
Seven days I drove along the dreary deep,   805
And with me drove the moon and all the stars;
And the wind fell, and on the seventh night
I heard the shingle grinding in the surge,
And felt the boat shock earth, and looking up,
Behold, the enchanted towers of Carbonek,   810
A castle like a rock upon a rock,
With chasm-like portals open to the sea,
And steps that met the breaker! there was none

Stood near it but a lion on each side
815 That kept the entry, and the moon was full.
Then from the boat I leapt, and up the stairs.
There drew my sword. With sudden-flaring manes
Those two great beasts rose upright like a man,
Each gript a shoulder, and I stood between;
820 And, when I would have smitten them, heard a voice,
'Doubt not, go forward; if thou doubt, the beasts
Will tear thee piecemeal.' Then with violence
The sword was dash'd from out my hand, and fell.
And up into the sounding hall I past;
825 But nothing in the sounding hall I saw,
No bench nor table, painting on the wall
Or shield of knight; only the rounded moon
Thro' the tall oriel on the rolling sea.
But always in the quiet house I heard,
830 Clear as a lark, high o'er me as a lark,
A sweet voice singing in the topmost tower
To the eastward: up I climb'd a thousand steps
With pain: as in a dream I seem'd to climb
For ever: at the last I reach'd a door,
835 A light was in the crannies, and I heard,
'Glory and joy and honour to our Lord
And to the Holy Vessel of the Grail.'
Then in my madness I essay'd the door;
It gave; and thro' a stormy glare, a heat
840 As from a seventimes-heated furnace, I,
Blasted and burnt, and blinded as I was,
With such a fierceness that I swoon'd away –
O, yet methought I saw the Holy Grail,
All pall'd in crimson samite, and around
845 Great angels, awful shapes, and wings and eyes.
And but for all my madness and my sin,
And then my swooning, I had sworn I saw
That which I saw; but what I saw was veil'd
And cover'd; and this Quest was not for me."

850 'So speaking, and here ceasing, Lancelot left
The hall long silent, till Sir Gawain – nay,
Brother, I need not tell thee foolish words, –

A reckless and irreverent knight was he,
Now bolden'd by the silence of his King, –
Well, I will tell thee: "O King, my liege," he said,   855
"Hath Gawain fail'd in any quest of thine?
When have I stinted stroke in foughten field?
But as for thine, my good friend Percivale,
Thy holy nun and thou have driven men mad,
Yea, made our mightiest madder than our least.   860
But by mine eyes and by mine ears I swear,
I will be deafer than the blue-eyed cat,
And thrice as blind as any noonday owl,
To holy virgins in their ecstasies,
Henceforward."

'"Deafer," said the blameless King,   865
"Gawain, and blinder unto holy things
Hope not to make thyself by idle vows,
Being too blind to have desire to see.
But if indeed there came a sign from heaven,
Blessèd are Bors, Lancelot and Percivale,   870
For these have seen according to their sight.
For every fiery prophet in old times,
And all the sacred madness of the bard,
When God made music thro' them, could but speak
His music by the framework and the chord;   875
And as ye saw it ye have spoken truth.

'"Nay – but thou errest, Lancelot: never yet
Could all of true and noble in knight and man
Twine round one sin, whatever it might be,
With such a closeness, but apart there grew,   880
Save that he were the swine thou spakest of,
Some root of knighthood and pure nobleness;
Whereto see thou, that it may bear its flower.

'"And spake I not too truly, O my knights?
Was I too dark a prophet when I said   885
To those who went upon the Holy Quest,
That most of them would follow wandering fires,
Lost in the quagmire? – lost to me and gone,

And left me gazing at a barren board,
890 And a lean Order – scarce return'd a tithe –
And out of those to whom the vision came
My greatest hardly will believe he saw;
Another hath beheld it afar off,
And leaving human wrongs to right themselves,
895 Cares but to pass into the silent life.
And one hath had the vision face to face,
And now his chair desires him here in vain,
However they may crown him otherwhere.

   '"And some among you held, that if the King
900 Had seen the sight he would have sworn the vow:
Not easily, seeing that the King must guard
That which he rules, and is but as the hind
To whom a space of land is given to plow.
Who may not wander from the allotted field
905 Before his work be done; but, being done,
Let visions of the night or of the day
Come, as they will; and many a time they come,
Until this earth he walks on seems not earth,
This light that strikes his eyeball is not light,
910 This air that smites his forehead is not air
But vision – yea, his very hand and foot –
In moments when he feels he cannot die,
And knows himself no vision to himself,
Nor the high God a vision, nor that One
915 Who rose again: ye have seen what ye have seen."

'So spake the King: I knew not all he meant.'

Pelleas and Ettarre

King Arthur made new knights to fill the gap
Left by the Holy Quest; and as he sat
In hall at old Caerleon, the high doors
Were softly sunder'd, and thro' these a youth,   5
Pelleas, and the sweet smell of the fields
Past, and the sunshine came along with him.

'Make me thy knight, because I know, Sir King,
All that belongs to knighthood, and I love.'
Such was his cry: for having heard the King
Had let proclaim a tournament – the prize   10
A golden circlet and a knightly sword,
Full fain had Pelleas for his lady won
The golden circlet, for himself the sword:
And there were those who knew him near the King,
And promised for him: and Arthur made him knight.   15

And this new knight, Sir Pelleas of the isles –
But lately come to his inheritance,
And lord of many a barren isle was he –
Riding at noon, a day or twain before,
Across the forest call'd of Dean, to find   20
Caerleon and the King, had felt the sun
Beat like a strong knight on his helm, and reel'd
Almost to falling from his horse; but saw
Near him a mound of even-sloping side,
Whereon a hundred stately beeches grew,   25
And here and there great hollies under them;
But for a mile all round was open space,
And fern and heath: and slowly Pelleas drew
To that dim day, then binding his good horse
To a tree, cast himself down; and as he lay   30
At random looking over the brown earth

Thro' that green-glooming twilight of the grove,
It seem'd to Pelleas that the fern without
Burnt as a living fire of emeralds,
35 So that his eyes were dazzled looking at it.
Then o'er it crost the dimness of a cloud
Floating, and once the shadow of a bird
Flying, and then a fawn; and his eyes closed.
And since he loved all maidens, but no maid
40 In special, half-awake he whisper'd, 'Where?
O where? I love thee, tho' I know thee not.
For fair thou art and pure as Guinevere,
And I will make thee with my spear and sword
As famous – O my Queen, my Guinevere,
45 For I will be thine Arthur when we meet.'

Suddenly waken'd with a sound of talk
And laughter at the limit of the wood,
And glancing thro' the hoary boles, he saw,
Strange as to some old prophet might have seem'd
50 A vision hovering on a sea of fire,
Damsels in divers colours like the cloud
Of sunset and sunrise, and all of them
On horses, and the horses richly trapt
Breast-high in that bright line of bracken stood:
55 And all the damsels talk'd confusedly,
And one was pointing this way, and one that,
Because the way was lost.

                              And Pelleas rose,
And loosed his horse, and led him to the light.
There she that seem'd the chief among them said,
60 'In happy time behold our pilot-star!
Youth, we are damsels-errant, and we ride,
Arm'd as ye see, to tilt against the knights
There at Caerleon, but have lost our way:
To right? to left? straight forward? back again?
Which? tell us quickly.'

                              Pelleas gazing thought,
'Is Guinevere herself so beautiful?'

For large her violet eyes look'd, and her bloom
A rosy dawn kindled in stainless heavens,
And round her limbs, mature in womanhood;
And slender was her hand and small her shape;   70
And but for those large eyes, the haunts of scorn,
She might have seem'd a toy to trifle with,
And pass and care no more. But while he gazed
The beauty of her flesh abash'd the boy,
As tho' it were the beauty of her soul: 75
For as the base man, judging of the good,
Puts his own baseness in him by default
Of will and nature, so did Pelleas lend
All the young beauty of his own soul to hers,
Believing her; and when she spake to him,   80
Stammer'd, and could not make her a reply.
For out of the waste islands had he come,
Where saving his own sisters he had known
Scarce any but the women of his isles,
Rough wives, that laugh'd and scream'd against the gulls,   85
Makers of nets, and living from the sea.

Then with a slow smile turn'd the lady round
And look'd upon her people; and as when
A stone is flung into some sleeping tarn,
The circle widens till it lip the marge,   90
Spread the slow smile thro' all her company.
Three knights were thereamong; and they too smiled,
Scorning him; for the lady was Ettarre,
And she was a great lady in her land.

Again she said, 'O wild and of the woods,   95
Knowest thou not the fashion of our speech?
Or have the Heavens but given thee a fair face,
Lacking a tongue?'

              'O damsel,' answer'd he,
'I woke from dreams; and coming out of gloom
Was dazzled by the sudden light, and crave   100
Pardon: but will ye to Caerleon? I
Go likewise: shall I lead you to the King?'

'Lead then,' she said; and thro' the woods they went.
And while they rode, the meaning in his eyes,
105 His tenderness of manner, and chaste awe,
His broken utterances and bashfulness,
Were all a burthen to her, and in her heart
She mutter'd, 'I have lighted on a fool,
Raw, yet so stale!' But since her mind was bent
110 On hearing, after trumpet blown, her name
And title, 'Queen of Beauty,' in the lists
Cried – and beholding him so strong, she thought
That peradventure he will fight for me,
And win the circlet: therefore flatter'd him,
115 Being so gracious, that he wellnigh deem'd
His wish by hers was echo'd; and her knights
And all her damsels too were gracious to him,
For she was a great lady.

                    And when they reach'd
Caerleon, ere they past to lodging, she,
120 Taking his hand, 'O the strong hand,' she said,
'See! look at mine! but wilt thou fight for me,
And win me this fine circlet, Pelleas,
That I may love thee?'

                    Then his helpless heart
Leapt, and he cried, 'Ay! wilt thou if I win?'
125 'Ay, that will I,' she answer'd, and she laugh'd,
And straitly nipt the hand, and flung it from her;
Then glanced askew at those three knights of hers,
Till all her ladies laugh'd along with her.

'O happy world,' thought Pelleas, 'all, meseems,
130 Are happy; I the happiest of them all.'
Nor slept that night for pleasure in his blood,
And green wood-ways, and eyes among the leaves;
Then being on the morrow knighted, sware
To love one only. And as he came away,
135 The men who met him rounded on their heels
And wonder'd after him, because his face
Shone like the countenance of a priest of old

234

Against the flame about a sacrifice
Kindled by fire from heaven: so glad was he.

Then Arthur made vast banquets, and strange knights   140
From the four winds came in: and each one sat,
Tho' served with choice from air, land, stream, and sea,
Oft in mid-banquet measuring with his eyes
His neighbour's make and might: and Pelleas look'd
Noble among the noble, for he dream'd   145
His lady loved him, and he knew himself
Loved of the King: and him his new-made knight
Worshipt, whose lightest whisper moved him more
Than all the rangèd reasons of the world.

Then blush'd and brake the morning of the jousts,   150
And this was call'd 'The Tournament of Youth:'
For Arthur, loving his young knight, withheld
His older and his mightier from the lists,
That Pelleas might obtain his lady's love,
According to her promise, and remain   155
Lord of the tourney. And Arthur had the jousts
Down in the flat field by the shore of Usk
Holden: the gilded parapets were crown'd
With faces, and the great tower fill'd with eyes
Up to the summit, and the trumpets blew.   160
There all day long Sir Pelleas kept the field
With honour: so by that strong hand of his
The sword and golden circlet were achieved.

Then rang the shout his lady loved: the heat
Of pride and glory fired her face; her eye   165
Sparkled; she caught the circlet from his lance,
And there before the people crown'd herself:
So for the last time she was gracious to him.

Then at Caerleon for a space – her look
Bright for all others, cloudier on her knight –   170
Linger'd Ettarre: and seeing Pelleas droop,
Said Guinevere, 'We marvel at thee much,
O damsel, wearing this unsunny face

To him who won thee glory!' And she said,
175 'Had ye not held your Lancelot in your bower,
My Queen, he had not won.' Whereat the Queen,
As one whose foot is bitten by an ant,
Glanced down upon her, turn'd and went her way.

But after, when her damsels, and herself,
180 And those three knights all set their faces home,
Sir Pelleas follow'd. She that saw him cried,
'Damsels – and yet I should be shamed to say it –
I cannot bide Sir Baby. Keep him back
Among yourselves. Would rather that we had
185 Some rough old knight who knew the worldly way,
Albeit grizzlier than a bear, to ride
And jest with: take him to you, keep him off,
And pamper him with papmeat, if ye will,
Old milky fables of the wolf and sheep,
190 Such as the wholesome mothers tell their boys.
Nay, should ye try him with a merry one
To find his mettle, good: and if he fly us,
Small matter! let him.' This her damsels heard,
And mindful of her small and cruel hand,
195 They, closing round him thro' the journey home,
Acted her hest, and always from her side
Restrain'd him with all manner of device,
So that he could not come to speech with her.
And when she gain'd her castle, upsprang the bridge,
200 Down rang the grate of iron thro' the groove,
And he was left alone in open field.

'These be the ways of ladies,' Pelleas thought,
'To those who love them, trials of our faith.
Yea, let her prove me to the uttermost,
205 For loyal to the uttermost am I.'
So made his moan; and, darkness falling, sought
A priory not far off, there lodged, but rose
With morning every day, and, moist or dry,
Full-arm'd upon his charger all day long
210 Sat by the walls, and no one open'd to him.

And this persistence turn'd her scorn to wrath.
Then calling her three knights, she charged them, 'Out!
And drive him from the walls.' And out they came,
But Pelleas overthrew them as they dash'd
Against him one by one; and these return'd,   215
But still he kept his watch beneath the wall.

Thereon her wrath became a hate; and once,
A week beyond, while walking on the walls
With her three knights, she pointed downward, 'Look,
He haunts me – I cannot breathe – besieges me;   220
Down! strike him! put my hate into your strokes,
And drive him from my walls.' And down they went,
And Pelleas overthrew them one by one;
And from the tower above him cried Ettarre,
'Bind him, and bring him in.'

              He heard her voice;   225
Then let the strong hand, which had overthrown
Her minion-knights, by those he overthrew
Be bounden straight, and so they brought him in.

Then when he came before Ettarre, the sight
Of her rich beauty made him at one glance   230
More bondsman in his heart than in his bonds.
Yet with good cheer he spake, 'Behold me, Lady,
A prisoner, and the vassal of thy will;
And if thou keep me in thy donjon here,
Content am I so that I see thy face   235
But once a day: for I have sworn my vows,
And thou hast given thy promise, and I know
That all these pains are trials of my faith,
And that thyself, when thou hast seen me strain'd
And sifted to the utmost, wilt at length   240
Yield me thy love and know me for thy knight.'

Then she began to rail so bitterly,
With all her damsels, he was stricken mute;
But when she mock'd his vows and the great King,

245   Lighted on words: 'For pity of thine own self,
        Peace, Lady, peace: is he not thine and mine?'
        'Thou fool,' she said, 'I never heard his voice
        But long'd to break away. Unbind him now,
        And thrust him out of doors; for save he be
250   Fool to the midmost marrow of his bones,
        He will return no more.' And those, her three,
        Laugh'd, and unbound, and thrust him from the gate.

        And after this, a week beyond, again
        She call'd them, saying, 'There he watches yet,
255   There like a dog before his master's door!
        Kick'd, he returns: do ye not hate him, ye?
        Ye know yourselves: how can ye bide at peace,
        Affronted with his fulsome innocence?
        Are ye but creatures of the board and bed,
260   No men to strike? Fall on him all at once,
        And if ye slay him I reck not: if ye fail,
        Give ye the slave mine order to be bound,
        Bind him as heretofore, and bring him in:
        It may be ye shall slay him in his bonds.'

265   She spake; and at her will they couch'd their spears,
        Three against one: and Gawain passing by,
        Bound upon solitary adventure, saw
        Low down beneath the shadow of those towers
        A villainy, three to one: and thro' his heart
270   The fire of honour and all noble deeds
        Flash'd, and he call'd, 'I strike upon thy side –
        The caitiffs!' 'Nay,' said Pelleas, 'but forbear;
        He needs no aid who doth his lady's will.'

        So Gawain, looking at the villainy done,
275   Forbore, but in his heat and eagerness
        Trembled and quiver'd, as the dog, withheld
        A moment from the vermin that he sees
        Before him, shivers, ere he springs and kills.

        And Pelleas overthrew them, one to three;
280   And they rose up, and bound, and brought him in.

Then first her anger, leaving Pelleas, burn'd
Full on her knights in many an evil name
Of craven, weakling, and thrice-beaten hound:
'Yet, take him, ye that scarce are fit to touch,
Far less to bind, your victor, and thrust him out,   285
And let who will release him from his bonds.
And if he comes again' – there she brake short;
And Pelleas answer'd, 'Lady, for indeed
I loved you and I deem'd you beautiful,
I cannot brook to see your beauty marr'd   290
Thro' evil spite: and if ye love me not,
I cannot bear to dream you so forsworn:
I had liefer ye were worthy of my love,
Than to be loved again of you – farewell;
And tho' ye kill my hope, not yet my love,   295
Vex not yourself: ye will not see me more.'

While thus he spake, she gazed upon the man
Of princely bearing, tho' in bonds, and thought,
'Why have I push'd him from me? this man loves,
If love there be: yet him I loved not.Why?   300
I deem'd him fool? yea, so? or that in him
A something – was it nobler than myself? –
Seem'd my reproach? He is not of my kind.
He could not love me, did he know me well.
Nay, let him go – and quickly.' And her knights   305
Laugh'd not, but thrust him bounden out of door.

Forth sprang Gawain, and loosed him from his bonds,
And flung them o'er the walls; and afterward,
Shaking his hands, as from a lazar's rag,
'Faith of my body,' he said, 'and art thou not –   310
Yea thou art he, whom late our Arthur made
Knight of his table; yea and he that won
The circlet? wherefore hast thou so defamed
Thy brotherhood in me and all the rest,
As let these caitiffs on thee work their will?'   315

And Pelleas answer'd, 'O, their wills are hers
For whom I won the circlet; and mine, hers,

239

Thus to be bounden, so to see her face,
Marr'd tho' it be with spite and mockery now,
320   Other than when I found her in the woods;
And tho' she hath me bounden but in spite,
And all to flout me, when they bring me in,
Let me be bounden, I shall see her face;
Else must I die thro' mine unhappiness.'

325   And Gawain answer'd kindly tho' in scorn,
'Why, let my lady bind me if she will,
And let my lady beat me if she will:
But an she send her delegate to thrall
These fighting hands of mine – Christ kill me then
330   But I will slice him handless by the wrist,
And let my lady sear the stump for him,
Howl as he may. But hold me for your friend:
Come, ye know nothing: here I pledge my troth,
Yea, by the honour of the Table Round,
335   I will be leal to thee and work thy work,
And tame thy jailing princess to thine hand.
Lend me thine horse and arms, and I will say
That I have slain thee. She will let me in
To hear the manner of thy fight and fall;
340   Then, when I come within her counsels, then
From prime to vespers will I chant thy praise
As prowest knight and truest lover, more
Than any have sung thee living, till she long
To have thee back in lusty life again,
345   Not to be bound, save by white bonds and warm,
Dearer than freedom. Wherefore now thy horse
And armour: let me go: be comforted:
Give me three days to melt her fancy, and hope
The third night hence will bring thee news of gold.'

350   Then Pelleas lent his horse and all his arms,
Saving the goodly sword, his prize, and took
Gawain's, and said, 'Betray me not, but help –
Art thou not he whom men call light-of-love?'

'Ay,' said Gawain, 'for women be so light.'

Then bounded forward to the castle walls,   355
And raised a bugle hanging from his neck,
And winded it, and that so musically
That all the old echoes hidden in the wall
Rang out like hollow woods at hunting-tide.

Up ran a score of damsels to the tower;   360
'Avaunt,' they cried, 'our lady loves thee not.'
But Gawain lifting up his vizor said,
'Gawain am I, Gawain of Arthur's court,
And I have slain this Pelleas whom ye hate:
Behold his horse and armour. Open gates,   365
And I will make you merry.'

                              And down they ran,
Her damsels, crying to their lady, 'Lo!
Pelleas is dead – he told us – he that hath
His horse and armour: will ye let him in?
He slew him! Gawain, Gawain of the court,   370
Sir Gawain – there he waits below the wall,
Blowing his bugle as who should say him nay.'

And so, leave given, straight on thro' open door
Rode Gawain, whom she greeted courteously.
'Dead, is it so?' she ask'd. 'Ay, ay,' said he,   375
'And oft in dying cried upon your name.'
'Pity on him,' she answer'd, 'a good knight,
But never let me bide one hour at peace.'
'Ay,' thought Gawain, 'and you be fair enow:
But I to your dead man have given my troth,   380
That whom ye loathe, him will I make you love.'

So those three days, aimless about the land,
Lost in a doubt, Pelleas wandering
Waited, until the third night brought a moon
With promise of large light on woods and ways.   385

Hot was the night and silent; but a sound
Of Gawain ever coming, and this lay –
Which Pelleas had heard sung before the Queen,

And seen her sadden listening – vext his heart,
390 And marr'd his rest – 'A worm within the rose.'

'A rose, but one, none other rose had I,
A rose, one rose, and this was wondrous fair,
One rose, a rose that gladden'd earth and sky,
One rose, my rose, that sweeten'd all mine air –
395 I cared not for the thorns; the thorns were there

'One rose, a rose to gather by and by,
One rose, a rose, to gather and to wear,
No rose but one – what other rose had I?
One rose, my rose; a rose that will not die, –
400 He dies who loves it, – if the worm be there.'

This tender rhyme, and evermore the doubt,
'Why lingers Gawain with his golden news?'
So shook him that he could not rest, but rode
Ere midnight to her walls, and bound his horse
405 Hard by the gates. Wide open were the gates,
And no watch kept; and in thro' these he past,
And heard but his own steps, and his own heart
Beating, for nothing moved but his own self,
And his own shadow. Then he crost the court,
410 And spied not any light in hall or bower,
But saw the postern portal also wide
Yawning; and up a slope of garden, all
Of roses white and red, and brambles mixt
And overgrowing them, went on, and found,
415 Here too, all hush'd below the mellow moon,
Save that one rivulet from a tiny cave
Came lightening downward, and so spilt itself
Among the roses, and was lost again.

Then was he ware of three pavilions rear'd
420 Above the bushes, gilden-peakt: in one,
Red after revel, droned her lurdane knights
Slumbering, and their three squires across their feet:
In one, their malice on the placid lip
Froz'n by sweet sleep, four of her damsels lay:

242

And in the third, the circlet of the jousts   425
Bound on her brow, were Gawain and Ettarre.

  Back, as a hand that pushes thro' the leaf
To find a nest and feels a snake, he drew:
Back, as a coward slinks from what he fears
To cope with, or a traitor proven, or hound   430
Beaten, did Pelleas in an utter shame
Creep with his shadow thro' the court again,
Fingering at his sword-handle until he stood
There on the castle-bridge once more, and thought,
'I will go back, and slay them where they lie.'   435

  And so went back, and seeing them yet in sleep
Said, 'Ye, that so dishallow the holy sleep,
Your sleep is death,' and drew the sword, and thought,
'What! slay a sleeping knight? the King hath bound
And sworn me to this brotherhood;' again,   440
'Alas that ever a knight should be so false.'
Then turn'd, and so return'd, and groaning laid
The naked sword athwart their naked throats,
There left it, and them sleeping; and she lay,
The circlet of the tourney round her brows,   445
And the sword of the tourney across her throat.

  And forth he past, and mounting on his horse
Stared at her towers that, larger than themselves
In their own darkness, throng'd into the moon.
Then crush'd the saddle with his thighs, and clench'd   450
His hands, and madden'd with himself and moan'd:

  'Would they have risen against me in their blood
At the last day? I might have answer'd them
Even before high God. O towers so strong,
Huge, solid, would that even while I gaze   455
The crack of earthquake shivering to your base
Split you, and Hell burst up your harlot roofs
Bellowing, and charr'd you thro' and thro' within,
Black as the harlot's heart – hollow as a skull!
Let the fierce east scream thro' your eyelet-holes,   460

And whirl the dust of harlots round and round
In dung and nettles! hiss, snake – I saw him there –
Let the fox bark, let the wolf yell. Who yells
Here in the still sweet summer night, but I –
465   I, the poor Pelleas whom she call'd her fool?
Fool, beast – he, she, or I? myself most fool;
Beast too, as lacking human wit – disgraced,
Dishonour'd all for trial of true love –
Love? – we be all alike: only the King
470   Hath made us fools and liars. O noble vows!
O great and sane and simple race of brutes
That own no lust because they have no law!
For why should I have loved her to my shame?
I loathe her, as I loved her to my shame.
475   I never loved her, I but lusted for her –
Away –'

He dash'd the rowel into his horse,
And bounded forth and vanish'd thro' the night.

Then she, that felt the cold touch on her throat,
Awaking knew the sword, and turn'd herself
480   To Gawain: 'Liar, for thou hast not slain
This Pelleas! here he stood, and might have slain
Me and thyself.' And he that tells the tale
Says that her ever-veering fancy turn'd
To Pelleas, as the one true knight on earth,
485   And only lover; and thro' her love her life
Wasted and pined, desiring him in vain.

But he by wild and way, for half the night,
And over hard and soft, striking the sod
From out the soft, the spark from off the hard,
490   Rode till the star above the wakening sun,
Beside that tower where Percivale was cowl'd,
Glanced from the rosy forehead of the dawn.
For so the words were flash'd into his heart
He knew not whence or wherefore: 'O sweet star,
495   Pure on the virgin forehead of the dawn!'
And there he would have wept, but felt his eyes

Harder and drier than a fountain bed
In summer: thither came the village girls
And linger'd talking, and they come no more
Till the sweet heavens have fill'd it from the heights   500
Again with living waters in the change
Of seasons: hard his eyes; harder his heart
Seem'd; but so weary were his limbs, that he,
Gasping, 'Of Arthur's hall am I, but here,
Here let me rest and die,' cast himself down,   505
And gulf'd his griefs in inmost sleep; so lay,
Till shaken by a dream, that Gawain fired
The hall of Merlin, and the morning star
Reel'd in the smoke, brake into flame, and fell.

He woke, and being ware of some one nigh,   510
Sent hands upon him, as to tear him, crying,
'False! and I held thee pure as Guinevere.'

But Percivale stood near him and replied,
'Am I but false as Guinevere is pure?
Or art thou mazed with dreams? or being one   515
Of our free-spoken Table hast not heard
That Lancelot' – there he check'd himself and paused.

Then fared it with Sir Pelleas as with one
Who gets a wound in battle, and the sword
That made it plunges thro' the wound again,   520
And pricks it deeper: and he shrank and wail'd,
'Is the Queen false?' and Percivale was mute.
'Have any of our Round Table held their vows?'
And Percivale made answer not a word.
'Is the King true?' 'The King!' said Percivale.   525
'Why then let men couple at once with wolves.
What! art thou mad?'

               But Pelleas, leaping up,
Ran thro' the doors and vaulted on his horse
And fled: small pity upon his horse had he,
Or on himself, or any, and when he met   530
A cripple, one that held a hand for alms –

245

Hunch'd as he was, and like an old dwarf-elm
That turns its back on the salt blast, the boy
Paused not, but overrode him, shouting, 'False,
535   And false with Gawain!' and so left him bruised
And batter'd, and fled on, and hill and wood
Went ever streaming by him till the gloom,
That follows on the turning of the world,
Darken'd the common path: he twitch'd the reins,
540   And made his beast that better knew it, swerve
Now off it and now on; but when he saw
High up in heaven the hall that Merlin built,
Blackening against the dead-green stripes of even,
'Black nest of rats,' he groan'd, 'ye build too high.'

545   Not long thereafter from the city gates
Issued Sir Lancelot riding airily,
Warm with a gracious parting from the Queen,
Peace at his heart, and gazing at a star
And marvelling what it was: on whom the boy,
550   Across the silent seeded meadow-grass
Borne, clash'd: and Lancelot, saying, 'What name
                hast thou
That ridest here so blindly and so hard?'
'No name, no name,' he shouted, 'a scourge am I
To lash the treasons of the Table Round.'
555   'Yea, but thy name?' 'I have many names,' he cried:
'I am wrath and shame and hate and evil fame,
And like a poisonous wind I pass to blast
And blaze the crime of Lancelot and the Queen.'
'First over me,' said Lancelot, 'shalt thou pass.'
560   'Fight therefore,' yell'd the youth, and either knight
Drew back a space, and when they closed, at once
The weary steed of Pelleas floundering flung
His rider, who call'd out from the dark field,
'Thou art false as Hell: slay me: I have no sword.'
565   Then Lancelot, 'Yea, between thy lips – and sharp;
But here will I disedge it by thy death.'
'Slay then,' he shriek'd, 'my will is to be slain,'
And Lancelot, with his heel upon the fall'n,

Rolling his eyes, a moment stood, then spake:
'Rise, weakling; I am Lancelot; say thy say.' 570

And Lancelot slowly rode his warhorse back
To Camelot, and Sir Pelleas in brief while
Caught his unbroken limbs from the dark field,
And follow'd to the city. It chanced that both
Brake into hall together, worn and pale. 575
There with her knights and dames was Guinevere.
Full wonderingly she gazed on Lancelot
So soon return'd, and then on Pelleas, him
Who had not greeted her, but cast himself
Down on a bench, hard-breathing. 'Have ye fought?' 580
She ask'd of Lancelot. 'Ay, my Queen,' he said.
'And thou hast overthrown him?' 'Ay, my Queen.'
Then she, turning to Pelleas, 'O young knight,
Hath the great heart of knighthood in thee fail'd
So far thou canst not bide, unfrowardly, 585
A fall from *him*?' Then, for he answer'd not,
'Or hast thou other griefs? If I, the Queen,
May help them, loose thy tongue, and let me know.'
But Pelleas lifted up an eye so fierce
She quail'd; and he, hissing 'I have no sword,' 590
Sprang from the door into the dark. The Queen
Look'd hard upon her lover, he on her;
And each foresaw the dolorous day to be:
And all talk died, as in a grove all song
Beneath the shadow of some bird of prey; 595
Then a long silence came upon the hall,
And Modred thought, 'The time is hard at hand.'

The Last Tournament

Dagonet, the fool, whom Gawain in his mood
Had made mock-knight of Arthur's Table Round,
At Camelot, high above the yellowing woods,
Danced like a wither'd leaf before the hall.
5   And toward him from the hall, with harp in hand,
And from the crown thereof a carcanet
Of ruby swaying to and fro, the prize
Of Tristram in the jousts of yesterday,
Came Tristram, saying, 'Why skip ye so, Sir Fool?'

10   For Arthur and Sir Lancelot riding once
Far down beneath a winding wall of rock
Heard a child wail. A stump of oak half-dead,
From roots like some black coil of carven snakes,
Clutch'd at the crag, and started thro' mid air
15   Bearing an eagle's nest: and thro' the tree
Rush'd ever a rainy wind, and thro' the wind
Pierced ever a child's cry: and crag and tree
Scaling, Sir Lancelot from the perilous nest,
This ruby necklace thrice around her neck,
20   And all unscarr'd from beak or talon, brought
A maiden babe; which Arthur pitying took,
Then gave it to his Queen to rear: the Queen
But coldly acquiescing, in her white arms
Received, and after loved it tenderly,
25   And named it Nestling; so forgot herself
A moment, and her cares; till that young life
Being smitten in mid heaven with mortal cold
Past from her; and in time the carcanet
Vext her with plaintive memories of the child:
30   So she, delivering it to Arthur, said,
'Take thou the jewels of this dead innocence,
And make them, an thou wilt, a tourney-prize.'

To whom the King, 'Peace to thine eagle-borne
Dead nestling, and this honour after death,
Following thy will! but, O my Queen, I muse   35
Why ye not wear on arm, or neck, or zone
Those diamonds that I rescued from the tarn,
And Lancelot won, methought, for thee to wear.'

'Would rather you had let them fall,' she cried,
'Plunge and be lost – ill-fated as they were,   40
A bitterness to me! – ye look amazed,
Not knowing they were lost as soon as given –
Slid from my hands, when I was leaning out
Above the river – that unhappy child
Past in her barge: but rosier luck will go   45
With these rich jewels, seeing that they came
Not from the skeleton of a brother-slayer,
But the sweet body of a maiden babe.
Perchance – who knows? – the purest of thy knights
May win them for the purest of my maids.'   50

She ended, and the cry of a great jousts
With trumpet-blowings ran on all the ways
From Camelot in among the faded fields
To furthest towers; and everywhere the knights
Arm'd for a day of glory before the King.   55

But on the hither side of that loud morn
Into the hall stagger'd, his visage ribb'd
From ear to ear with dogwhip-weals, his nose
Bridge-broken, one eye out, and one hand off,
And one with shatter'd fingers dangling lame,   60
A churl, to whom indignantly the King,

'My churl, for whom Christ died, what evil beast
Hath drawn his claws athwart thy face? or fiend?
Man was it who marr'd heaven's image in thee thus?'

Then, sputtering thro' the hedge of splinter'd teeth,   65
Yet strangers to the tongue, and with blunt stump
Pitch-blacken'd sawing the air, said the maim'd churl,

'He took them and he drave them to his tower –
Some hold he was a table-knight of thine –
70 A hundred goodly ones – the Red Knight, he –
Lord, I was tending swine, and the Red Knight
Brake in upon me and drave them to his tower;
And when I call'd upon thy name as one
That doest right by gentle and by churl,
75 Maim'd me and maul'd, and would outright have slain,
Save that he sware me to a message, saying,
"Tell thou the King and all his liars, that I
Have founded my Round Table in the North,
And whatsoever his own knights have sworn
80 My knights have sworn the counter to it – and say
My tower is full of harlots, like his court,
But mine are worthier, seeing they profess
To be none other than themselves – and say
My knights are all adulterers like his own,
85 But mine are truer, seeing they profess
To be none other; and say his hour is come,
The heathen are upon him, his long lance
Broken, and his Excalibur a straw."'

Then Arthur turn'd to Kay the seneschal,
90 'Take thou my churl, and tend him curiously
Like a king's heir, till all his hurts be whole.
The heathen – but that ever-climbing wave,
Hurl'd back again so often in empty foam,
Hath lain for years at rest – and renegades,
95 Thieves, bandits, leavings of confusion, whom
The wholesome realm is purged of otherwhere,
Friends, thro' your manhood and your fëalty, – now
Make their last head like Satan in the North.
My younger knights, new-made, in whom your flower
100 Waits to be solid fruit of golden deeds,
Move with me toward their quelling, which achieved,
The loneliest ways are safe from shore to shore.
But thou, Sir Lancelot, sitting in my place
Enchair'd to-morrow, arbitrate the field;
105 For wherefore shouldst thou care to mingle with it,

Only to yield my Queen her own again?
Speak, Lancelot, thou art silent: is it well?'

Thereto Sir Lancelot answer'd, 'It is well:
Yet better if the King abide, and leave
The leading of his younger knights to me.   110
Else, for the King has will'd it, it is well.'

Then Arthur rose and Lancelot follow'd him,
And while they stood without the doors, the King
Turn'd to him saying, 'Is it then so well?
Or mine the blame that oft I seem as he   115
Of whom was written, "A sound is in his ears"?
The foot that loiters, bidden go, – the glance
That only seems half-loyal to command, –
A manner somewhat fall'n from reverence –
Or have I dream'd the bearing of our knights   120
Tells of a manhood ever less and lower?
Or whence the fear lest this my realm, uprear'd,
By noble deeds at one with noble vows,
From flat confusion and brute violences,
Reel back into the beast, and be no more?'   125

He spoke, and taking all his younger knights,
Down the slope city rode, and sharply turn'd
North by the gate. In her high bower the Queen,
Working a tapestry, lifted up her head,
Watch'd her lord pass, and knew not that she sigh'd.   130
Then ran across her memory the strange rhyme
Of bygone Merlin, 'Where is he who knows?
From the great deep to the great deep he goes.'

But when the morning of a tournament,
By these in earnest those in mockery call'd   135
The Tournament of the Dead Innocence,
Brake with a wet wind blowing, Lancelot,
Round whose sick head all night, like birds of prey,
The words of Arthur flying shriek'd, arose,
And down a streetway hung with folds of pure   140

251

White samite, and by fountains running wine,
Where children sat in white with cups of gold,
Moved to the lists, and there, with slow sad steps
Ascending, fill'd his double-dragon'd chair.

145   He glanced and saw the stately galleries,
Dame, damsel, each thro' worship of their Queen
White-robed in honour of the stainless child,
And some with scatter'd jewels, like a bank
Of maiden snow mingled with sparks of fire.
150   He look'd but once, and vail'd his eyes again.

The sudden trumpet sounded as in a dream
To ears but half-awaked, then one low roll
Of Autumn thunder, and the jousts began:
And ever the wind blew, and yellowing leaf
155   And gloom and gleam, and shower and shorn plume
Went down it. Sighing weariedly, as one
Who sits and gazes on a faded fire,
When all the goodlier guests are past away,
Sat their great umpire, looking o'er the lists.
160   He saw the laws that ruled the tournament
Broken, but spake not; once, a knight cast down
Before his throne of arbitration cursed
The dead babe and the follies of the King;
And once the laces of a helmet crack'd,
165   And show'd him, like a vermin in its hole,
Modred, a narrow face: anon he heard
The voice that billow'd round the barriers roar
An ocean-sounding welcome to one knight,
But newly-enter'd, taller than the rest,
170   And armour'd all in forest green, whereon
There tript a hundred tiny silver deer,
And wearing but a holly-spray for crest,
With ever-scattering berries, and on shield
A spear, a harp, a bugle – Tristram – late
175   From overseas in Brittany return'd,
And marriage with a princess of that realm,
Isolt the White – Sir Tristram of the Woods –
Whom Lancelot knew, had held sometime with pain

His own against him, and now yearn'd to shake
The burthen off his heart in one full shock   180
With Tristram ev'n to death: his strong hands gript
And dinted the gilt dragons right and left,
Until he groan'd for wrath – so many of those,
That ware their ladies' colours on the casque,
Drew from before Sir Tristram to the bounds,   185
And there with gibes and flickering mockeries
Stood, while he mutter'd, 'Craven crests! O shame!
What faith have these in whom they sware to love?
The glory of our Round Table is no more.'

    So Tristram won, and Lancelot gave, the gems,   190
Not speaking other word than 'Hast thou won?
Art thou the purest, brother? See, the hand
Wherewith thou takest this, is red!' to whom
Tristram, half plagued by Lancelot's languorous mood,
Made answer, 'Ay, but wherefore toss me this   195
Like a dry bone cast to some hungry hound?
Let be thy fair Queen's fantasy. Strength of heart
And might of limb, but mainly use and skill,
Are winners in this pastime of our King.
My hand – belike the lance hath dript upon it –   200
No blood of mine, I trow; but O chief knight,
Right arm of Arthur in the battlefield,
Great brother, thou nor I have made the world;
Be happy in thy fair Queen as I in mine.'

    And Tristram round the gallery made his horse   205
Caracole; then bow'd his homage, bluntly saying,
'Fair damsels, each to him who worships each
Sole Queen of Beauty and of love, behold
This day my Queen of Beauty is not here.'
And most of these were mute, some anger'd, one   210
Murmuring, 'All courtesy is dead,' and one,
'The glory of our Round Table is no more.'

    Then fell thick rain, plume droopt and mantle clung,
And pettish cries awoke, and the wan day
Went glooming down in wet and weariness: 215

But under her black brows a swarthy one
Laugh'd shrilly, crying, 'Praise the patient saints,
Our one white day of Innocence hath past,
Tho' somewhat draggled at the skirt. So be it.
220 The snowdrop only, flowering thro' the year,
Would make the world as blank as Winter-tide.
Come – let us gladden their sad eyes, our Queen's
And Lancelot's, at this night's solemnity
With all the kindlier colours of the field.'

225 So dame and damsel glitter'd at the feast
Variously gay: for he that tells the tale
Liken'd them, saying, as when an hour of cold
Falls on the mountain in midsummer snows,
And all the purple slopes of mountain flowers
230 Pass under white, till the warm hour returns
With veer of wind, and all are flowers again;
So dame and damsel cast the simple white,
And glowing in all colours, the live grass,
Rose-campion, bluebell, kingcup, poppy, glanced
235 About the revels, and with mirth so loud
Beyond all use, that, half-amazed, the Queen,
And wroth at Tristram and the lawless jousts,
Brake up their sports, then slowly to her bower
Parted, and in her bosom pain was lord.

240 And little Dagonet on the morrow morn,
High over all the yellowing Autumn-tide,
Danced like a wither'd leaf before the hall.
Then Tristram saying, 'Why skip ye so, Sir Fool?'
Wheel'd round on either heel, Dagonet replied,
245 'Belike for lack of wiser company;
Or being fool, and seeing too much wit
Makes the world rotten, why, belike I skip
To know myself the wisest knight of all.'
'Ay, fool,' said Tristram, 'but 'tis eating dry
250 To dance without a catch, a roundelay
To dance to.' Then he twangled on his harp,
And while he twangled little Dagonet stood
Quiet as any water-sodden log

Stay'd in the wandering warble of a brook;
But when the twangling ended, skipt again;   255
And being ask'd, 'Why skipt ye not, Sir Fool?'
Made answer, 'I had liefer twenty years
Skip to the broken music of my brains
Than any broken music thou canst make.'
Then Tristram, waiting for the quip to come,   260
'Good now, what music have I broken, fool?'
And little Dagonet, skipping, 'Arthur, the King's;
For when thou playest that air with Queen Isolt,
Thou makest broken music with thy bride,
Her daintier namesake down in Brittany –   265
And so thou breakest Arthur's music too.'
'Save for that broken music in thy brains,
Sir Fool,' said Tristram, 'I would break thy head.
Fool, I came late, the heathen wars were o'er,
The life had flown, we sware but by the shell –   270
I am but a fool to reason with a fool –
Come, thou art crabb'd and sour: but lean me down,
Sir Dagonet, one of thy long asses' ears,
And harken if my music be not true.

' "Free love – free field – we love but while we may: 275
The woods are hush'd, their music is no more:
The leaf is dead, the yearning past away:
New leaf, new life – the days of frost are o'er:
New life, new love, to suit the newer day:
New loves are sweet as those that went before: 280
Free love – free field – we love but while we may."

'Ye might have moved slow measure to my tune,
Not stood stockstill. I made it in the woods,
And heard it ring as true as tested gold.'

But Dagonet with one foot poised in his hand,   285
'Friend, did ye mark that fountain yesterday
Made to run wine? – but this had run itself
All out like a long life to a sour end –
And them that round it sat with golden cups
To hand the wine to whosoever came –   290

The twelve small damosels white as Innocence,
In honour of poor Innocence the babe,
Who left the gems which Innocence the Queen
Lent to the King, and Innocence the King
295   Gave for a prize – and one of those white slips
Handed her cup and piped, the pretty one,
"Drink, drink, Sir Fool," and thereupon I drank,
Spat – pish – the cup was gold, the draught was mud.'

And Tristram, 'Was it muddier than thy gibes?
300   Is all the laughter gone dead out of thee? –
Not marking how the knighthood mock thee, fool –
"Fear God: honour the King – his one true knight –
Sole follower of the vows" – for here be they
Who knew thee swine enow before I came,
305   Smuttier than blasted grain: but when the King
Had made thee fool, thy vanity so shot up
It frighted all free fool from out thy heart;
Which left thee less than fool, and less than swine,
A naked aught – yet swine I hold thee still,
310   For I have flung thee pearls and find thee swine.'

And little Dagonet mincing with his feet,
'Knight, an ye fling those rubies round my neck
In lieu of hers, I'll hold thou hast some touch
Of music, since I care not for thy pearls.
315   Swine? I have wallow'd, I have wash'd – the world
Is flesh and shadow – I have had my day.
The dirty nurse, Experience, in her kind
Hath foul'd me – an I wallow'd, then I wash'd –
I have had my day and my philosophies –
320   And thank the Lord I am King Arthur's fool.
Swine, say ye? swine, goats, asses, rams and geese
Troop'd round a Paynim harper once, who thrumm'd
On such a wire as musically as thou
Some such fine song – but never a king's fool.'

325   And Tristram, 'Then were swine, goats, asses, geese
The wiser fools, seeing thy Paynim bard
Had such a mastery of his mystery
That he could harp his wife up out of hell.'

Then Dagonet, turning on the ball of his foot,
'And whither harp'st thou thine? down! and thyself   330
Down! and two more: a helpful harper thou,
That harpest downward! Dost thou know the star
We call the harp of Arthur up in heaven?'

And Tristram, 'Ay, Sir Fool, for when our King
Was victor wellnigh day by day, the knights,   335
Glorying in each new glory, set his name
High on all hills, and in the signs of heaven.'

And Dagonet answer'd, 'Ay, and when the land
Was freed, and the Queen false, ye set yourself
To babble about him, all to show your wit –   340
And whether he were King by courtesy,
Or King by right – and so went harping down
The black king's highway, got so far, and grew
So witty that ye play'd at ducks and drakes
With Arthur's vows on the great lake of fire.   345
Tuwhoo! do ye see it? do ye see the star?'

'Nay, fool,' said Tristram, 'not in open day.'
And Dagonet, 'Nay, nor will: I see it and hear.
It makes a silent music up in heaven,
And I, and Arthur and the angels hear,   350
And then we skip.' 'Lo, fool,' he said, 'ye talk
Fool's treason: is the King thy brother fool?'
Then little Dagonet clapt his hands and shrill'd,
'Ay, ay, my brother fool, the king of fools!
Conceits himself as God that he can make   355
Figs out of thistles, silk from bristles, milk
From burning spurge, honey from hornet-combs,
And men from beasts – Long live the king of fools!'

And down the city Dagonet danced away;
But thro' the slowly-mellowing avenues   360
And solitary passes of the wood
Rode Tristram toward Lyonnesse and the west.
Before him fled the face of Queen Isolt
With ruby-circled neck, but evermore

365　Past, as a rustle or twitter in the wood
　　　Made dull his inner, keen his outer eye
　　　For all that walk'd, or crept, or perch'd, or flew.
　　　Anon the face, as, when a gust hath blown,
　　　Unruffling waters re-collect the shape
370　Of one that in them sees himself, return'd;
　　　But at the slot or fewmets of a deer,
　　　Or ev'n a fall'n feather, vanish'd again.

　　　So on for all that day from lawn to lawn
　　　Thro' many a league-long bower he rode. At length
375　A lodge of intertwisted beechen-boughs
　　　Furze-cramm'd, and bracken-rooft, the which himself
　　　Built for a summer day with Queen Isolt
　　　Against a shower, dark in the golden grove
　　　Appearing, sent his fancy back to where
380　She lived a moon in that low lodge with him:
　　　Till Mark her lord had past, the Cornish King,
　　　With six or seven, when Tristram was away,
　　　And snatch'd her thence; yet dreading worse than shame
　　　Her warrior Tristram, spake not any word,
385　But bode his hour, devising wretchedness.

　　　And now that desert lodge to Tristram lookt
　　　So sweet, that halting, in he past, and sank
　　　Down on a drift of foliage random-blown;
　　　But could not rest for musing how to smoothe
390　And sleek his marriage over to the Queen.
　　　Perchance in lone Tintagil far from all
　　　The tonguesters of the court she had not heard.
　　　But then what folly had sent him overseas
　　　After she left him lonely here? a name?
395　Was it the name of one in Brittany,
　　　Isolt, the daughter of the King? 'Isolt
　　　Of the white hands' they call'd her: the sweet name
　　　Allured him first, and then the maid herself,
　　　Who served him well with those white hands of hers,
400　And loved him well, until himself had thought
　　　He loved her also, wedded easily,
　　　But left her all as easily, and return'd.

The black-blue Irish hair and Irish eyes
Had drawn him home – what marvel? then he laid
His brows upon the drifted leaf and dream'd.   405

He seem'd to pace the strand of Brittany
Between Isolt of Britain and his bride,
And show'd them both the ruby-chain, and both
Began to struggle for it, till his Queen
Graspt it so hard, that all her hand was red.   410
Then cried the Breton, 'Look, her hand is red!
These be no rubies, this is frozen blood,
And melts within her hand – her hand is hot
With ill desires, but this I gave thee, look,
Is all as cool and white as any flower.'   415
Follow'd a rush of eagle's wings, and then
A whimpering of the spirit of the child,
Because the twain had spoil'd her carcanet.

He dream'd; but Arthur with a hundred spears
Rode far, till o'er the illimitable reed,   420
And many a glancing plash and sallowy isle,
The wide-wing'd sunset of the misty marsh
Glared on a huge machicolated tower
That stood with open doors, whereout was roll'd   425
A roar of riot, as from men secure
Amid their marshes, ruffians at their ease
Among their harlot-brides, an evil song.
'Lo there,' said one of Arthur's youth, for there,
High on a grim dead tree before the tower,   430
A goodly brother of the Table Round
Swung by the neck: and on the boughs a shield
Showing a shower of blood in a field noir,
And therebeside a horn, inflamed the knights
At that dishonour done the gilded spur,   435
Till each would clash the shield, and blow the horn.
But Arthur waved them back. Alone he rode.
Then at the dry harsh roar of the great horn,
That sent the face of all the marsh aloft
An ever upward-rushing storm and cloud   440
Of shriek and plume, the Red Knight heard, and all,

Even to tipmost lance and topmost helm,
In blood-red armour sallying, howl'd to the King,

    'The teeth of Hell flay bare and gnash thee flat! –
Lo! art thou not that eunuch-hearted King
445 Who fain had clipt free manhood from the world –
The woman-worshipper? Yea, God's curse, and I!
Slain was the brother of my paramour
By a knight of thine, and I that heard her whine
And snivel, being eunuch-hearted too,
450 Sware by the scorpion-worm that twists in hell,
And stings itself to everlasting death,
To hang whatever knight of thine I fought
And tumbled. Art thou King? – Look to thy life!'

    He ended: Arthur knew the voice; the face
455 Wellnigh was helmet-hidden, and the name
Went wandering somewhere darkling in his mind.
And Arthur deign'd not use of word or sword,
But let the drunkard, as he stretch'd from horse
To strike him, overbalancing his bulk,
460 Down from the causeway heavily to the swamp
Fall, as the crest of some slow-arching wave,
Heard in dead night along that table-shore,
Drops flat, and after the great waters break
Whitening for half a league, and thin themselves,
465 Far over sands marbled with moon and cloud,
From less and less to nothing; thus he fell
Head-heavy; then the knights, who watch'd him, roar'd
And shouted and leapt down upon the fall'n;
There trampled out his face from being known,
470 And sank his head in mire, and slimed themselves:
Nor heard the King for their own cries, but sprang
Thro' open doors, and swording right and left
Men, women, on their sodden faces, hurl'd
The tables over and the wines, and slew
475 Till all the rafters rang with woman-yells,
And all the pavement stream'd with massacre:
Then, echoing yell with yell, they fired the tower,
Which half that autumn night, like the live North,

Red-pulsing up thro' Alioth and Alcor,
Made all above it, and a hundred meres   480
About it, as the water Moab saw
Come round by the East, and out beyond them flush'd
The long low dune, and lazy-plunging sea.

So all the ways were safe from shore to shore,   485
But in the heart of Arthur pain was lord.

Then, out of Tristram waking, the red dream
Fled with a shout, and that low lodge return'd,
Mid-forest, and the wind among the boughs.
He whistled his good warhorse left to graze
Among the forest greens, vaulted upon him,   490
And rode beneath an ever-showering leaf,
Till one lone woman, weeping near a cross,
Stay'd him. 'Why weep ye?' 'Lord,' she said, 'my man
Hath left me or is dead;' whereon he thought –
'What, if she hate me now? I would not this.   495
What, if she love me still? I would not that.
I know not what I would' – but said to her,
'Yet weep not thou, lest, if thy mate return,
He find thy favour changed and love thee not' –
Then pressing day by day thro' Lyonnesse   500
Last in a roky hollow, belling, heard
The hounds of Mark, and felt the goodly hounds
Yelp at his heart, but turning, past and gain'd
Tintagil, half in sea, and high on land,
A crown of towers.

                         Down in a casement sat,   505
A low sea-sunset glorying round her hair
And glossy-throated grace, Isolt the Queen.
And when she heard the feet of Tristram grind
The spiring stone that scaled about her tower,
Flush'd, started, met him at the doors, and there   510
Belted his body with her white embrace,
Crying aloud, 'Not Mark – not Mark, my soul!
The footstep flutter'd me at first: not he:
Catlike thro' his own castle steals my Mark,

515 But warrior-wise thou stridest thro' his halls
Who hates thee, as I him – ev'n to the death.
My soul, I felt my hatred for my Mark
Quicken within me, and knew that thou wert nigh.'
To whom Sir Tristram smiling, 'I am here.
520 Let be thy Mark, seeing he is not thine.'

And drawing somewhat backward she replied,
'Can he be wrong'd who is not ev'n his own,
But save for dread of thee had beaten me,
Scratch'd, bitten, blinded, marr'd me somehow – Mark?
525 What rights are his that dare not strike for them?
Not lift a hand – not, tho' he found me thus!
But harken! have ye met him? hence he went
To-day for three days' hunting – as he said –
And so returns belike within an hour.
530 Mark's way, my soul! – but eat not thou with Mark,
Because he hates thee even more than fears;
Nor drink: and when thou passest any wood
Close vizor, lest an arrow from the bush
Should leave me all alone with Mark and hell.
535 My God, the measure of my hate for Mark
Is as the measure of my love for thee.'

So, pluck'd one way by hate and one by love,
Drain'd of her force, again she sat, and spake
To Tristram, as he knelt before her, saying,
540 'O hunter, and O blower of the horn,
Harper, and thou hast been a rover too,
For, ere I mated with my shambling king,
Ye twain had fallen out about the bride
Of one – his name is out of me – the prize,
545 If prize she were – (what marvel – she could see) –
Thine, friend; and ever since my craven seeks
To wreck thee villainously: but, O Sir Knight,
What dame or damsel have ye kneel'd to last?'

And Tristram, 'Last to my Queen Paramount,
550 Here now to my Queen Paramount of love
And loveliness – ay, lovelier than when first

262

Her light feet fell on our rough Lyonnesse,
Sailing from Ireland.'

         Softly laugh'd Isolt;
'Flatter me not, for hath not our great Queen
My dole of beauty trebled?' and he said,   555
'Her beauty is her beauty, and thine thine,
And thine is more to me – soft, gracious, kind –
Save when thy Mark is kindled on thy lips
Most gracious; but she, haughty, ev'n to him,
Lancelot; for I have seen him wan enow   560
To make one doubt if ever the great Queen
Have yielded him her love.'

         To whom Isolt,
'Ah then, false hunter and false harper, thou
Who brakest thro' the scruple of my bond,
Calling me thy white hind, and saying to me   565
That Guinevere had sinn'd against the highest,
And I – misyoked with such a want of man –
That I could hardly sin against the lowest.'

He answer'd, 'O my soul, be comforted!
If this be sweet, to sin in leading-strings,   570
If here be comfort, and if ours be sin,
Crown'd warrant had we for the crowning sin
That made us happy: but how ye greet me – fear
And fault and doubt – no word of that fond tale –
Thy deep heart-yearnings, thy sweet memories   575
Of Tristram in that year he was away.'

And, saddening on the sudden, spake Isolt,
'I had forgotten all in my strong joy
To see thee – yearnings? – ay! for, hour by hour,
Here in the never-ended afternoon,   580
O sweeter than all memories of thee,
Deeper than any yearnings after thee
Seem'd those far-rolling, westward-smiling seas,
Watch'd from this tower. Isolt of Britain dash'd
Before Isolt of Brittany on the strand,   585

Would that have chill'd her bride-kiss? Wedded her?
Fought in her father's battles? wounded there?
The King was all fulfill'd with gratefulness,
And she, my namesake of the hands, that heal'd
590   Thy hurt and heart with unguent and caress –
Well – can I wish her any huger wrong
Than having known thee? her too hast thou left
To pine and waste in those sweet memories.
O were I not my Mark's, by whom all men
595   Are noble, I should hate thee more than love.'

And Tristram, fondling her light hands, replied,
'Grace, Queen, for being loved: she loved me well.
Did I love her? the name at least I loved.
Isolt? – I fought his battles, for Isolt!
600   The night was dark; the true star set. Isolt!
The name was ruler of the dark – Isolt?
Care not for her! patient, and prayerful, meek,
Pale-blooded, she will yield herself to God.'

And Isolt answer'd, 'Yea, and why not I?
605   Mine is the larger need, who am not meek,
Pale-blooded, prayerful. Let me tell thee now.
Here one black, mute midsummer night I sat,
Lonely, but musing on thee, wondering where,
Murmuring a light song I had heard thee sing,
610   And once or twice I spake thy name aloud.
Then flash'd a levin-brand; and near me stood,
In fuming sulphur blue and green, a fiend –
Mark's way to steal behind one in the dark –
For there was Mark: "He has wedded her," he said,
615   Not said, but hiss'd it: then this crown of towers
So shook to such a roar of all the sky,
That here in utter dark I swoon'd away,
And woke again in utter dark, and cried,
"I will flee hence and give myself to God" –
620   And thou wert lying in thy new leman's arms.'

Then Tristram, ever dallying with her hand,
'May God be with thee, sweet, when old and gray,

264

And past desire!' a saying that anger'd her.
'"May God be with thee, sweet, when thou art old,
And sweet no more to me!" I need Him now.   625
For when had Lancelot utter'd aught so gross
Ev'n to the swineherd's malkin in the mast?
The greater man, the greater courtesy.
Far other was the Tristram, Arthur's knight!
But thou, thro' ever harrying thy wild beasts –   630
Save that to touch a harp, tilt with a lance
Becomes thee well – art grown wild beast thyself.
How darest thou, if lover, push me even
In fancy from thy side, and set me far
In the gray distance, half a life away,   635
Her to be loved no more? Unsay it, unswear!
Flatter me rather, seeing me so weak,
Broken with Mark and hate and solitude,
Thy marriage and mine own, that I should suck
Lies like sweet wines: lie to me: I believe.   640
Will ye not lie? not swear, as there ye kneel,
And solemnly as when ye sware to him,
The man of men, our King – My God, the power
Was once in vows when men believed the King!
They lied not then, who sware, and thro' their vows 645
The King prevailing made his realm: – I say,
Swear to me thou wilt love me ev'n when old,
Gray-hair'd, and past desire, and in despair.'

    Then Tristram, pacing moodily up and down,
'Vows! did you keep the vow you made to Mark   650
More than I mine? Lied, say ye? Nay, but learnt,
The vow that binds too strictly snaps itself –
My knighthood taught me this – ay, being snapt –
We run more counter to the soul thereof
Than had we never sworn. I swear no more.   655
I swore to the great King, and am forsworn.
For once – ev'n to the height – I honour'd him.
"Man, is he man at all?" methought, when first
I rode from our rough Lyonnesse, and beheld
That victor of the Pagan throned in hall –   660
His hair, a sun that ray'd from off a brow

Like hillsnow high in heaven, the steel-blue eyes,
The golden beard that clothed his lips with light –
Moreover, that weird legend of his birth,
665 With Merlin's mystic babble about his end
Amazed me; then, his foot was on a stool
Shaped as a dragon; he seem'd to me no man,
But Michaël trampling Satan; so I sware,
Being amazed: but this went by – The vows!
670 O ay – the wholesome madness of an hour –
They served their use, their time; for every knight
Believed himself a greater than himself,
And every follower eyed him as a God;
Till he, being lifted up beyond himself,
675 Did mightier deeds than elsewise he had done,
And so the realm was made; but then their vows –
First mainly thro' that sullying of our Queen –
Began to gall the knighthood, asking whence
Had Arthur right to bind them to himself?
680 Dropt down from heaven? wash'd up from out the deep?
They fail'd to trace him thro' the flesh and blood
Of our old kings: whence then? a doubtful lord
To bind them by inviolable vows,
Which flesh and blood perforce would violate:
685 For feel this arm of mine – the tide within
Red with free chase and heather-scented air,
Pulsing full man; can Arthur make me pure
As any maiden child? lock up my tongue
From uttering freely what I freely hear?
690 Bind me to one? The wide world laughs at it.
And worldling of the world am I, and know
The ptarmigan that whitens ere his hour
Woos his own end; we are not angels here
Nor shall be: vows – I am woodman of the woods,
695 And hear the garnet-headed yaffingale
Mock them: my soul, we love but while we may;
And therefore is my love so large for thee,
Seeing it is not bounded save by love.'

Here ending, he moved toward her, and she said,
700 'Good: an I turn'd away my love for thee

To some one thrice as courteous as thyself –
For courtesy wins woman all as well
As valour may, but he that closes both
Is perfect, he is Lancelot – taller indeed,
Rosier and comelier, thou – but say I loved   705
This knightliest of all knights, and cast thee back
Thine own small saw, "We love but while we may,"
Well then, what answer?'

                 He that while she spake,
Mindful of what he brought to adorn her with,
The jewels, had let one finger lightly touch   710
The warm white apple of her throat, replied,
'Press this a little closer, sweet, until –
Come, I am hunger'd and half-anger'd – meat,
Wine, wine – and I will love thee to the death,
And out beyond into the dream to come.'   715

So then, when both were brought to full accord,
She rose, and set before him all he will'd;
And after these had comforted the blood
With meats and wines, and satiated their hearts –
Now talking of their woodland paradise,   720
The deer, the dews, the fern, the founts, the lawns;
Now mocking at the much ungainliness,
And craven shifts, and long crane legs of Mark –
Then Tristram laughing caught the harp, and sang:

'Ay, ay, O ay – the winds that bend the brier!   725
A star in heaven, a star within the mere!
Ay, ay, O ay – a star was my desire,
And one was far apart, and one was near:
Ay, ay, O ay – the winds that bow the grass!
And one was water and one star was fire,   730
And one will ever shine and one will pass.
Ay, ay, O ay – the winds that move the mere.'

Then in the light's last glimmer Tristram show'd
And swung the ruby carcanet. She cried,
'The collar of some Order, which our King   735

Hath newly founded, all for thee, my soul,
For thee, to yield thee grace beyond thy peers.'

'Not so, my Queen,' he said, 'but the red fruit
Grown on a magic oak-tree in mid-heaven,
740 And won by Tristram as a tourney-prize,
And hither brought by Tristram for his last
Love-offering and peace-offering unto thee.'

He spoke, he turn'd, then, flinging round her neck,
Claspt it, and cried 'Thine Order, O my Queen!'
745 But, while he bow'd to kiss the jewell'd throat,
Out of the dark, just as the lips had touch'd,
Behind him rose a shadow and a shriek –
'Mark's way,' said Mark, and clove him thro' the brain.

That night came Arthur home, and while he climb'd,
750 All in a death-dumb autumn-dripping gloom,
The stairway to the hall, and look'd and saw
The great Queen's bower was dark, – about his feet
A voice clung sobbing till he question'd it,
'What art thou?' and the voice about his feet
755 Sent up an answer, sobbing, 'I am thy fool,
And I shall never make thee smile again.'

Guinevere

Queen Guinevere had fled the court, and sat
There in the holy house at Almesbury
Weeping, none with her save a little maid,
A novice: one low light betwixt them burn'd
Blurr'd by the creeping mist, for all abroad, 5
Beneath a moon unseen albeit at full,
The white mist, like a face-cloth to the face,
Clung to the dead earth, and the land was still.

For hither had she fled, her cause of flight
Sir Modred; he that like a subtle beast 10
Lay couchant with his eyes upon the throne,
Ready to spring, waiting a chance: for this
He chill'd the popular praises of the King
With silent smiles of slow disparagement;
And tamper'd with the Lords of the White Horse, 15
Heathen, the brood by Hengist left; and sought
To make disruption in the Table Round
Of Arthur, and to splinter it into feuds
Serving his traitorous end; and all his aims
Were sharpen'd by strong hate for Lancelot. 20

For thus it chanced one morn when all the court,
Green-suited, but with plumes that mock'd the may,
Had been, their wont, a-maying and return'd,
That Modred still in green, all ear and eye,
Climb'd to the high top of the garden-wall 25
To spy some secret scandal if he might,
And saw the Queen who sat betwixt her best
Enid, and lissome Vivien, of her court
The wiliest and the worst; and more than this
He saw not, for Sir Lancelot passing by 30
Spied where he couch'd, and as the gardener's hand

Picks from the colewort a green caterpillar,
So from the high wall and the flowering grove
Of grasses Lancelot pluck'd him by the heel,
35   And cast him as a worm upon the way;
But when he knew the Prince tho' marr'd with dust,
He, reverencing king's blood in a bad man,
Made such excuses as he might, and these
Full knightly without scorn; for in those days
40   No knight of Arthur's noblest dealt in scorn;
But, if a man were halt or hunch'd, in him
By those whom God had made full-limb'd and tall,
Scorn was allow'd as part of his defect,
And he was answer'd softly by the King
45   And all his Table. So Sir Lancelot holp
To raise the Prince, who rising twice or thrice
Full sharply smote his knees, and smiled, and went:
But, ever after, the small violence done
Rankled in him and ruffled all his heart,
50   As the sharp wind that ruffles all day long
A little bitter pool about a stone
On the bare coast.

                    But when Sir Lancelot told
This matter to the Queen, at first she laugh'd
Lightly, to think of Modred's dusty fall,
55   Then shudder'd, as the village wife who cries
'I shudder, some one steps across my grave;'
Then laugh'd again, but faintlier, for indeed
She half-foresaw that he, the subtle beast,
Would track her guilt until he found, and hers
60   Would be for evermore a name of scorn.
Henceforward rarely could she front in hall,
Or elsewhere, Modred's narrow foxy face,
Heart-hiding smile, and gray persistent eye:
Henceforward too, the Powers that tend the soul,
65   To help it from the death that cannot die,
And save it even in extremes, began
To vex and plague her. Many a time for hours,
Beside the placid breathings of the King,
In the dead night, grim faces came and went

Before her, or a vague spiritual fear –   70
Like to some doubtful noise of creaking doors,
Heard by the watcher in a haunted house,
That keeps the rust of murder on the walls –
Held her awake: or if she slept, she dream'd
An awful dream; for then she seem'd to stand   75
On some vast plain before a setting sun,
And from the sun there swiftly made at her
A ghastly something, and its shadow flew
Before it, till it touch'd her, and she turn'd –
When lo! her own, that broadening from her feet,   80
And blackening, swallow'd all the land, and in it
Far cities burnt, and with a cry she woke.
And all this trouble did not pass but grew;
Till ev'n the clear face of the guileless King,
And trustful courtesies of household life,   85
Became her bane; and at the last she said,
'O Lancelot, get thee hence to thine own land,
For if thou tarry we shall meet again,
And if we meet again, some evil chance
Will make the smouldering scandal break and blaze   90
Before the people, and our lord the King.'
And Lancelot ever promised, but remain'd,
And still they met and met. Again she said,
'O Lancelot, if thou love me get thee hence.'
And then they were agreed upon a night   95
(When the good King should not be there) to meet
And part for ever. Vivien, lurking, heard..
She told Sir Modred. Passion-pale they met
And greeted. Hands in hands, and eye to eye,
Low on the border of her couch they sat   100
Stammering and staring. It was their last hour,
A madness of farewells. And Modred brought
His creatures to the basement of the tower
For testimony; and crying with full voice
'Traitor, come out, ye are trapt at last,' aroused
Lancelot, who rushing outward lionlike
Leapt on him, and hurl'd him headlong, and he fell 105
Stunn'd, and his creatures took and bare him off,
And all was still: then she, 'The end is come,

110 And I am shamed for ever;' and he said,
    'Mine be the shame; mine was the sin: but rise,
    And fly to my strong castle overseas:
    There will I hide thee, till my life shall end,
    There hold thee with my life against the world.'
115 She answer'd, 'Lancelot, wilt thou hold me so?
    Nay, friend, for we have taken our farewells.
    Would God that thou couldst hide me from myself!
    Mine is the shame, for I was wife, and thou
    Unwedded: yet rise now, and let us fly,
120 For I will draw me into sanctuary,
    And bide my doom.' So Lancelot got her horse,
    Set her thereon, and mounted on his own,
    And then they rode to the divided way,
    There kiss'd, and parted weeping: for he past,
125 Love-loyal to the least wish of the Queen,
    Back to his land; but she to Almesbury
    Fled all night long by glimmering waste and weald,
    And heard the Spirits of the waste and weald
    Moan as she fled, or thought she heard them moan:
130 And in herself she moan'd 'Too late, too late!'
    Till in the cold wind that foreruns the morn,
    A blot in heaven, the Raven, flying high,
    Croak'd, and she thought, 'He spies a field of death;
    For now the Heathen of the Northern Sea,
135 Lured by the crimes and frailties of the court,
    Begin to slay the folk, and spoil the land.'

    And when she came to Almesbury she spake
    There to the nuns, and said, 'Mine enemies
    Pursue me, but, O peaceful Sisterhood,
140 Receive, and yield me sanctuary, nor ask
    Her name to whom ye yield it, till her time
    To tell you:' and her beauty, grace and power,
    Wrought as a charm upon them, and they spared
    To ask it.

                    So the stately Queen abode
145 For many a week, unknown, among the nuns;
    Nor with them mix'd, nor told her name, nor sought,

Wrapt in her grief, for housel or for shrift,
But communed only with the little maid,
Who pleased her with a babbling heedlessness
Which often lured her from herself; but now,   150
This night, a rumour wildly blown about
Came, that Sir Modred had usurp'd the realm,
And leagued him with the heathen, while the King
Was waging war on Lancelot: then she thought,
'With what a hate the people and the King   155
Must hate me,' and bow'd down upon her hands
Silent, until the little maid, who brook'd
No silence, brake it, uttering 'Late! so late!
What hour, I wonder, now?' and when she drew
No answer, by and by began to hum   160
An air the nuns had taught her; 'Late, so late!'
Which when she heard, the Queen look'd up, and said,
'O maiden, if indeed ye list to sing,
Sing, and unbind my heart that I may weep.'
Whereat full willingly sang the little maid.   165

   'Late, late, so late! and dark the night and chill!
Late, late, so late! but we can enter still.
Too late, too late! ye cannot enter now.

   'No light had we: for that we do repent;
And learning this, the bridegroom will relent.   170
Too late, too late! ye cannot enter now.

   'No light: so late! and dark and chill the night!
O let us in, that we may find the light!
Too late, too late: ye cannot enter now.

   'Have we not heard the bridegroom is so sweet?   175
O let us in, tho' late, to kiss his feet!
No, no, too late! ye cannot enter now.'

   So sang the novice, while full passionately,
Her head upon her hands, remembering
Her thought when first she came, wept the sad Queen.   180
Then said the little novice prattling to her,

'O pray you, noble lady, weep no more;
But let my words, the words of one so small,
Who knowing nothing knows but to obey,
185 And if I do not there is penance given –
Comfort your sorrows; for they do not flow
From evil done; right sure am I of that,
Who see your tender grace and stateliness.
But weigh your sorrows with our lord the King's,
190 And weighing find them less; for gone is he
To wage grim war against Sir Lancelot there,
Round that strong castle where he holds the Queen;
And Modred whom he left in charge of all,
The traitor – Ah sweet lady, the King's grief
195 For his own self, and his own Queen, and realm,
Must needs be thrice as great as any of ours.
For me, I thank the saints, I am not great.
For if there ever come a grief to me
I cry my cry in silence, and have done.
200 None knows it, and my tears have brought me good:
But even were the griefs of little ones
As great as those of great ones, yet this grief
Is added to the griefs the great must bear,
That howsoever much they may desire
205 Silence, they cannot weep behind a cloud:
As even here they talk at Almesbury
About the good King and his wicked Queen,
And were I such a King with such a Queen,
Well might I wish to veil her wickedness,
210 But were I such a King, it could not be.'

Then to her own sad heart mutter'd the Queen,
'Will the child kill me with her innocent talk?'
But openly she answer'd, 'Must not I,
If this false traitor have displaced his lord,
215 Grieve with the common grief of all the realm?'

'Yea,' said the maid, 'this is all woman's grief,
That *she* is woman, whose disloyal life
Hath wrought confusion in the Table Round
Which good King Arthur founded, years ago,

With signs and miracles and wonders, there   220
At Camelot, ere the coming of the Queen.'

    Then thought the Queen within herself again,
'Will the child kill me with her foolish prate?'
But openly she spake and said to her,
'O little maid, shut in by nunnery walls,   225
What canst thou know of Kings and Tables Round,
Or what of signs and wonders, but the signs
And simple miracles of thy nunnery?'

    To whom the little novice garrulously,
'Yea, but I know: the land was full of signs   230
And wonders ere the coming of the Queen.
So said my father, and himself was knight
Of the great Table – at the founding of it;
And rode thereto from Lyonnesse, and he said
That as he rode, an hour or maybe twain   235
After the sunset, down the coast, he heard
Strange music, and he paused, and turning – there,
All down the lonely coast of Lyonnesse,
Each with a beacon-star upon his head,
And with a wild sea-light about his feet,   240
He saw them – headland after headland flame
Far on into the rich heart of the west:
And in the light the white mermaiden swam,
And strong man-breasted things stood from the sea,
And sent a deep sea-voice thro' all the land,   245
To which the little elves of chasm and cleft
Made answer, sounding like a distant horn.
So said my father – yea, and furthermore,
Next morning, while he past the dim-lit woods,
Himself beheld three spirits mad with joy   250
Come dashing down on a tall wayside flower,
That shook beneath them, as the thistle shakes
When three gray linnets wrangle for the seed:
And still at evenings on before his horse
The flickering fairy-circle wheel'd and broke   255
Flying, and link'd again, and wheel'd and broke
Flying, for all the land was full of life.

And when at last he came to Camelot,
A wreath of airy dancers hand-in-hand
260   Swung round the lighted lantern of the hall;
And in the hall itself was such a feast
As never man had dream'd; for every knight
Had whatsoever meat he long'd for served
By hands unseen; and even as he said
265   Down in the cellars merry bloated things
Shoulder'd the spigot, straddling on the butts
While the wine ran: so glad were spirits and men
Before the coming of the sinful Queen.'

Then spake the Queen and somewhat bitterly,
270   'Were they so glad? ill prophets were they all,
Spirits and men: could none of them foresee,
Not even thy wise father with his signs
And wonders, what has fall'n upon the realm?'

To whom the novice garrulously again,
275   'Yea, one, a bard; of whom my father said,
Full many a noble war-song had he sung,
Ev'n in the presence of an enemy's fleet,
Between the steep cliff and the coming wave;
And many a mystic lay of life and death
280   Had chanted on the smoky mountain-tops,
When round him bent the spirits of the hills
With all their dewy hair blown back like flame:
So said my father – and that night the bard
Sang Arthur's glorious wars, and sang the King
285   As wellnigh more than man, and rail'd at those
Who call'd him the false son of Gorloïs:
For there was no man knew from whence he came;
But after tempest, when the long wave broke
All down the thundering shores of Bude and Bos,
290   There came a day as still as heaven, and then
They found a naked child upon the sands
Of dark Tintagil by the Cornish sea;
And that was Arthur; and they foster'd him
Till he by miracle was approven King:
295   And that his grave should be a mystery

From all men, like his birth; and could he find
A woman in her womanhood as great
As he was in his manhood, then, he sang,
The twain together well might change the world.
But even in the middle of his song   300
He falter'd, and his hand fell from the harp,
And pale he turn'd, and reel'd, and would have fall'n,
But that they stay'd him up; nor would he tell
His vision; but what doubt that he foresaw
This evil work of Lancelot and the Queen?'   305

     Then thought the Queen, 'Lo! they have set her on,
Our simple-seeming Abbess and her nuns,
To play upon me,' and bow'd her head nor spake.
Whereat the novice crying, with clasp'd hands,
Shame on her own garrulity garrulously,   310
Said the good nuns would check her gadding tongue
Full often, 'and, sweet lady, if I seem
To vex an ear too sad to listen to me,
Unmannerly, with prattling and the tales
Which my good father told me, check me too   315
Nor let me shame my father's memory, one
Of noblest manners, tho' himself would say
Sir Lancelot had the noblest; and he died,
Kill'd in a tilt, come next, five summers back,
And left me; but of others who remain,   320
And of the two first-famed for courtesy –
And pray you check me if I ask amiss –
But pray you, which had noblest, while you moved
Among them, Lancelot or our lord the King?'

     Then the pale Queen look'd up and answer'd her,   325
'Sir Lancelot, as became a noble knight,
Was gracious to all ladies, and the same
In open battle or the tilting-field
Forbore his own advantage, and the King
In open battle or the tilting-field   330
Forbore his own advantage, and these two
Were the most nobly-manner'd men of all;
For manners are not idle, but the fruit
Of loyal nature, and of noble mind.'

335 'Yea,' said the maid, 'be manners such fair fruit?
Then Lancelot's needs must be a thousand-fold
Less noble, being, as all rumour runs,
The most disloyal friend in all the world.'

To which a mournful answer made the Queen:
340 'O closed about by narrowing nunnery-walls,
What knowest thou of the world, and all its lights
And shadows, all the wealth and all the woe?
If ever Lancelot, that most noble knight,
Were for one hour less noble than himself,
345 Pray for him that he scape the doom of fire,
And weep for her who drew him to his doom.'

'Yea,' said the little novice, 'I pray for both;
But I should all as soon believe that his,
Sir Lancelot's, were as noble as the King's,
350 As I could think, sweet lady, yours would be
Such as they are, were you the sinful Queen.'

So she, like many another babbler, hurt
Whom she would soothe, and harm'd where she
        would heal;
For here a sudden flush of wrathful heat
355 Fired all the pale face of the Queen, who cried,
'Such as thou art be never maiden more
For ever! thou their tool, set on to plague
And play upon, and harry me, petty spy
And traitress.' When that storm of anger brake
360 From Guinevere, aghast the maiden rose,
White as her veil, and stood before the Queen
As tremulously as foam upon the beach
Stands in a wind, ready to break and fly,
And when the Queen had added 'Get thee hence,'
365 Fled frighted. Then that other left alone
Sigh'd, and began to gather heart again,
Saying in herself, 'The simple, fearful child
Meant nothing, but my own too-fearful guilt,
Simpler than any child, betrays itself.
370 But help me, heaven, for surely I repent.

For what is true repentance but in thought –
Not ev'n in inmost thought to think again
The sins that made the past so pleasant to us:
And I have sworn never to see him more,
To see him more.'

           And ev'n in saying this,   375
Her memory from old habit of the mind
Went slipping back upon the golden days
In which she saw him first, when Lancelot came,
Reputed the best knight and goodliest man,
Ambassador, to lead her to his lord   380
Arthur, and led her forth, and far ahead
Of his and her retinue moving, they,
Rapt in sweet talk or lively, all on love
And sport and tilts and pleasure, (for the time
Was maytime, and as yet no sin was dream'd,)   385
Rode under groves that look'd a paradise
Of blossom, over sheets of hyacinth
That seem'd the heavens upbreaking thro' the earth,
And on from hill to hill, and every day
Beheld at noon in some delicious dale   390
The silk pavilions of King Arthur raised
For brief repast or afternoon repose
By couriers gone before; and on again,
Till yet once more ere set of sun they saw
The Dragon of the great Pendragonship,   395
That crown'd the state pavilion of the King,
Blaze by the rushing brook or silent well.

  But when the Queen immersed in such a trance,
And moving thro' the past unconsciously,
Came to that point where first she saw the King   400
Ride toward her from the city, sigh'd to find
Her journey done, glanced at him, thought him cold,
High, self-contain'd, and passionless, not like him,
'Not like my Lancelot' – while she brooded thus
And grew half-guilty in her thoughts again,   405
There rode an armèd warrior to the doors.
A murmuring whisper thro' the nunnery ran,

Then on a sudden a cry, 'The King.' She sat
Stiff-stricken, listening; but when armèd feet
410   Thro' the long gallery from the outer doors
Rang coming, prone from off her seat she fell,
And grovell'd with her face against the floor:
There with her milkwhite arms and shadowy hair
She made her face a darkness from the King:
415   And in the darkness heard his armèd feet
Pause by her; then came silence, then a voice,
Monotonous and hollow like a Ghost's
Denouncing judgment, but tho' changed, the King's:

'Liest thou here so low, the child of one
420   I honour'd, happy, dead before thy shame?
Well is it that no child is born of thee.
The children born of thee are sword and fire,
Red ruin, and the breaking up of laws,
The craft of kindred and the Godless hosts
425   Of heathen swarming o'er the Northern Sea;
Whom I, while yet Sir Lancelot, my right arm,
The mightiest of my knights, abode with me,
Have everywhere about this land of Christ
In twelve great battles ruining overthrown.
430   And knowest thou now from whence I come – from him,
From waging bitter war with him: and he,
That did not shun to smite me in worse way,
Had yet that grace of courtesy in him left,
He spared to lift his hand against the King
435   Who made him knight: but many a knight was slain;
And many more, and all his kith and kin
Clave to him, and abode in his own land.
And many more when Modred raised revolt,
Forgetful of their troth and fealty, clave
440   To Modred, and a remnant stays with me.
And of this remnant will I leave a part,
True men who love me still, for whom I live,
To guard thee in the wild hour coming on,
Lest but a hair of this low head be harm'd.
445   Fear not: thou shalt be guarded till my death.
Howbeit I know, if ancient prophecies

Have err'd not, that I march to meet my doom.
Thou hast not made my life so sweet to me,
That I the King should greatly care to live;
For thou hast spoilt the purpose of my life.   450
Bear with me for the last time while I show,
Ev'n for thy sake, the sin which thou hast sinn'd.
For when the Roman left us, and their law
Relax'd its hold upon us, and the ways
Were fill'd with rapine, here and there a deed   455
Of prowess done redress'd a random wrong.
But I was first of all the kings who drew
The knighthood-errant of this realm and all
The realms together under me, their Head,
In that fair Order of my Table Round,   460
A glorious company, the flower of men,
To serve as model for the mighty world,
And be the fair beginning of a time.
I made them lay their hands in mine and swear
To reverence the King, as if he were   465
Their conscience, and their conscience as their King,
To break the heathen and uphold the Christ,
To ride abroad redressing human wrongs.
To speak no slander, no, nor listen to it,
To honour his own word as if his God's,   470
To lead sweet lives in purest chastity,
To love one maiden only, cleave to her,
And worship her by years of noble deeds,
Until they won her; for indeed I knew
Of no more subtle master under heaven   475
Than is the maiden passion for a maid,
Not only to keep down the base in man,
But teach high thought, and amiable words
And courtliness, and the desire of fame,
And love of truth, and all that makes a man.   480
And all this throve before I wedded thee,
Believing, "lo mine helpmate, one to feel
My purpose and rejoicing in my joy."
Then came thy shameful sin with Lancelot;
Then came the sin of Tristram and Isolt;   485
Then others, following these my mightiest knights,

And drawing foul ensample from fair names,
Sinn'd also, till the loathsome opposite
Of all my heart had destined did obtain,
490 And all thro' thee! so that this life of mine
I guard as God's high gift from scathe and wrong,
Not greatly care to lose; but rather think
How sad it were for Arthur, should he live,
To sit once more within his lonely hall,
495 And miss the wonted number of my knights,
And miss to hear high talk of noble deeds
As in the golden days before thy sin.
For which of us, who might be left, could speak
Of the pure heart, nor seem to glance at thee?
500 And in thy bowers of Camelot or of Usk
Thy shadow still would glide from room to room,
And I should evermore be vext with thee
In hanging robe or vacant ornament,
Or ghostly footfall echoing on the stair.
505 For think not, tho' thou wouldst not love thy lord,
Thy lord has wholly lost his love for thee.
I am not made of so slight elements.
Yet must I leave thee, woman, to thy shame.
I hold that man the worst of public foes
510 Who either for his own or children's sake,
To save his blood from scandal, lets the wife
Whom he knows false, abide and rule the house:
For being thro' his cowardice allow'd
Her station, taken everywhere for pure,
515 She like a new disease, unknown to men,
Creeps, no precaution used, among the crowd,
Makes wicked lightnings of her eyes, and saps
The fealty of our friends, and stirs the pulse
With devil's leaps, and poisons half the young.
520 Worst of the worst were that man he that reigns!
Better the King's waste hearth and aching heart
Than thou reseated in thy place of light,
The mockery of my people, and their bane.'

He paused, and in the pause she crept an inch
525 Nearer, and laid her hands about his feet.

Far off a solitary trumpet blew.
Then waiting by the doors the warhorse neigh'd
As at a friend's voice, and he spake again:

   'Yet think not that I come to urge thy crimes,
I did not come to curse thee, Guinevere, 530
I, whose vast pity almost makes me die
To see thee, laying there thy golden head,
My pride in happier summers, at my feet.
The wrath which forced my thoughts on that fierce law,
The doom of treason and the flaming death, 535
(When first I learnt thee hidden here) is past.
The pang – which while I weigh'd thy heart with one
Too wholly true to dream untruth in thee,
Made my tears burn – is also past – in part.
And all is past, the sin is sinn'd, and I, 540
Lo! I forgive thee, as Eternal God
Forgives: do thou for thine own soul the rest.
But how to take last leave of all I loved?
O golden hair, with which I used to play
Not knowing! O imperial-moulded form, 545
And beauty such as never woman wore,
Until it came a kingdom's curse with thee –
I cannot touch thy lips, they are not mine,
But Lancelot's: nay, they never were the King's.
I cannot take thy hand; that too is flesh, 550
And in the flesh thou hast sinn'd; and mine own flesh,
Here looking down on thine polluted, cries
"I loathe thee:" yet not less, O Guinevere,
For I was ever virgin save for thee,
My love thro' flesh hath wrought into my life 555
So far, that my doom is, I love thee still.
Let no man dream but that I love thee still.
Perchance, and so thou purify thy soul,
And so thou lean on our fair father Christ,
Hereafter in that world where all are pure 560
We two may meet before high God, and thou
Wilt spring to me, and claim me thine, and know
I am thine husband – not a smaller soul,
Nor Lancelot, nor another. Leave me that,

565 I charge thee, my last hope. Now must I hence.
Thro' the thick night I hear the trumpet blow:
They summon me their King to lead mine hosts
Far down to that great battle in the west,
Where I must strike against the man they call
570 My sister's son – no kin of mine, who leagues
With Lords of the White Horse, heathen, and knights,
Traitors – and strike him dead, and meet myself
Death, or I know not what mysterious doom.
And thou remaining here wilt learn the event;
575 But hither shall I never come again,
Never lie by thy side; see thee no more –
Farewell!'

                    And while she grovell'd at his feet,
She felt the King's breath wander o'er her neck,
And in the darkness o'er her fallen head,
580 Perceived the waving of his hands that blest.

        Then, listening till those armèd steps were gone,
Rose the pale Queen, and in her anguish found
The casement: 'peradventure,' so she thought,
'If I might see his face, and not be seen.'
585 And lo, he sat on horseback at the door!
And near him the sad nuns with each a light
Stood, and he gave them charge about the Queen,
To guard and foster her for evermore.
And while he spake to these his helm was lower'd,
590 To which for crest the golden dragon clung
Of Britain; so she did not see the face,
Which then was as an angel's, but she saw,
Wet with the mists and smitten by the lights,
The Dragon of the great Pendragonship
595 Blaze, making all the night a steam of fire.
And even then he turn'd; and more and more
The moony vapour rolling round the King,
Who seem'd the phantom of a Giant in it,
Enwound him fold by fold, and made him gray
600 And grayer, till himself became as mist
Before her, moving ghostlike to his doom.

Then she stretch'd out her arms and cried aloud
'Oh Arthur!' there her voice brake suddenly,
Then – as a stream that spouting from a cliff
Fails in mid air, but gathering at the base   605
Re-makes itself, and flashes down the vale –
Went on in passionate utterance:

                        'Gone – my lord!
Gone thro' my sin to slay and to be slain!
And he forgave me, and I could not speak.
Farewell? I should have answer'd his farewell.   610
His mercy choked me. Gone, my lord the King,
My own true lord! how dare I call him mine?
The shadow of another cleaves to me,
And makes me one pollution: he, the King,
Call'd me polluted: shall I kill myself?   615
What help in that? I cannot kill my sin,
If soul be soul; nor can I kill my shame;
No, nor by living can I live it down.
The days will grow to weeks, the weeks to months,
The months will add themselves and make the years,   620
The years will roll into the centuries,
And mine will ever be a name of scorn.
I must not dwell on that defeat of fame.
Let the world be; that is but of the world.
What else? what hope? I think there was a hope,   625
Except he mock'd me when he spake of hope;
His hope he call'd it; but he never mocks,
For mockery is the fume of little hearts.
And blessèd be the King, who hath forgiven
My wickedness to him, and left me hope   630
That in mine own heart I can live down sin
And be his mate hereafter in the heavens
Before high God. Ah great and gentle lord,
Who wast, as is the conscience of a saint
Among his warring senses, to thy knights –   635
To whom my false voluptuous pride, that took
Full easily all impressions from below,
Would not look up, or half-despised the height
To which I would not or I could not climb –

640 I thought I could not breathe in that fine air
That pure severity of perfect light –
I yearn'd for warmth and colour which I found
In Lancelot – now I see thee what thou art,
Thou art the highest and most human too,
645 Not Lancelot, nor another. Is there none
Will tell the King I love him tho' so late?
Now – ere he goes to the great Battle? none:
Myself must tell him in that purer life,
But now it were too daring. Ah my God,
650 What might I not have made of thy fair world,
Had I but loved thy highest creature here?
It was my duty to have loved the highest:
It surely was my profit had I known:
It would have been my pleasure had I seen.
655 We needs must love the highest when we see it,
Not Lancelot, nor another.'

                                    Here her hand
Grasp'd, made her vail her eyes: she look'd and saw
The novice, weeping, suppliant, and said to her,
'Yea, little maid, for am *I* not forgiven?'
660 Then glancing up beheld the holy nuns
All round her, weeping; and her heart was loosed
Within her, and she wept with these and said,

        'Ye know me then, that wicked one, who broke
The vast design and purpose of the King.
665 O shut me round with narrowing nunnery-walls,
Meek maidens, from the voices crying "shame."
I must not scorn myself: he loves me still.
Let no one dream but that he loves me still.
So let me, if you do not shudder at me,
670 Nor shun to call me sister, dwell with you;
Wear black and white, and be a nun like you,
Fast with your fasts, not feasting with your feasts;
Grieve with your griefs, not grieving at your joys,
But not rejoicing; mingle with your rites;
675 Pray and be pray'd for; lie before your shrines;
Do each low office of your holy house;

Walk your dim cloister, and distribute dole
To poor sick people, richer in His eyes
Who ransom'd us, and haler too than I;
And treat their loathsome hurts and heal mine own;   680
And so wear out in almsdeed and in prayer
The sombre close of that voluptuous day,
Which wrought the ruin of my lord the King.'

    She said: they took her to themselves; and she
Still hoping, fearing 'is it yet too late?'   685
Dwelt with them, till in time their Abbess died.
Then she, for her good deeds and her pure life,
And for the power of ministration in her,
And likewise for the high rank she had borne,
Was chosen Abbess, there, an Abbess, lived   690
For three brief years, and there, an Abbess, past
To where beyond these voices there is peace.

The Passing of Arthur

That story which the bold Sir Bedivere,
First made and latest left of all the knights,
Told, when the man was no more than a voice
In the white winter of his age, to those
5   With whom he dwelt, new faces, other minds.

    For on their march to westward, Bedivere,
Who slowly paced among the slumbering host,
Heard in his tent the moanings of the King:

    'I found Him in the shining of the stars,
10   I mark'd Him in the flowering of His fields,
But in His ways with men I find Him not.
I waged His wars, and now I pass and die.
O me! for why is all around us here
As if some lesser god had made the world,
15   But had not force to shape it as he would,
Till the High God behold it from beyond,
And enter it, and make it beautiful?
Or else as if the world were wholly fair,
But that these eyes of men are dense and dim,
20   And have not power to see it as it is:
Perchance, because we see not to the close; –
For I, being simple, thought to work His will,
And have but stricken with the sword in vain;
And all whereon I lean'd in wife and friend
25   Is traitor to my peace, and all my realm
Reels back into the beast, and is no more.
My God, thou hast forgotten me in my death:
Nay – God my Christ – I pass but shall not die.'

    Then, ere that last weird battle in the west,
30   There came on Arthur sleeping, Gawain kill'd

In Lancelot's war, the ghost of Gawain blown
Along a wandering wind, and past his ear
Went shrilling, 'Hollow, hollow all delight!
Hail, King! to-morrow thou shalt pass away.
Farewell! there is an isle of rest for thee.   35
And I am blown along a wandering wind,
And hollow, hollow, hollow all delight.'
And fainter onward, like wild birds that change
Their season in the night and wail their way
From cloud to cloud, down the long wind the dream   40
Shrill'd; but in going mingled with dim cries
Far in the moonlit haze among the hills,
As of some lonely city sack'd by night,
When all is lost, and wife and child with wail
Pass to new lords; and Arthur woke and call'd,   45
'Who spake? A dream. O light upon the wind,
Thine, Gawain, was the voice – are these dim cries
Thine? or doth all that haunts the waste and wild
Mourn, knowing it will go along with me?'

This heard the bold Sir Bedivere and spake: 50
'O me, my King, let pass whatever will,
Elves, and the harmless glamour of the field;
But in their stead thy name and glory cling
To all high places like a golden cloud
For ever: but as yet thou shalt not pass.   55
Light was Gawain in life, and light in death
Is Gawain, for the ghost is as the man;
And care not thou for dreams from him, but rise –
I hear the steps of Modred in the west,
And with him many of thy people, and knights   60
Once thine, whom thou hast loved, but grosser grown
Than heathen, spitting at their vows and thee.
Right well in heart they know thee for the King.
Arise, go forth and conquer as of old.'

Then spake King Arthur to Sir Bedivere: 65
'Far other is this battle in the west
Whereto we move, than when we strove in youth,
And brake the petty kings, and fought with Rome,

Or thrust the heathen from the Roman wall,
70 And shook him thro' the north. Ill doom is mine
To war against my people and my knights.
The king who fights his people fights himself.
And they my knights, who loved me once, the stroke
That strikes them dead is as my death to me.
75 Yet let us hence, and find or feel a way
Thro' this blind haze, which ever since I saw
One lying in the dust at Almesbury,
Hath folded in the passes of the world.'

80   Then rose the King and moved his host by night,
And ever push'd Sir Modred, league by league,
Back to the sunset bound of Lyonnesse –
A land of old upheaven from the abyss
By fire, to sink into the abyss again;
85 Where fragments of forgotten peoples dwelt,
And the long mountains ended in a coast
Of ever-shifting sand, and far away
The phantom circle of a moaning sea.
There the pursuer could pursue no more,
90 And he that fled no further fly the King;
And there, that day when the great light of heaven
Burn'd at his lowest in the rolling year,
On the waste sand by the waste sea they closed.
Nor ever yet had Arthur fought a fight
95 Like this last, dim, weird battle of the west.
A deathwhite mist slept over sand and sea:
Whereof the chill, to him who breathed it, drew
Down with his blood, till all his heart was cold
With formless fear; and ev'n on Arthur fell
Confusion, since he saw not whom he fought.
100 For friend and foe were shadows in the mist,
And friend slew friend not knowing whom he slew;
And some had visions out of golden youth,
And some beheld the faces of old ghosts
Look in upon the battle; and in the mist
105 Was many a noble deed, many a base,
And chance and craft and strength in single fights,
And ever and anon with host to host

Shocks, and the splintering spear, the hard mail hewn,
Shield-breakings, and the clash of brands, the crash
Of battleaxes on shatter'd helms, and shrieks   110
After the Christ, of those who falling down
Look'd up for heaven, and only saw the mist;
And shouts of heathen and the traitor knights,
Oaths, insult, filth, and monstrous blasphemies,
Sweat, writhings, anguish, labouring of the lungs   115
In that close mist, and cryings for the light,
Moans of the dying, and voices of the dead.

Last, as by some one deathbed after wail
Of suffering, silence follows, or thro' death
Or deathlike swoon, thus over all that shore,   120
Save for some whisper of the seething seas,
A dead hush fell; but when the dolorous day
Grew drearier toward twilight falling, came
A bitter wind, clear from the North, and blew
The mist aside, and with that wind the tide   125
Rose, and the pale King glanced across the field
Of battle: but no man was moving there;
Nor any cry of Christian heard thereon,
Nor yet of heathen; only the wan wave
Brake in among dead faces, to and fro   130
Swaying the helpless hands, and up and down
Tumbling the hollow helmets of the fallen,
And shiver'd brands that once had fought with Rome,
And rolling far along the gloomy shores
The voice of days of old and days to be.   135

Then spake King Arthur to Sir Bedivere,
And whiter than the mist that all day long
Had held the field of battle was the King:

'Hearest thou this great voice that shakes the world,
And wastes the narrow realm whereon we move,   140
And beats upon the faces of the dead,
My dead, as tho' they had not died for me? –
O Bedivere, for on my heart hath fall'n
Confusion, till I know not what I am,

145   Nor whence I am, nor whether I be King.
      Behold, I seem but King among the dead.'

      Then spake the bold Sir Bedivere: 'My King,
      King everywhere! and so the dead have kings,
      There also will I worship thee as King.
150   Yet still thy life is whole, and still I live
      Who love thee; but who hates thee, he that brought
      The heathen back among us, yonder stands,
      Modred, unharm'd, the traitor of thine house.'

      Then spake the King: 'My house hath been my doom.
155   But call not thou this traitor of my house
      Who hath but dwelt beneath one roof with me.
      My house are rather they who sware my vows,
      Yea, even while they brake them, own'd me King.
      And well for thee, saying in my dark hour,
160   When all the purport of my throne hath fail'd,
      That quick or dead thou holdest me for King.
      King am I, whatsoever be their cry;
      And one last act of kinghood shalt thou see
      Yet, ere I pass.' And uttering this the King
165   Made at the man: then Modred smote his liege
      Hard on that helm which many a heathen sword
      Had beaten thin; while Arthur at one blow,
      Striking the last stroke with Excalibur,
      Slew him, and all but slain himself, he fell.

170   So all day long the noise of battle roll'd
      Among the mountains by the winter sea;
      Until King Arthur's Table, man by man,
      Had fall'n in Lyonnesse about their lord,
      King Arthur. Then, because his wound was deep,
175   The bold Sir Bedivere uplifted him,
      And bore him to a chapel nigh the field,
      A broken chancel with a broken cross,
      That stood on a dark strait of barren land:
      On one side lay the Ocean, and on one
180   Lay a great water, and the moon was full.

Then spake King Arthur to Sir Bedivere:
'The sequel of to-day unsolders all
The goodliest fellowship of famous knights
Whereof this world holds record. Such a sleep
They sleep – the men I loved. I think that we   185
Shall never more, at any future time,
Delight our souls with talk of knightly deeds
Walking about the gardens and the halls
Of Camelot, as in the days that were.
I perish by this people which I made, –   190
Tho' Merlin sware that I should come again
To rule once more; but, let what will be, be,
I am so deeply smitten thro' the helm
That without help I cannot last till morn.
Thou therefore take my brand Excalibur,   195
Which was my pride: for thou rememberest how
In those old days, one summer noon, an arm
Rose up from out the bosom of the lake,
Clothed in white samite, mystic, wonderful,
Holding the sword – and how I row'd across   200
And took it, and have worn it, like a king;
And, wheresoever I am sung or told
In aftertime, this also shall be known:
But now delay not: take Excalibur,
And fling him far into the middle mere: 205
Watch what thou seëst, and lightly bring me word.'

To him replied the bold Sir Bedivere:
'It is not meet, Sir King, to leave thee thus,
Aidless, alone, and smitten thro' the helm –
A little thing may harm a wounded man;   210
Yet I thy hest will all perform at full,
Watch what I see, and lightly bring thee word.'

So saying, from the ruin'd shrine he stept,
And in the moon athwart the place of tombs,
Where lay the mighty bones of ancient men,   215
Old knights, and over them the sea-wind sang
Shrill, chill, with flakes of foam. He, stepping down

By zigzag paths, and juts of pointed rock,
Came on the shining levels of the lake.

220   There drew he forth the brand Excalibur,
And o'er him, drawing it, the winter moon,
Brightening the skirts of a long cloud, ran forth
And sparkled keen with frost against the hilt:
For all the haft twinkled with diamond sparks,
225 Myriads of topaz-lights, and jacinth-work
Of subtlest jewellery. He gazed so long
That both his eyes were dazzled as he stood,
This way and that dividing the swift mind,
In act to throw: but at the last it seem'd
230 Better to leave Excalibur conceal'd
There in the many-knotted waterflags,
That whistled stiff and dry about the marge.
So strode he back slow to the wounded King.

    Then spake King Arthur to Sir Bedivere:
235 'Hast thou perform'd my mission which I gave?
What is it thou hast seen? or what hast heard?'

    And answer made the bold Sir Bedivere:
I heard the ripple washing in the reeds,
And the wild water lapping on the crag.'

240   To whom replied King Arthur, faint and pale:
'Thou hast betray'd thy nature·and thy name,
Not rendering true answer, as beseem'd
Thy fealty, nor like a noble knight:
For surer sign had follow'd, either hand,
245 Or voice, or else a motion of the mere.
This is a shameful thing for men to lie.
Yet now, I charge thee, quickly go again,
As thou art lief and dear, and do the thing
I bad thee, watch, and lightly bring me word.'

250   Then went Sir Bedivere the second time
Across the ridge, and paced beside the mere,
Counting the dewy pebbles, fix'd in thought;

But when he saw the wonder of the hilt,
How curiously and strangely chased, he smote
His palms together, and he cried aloud: 255

'And if indeed I cast the brand away,
Surely a precious thing, one worthy note,
Should thus be lost for ever from the earth,
Which might have pleased the eyes of many men.
What good should follow this, if this were done?   260
What harm, undone? Deep harm to disobey,
Seeing obedience is the bond of rule.
Were it well to obey then, if a king demand
An act unprofitable, against himself?
The King is sick, and knows not what he does.   265
What record, or what relic of my lord
Should be to aftertime, but empty breath
And rumours of a doubt? But were this kept,
Stored in some treasure-house of mighty kings,
Some one might show it at a joust of arms,   270
Saying, "King Arthur's sword, Excalibur,
Wrought by the lonely maiden of the Lake.
Nine years she wrought it, sitting in the deeps
Upon the hidden bases of the hills."
So might some old man speak in the aftertime   275
To all the people, winning reverence.
But now much honour and much fame were lost.'

So spake he, clouded with his own conceit,
And hid Excalibur the second time,
And so strode back slow to the wounded King.   280

Then spoke King Arthur, breathing heavily:
'What is it thou hast seen? or what hast heard?'

And answer made the bold Sir Bedivere:
'I heard the water lapping on the crag,
And the long ripple washing in the reeds.'   285

To whom replied King Arthur, much in wrath:
'Ah, miserable and unkind, untrue,

Unknightly, traitor-hearted! Woe is me!
Authority forgets a dying king,
290 Laid widow'd of the power in his eye
That bow'd the will. I see thee what thou art,
For thou, the latest-left of all my knights,
In whom should meet the offices of all,
Thou wouldst betray me for the precious hilt;
295 Either from lust of gold, or like a girl
Valuing the giddy pleasure of the eyes.
Yet, for a man may fail in duty twice,
And the third time may prosper, get thee hence:
But, if thou spare to fling Excalibur,
300 I will arise and slay thee with my hands.

Then quickly rose Sir Bedivere, and ran,
And, leaping down the ridges lightly, plunged
Among the bulrush beds, and clutch'd the sword,
And strongly wheel'd and threw it. The great brand
305 Made lightnings in the splendour of the moon,
And flashing round and round, and whirl'd in an arch,
Shot like a streamer of the northern morn,
Seen where the moving isles of winter shock
By night, with noises of the Northern Sea.
310 So flash'd and fell the brand Excalibur:
But ere he dipt the surface, rose an arm
Clothed in white samite, mystic, wonderful,
And caught him by the hilt, and brandish'd him
Three times, and drew him under in the mere.
315 And lightly went the other to the King.

Then spoke King Arthur, drawing thicker breath
'Now see I by thine eyes that this is done.
Speak out: what is it thou hast heard, or seen?'

And answer made the bold Sir Bedivere:
320 'Sir King, I closed mine eyelids, lest the gems
Should blind my purpose, for I never saw,
Nor shall see, here or elsewhere, till I die,
Not tho' I live three lives of mortal men,
So great a miracle as yonder hilt.

Then with both hands I flung him, wheeling him;   325
But when I look'd again, behold an arm,
Clothed in white samite, mystic, wonderful,
That caught him by the hilt, and brandish'd him
Three times, and drew him under in the mere.'

And answer made King Arthur, breathing hard: 330
'My end draws nigh; 'tis time that I were gone.
Make broad thy shoulders to receive my weight,
And bear me to the margin; yet I fear
My wound hath taken cold, and I shall die.'

So saying, from the pavement he half rose,   335
Slowly, with pain, reclining on his arm,
And looking wistfully with wide blue eyes
As in a picture. Him Sir Bedivere
Remorsefully regarded thro' his tears,
And would have spoken, but he found not words;   340
Then took with care, and kneeling on one knee,
O'er both his shoulders drew the languid hands,
And rising bore him thro' the place of tombs.

But, as he walk'd, King Arthur panted hard,
Like one that feels a nightmare on his bed   345
When all the house is mute. So sigh'd the King,
Muttering and murmuring at his ear, 'Quick, quick!
I fear it is too late, and I shall die.'
But the other swiftly strode from ridge to ridge,
Clothed with his breath, and looking, as he walk'd,   350
Larger than human on the frozen hills.
He heard the deep behind him, and a cry
Before. His own thought drove him like a goad.
Dry clash'd his harness in the icy caves
And barren chasms, and all to left and right   355
The bare black cliff clang'd round him, as he based
His feet on juts of slippery crag that rang
Sharp-smitten with the dint of armèd heels –
And on a sudden, lo! the level lake,
And the long glories of the winter moon.   360

Then saw they how there hove a dusky barge,
Dark as a funeral scarf from stem to stern,
Beneath them; and descending they were ware
365 That all the decks were dense with stately forms,
Black-stoled, black-hooded, like a dream – by these
Three Queens with crowns of gold: and from them rose
A cry that shiver'd to the tingling stars,
And, as it were one voice, an agony
370 Of lamentation, like a wind that shrills
All night in a waste land, where no one comes,
Or hath come, since the making of the world.

Then murmur'd Arthur, 'Place me in the barge.'
So to the barge they came. There those three Queens
Put forth their hands, and took the King, and wept.
375 But she, that rose the tallest of them all
And fairest, laid his head upon her lap,
And loosed the shatter'd casque, and chafed his hands,
And call'd him by his name, complaining loud,
And dropping bitter tears against a brow
380 Striped with dark blood: for all his face was white
And colourless, and like the wither'd moon
Smote by the fresh beam of the springing east;
And all his greaves and cuisses dash'd with drops
Of onset; and the light and lustrous curls –
385 That made his forehead like a rising sun
High from the daïs-throne – were parch'd with dust;
Or, clotted into points and hanging loose,
Mix'd with the knightly growth that fringed his lips.
So like a shatter'd column lay the King;
390 Not like that Arthur who, with lance in rest,
From spur to plume a star of tournament,
Shot thro' the lists at Camelot, and charged
Before the eyes of ladies and of kings.

Then loudly cried the bold Sir Bedivere:
395 'Ah! my Lord Arthur, whither shall I go?
Where shall I hide my forehead and my eyes?
For now I see the true old times are dead,
When every morning brought a noble chance,

And every chance brought out a noble knight.
Such times have been not since the light that led   400
The holy Elders with the gift of myrrh.
But now the whole Round Table is dissolved
Which was an image of the mighty world,
And I, the last, go forth companionless,
And the days darken round me, and the years,   405
Among new men, strange faces, other minds.'

　　And slowly answer'd Arthur from the barge:
'The old order changeth, yielding place to new,
And God fulfils himself in many ways,
Lest one good custom should corrupt the world.   410
Comfort thyself: what comfort is in me?
I have lived my life, and that which I have done
May He within himself make pure! but thou,
If thou shouldst never see my face again,
Pray for my soul. More things are wrought by prayer   415
Than this world dreams of. Wherefore, let thy voice
Rise like a fountain for me night and day.
For what are men better than sheep or goats
That nourish a blind life within the brain,
If, knowing God, they lift not hands of prayer   420
Both for themselves and those who call them friend?
For so the whole round earth is every way
Bound by gold chains about the feet of God.
But now farewell. I am going a long way
With these thou seëst – if indeed I go   425
(For all my mind is clouded with a doubt) –
To the island-valley of Avilion;
Where falls not hail, or rain, or any snow,
Nor ever wind blows loudly; but it lies
Deep-meadow'd, happy, fair with orchard lawns   430
And bowery hollows crown'd with summer sea,
Where I will heal me of my grievous wound.'

　　So said he, and the barge with oar and sail
Moved from the brink, like some full-breasted swan
That, fluting a wild carol ere her death,   435
Ruffles her pure cold plume, and takes the flood

299

With swarthy webs. Long stood Sir Bedivere
Revolving many memories, till the hull
Look'd one black dot against the verge of dawn.
440 And on the mere the wailing died away.

But when that moan had past for evermore,
The stillness of the dead world's winter dawn
Amazed him, and he groan'd, 'The King is gone.'
And therewithal came on him the weird rhyme,
445 'From the great deep to the great deep he goes.'

Whereat he slowly turn'd and slowly clomb
The last hard footstep of that iron crag;
Thence mark'd the black hull moving yet, and cried,
'He passes to be King among the dead,
450 And after healing of his grievous wound
He comes again; but – if he come no more –
O me, be yon dark Queens in yon black boat,
Who shriek'd and wail'd, the three whereat we gazed
On that high day, when, clothed with living light,
455 They stood before his throne in silence, friends
Of Arthur, who should help him at his need?'

Then from the dawn it seem'd there came, but faint
As from beyond the limit of the world,
Like the last echo born of a great cry,
460 Sounds, as if some fair city were one voice
Around a king returning from his wars.

Thereat once more he moved about, and clomb
Ev'n to the highest he could climb, and saw,
Straining his eyes beneath an arch of hand,
465 Or thought he saw, the speck that bare the King,
Down that long water opening on the deep
Somewhere far off, pass on and on, and go
From less to less and vanish into light.
And the new sun rose bringing the new year.

To the Queen

O loyal to the royal in thyself,
And loyal to thy land, as this to thee —
Bear witness, that rememberable day,
When, pale as yet, and fever-worn, the Prince
Who scarce had pluck'd his flickering life again   5
From halfway down the shadow of the grave,
Past with thee thro' thy people and their love,
And London roll'd one tide of joy thro' all
Her trebled millions, and loud leagues of man
And welcome! witness, too, the silent cry,   10
The prayer of many a race and creed, and clime —
Thunderless lightnings striking under sea
From sunset and sunrise of all thy realm,
And that true North, whereof we lately heard
A strain to shame us 'keep you to yourselves;   15
So loyal is too costly! friends – your love
Is but a burthen: loose the bond, and go.'
Is this the tone of empire? here the faith
That made us rulers? this, indeed, her voice
And meaning, whom the roar of Hougoumont   20
Left mightiest of all peoples under heaven?
What shock has fool'd her since, that she should speak
So feebly? wealthier – wealthier – hour by hour!
The voice of Britain, or a sinking land,
Some third-rate isle half-lost among her seas?   25
There rang her voice, when the full city peal'd
Thee and thy Prince! The loyal to their crown
Are loyal to their own far sons, who love
Our ocean-empire with her boundless homes
For ever-broadening England, and her throne   30
In our vast Orient, and one isle, one isle,
That knows not her own greatness? if she knows
And dreads it we are fall'n. — But thou, my Queen,

301

To the Queen

Not for itself, but thro' thy living love
For one to whom I made it o'er his grave
Sacred, accept this old imperfect tale,
New-old, and shadowing Sense at war with Soul,
Ideal manhood closed in real man,
Rather than that gray king, whose name, a ghost,
Streams like a cloud, man-shaped, from mountain peak,
And cleaves to cairn and cromlech still; or him
Of Geoffrey's book, or him of Malleor's, one
Touch'd by the adulterous finger of a time
That hover'd between war and wantonness,
And crownings and dethronements: take withal
Thy poet's blessing, and his trust that Heaven
Will blow the tempest in the distance back
From thine and ours: for some are scared, who mark,
Or wisely or unwisely, signs of storm,
Waverings of every vane with every wind,
And wordy trucklings to the transient hour,
And fierce or careless looseners of the faith,
And Softness breeding scorn of simple life,
Or Cowardice, the child of lust for gold,
Or Labour, with a groan and not a voice,
Or Art with poisonous honey stol'n from France,
And that which knows, but careful for itself,
And that which knows not, ruling that which knows
To its own harm: the goal of this great world
Lies beyond sight: yet – if our slowly-grown
And crown'd Republic's crowning common-sense,
That saved her many times, not fail – their fears
Are morning shadows huger than the shapes
That cast them, not those gloomier which forego
The darkness of that battle in the West,
Where all of high and holy dies away.

Notes

For this annotation I have selected the best edited Malory that Tennyson possessed, Thomas Wright's edition of 1858. In the notes the following abbreviations have been used:

T.	=	Tennyson
H.T.	=	Hallam Tennyson
CA	=	The Coming of Arthur
GL	=	Gareth and Lynette
MG	=	The Marriage of Geraint
GE	=	Geraint and Enid
BB	=	Balin and Balan
MV	=	Merlin and Vivien
LE	=	Lancelot and Elaine
HG	=	The Holy Grail
PE	=	Pelleas and Ettarre
LT	=	The Last Tournament
G	=	Guinevere
PA	=	The Passing of Arthur

Dedication

Published 1862. 'To the Prince Consort' (T.), who had died on 14 December 1861. It was written by about Christmas 1861.

1. *These to His Memory – since he held them dear*: Prince Albert had asked Tennyson to inscribe a copy of the *Idylls*, 17 May 1860.
4. *I dedicate, I consecrate with tears*: cf. Catullus, *Fragmenta 2*: *'tibi dedico consecroque'.*
5. *Idylls*: 'Regarding the Greek derivation, I spelt my Idylls with two *l*'s mainly to divide them from the ordinary pastoral idyls usually spelt with one *l*. These idylls group themselves round one central figure' (T.). Tennyson pronounced the word with an I as in 'idle'.
6. *my king's ideal knight*: 'The first reading ("my own ideal knight") was altered because Leslie Stephen and others called King Arthur a portrait of the Prince Consort' (H.T.).
7–10. These lines, despite being set within quotation marks, are in fact a selective paraphrase of G 465–72. Several also occur separately in the *Idylls*.
12. *Commingled*: mixed intimately with.
    the gloom of imminent war: 'Owing to the *Trent* affair (1861), when two Southern Commissioners accredited to Great Britain and France by the Confederate States were taken off a British steamship, the *Trent*, by the captain of the Federal man-of-war *San Jacinto*. The Queen and the Prince Consort were said to have averted war by their modification of a dispatch' (T.).
36–7. *Far-sighted summoner of War and Waste/To fruitful strifes and rivalries of peace*: 'The Prince Consort's work in the planning of the International Exhibitions of 1851 and 1862' (H.T.).
40. *thy land*: 'Saxe-Coburg Gotha' (T.).
49. *o'ershadow: OED* 2, to protect.

The Coming of Arthur

Published in December 1869 (dated 1870) as the first poem of *The Holy Grail and Other Poems*. Composed early in 1869. Significant additions, some ninety lines in all, were made by 1873. Some form of the poem was envisaged from the outset (see 'Guinevere', which was published in 1859, ll. 274–305, for a foreshadowing). The plot and characterization are almost entirely original.

To introduce his series Tennyson comments:

'How much of history we have in the story of Arthur is doubtful. Let not my readers press too hardly on details whether for history or for allegory. Some think that King Arthur may be taken to typify conscience. He is anyhow meant to be a man who spent himself in the cause of honour, duty and self-sacrifice, who felt and aspired with his nobler knights, though with a stronger and a clearer conscience than any of them, "reverencing his conscience as his king". "In short, God had not made since Adam was, the man more perfect than Arthur," as an older writer says. "Major praeteritis majorque futuris Regibus." The vision of Arthur as I have drawn him came upon me when, little more than a boy, I first lighted upon Malory.

> þe time cõ þe wes icoren:
> þa wes Arður iboren.
> Sone swa he com an eorðe:
> aluen hine iuengen.
> heo bigolen þat child:
> mid galdere swiðe stronge.
> heo ʒeuē him mihte:
> to beon bezst alre cnihten.
> heo ʒeuen him an oðer þing:
> þat he scolde beon riche king.
> heo ʒiuen hī þat þridde:
> þat he scolde longe libben.
> heo ʒifen him þat kine-bern:
> custen swiðe gode.
> þat he wes mete-custi:
> of alle quikemonnen.
> þis þe alue him ʒef:
> And al swa þat child iþæh.

Layamon's *Brut*, Madden, vol. ii 384.

'(The time came that was chosen, then was Arthur born. So soon as he came on earth, elves took him; they enchanted the child with magic most strong, they gave him might to be the best of all knights; they gave him another thing, that he should be a rich king; they gave him the third, that he should live long; they gave to him, the child, virtues most good, so that he was *most* generous of all men alive: This the elves gave him, and thus the child thrived.)

'The Coming of Arthur is on the night of the New Year; when he is wedded "the world is white with May"; on a summer night the vision of the Holy Grail appears; and the "Last Tournament" is in the "yellowing autumn-tide". Guinevere flees thro' the mists of autumn, and Arthur's death takes place at midnight in mid-winter. The form of the *Coming of Arthur* and of the *Passing* is purposely more archaic than that of the other Idylls. The blank verse throughout each of the twelve Idylls varies according to the subject.'

5. *For many a petty king*: 'This explains the existence of Leodogran, one of the petty princes. "Cameliard is apparently", according to Wright, "the district called Carmelide in the English metrical romance of *Merlin*, on the border of which was a town called 'Breckenho' (Brecknock)" – T. Wright's edition of the *Mort d'Arthure*' (T.).

8. *the heathen host*: Jutes, Angles and Saxons.

13. *Aurelius*: 'Aurelius (Emrys) Ambrosius was brother of King Uther' (T.). H.T. adds: 'For the histories of Aurelius and Uther see Geoffrey of Monmouth's *Chronicle*, Bks v and vi.'

17. *puissance*: power.
    Table Round: 'A table called King Arthur's is kept at Winchester. It was supposed to symbolize the world, being flat and round' (T.).

18. *Drew all their petty princedoms under him*: 'The several petty princedoms were under one head, the "pendragon"' (T.).

24. *rooted*: of swine, to turn up the soil by grubbing with the snout.

31. *And mock their foster-mother on four feet*: 'Imitate the wolf by going on four feet' (T.).

32. *they grew up to wolf-like men*: 'Compare what is told of in some parts of India (*Journal of Anthropological Society of Bombay*, vol. i) and of the loupgarous and were-wolves of France and Germany' (T.).

34. *Groan'd for the Roman legions here again*: 'Cf. *Groans of the Britons*, by Gildas' (T.).

35. *Cæsar's eagle*: imperial protection, symbolized by the legionary standards.

36. *Urien*] *1873*; Rience *1869–70*. 'King of North Wales' (T.).

39. *Spitting the child*: impale it upon sharp pointed weapons ('Your naked Infants spitted upon Pykes' – *Henry V* III 338).

42. *Tho' not without an uproar*: as in Malory I 6.

47–57. Tennyson's invention.

50. *The golden symbol of his kinglihood*: 'The golden dragon' (T.). *kinglihood*: kingly or royal state (Tennyson's coinage).

58. *drave*: archaic form of drove.

66] *1873; not 1869–70.*

67. *Made head against*: to advance against, resist successfully.

72. *Gorloïs*: name from Geoffrey of Monmouth, but Tennyson's spelling is from Spenser, *Faerie Queene* III iii 27.

73. *Anton*: Ector in Malory, Antor in other versions. Arthur's foster-father.

84. *saving*: excepting.

94–133] *1873; not 1869–70.*

102. *clarions shrilling unto blood*: shrill-sounding trumpet with a narrow tube, formerly much used as a signal in war ('Clariouns/That in the bataille blowen blody sounes' – Chaucer, *Knight's Tale* 1653).

103. *The long-lanced battle let their horses run*: Malory i 15: 'then either battaile let their horses runne as fast as they might'.

111–15. Kings opposing Arthur in Malory. For metrical and other effects Tennyson modifies some names.

118. *brake*: broke.

123. *And in the heart of Arthur joy was lord*: cf. LT 485: 'But in the heart of Arthur pain was lord.'

124–5. *his warrior whom he loved/And honoured most*: Lancelot.

127. *the fire of God*: cf. LE 314–15: 'Yet in this heathen war the fire of God/Fills him.'

132. *Man's word is God in man*: repeated BB 8. Cf. also LE 143: 'a King who honours his own word,/As if it were his God's?', and G 470: 'To honour his own word as if his God's.'

134. *foughten field*: battlefield, as in *Paradise Lost* vi 410.

137. *aught*: anything whatever.

139. Tennyson develops Leodogran for his own purposes. Malory's Leodogran has no doubts.

141. *holp*: archaic form of help.

152–3. *Merlin's master (so they call him) Bleys . . . wrote/All things and whatsoever Merlin did*: Malory i 15: 'All the batayles that were done in king Arthurs dayes Merlyn caused Bleyse his master to write them.' The retirement of Bleys from magic because of the superior power of Merlin is Tennyson's addition.

157. *annal-book*: year-book or chronicle.

176. *breathed: OED* 12, to give utterance to.

185–222. Bedivere's account of Arthur's origin and birth in all important details follows Malory.

187. *Ygerne*: spelling as in Layamon's *Brut*.

189. *Lot's wife, the Queen of Orkney, Bellicent*: name from Wright's edn of Malory. 'The kingdom of Orkney and Lothian composed the North and East of Scotland' (T.).

205. *moons*: months.

208. *the night of the new year*: the opening of Tennyson's year cycle.

211–13. *and all as soon as born/Deliver'd at a secret postern-gate/To Merlin*: Malory i 3: 'And when the child is borne, let it bee delivered unto mee at yonder privie postern unchristned.'
postern-gate: back gate.

233. *craft*: occult art, magic.

234. *And while the people clamour'd for a king*: Tennyson quotes Malory i 7: 'wherefore all the comons cryed at once: "We will have Arthur unto our king."'

250] *1873; not 1869–70.*

252. *enow*: enough; *body enow*: 'strength' (T.).

267. *comfortable*: strengthening or supporting, morally or spiritually.

272. *the Crucified*: in stained glass the figure of Christ on the cross.

274. *vert*: green, especially in heraldry.

275. *three fair queens*: Malory xxi 6. Tennyson has introduced them at the inception.

279. *mage*: magician.
wit: intellect, intelligence.

282. *the Lady of the Lake*: 'The Lady of the Lake in the old legends is the Church' (T.). Her gift to Arthur of a sword is in Malory i 25.

284. *samite*: a rich silk fabric.

290. *A voice as of the waters*: Tennyson compares Revelation xiv 2: 'I heard a voice from heaven, as the voice of many waters.'

294. *Excalibur*: 'Said to mean "cut steel". In the Romance of *Merlin* the sword bore the following inscription: "Ich am y-hote Escalabore/Unto a king a fair tresore", and it is added: "On Inglis is this writing/Kerve steel and yren and al thing"' (T.).

296. *That rose from out the bosom of the lake*: see P A 198: 'Rose up from out the bosom of the lake.'

298. *Urim*: Exodus xxviii 30: 'And thou shalt put in the breastplate of judgment the Urim and the Thummim' (oraculous gems) and the armour of the Son of God; *Paradise Lost* vi 760–61: 'He in celestial panoply all arm'd/Of radiant Urim, work divinely wrought.'

306–7. Ecclesiastes iii 6: 'A time to get, and a time to lose; a time to keep, and a time to cast away.'

307. *brand*: sword.

315. *Daughter of Gorloïs and Ygerne am I*: as in Malory and Arthurian romance, though there known as Margawse.

319–24. Invented by Tennyson, as is all the dialogue in the poem.

325–30. Using the exaggerated division of Celts into Brythonic and Goidelic, dark and fair.

346–7. *Merlin, who, they say, can walk / Unseen at pleasure*: as often in Malory.

362. *changeling*: a child secretly substituted for another in infancy.

363. *told me that himself / And Merlin ever served about the King*: in Malory Merlin alone.

365–85. Uther's death counterbalanced by Arthur's coming is unique to Tennyson. In Geoffrey of Monmouth Uther dies when Arthur is fifteen. In Malory Arthur is two at the time of the death.

372. *dreary*: dismal, gloomy.

373–4. *the shape thereof / A dragon wing'd*: the first association of the dragon with Arthur, stemming from Geoffrey of Monmouth's Historia IX 4, where Arthur wears a helmet with dragon for crest. Arthur's dragon recurs in LE 433–5, HG 263, LT 182, 667, G 395, 590–94.

379. *a ninth one, gathering half the deep*: noted from Edward Davies's *Mythology and Rites of the British Druids*, 1809, p. 509.

393. *seer*: one to whom divine revelations are made in visions.

402. 'The truth appears in different guise to divers persons. The one fact is that man comes from the great deep and returns to it. This is an echo of the triads of the Welsh bards' (T.).

410. The line is repeated LT 133, PA 445.

420. *Tho' men may wound him that he will not die*: Malory xxi 7: 'Some men yet say in many parts of England that king Arthur is not dead, but had by the will of our Lord Jesu Christ into another place; and men say that hee will come againe, and hee shall winne the holy crosse.'

431. *hind*: servant.

432. *glimpsed*: shone faintly or intermittently, glimmered.

451. In Malory iii 1 it is Merlin who conducts Guinevere to Arthur.

452. *Dubric the high saint*: 'Archbishop of Caerleon. His crozier is said to be at St David's' (T.). Form of name and epic tag from Layamon's *Brut*.

456. *the fair beginners of a nobler time*: cf. G 463.

459–69] *1873; not 1869–70.*

464. *A voice as of the waters*: see note to l. 290.

475–502] *1873: not 1869–70.* 'My father wrote to my mother that this Viking song, a pendant to Merlin's song, "rings like a grand music".

This and Leodogran's dream give the drift and grip of the poem, which describes the aspirations and ambitions of Arthur and his knights, doomed to downfall – the hints of coming doom being heard throughout' (H. T.).

476–7. *Great Lords from Rome before the portal stood,/In scornful stillness gazing as they past*: 'Because Rome had been the Lord of Britain' (T.).

499. *The King will follow Christ, and we the King*: 1 Corinthians xi 1: 'Be ye followers of me, even as I also am of Christ.'

503–13. Based on Malory v 1–3.

508. *The old order changeth, yielding place to new*: repeated PA 408.

511. *To drive the heathen from your Roman wall*: 'A line of forts built by Agricola betwixt the Firth of Forth and the Clyde, forty miles long' (T.).

512. *No tribute will we pay*: Malory v 8.

517. *twelve great battles*: the earliest record of Arthur, the chronicle of Nennius. Tennyson uses the entire Nennius battle list in LE 284–307. The twelve battles are mentioned in various contexts: BB 85, HG 248–50, 311, G 429.

Gareth and Lynette

Published 1872. Begun by 19 August 1869 and sent to the press 9 July 1872. All except the beginning is based on Malory vii.

2. *showerful*: abounding in showers. Tennyson's coinage.

3. *spate*: 'the river in flood' (T.)

8. *precipitancy*: the quality of a headlong descent or fall, or of a very rapid onward movement.

18. *Heaven yield her for it*: cf. 'And the gods yield you for't' – *Antony and Cleopatra* IV ii 33.

20. *discaged*: to uncage, release from a cage.

21. *ever-highering*: 'He invents a verb in his youthful exuberance' (T.).

25–6. *Why, Gawain, when he came/With Modred hither*: 'Gawain and Modred, brothers of Gareth' (T.). In Malory there was also Agravaine, eliminated from the plot by Tennyson.

29. *so shook him in the saddle*: to be shaken in the saddle is one of several chivalric disgraces listed in Clark and Wormull's *Introduction to Heraldry*, 1779, p. 54 (of which Tennyson had a copy) and so Gawain's admission in the following line 'Thou hast half prevail'd against me' minimizes his brother's prowess.

46. *Book of Hours*: a book containing the prayers or offices appointed to be

said at the seven stated times of the day allotted to prayer, often as here elaborately illuminated.

47. *haunting: OED* 3, to frequent or be much about (a place).

50. *An*: archaic form of if.

51. *a leash of kings*: 'Three kings. Cf. a leash of dogs' (T.).

56. *clomb*: archaic past tense of climb.

68. *flurried*: bewildered or confused as by haste or noise.

71. *bemoan'd*: moaned for, lamented.

73–80. Lot's fate in Malory is very different. He dies in battle against Arthur.

90. *burns*: in Scottish and northern dialects mountain brooks and streams.

91. *So make thy manhood mightier day by day*: an echo of the battle anthem sung by the knights, CA 497: 'Blow, for our Sun is mightier day by day!'

93. *comfortable*: pleasant, enjoyable.

94. *prone year*: figurative for declining into age.

111. *fronted*: faced, looked.

149–54. In Malory Gareth himself requests these conditions of the king at the outset.

162. *thrall*: serf, bondman, slave.

172. *outward purpose*: 'purpose to go' (T.).

187. *Royal mount*: note that the adjective is capitalized.

202. *glamour*: magic, enchantment, spell.

212. *The Lady of the Lake*: 'The Lady of the Lake in the old romances of Lancelot instructs him in the mysteries of the Christian faith' (T.).

219. *sacred fish*: ancient symbol of Christianity.

223. *inveterately*: in a manner confirmed by long existence or practice.

225–6. *those three Queens, the friends/Of Arthur, who should help him at his need*: see CA 275 and note.

229. *dragon-boughts*: 'folds of the dragons' tails' (T.). 'His huge long tayle wound up in hundred foldes,/Does overspred his long bras-scaly backe,/Whose wreathed boughts when ever he unfoldes,/Bespotted as with shields of red and black' – *Faerie Queene* I xi ll.

elvish: having the nature of an elf, supernatural, weird.

236–7. *an ancient man,/Long-bearded*: 'Merlin' (T.).

249–52. 'Refraction by mirage' (T.).

253. *Take thou the truth as thou hast told it me*: 'Ironical' (T.).

257. *Toward the sunrise*: 'The religions and the arts that came from the East' (T.).

269–70. *Pass not beneath this gateway, but abide/Without, among the cattle of the field*: 'Be a mere beast' (T.).

272–4. *They are building still, seeing the city is built/To music, therefore never built at all,/And therefore built for ever*: 'By the Muses' (T.).

285. *I know thee who thou art*: Luke iv 34: 'I know thee who thou art; the Holy One of God.'

302. *had made it spire to heaven*: 'Symbolizing the divine' (T.).

326–41. Based on Malory i 7: 'And many complaints were made unto king Arthur of great wrongs that were done since the death of Utherpendragon, of many lands that were bereved of lords, knights, ladyes, and gentlemen. Wherefore king Arthur made the lands for to be rendred againe unto them that ought (owned) them.'

327. *boon*: the asking of a chivalric favour.

345. *the Barons' war*: see CA 94–133.

350. *thrall'd*: imprisoned.

355. *wreak*: revenge, avenge.

359. *Sir Kay, the seneschal*: 'In the *Roman de la Rose* Sir Kay is given as a pattern of rough discourtesy' (T.).
seneschal: steward.

361. *railer*: reviler.

362. *gyve and gag*: prevented by fetters and gag from motion and speech.

367. *Aurelius Emrys*: see note to CA 13.

376–410. This episode has no counterpart in Malory and Arthurian romance.

380. *charlock*: field mustard.

391. *fëalty*: the obligation of fidelity on the part of a feudal tenant or vassal to his lord.

398. *blazon'd*: painted with a heraldic device.

411. *reave*: forcibly deprive of something.

419. *churl*: bondman or serf, one with no rank or status.

422. *Lest we should lap him up in cloth of lead*: 'King Pandion he is dead;/All thy friends are lapped in lead' – *The Passionate Pilgrim*, 'As it fell upon a day' 23–4.

423–7. A synopsis of the activities of Mark in Malory viii 13, ix 19, 37, x 7, 26–7.

428. *suppliant*: humble petitioner.

431–6. Malory vii 1: 'Right so came into the hall two men well beseene and richly, and upon their shoulders there leaned the goodliest young man and the fairest that ever they saw, and he was large, long, and broad in the shoulders, and well visaged, and the fairest and the largest hands that ever man saw, but he fared as though he might not goe nor beare himselfe, but if hee leaned upon their shoulders.'

436–40. Malory vii 1: '"Now, sir," said he, "this is my petition for this feast, that ye will give me meate and drinke sufficiently for these twelve-monethes, and at that day I will aske mine other two giftes." "My faire sonne," said king Arthur, "aske better, I counsaile thee, for this is but a simple asking, for my heart giveth mee to thee greatly that thou art come of men of worship . . . Yee shall have meate and drinke enough; I never defended that none, neither my friend nor foe. But what is thy name? I would faine know." "I can not tell you," said hee. "That have I marvaile of thee," said the king, 'that thou knowest not thine owne name, and thou art one of the goodliest young men that ever I saw." '

441–2. Malory vii 1: 'Then the noble king Arthur betooke him unto the steward sir Kay, and charged him that hee should give him of all manner of meates and drinkes of the best, "and also that he have all manner of finding, as though hee were a lords sonne." '

443. *mien*: facial expression.

446–50. Malory vii 1–2: "Upon paine of my life he was brought up and fostred in some abbey, and howsomever it was they failed of meate and drinke, and so hither he is come for sustenance . . . and into the kitchen I shall bring him, and there he shall have fat browesse every day, that he shall bee as fat by the twelve-monethes end as a porke hog."

447. *brewis*: 'broth' (T.).

451–9. Malory vii 2 includes: 'And especially sir Launcelot, for hee bad sir Kay leave his mocking, "for I dare lay my head he shall prove a man of great worship." '

454. *fluent*: growing in abundant quantity and falling in graceful curves.

463–5. Malory vii 1: "'That shall little neede," said sir Kay, "to doe such cost upon him, for I dare well undertake that hee is a villaine borne, and never will make man, for and hee had beene come of a gentleman, hee would have asked of you horse and harneis, but such as hee is hath asked. And sithen hee hath no name, I shall give him a name, that shal be Beaumains, that is to say, faire hands." '

463. *Tut*: a characteristic of Kay. See also ll. 702, 715.

465–7. Tennyson's addition to Malory.

470–72. Malory vii 2: 'And so sir Kay had got him a place, and sat downe to meate. So Beaumains went to the hall dore, and sat him downe among boyes and lads, and there hee eate sadly.'

476. *broach*: 'spit' (T.).

485. *For Lancelot was the first in Tournament,/But Arthur mightiest on the battle-field*: see LE 309–16 and G 325–34.

487–94. Cf. Bellicent's account in CA 358–91.

489. *tarns*: small mountain lakes having no significant tributaries.

490. *Caer-Eryri's highest*: 'Snowdon' (T.).

491. *the Prophet*: Merlin.

492–3. *He passes to the Isle Avilion,/He passes and is heal'd and cannot die*: see CA 420–21 and PA 28. Avilion is a variant of Avalon.

496. *roundelay*: a short simple song with a refrain.

506–14. Malory vii 2: 'But ever when hee knew of any justing of knights, that would he see and hee might . . . And where as were any masteries done, there would hee be; and there might none cast the barre or stone to him by two yards.'

515–72. Added to Malory.

519. *Between the in-crescent and de-crescent moon*: between the waxing and waning of the moon, chiefly in heraldry.

521–6. Similar to a memory of Tennyson's own childhood, *Memoir* i 4.

542. *hardihood*: boldness, audacity.

549. *mellow*: good-humoured, genial, jovial.

555–6. In Malory it is Lancelot himself who makes Gareth knight.

573–96. Malory vii 2: 'Right so there came in a damosell, and saluted the king, and praied him for succour. "For whom?" said the king: "what is the adventure?" "Sir," said she, "I have a lady of great worship and renown, and she is besieged with a tyrant, so that shee may not goe out of her castle, and because that heere in your court are called the noblest knights of the world, I come unto you and pray you for succour." "What call ye your lady, and where dwelleth she, and who is hee and what is his name that hath besieged her?" "Sir king," said shee, "as for my ladies name, that shall not bee knowne for me as at this time; but I let you wit shee is a lady of great worship, and of great lands. And as for the tyrant that besiegeth her and destroyeth her land, hee is called the red knight of the reede lands." "I know him not," said the king . . . there bee knights heere that would doe their power to rescew your lady, but because ye wil not tell her name nor where she dwelleth, therefore none of my knights that be here now shall goe with you by my will." "Then must I speake (seek) further," said the damosell.'

584. *lonest hold*: most remote castle or keep.

624. *And wears a helmet mounted with a skull*: 'Upon his head he wore an Helmet light,/Made of a dead mans skull, that seemd a ghastly sight' of Maleger, *Faerie Queene* II xi 22.

630–49. Malory vii 3: 'Then with these words came before the king Beaumains, while the damosel was there; and thus he said: "Sir king, God thanke you, I have beene this twelve monethes in your kitchen, and have had my full sustenance, and now I will aske my two gifts that bee behind." "Ask upon my perill," said the king. "Sir, these shal be my two gifts: first, that ye will grant mee to have this adventure of the damosell, for it belongeth to me." "Thou shalt have it," said the king; "I graunt it thee." "Then, sir, this is now the other gift; that ye shall bid sir Launcelot du Lake to make me a knight, for of him I will bee made knight, and else of none; and when I am past, I pray you let him ride after mee, and make mee knight when I require him." "All this shall be done," said the king. "Fie on thee," said the damosell; "shall I have none but one that is your kitchen page?" Then was shee wroth, and tooke her horse and departed.'

665. *casque*: helmet.

665–85. Malory vii 3–4: 'And with that there came one to Beaumains, and told him that his horse and armour was come for him, and there was a dwarfe come with al things that him needed in the richest manner. Thereat all the court had much marvaile from whence came all that geare. So when hee was armed, there was none but few so goodly a man as hee was. And right so he came into the hall, and tooke his leave of king Arthur and of sir Gawaine, and of sir Launcelot, and prayed him that he would hie after him; and so departed and rode after the damosell. But there went many after to behold how well he was horsed and trapped in cloth of gold, but hee had neither shield nor speare.'

670–73. *and flash'd as those/Dull-coated things, that making slide apart/Their dusk wing-cases, all beneath there burns/A jewell'd harness, ere they pass and fly*: 'Certain insects which have brilliant bodies underneath dull wing-cases' (T.).

678. *trenchant*: having a keen edge.

681. *lustier*: more vigorously.

690–718. Malory vii 4: 'Then sir Kay said openly in the hall: "I will ride after my boy of the kitching, for to wit whether hee will know mee for his better." Sir Launcelot and sir Gawaine said, "yet abide at home." So sir Kay made him ready, and tooke his horse and his speare, and rode after him.'

726. *And there were none but few goodlier than he*: Malory vii 3: 'So when hee was armed there was none but few so goodly a man as he was.'

728–9. *as one/That smells a foul-fresh'd agaric in the holt*: 'An evil-smelling fungus of the wood common at Aldworth' (T.).

733. Malory vii 5: '"What doest thou heere? thou stinkest all of the kitching; thy clothes bee all bawdy (dirty) of the grease and tallow."'

735–40. Malory vii 4: 'And right as Beaumains overtooke the damosell, so came sir Kay, and said: "What, sir Beaumains, know yee not mee?" Then hee turned his horse, and knew that it was sir Kay, which had done him all the despite that yee have heard afore. "Yee," said Beaumains, "I know you for an ungentle knight of the court, and therefore beware of me." Therewith sir Kay put his speare in the rest, and runne straight to him, and Beaumains came as fast upon him with his sword in his hand; and so hee put away the speare with his sword, and with a foyne thrust him through the side, that sir Kaye fell downe as hee had beene dead; and he alight downe, and tooke sir Kays shield and his speare, and start upon his owne horse and rode his way.'

Notes to Gareth and Lynette

746–52. Malory vii 5: '"Wenest thou," said shee, "that I alow thee for
yonder knight that thou hast slaine? nay, truely, for thou slewest him
unhappily and cowardly, therefore returne againe, bawdy kitching page.
I know thee well, for sir Kay named thee Beaumains. What art thou but
a luske and a turner of broaches and a washer of dishes!"'

748. *device*: trick, stratagem.

751. *loon*: a boor, lout, clown, untaught and ill-bred person.

753–6. Malory vii 5: '"Damosell," said sir Beaumains, "say to mee what
ye list, I wil not goe from you whatsoever yee say, for I have undertaken
of king Arthur for to atchieve your adventure, and I shall finish it to the
end, or I shall die therefore."'

756–62. Malory vii 5: '"Fie on thee, kitching knave. Wilt thou finish mine
adventure? thou shalt anon bee met withall, that thou wouldest not, for
all the broth that ever thou suppest, once looke him in the face."'

763. *assay*: put to the test.
   '*I shall assay,' said Gareth with a smile*: Malory vii 5: '"I shall assay," said
   Beaumains.'

781–3. Malory vii 5: 'So as they thus rode in the wood, there came a man
flying all that he might. "Whether wilt thou?" said Beaumains. "O
Lord," said he, "helpe mee, for hereby in a slade (sludge) are six theeves
which have taken my lord and bound him, and I am afraid least they
will slay him."' Another of Tennyson's editions has "sludge" for
"slade" and presumably ll. 789–96 were suggested by it.

791. *haling*: hauling, pulling.

791–6. Malory vii 5: 'And so they rode together till they came there as the
knight was bound, and then hee rode unto the theeves, and strake one at
the first strooke to death, and then another, and at the third strooke hee
slew the third thiefe; and then the other three fled, and hee rod after and
overtooke them, and then those three theeves turned againe and hard
assailed sir Beaumains; but at the last hee slew them: and then returned
and unbound the knight.'

799. *caitiff*: vile, base, mean.

809. *fain*: gladly, willingly.

810–23. Malory vii 5: '"Sir," said sir Beaumains, "I will no reward have; I
was this day made knight of the noble sir Launcelot, and therefore I will
have no reward, but God reward me. And also I must follow this
damosell." And when hee came nigh her, shee bad him ride from her,
"for thou smellest all of the kitching. Wenest thou that I have joy of
thee? for all this deede that thou hast done, is but mishapned thee. But
thou shalt see a sight that shall make thee to turne againe, and that
lightly."'

316

810. *guerdon*: reward.

811. *for the deed's sake have I done the deed*: echoing the king's words, l. 559.

813. *harbourage*: shelter, lodging.

825–46. Malory vii 5: 'Then the same knight which was rescued of the theeves rode after the damosell, and prayed her to lodge with him all that night. And because it was neere night, the damosell rode with him to his castle, and there they had great cheere. And at supper the knight set sir Beaumains before the damosell. "Fie, fie," said shee, "sir knight, yee are uncurteous for to set a kitching page before me: him beseemeth better to sticke a swine then to sit before a damosell of high parentage."'

826. *All in a full-fair manor and a rich*: Malory iv 7: 'and so he keepeth from him a full fair manor and a rich'.

828. *viand*: provisions, victuals.

829. *cate*: dainty, delicacy.

839. *frontless*: 'shameless' (T.).

847–51. Malory vii 5: 'Then the knight was ashamed of her words, and tooke him up and sat before him at a side boord, and set himselfe before him. And so all that night they had good and merry rest.'

848–9. *left/ The damsel by the peacock in his pride*: 'Brought in on the trencher with his tail-feathers left' (T.). Hallam Tennyson quotes Edward Stanley's *History of Birds*: when it was served, 'all the guests, male and female, took a solemn vow; the knights vowing bravery, and the ladies engaging to be loving and faithful'.

862. *I but speak for thine avail*: Malory vii 6: 'I say it for thine availe'.
   avail: advantage, profit.

871. *stoat*: European ermine.

873. *ruth*: pity, compassion.

880–82. *and thou wilt find/ My fortunes all as fair as hers who lay/ Among the ashes and wedded the King's son*: 'Cinderella's' (T.).

883. *Then to the shore of one of those long loops*: 'The three loops of the river typify the three ages of life; and the guardians at the crossing the temptations of these ages' (T.).

889. *Lent-lily*: 'daffodil' (T.).

893–900. Malory vii 7: 'With that the blacke knight came to the damosell, and said, "faire damosell, have yee brought this knight from king Arthurs court to be your champion?" "Nay, faire knight," said shee, "this is but a kitching knave, that hath beene fed in king Arthurs kitching for almes."'

896. In Malory there is a succession of knights, among them the Black Knight, the Green Knight, and the Red Knight. Tennyson reorganizes details according to his allegory of time and colour.

901–7. Partly suggested by Malory vii 11 and containing in l. 904 a detail
from Malory vii 8: 'And there he blew three deadly notes, and there
came three damsels that lightly armed him.'

908. *Avanturine*: 'sometimes called the Panther-stone – a kind of gray-green
or brown quartz with sparkles in it' (T.).

914. *Immingled*: mixed or blended intimately.

918–20. Malory vii 7: 'When the damosell saw the blacke knight, shee bad
sir Beaumains flee downe the valey, for his horse was not sadled. "I
thanke you," said sir Beaumains, "for alwayes yee will have mee a
coward."'

921–4. Malory vii 11: '"Damosell," said sir Beaumains, "yee are to blame
so to rebuke me, for I had rather to doe five battailes then so to be
rebuked. Let him come, and then let him doe his worst... All the
missaying that ye missayed mee furthered me in my battailes."'

922. *Far liefer*: far more willingly.

929–36. Malory vii 7: '"Wherefore commeth he in such aray?" said the
knight, "it is great shame that he beareth you company... I shall put
him downe upon his feete, and his horse and his armour he shall leave
with me, for it were shame for mee to doe him any more harme... for it
beseemeth not a kitchin knave to ride with such a lady."'

930. *Such fight not I, but answer scorn with scorn*: cf. Zephon, *Paradise Lost* iv 834:
'answering scorn with scorn'.

936–48. Malory vii 7: '"Thou liest," said sir Beaumains, "I am a gentle-
man borne, and of more high linage then thou art, and that I will prove
upon thy body." Then in great wrath they departed with their horses,
and came together as it had beene thunder, and the blacke knights
speare brake, and sir Beaumains thrust him through both his sides, and
therewith his speare brake, and the truncheon stucke still in his side, but
neverthelesse the blacke knight drew his sword and smote many eager
strookes and of great might, and hurt sir Beaumains full sore. But at the
last the blacke knight within an houre and a halfe fell downe from his
horse in a sound (swoon), and there died forthwith.'

942. *crupper*: leathern strap buckled to the back of the saddle and passing
under the horse's tail, to prevent the saddle from slipping forwards.

947. *Till Gareth's shield was cloven*: from another combat, Malory vii 8.

949–59. Based on Malory vii 8.

967–9. Malory vii 7: '"Away, kitchen knave, goe out of the wind, for the
smell of thy baudy cloathes grieveth me."'

972. Malory vii 7: '"Alas! that ever such a knave as thou art should by mis-
hap sley so good a knight as thou has slaine, but all this is through
thine unhappinesses."'

980. Malory vii 7: '"But hereby is a knight that shall pay thee all thy payment."'

1002–5. *As if the flower... all sun*: 'The dandelion' (T.).

1008–11. Malory vii 8: '"Is that my brother the blacke knight that ye have brought with you?" "Nay, nay," said she, "this unhappie kitchin knave hath slaine your brother through unhappinesse."'

1009. *athwart*: across from side to side, transversely.

1013. *cipher*: empty.

1015–31. Malory vii 6: 'And therewith hee rashed into the water, and in the midest of the water either brake their speares to their hands, and then they drew their swords and smote at other egerly; and at the last, sir Beaumains smote the other upon the helme that his head was astonied, and therewith hee fell downe into the water, and there was drowned ... "Alas," said shee, "that ever kitching page should have the fortune to destroy such two doughty knights! thou weenest thou hast done doughtily, and that is not so, for the first knights horse stumbled and there he was drowned in the water, and never it was by thy force and might; and the last knight by mishap thou camest behind him and shamefully thou slewest him."'

1029. *point*: of the compass.

1033. *unhappiness*: 'mischance' (T.).

1044. *our good King*: this heroic epithet for Arthur also occurs GL 1143, MG 152, BB 525, MV 781, LE 278, G 96, 207, 219.

1052. *mavis*: song-thrush
merle: blackbird.

1060. *bow*: an arch of masonry: *bridge of treble bow*: bridge comprising three arches.

1067. *only wrapt in harden'd skins*: 'Allegory of habit' (T.).

1071. *'O brother-star, why shine ye here so low?'*: Hallam Tennyson notes that 'Gareth has taken the shield of the Morning-Star.' Gareth's original shield was destroyed – see l. 947.

1092ff. Cf. the fight with Maleger, *Faerie Queene* II xi 20–46.

1130. *trefoil*: the three-leaved clover, in heraldry symbolizing fidelity and constancy in love.

1135–6. *Shamed am I that I so rebuked, reviled,/Missaid thee*: '"Alas," said shee, "faire sir Beaumains, forgive me all that I have missayed and misdone against you."'

1141. *mazed my wit*: confused my mind.

1155. *hern*: heron.

1163. *comb*: a deep hollow or valley.

1172–5. Tennyson comments: 'Years ago when I was visiting the Howards at Naworth castle, I drove over to the little river Gelt to see the inscription carved upon ·the crags. It seemed to me very pathetic, this sole record of the vexillary or standard-bearer of the sacred Legion (Augusta). This is the inscription: VEX.LLEG.II AVG. ON. AP. APRO E MAXIMO CONSULIBUS SUB AGRICOLA OP. OFICINA MERCATI.' Of the 'figures', Hallam Tennyson says: 'Symbolical of the temptations of youth, of middle-age, of later life, and of death overcome by the youthful and joyous Gareth.'

1182. *dislocated Kay*: from being 'shoulder-slipt', l. 740. Malory's Kay suffers more severely.

1184. *error*: wayward direction or track.

1185–93. Suggested by Gareth's jousting with Lancelot, Malory vii 4.

1189. *felon*: wicked.

1198. *'Why laugh ye? that ye blew your boast in vain?'*: Malory vii 11: '"Fie, fie," said the damosel, "that ever such a stinking knave should blow such a boast."'

1229. *Thrown have I been, nor once, but many a time*: as in Malory ix 4.

1236. *wreak'd*: executed, carried out.

1251. *lusty*: refreshed, renewed in strength.

1253. *rated*: scolded.

1266. *Peradventure*: by chance, by accident.

1274. *agape*: in an attitude or state of wondering expectation.

1275. *ramp*: to assume a threatening posture.

1281. *Arthur's harp*: 'Lyra' (T.).

1284–5. *A star shot: 'Lo,' said Gareth, 'the foe falls!'/An owl whoopt: 'Hark the victor pealing there!'* 'When the falling stars are shooting,/And the answer'd owls are hooting,/And the silent leaves are still/In the shadows of the hill/Shall my soul be upon thine/With a power and with a sign' – Byron, *Manfred* I i 197–202.

1303. *mouthpiece*: spokesman.

1306. *tare*: tore.

1318. *Instant*: pressing, urgent, importunate.

1330. *crimson*: 'sunrise' (T.).

1331ff. *Black, with black banner, and a long black horn/Beside it hanging*: Malory vii 6–7: 'And then they came to a blacke laund, and there was a blacke hawthorne, and thereon hung a blacke baner, and on the other side there hung a blacke shield, and by it stood a blacke speare and a long, and a greate blacke horse covered with silke, and blacke stone fast by it. There sate a knight all armed in blacke harnies, and his name was the knight of the blacke laundes.'

1340. Malory vii 16: '"Sir," said the damosell Lynet unto sir Beaumains, "looke that yee be mery and light, for yonder is your deadly enemy, and at yonder window is my lady my sister dame Lyones." "Where?" said sir Beaumains. "Yonder," saith the damosell, and pointed with her finger. "That is sooth," said sir Beaumains, "she seemeth afarre the fairest lady that ever I looked upon, and truely," said hee, "I aske no better quarrell then now to doe battaile, for truely shee shall bee my lady, and for her will I fight."

1348. *And crown'd with fleshless laughter*: 'With a grinning skull' (T.).

1367. *blink*: shut the eyes to.

1372. *throughly*: thoroughly.

1392-4. Hallam Tennyson glosses this 'Malory' and 'my father'.

The Marriage of Geraint

Published 1859, the first part of 'Enid'. Composition begun 16 April 1856. Completed by 5 November. The title 'Enid' was expanded to 'Geraint and Enid' in 1870; the poem was divided into two parts in 1873; and the final titles were given in 1886. Based on Geraint, Son of Erbin, in the *Mabinogion*, translated by Lady Charlotte Guest 1840, collected 1849, vol. ii.

2. *tributary*: dependent, paying tribute to.

4. *Had married Enid*: first reading 'wedded'. 'He found out that the "E" in "Enid" was pronounced short (as if it were spelt "Ennid") and so altered the phrase in the proofs "wedded Enid" to "married Enid" ' (H.T.).

13. *fronted*: came before.

24-9. *But when a rumour rose about the Queen . . .*: added to *Mabinogion*, so that Tennyson could link these two idylls with his main theme.

33-41. *He made his pretext*: in *Mabinogion*, this is no pretext; Geraint needs 'to protect his dominions and his boundaries, seeing that his father was unable to do so'.

41. *marches*: borders.

44-5. *to the shores/Of Severn, and they past to their own land*: 'Geraint was at Caerleon, and would have to cross the Bristol Channel to go to Devon' (T.). 'I like the *t* – the strong perfect in verbs ending in *s, p*, and *x* – past, slipt, vext' (T.).

46-68. *Mabinogion*: 'He began to love ease and pleasure, for there was no one who was worth his opposing. And he loved his wife, and liked to continue in the palace, with minstrelsy and diversions. And for a long time he abode at home. And after that he began to shut himself up in the chamber of his wife, and he took no delight in anything besides, insomuch that he gave up the friendship of his nobles, together with his hunting and his amusements, and lost the hearts of all the host in his Court; and there was murmuring and scoffing concerning him among the inhabitants of the palace, on account of his relinquishing so completely their companionship for the love of his wife ... "There is nothing more hateful to me than this." And she knew not what she should do, for, although it was hard for her to own this to Geraint, yet was it not more easy for her to listen to what she heard, without warning Geraint concerning it. And she was very sorrowful.'

60. *uxoriousness*: wife-worship.

69–108. *Mabinogion*: 'And one morning in the summer time, they were upon their couch, and Geraint lay upon the edge of it. And Enid was without sleep in the apartment which had windows of glass. And the sun shone upon the couch. And the clothes had slipped from off his arms and his breast, and he was asleep. Then she gazed upon the marvellous beauty of his appearance, and she said, "Alas, and am I the cause that these arms and this breast have lost their glory and the warlike fame which they once so richly enjoyed!"' Tennyson adds words capable of misconstruction.

76–8. *And arms on which the standing muscle sloped,/As slopes a wild brook o'er a little stone,/Running too vehemently to break upon it*: Tennyson remarks: 'I made this simile from a stream, and it is different, though like Theocritus, *Idyll* xxii 48ff.:

> ἐν δὲ μύες στερεοῖσι βραχίοσιν ἄκρον ὑπ' ὦμον
> ἕστασαν ἠύτε πέτροι ὀλοίτροχοι οὕστε κυλίνδων
> χειμάρρους ποταμὸς μεγάλαις περιέξεσε δίναις

('Moreover, the sinews upon his brawny arms upstood beside the shoulder like the boulder-stones some torrent hath rolled and rounded in his swirling eddies.') Hallam Tennyson adds: 'When some one objected that he had taken this simile from Theocritus, he answered: "It is quite different. Geraint's muscles are not compared to the rounded stones, but to the stream pouring vehemently over them."'

86. *all-puissant*: omnipotent.

95. *mightful*: mighty, powerful.

109–18. *Mabinogion*: 'And as she said this, the tears dropped from her eyes, and they fell upon his breast. And the tears she shed, and the words she had spoken, awoke him; and another thing contributed to awaken him, and that was the idea that it was not in thinking of him that she spoke thus, but that it was because she loved some other man more than him.'

121. *manful*: characterized by manly courage and resolution.

124–33. *Mabinogion*: 'And thereupon Geraint was troubled in his mind, and he called his squire; and when he came to him, "Go quickly," said he, "and prepare my horse and my arms, and make them ready. And do thou arise," said he to Enid, "and apparel thyself; and cause thy horse to be accoutred, and clothe thee in the worst riding-dress that thou hast in thy possession." . . . So she arose, and clothed herself in her meanest garments. "I know nothing, Lord", said she, "of thy meaning," "Neither wilt thou know at this time," said he.'

126. *charger*: a horse ridden in charging the enemy.
palfrey: small saddle-horse for ladies.

136. *cedarn*: made of cedar.

138. *With sprigs of summer*: 'Lavender' (T.).

146. *old Caerleon upon Usk*: 'Arthur's capital, *castra Legionis*, is in Monmouthshire on the Usk, which flows into the Bristol Channel' (T.).

147–56. *Mabinogion*: '"I am one of thy foresters, Lord, in the forest of Dean . . ." "Tell me thine errand," said Arthur. "I will do so, Lord," said he. "In the Forest I saw a stag, the like of which beheld I never yet." "What is there about him," asked Arthur, "that thou never yet didst see his like?" "He is of pure white, Lord, and he does not herd with any other animal through stateliness and pride, so royal is his bearing . . ." "It seems best to me," said Arthur, "to go and hunt him to-morrow at break of day; and to cause general notice thereof to be given to-night in all quarters of the Court." . . . Then Gwenhwyvar said to Arthur, "Wilt thou permit me, Lord," said she, "to go to-morrow to see and hear the hunt of the stag of which the young man spoke?" "I will, gladly," said Arthur. "Then will I go," said she."'

149. *notice*: intimation, intelligence.

157–9. *Mabinogion*: 'And Arthur wondered that Gwenhwyvar did not awake, and did not move in her bed; and the attendants wished to awaken her. "Disturb her not," said Arthur, "for she had rather sleep than go to see the hunting."' Tennyson's addition stresses a theme of the *Idylls*.

160–83. *Mabinogion*: '. . . and Gwenhwyvar and one of her maidens mounted them, and went through the Usk, and followed the track of the men and the horses. And as they rode thus, they heard a loud and rushing sound; and they looked behind them, and beheld a knight upon a hunter foal of mighty size; and the rider was a fair-haired youth, barelegged, and of princely mien, and a golden-hilted sword was at his side, and a robe and surcoat of satin were upon him, and two low shoes of leather upon his feet; and around him was a scarf of blue purple, at each corner of which was a golden apple . . . "From this place," said she, "we shall hear when the dogs are let loose."'

176. *queenhood*: the rank or dignity of a queen. Tennyson's coinage.

185. *Cavall*: mentioned as a hound of Arthur's in *Mabinogion*.

186. *hound of deepest mouth*: Tennyson compares *Midsummer Night's Dream* IV i 122: 'matched in mouth like bells'. See also *1 Henry VI* II iv 12: 'Between two dogs, which hath the deeper mouth.'

186–214. Following *Mabinogion*, but tempering details. See notes below.

190. *haughtiest lineaments: The Princess* ii 425. Disdainful look and bearing.

201. *Mabinogion*: 'Then the maiden turned her horse's head towards the knight; but the dwarf overtook him, and struck him as he had done the maiden, so that the blood coloured the scarf that Geraint wore. Then Geraint put his hand upon the hilt of his sword, but he took counsel with himself, and considered that it would be no vengeance for him to slay the dwarf, and to be attacked unarmed by the armed knight, so he returned to where Gwenhwyvar was.'

215–31. As in *Mabinogion*.

217. *earths*: burrows.

239. *Mabinogion*: 'And they went along a fair, and even, and lofty ridge of ground.'

242–55. Expanding *Mabinogion*.

255–92. *Mabinogion*: 'And every house he saw was full of men, and arms, and horses. And they were polishing shields, and burnishing swords, and washing armour, and shoeing horses.' In *Mabinogion*, Geraint's enemies (the knight, the lady and the dwarf) are warmly welcomed in the city.

274. *pips*: 'a bird-disease' (T.).

276. *bourg*: town under the shadow of a castle.

281. *harbourage*: lodging, shelter.

288. *scantly*: scarcely, hardly, barely.

293–325. Expanded from *Mabinogion*: 'At a little distance from the town he saw an old palace in ruins, wherein was a hall that was falling to decay. And as he knew not anyone in the town, he went towards the old palace; and when he came near to the palace, he saw but one chamber, and a bridge of marble-stone leading to it. And upon the bridge he saw sitting a hoary-headed man, upon whom were tattered garments.'

293. *spleenful*: passionate, irritable.

304. *So that*: provided that.

317–19. 'These lines were made at Middleham Castle' (T.).

319. *wilding*: growing wild.

322–3. 'Tintern Abbey' (T.). These lines had originally been part of *The Princess* (Prologue in MS.).

326–60. Not in *Mabinogion*.

330. *lander*: one who lands or goes ashore. Tennyson's coinage.

339. *coppice*: small wood or thicket grown for the purpose of periodic cutting.

347–58. Hallam Tennyson notes: 'This song of noble and enduring womanhood has its refrain in "Però giri Fortuna la sua ruota,/Come le piace"' (Dante, *Inferno* xv 95–6). Sir Charles Tennyson (*Cornhill* cliii (1936) 535) quotes from the Harvard MS. another version of the song:

> Come in, the ford is roaring on the plain,
> The distant hills are pale across the rain;
> Come in, come in, for open is the gate.
>
> Come in, poor man, and let the tempest blow.
> Let Fortune frown and old possession go,
> But health is wealth in high or low estate;
>
> Tho' Fortune frown thou shalt not hear us rail,
> The frown of Fortune never turn'd us pale,
> For man is man and master of his fate.
>
> Turn, Fortune, turn thy wheel with smile or frown,
> With thy false wheel we go not up or down,
> Our hoard is little but our hearts are great.
>
> Smile and we smile, the lords of many lands,
> Frown and we smile, the lords of our own hands,
> For man is man and master of his fate.
>
> The river ford will fall on yonder plain,
> The flying rainbow chase the flying rain,
> The sun at last will smile however late;
>
> Come in, come in, whoever lingers there,
> Nor scorn the ruin'd house and homely fare,
> The house is poor but open is the gate.

360–68. *Mabinogion*: 'And in the chamber he beheld an old decrepit woman, sitting on a cushion, with old, tattered garments of satin upon her; and it seemed to him that he had never seen a woman fairer than she must have been, when in the fulness of youth. And beside her was a maiden, upon whom were a vest and a veil, that were old, and beginning to be worn out. And truly, he never saw a maiden more full of comeliness, and grace, and beauty, than she.'

361. *mount*: an artificial mound of earth or stones.

364. *vermeil-white*: vermeil is a bright scarlet or red colour.

368. *rood*: 'Rood (originally the same as "rod") is the old word for cross' (T.).

375–81. Not in *Mabinogion*.

382–9. *Mabinogion*: 'And the hoary-headed man said to the maiden, "There is no attendant for the horse of this youth but thyself." "I will render the best service I am able," said she, "both to him and to his horse." And to the town went the maiden. And behold! the maiden came back and a youth with her, bearing on his back a costrel full of good purchased mead, and a quarter of a young bullock. And in the hands of the maiden was a quantity of white bread, and she had some manchet bread in her veil, and she came into the chamber.'

386. *costrel*: 'a bottle with ear or ears, by which it could be hung from the waist (*costrer*, by the side), hence sometimes called "pilgrim's bottle"' (T.).

389. *manchet bread*: 'little loaves or rolls made of fine wheat flour' (T.).

396. *trencher*: plate or platter.

398. *the wine made summer in his veins*: cf. *The Princess* i 183: 'The summer of the vine in all his veins.'

403–65. Expanded with reorganization from *Mabinogion*: 'And when they had finished eating, Geraint talked with the hoary-headed man, and he asked him in the first place, to whom belonged the palace that he was in. "Truly," said he, "it was I that built it, and to me also belonged the city and the castle which thou sawest." "Alas!" said Geraint, "how is it that thou hast lost them now?" "I lost a great Earldom as well as these," said he, "and this is how I lost them. I had a nephew, the son of my brother, and I took his possessions to myself; and when he came to his strength, he demanded of me his property, but I withheld it from him. So he made war upon me, and wrested from me all that I possessed."' Hallam Tennyson comments: 'In the *Mabinogion* Earl Yniol is the wrong-doer, and has earned his reward; but the poet has made the story more interesting and more poetic by making the tale of wrong-doing a calumny on the part of the Earl's nephew.' He also notes another aspect of this re-arrangement: 'In the Idyll, for the greater unity of the tale, the nephew and the knight of the Sparrow-hawk are one.'

412. *under-shapen*: deformed and dwarfish. Tennyson's coinage.

426–8. Not in *Mabinogion*. Geraint's reputation was celebrated by the Welsh bards.

432. *at Camelot*: Arthur's principal court; Geraint's adventures relate to Caerleon.

437. *grateful*: agreeable, acceptable.

440. *Limours*: introduced from later in *Mabinogion*. However, Tennyson's characterization is entirely his own.

465–73. Not in *Mabinogion*.

480–85. *Mabinogion*: 'In the midst of a meadow which is here, two forks will be set up, and upon the forks a silver rod, and upon the silver rod a Sparrow-Hawk . . . and no man can joust for the Sparrow-Hawk, except the lady he loves best be with him.'

495–503. *Mabinogion*: 'And if ... thou wilt permit me, Sir, to challenge for yonder maiden that is thy daughter, I will engage, if I escape from the tournament, to love the maiden as long as I live; and if I do not escape, she will remain unsullied as before.'

504–32. Not in *Mabinogion*.

522. *coursed one another*: followed one another.

531–2. *She found no rest, and ever fail'd to draw/The quiet night into her blood*: Hallam Tennyson compares *Aeneid* iv 529–31: '*neque umquam/solvitur in somnos, oculisve aut pectore noctem/accipit*' ('She never sinks to sleep, nor draws the night into eyes or heart').

543. *The chair of Idris*: 'Idris was one of the three primitive Bards. Cader Idris, the noblest mountain next to Snowdon in N. Wales' (T.).

562–74. As in *Mabinogion*.

563. *dishorsed*: unhorsed, dismounted. Tennyson's coinage.

565–6. *and now and then from distant walls/There came a clapping as of phantom hands*: 'This is an echo of the sword-clash' (T.).

567. *breathed*: paused, rested.

584–5. This addition to *Mabinogion* was necessitated by Tennyson's changes.

592–6. *Mabinogion* later gives a detailed account of Edyrn's return to the court, which suggested Tennyson's handling of the close of 'Geraint and Enid'.

595–6. *and fell at last/In the great battle fighting for the King*: Tennyson's addition.

609ff. Hallam Tennyson quotes *Mabinogion*: '"Where is the Earl Ynywl," said Geraint, "and his wife, and his daughter:" "They are in the chamber yonder," said the Earl's chamberlain, "arraying themselves in garments which the Earl has caused to be brought for them." "Let not the damsel array herself," said he, "except in her vest and her veil, until she come to the Court of Arthur, to be clad by Gwenhwyvar, in such garments as she may choose." So the maiden did not array herself.' From this point Tennyson considerably expands, through to l. 826.

631. *branch'd*: adorned with a figured pattern in embroidery.
flower'd: embellished with figures of flowers.

647. *bethought*: recollected.

661. *turkis*: turquoise.

672. *mixen*: dung-hill.

684. *trow*: believe.

724. *ragged-robin*: popular name for a well-known English flower.

730–31. *like those of old/That lighted on Queen Esther*: see Esther ii 1–4.

742–3. *And call'd her like that maiden in the tale,/Whom Gwydion made by glamour out of flowers*: Tennyson quotes from *Mabinogion*, 'The Tale of Math, son of Mathonwy': 'So they took the blossoms of the oak, and the blossoms of the broom, and the blossoms of the meadow-sweet, and produced from them a maiden, the fairest and most graceful that man ever saw. And they baptized her and gave her the name of Blodeuwedd' (flower-vision).

744–6. *And sweeter than the bride of Cassivelaun,/Flur, for whose love the Roman Cæsar first/Invaded Britain*: Hallam Tennyson comments: 'The love of a British maiden named Flur, who was betrothed to Cassivelaunus, according to the Welsh legend, led Caesar to invade Britain', from *Mabinogion*, 'Manawyddan the Son of Llyr'.

764. *flaws*: Hallam Tennyson compares *Hamlet* V i 210: 'the winter's flaw' – gusts of wind.

774. *As careful robins eye the delver's toil*: cf. 'Early Spring' (1833) 11–12: 'Earnest as redbreasts eye/The delver's toil.'

799. *weal*: welfare, well-being, happiness.

802. *dusky*: gloomy.

811. *intermitted*: interrupted.

818. *gaudy-day*: 'Holiday – now only used for special feast-days at the Universities' (H. T.).

826–7. *Now thrice that morning Guinevere had climb'd/The giant tower*: Geoffrey of Monmouth notes a Giant's Tower at Caerleon. In *Mabinogion* Guinevere places a watch on the ramparts.

836. *Mabinogion*: 'And the choicest of all Gwenhwyvar's apparel was given to the maiden.'

838. *Dubric, the high saint*: no dignitary is mentioned in *Mabinogion*. The name and epithet are derived from Layamon's *Brut*.

Geraint and Enid

Published 1859, the second half of 'Enid'. The title 'Enid' was expanded to 'Geraint and Enid' in 1870; the poem was divided into two parts in 1873; and the final titles were given in 1886.

1. *O purblind race of miserable men*: Hallam Tennyson compares Lucretius ii 14: '*O miseras hominum mentes, O pectora caeca*' ('O pitiable minds of men, O blind intelligences!').
purblind: totally or morally blind.

6–7. *until we pass and reach/That other, where we see as we are seen*: 1 Corinthians xiii 12: 'Now we see through a glass, darkly; but then face to face: now I know in part; but then shall I know even as also I am known.'

12. *perforce*: compulsorily, of necessity.

14–18. *Mabinogion*: 'And he desired Enid to mount her horse, and to ride forward, and to keep a long way before him. "And whatever thou mayest see, and whatever thou mayest hear concerning me," said he, "do thou not turn back. And unless I speak to thee, say not thou one word either."'

20–27. Not in *Mabinogion*.

30. *Mabinogion*: 'And he did not choose the pleasantest and most frequented road, but that which was the wildest and most beset by thieves.'

30. *holds*: strongholds, fortresses.

31. *Gray swamps and pools, waste places of the hern*: adapted from an unpublished stanza of 'Come not, when I am dead' (*c.* 1838): 'By swamps and pools, waste places of the hern.'

33. *Round*: brisk.

35–54. Not in *Mabinogion*.

51. *In every wavering brake an ambuscade*: suggesting Juvenal x 19–21.
      brake: a clump of bushes, thicket.
      ambuscade: ambush.

55–100. Based closely on *Mabinogion*, where however there are four attackers.

58. *caitiffs*: villains.

86. *cubit*: an ancient measure of length, between 18 and 22 inches.

101–15. Not in *Mabinogion*.

118–45. Based closely on *Mabinogion*.

146–52. Not in *Mabinogion*.

153–78. Expanding *Mabinogion*.

159. *corselet*: defensive armour covering the body.

161. *as he that tells the tale*: Tennyson.

169–70. *On whom the victor, to confound them more,/Spurr'd with his terrible war-cry*: not in *Mabinogion*. Perhaps an allusion to elegy on Geraint composed by Llywarch Hên, which opens: 'Before Geraint, the terror of the foe,/I saw steeds fatigued with the toil of battle./And after the shout was given, how dreadful was the onset.'

170–75. 'A memory of what I heard near Festiniog, but the scenery imagined is vaster' (T.).

171. *torrent*: rushing like a torrent.

186–94. Not in *Mabinogion*, which has a further episode with five attackers, thus making Enid drive twelve horses in all.

189. *disedge*: alleviate.

195–9. *Mabinogion*: 'And early in the day they left the wood, and they came to an open country, with meadows on one hand, and mowers mowing the meadows.'

198. *chased*: set like a jewel.

209. *meet*: suitable.

210–31. Based on *Mabinogion*.

232–40. Expanded from *Mabinogion*.

241–69. Not in *Mabinogion*, which simply remarks: 'And Geraint went to sleep; and so did Enid also.'

245. *errant*: wandering.

247. *doom*: 'judgment' (T.).

250. *ruth*: contrition, repentance, remorse.

255. *daws*: jackdaws.

258. *annulet*: a little ring.

267. *supporters*: figures represented as holding up or standing beside the shield, one on each side of the shield.

274. *roisterers*: swaggering or noisy revellers.

276–7. In *Mabinogion*, the Earl is not her previous suitor, though 'he set all his thoughts and his affections upon her'.

278. *pliant*: yielding, compliant.

306–47. Again expanding and modifying *Mabinogion*.

348–51. Not in *Mabinogion*.

352. *Mabinogion*: 'and she considered that it was advisable to encourage him in his request'.

356. *practise on*: to delude.

359–64. Not in *Mabinogion*.

373–5. *Mabinogion*: 'At midnight she arose, and placed all Geraint's armour together, so that it might be ready to put on.' Tennyson's ll. 387–9 are his addition.

376. *overtoil'd*: worn out or exhausted by excessive toil.

409. In *Mabinogion*, the remaining eleven.

418–35. Not in *Mabinogion*.

426. *mismated*: ill-matched.

431. See note to MG 774.

434. Identical to MG 775.

436–66. Expanded from *Mabinogion*.

439. *Doorm*: in *Mabinogion* Limours. 'The Bull' is Tennyson's designation.

442. *rood*: rod, a unit of measure between six and eight yards.

449. *bicker*: disturb, flash through.

450–56. In *Mabinogion*, Enid simply speaks.

458–9. *Borne on a black horse, like a thunder-cloud/Whose skirts are loosen'd by the breaking storm*: 'The horse's mane is compared to the skirts of the rain-cloud' (T.).

467–79. Not in *Mabinogion*, where Geraint has hereafter various combats, is wounded, meets Arthur, rests and is healed.

475. *cressy*: abounding in cresses.

490. 'Shall we go hungry, or shall we take his spoils and pay for our dinner with them?' (T.).

491. 'Enid shrinks from taking anything from her old lover' (T.).

500. *So fared it with Geraint*: in *Mabinogion*, Geraint is wounded by a dwarf and faints. Doorm (there named Limours) comes upon Enid, who is with a damsel whose husband has been killed by giants.

502. *Bled underneath his armour secretly*: in *Mabinogion* 'And the heat of the sun was very great, and through the blood and sweat, Geraint's armour cleaved to his flesh.'

509–35. Not in *Mabinogion*.

531–2. *made/The long way smoke beneath him in his fear*: echoing *Faerie Queene* II v 3: 'But prickt so fiers, that underneath his feete/The smouldering dust did round about him smoke.'

534. *scour'd*: ran off.

coppices: copses, thickets of small trees cut periodically for wood.

536–78. Expanding *Mabinogion*.

542. *'No, no, not dead!' she answer'd*: in *Mabinogion*, Enid thought Geraint was dead, and it was the Earl who 'thought that there still remained some life in Geraint'.

549. *quicken*: enliven

568. *All in the hollow of his shield*: *Mabinogion*: 'He had him carried with him in the hollow of his shield.'

572. *settle*: bench, chair.

597–607. Not in *Mabinogion*.

601. *beeves*: oxen, cattle.

608–717. Tennyson greatly expands this, though the main events are in *Mabinogion* (the brief commands to eat, drink and change apparel, and the blow).

627. *forage*: loot, booty.

631. *old serpent*: Revelation xii 9: 'And the great dragon was cast out, that old serpent, called the Devil, and Satan.' 'My father would quote this simile as good' (H. T.).

674. *flout*: a mocking speech or action.

679. *weed*: 'garment' (T.)

687–9. 'I made these lines on the High Down one morning at Freshwater' (T.).

693–4. *harder to be moved/Than hardest tyrants in their day of power*: 'The worst tyrants are those who have long been tyrannized over, if they have tyrannous natures' (T.).

716–17. *unknightly with flat hand,/However lightly, smote her on the cheek*: In *Mabinogion*: 'and he gave her a box on the ear'.

718–21. As in *Mabinogion*.

727–8. In *Mabinogion*, merely 'he clove him in twain'.

733–44. *Mabinogion*: 'He was grieved for two causes; one was, to see that Enid had lost her colour and her wonted aspect; and the other, to know that she was in the right.'

762ff. In *Mabinogion* there are other adventures, but the rest of Tennyson's poem is his own.

762–3. *since high in Paradise/O'er the four rivers the first roses blew*: Genesis ii 10: 'And a river went out of Eden to water the garden; and from thence it was parted, and became into four heads.'

768–70. *came a happy mist/Like that which kept the heart of Eden green/Before the useful trouble of the rain*: Genesis ii 6: 'But there went up a mist from the earth and watered the whole face of the ground.'

780ff.. Tennyson's version ends with Edyrn's encounter with Gareth, and his account of his conversion.

811. *the blameless King*: heroic epithet repeated GE 931, 969, BB 472, MV 162, 777, HG 865.

833. *And, toppling all antagonism*: repeating MG 491.

864. *Dubric, the high saint*: see notes to CA 452, MG 838.

902. *the vicious quitch*: a species of grass. Emily Lady Tennyson's letter diary records at this time Tennyson's efforts to eradicate this from his Farringford lawn.

903. *of blood*: inherited.

922. *leech*: doctor, surgeon.

925. *tendance*: attention, care.

929. *the sacred Dee*: Tennyson compares *Lycidas* 55: 'Where Deva spreads her wisard stream.' In Welsh Dee means sacred river.

932. *Uther*: see note to CA 13.

935. *Men weed the white horse on the Berkshire hills*: 'The white horse near Wantage on the Berkshire hills which commemorates the victory at Ashdown of the English under Alfred over the Danes (871). The white horse was the emblem of the English or Saxons, as the raven was of the Danes, and as the dragon was of the Britons' (T.).

939. *chairs*: places of authority.

967–9. *and fell/Against the heathen of the Northern Sea/In battle, fighting for the blameless King*: Hallam Tennyson quotes, from the notes to *Mabinogion*, Llywarch Hen's elegy on Geraint's death in the battle of Llongborth. Mrs Patmore, by request, sent a copy of the elegy to Tennyson in November 1857 (Patmore, *Memoir* (1900) ii 308).

Balin and Balan

Published 1885. Written 1872–4. Complete transformation of Malory Book ii, with the added characters of Guinevere, Lancelot and Vivien.

1. *Pellam the King, who held and lost with Lot*: not in Malory.
8. *Man's word is God in man*: repetition of CA 132.
9–10. *two strange knights/Who sit near Camelot at a fountain-side*: not in Malory's account of Balin.
13. *undertake*: enter into combat with.
23. *Brethren*: Tennyson preserves their relationship in Malory, but adds twinhood – see l. 617.
23–5. *to right and left the spring, that down,/From underneath a plume of lady-fern,/Sang, and the sand danced at the bottom of it*: 'suggested by a spring which rises near the house at Aldworth' (H.T.).
36. *Paynim*: pagan, heathen.
45. *pursuivant*: royal or state messenger with power to execute warrants.
51. *Balin, 'the Savage' – that addition thine*: in Malory Balin le savage from the first.
55. *half slew him*: in Malory the man is slain. He is further 'cousin to Arthur'.
61. *Saving for Balan*: Balin's brother has no such role in Malory.
78. *The Lost one Found was greeted as in Heaven*: echoing Luke xv 4–7.
80. *garlandage*: display of garlands. Tennyson's coinage.
85. *twelve battles*: the twelve battles listed by Nennius: see note to CA 517.
97. *heat*: passion.
98–9. *Saint/Arimathæan Joseph*: Joseph of Arimathea, reputed to have brought the Cross to Britain, leaving it at Glastonbury.
107. *arks*: receptacles, coffers.
114. *Garlon, mine heir*: in Malory Garlon is brother to Pellam.
118ff. *spear-stricken from behind*: as of others attacked by Garlon in Malory, but there is no embassage, nor is Garlon in any way equated with a spirit of slander.
128. *the cave*: not in Malory.
151. *moons*: months.
157. *Lancelot*: plays no part here in Malory.
181. *an*: if.
182–3. *as he/That brought her thither*: Lancelot. See CA 446–51, G 375–404.
191. *cognizance*: badge, device or emblem.

193. *langued gules*: 'red-tongued – language of heraldry' (H.T.).

204. *earnest*: promise.

226–9. *Thus, as a hearth lit in a mountain home,/And glancing on the window, when the gloom/Of twilight deepens round it, seems a flame/That rages in the woodland far below*: 'Suggested by what he often saw from his own study at Aldworth' (H.T.).

235–75. Not in Malory.

241. *counter door*: door opposite.

289. *hoarhead woodman*: in part suggested by a hoary-headed man in Malory.

302. *fabler*: one who invents fictitious stories.

309–10. *rocks/Roof-pendent*: stalactites.

310. *others from the floor,/Tusklike, arising*: stalagmites.

329. *donjon*: great tower or innermost keep of a castle.

330. *ivytods*: ivy bushes.

332–420. Sketchily based on Malory ii 14 where Balin enters Pellam's castle and is accosted by Pellam's brother, Garlon, at a feast: 'Then was Balin wel received, and brought to a chamber and unarmed him; and there were brought him robes to his pleasure, and would have had Balin leave his sword behinde him. "Nay," said Balin, "that will I not doe, for it is the custome of my countrey a knight alway to keepe his weapon with him, and that custome will I keepe, or else I will depart as I came." Then they gave him leave to were his sword. And so he went to the castle, and was set among knights of worship, and his lady afore him. Soone Balin asked a knight, "Is there not a knight in this court whose name is Garlon?" "Yonder he goeth," said the knight, "he with that blacke face; he is the marvailest knight that is now living, for he destroyeth many good knights, for he goeth invisible." "Ah, wel," said Balin, "is that he?" Then Balin advised him long: "If I slay him heere, I shall not scape; and if I leave him now, peradventure I shall never meete with him againe at such a steven; and much harm he will doe and he live." Therewith this Garlon espied that this Balin beheld him, and then he came and smote Balin on the face with the backe of his hand, and said, 'Knight, why beholdest thou me so? for shame therefore, eate thy meate and doe that thou came for." "Thou saist sooth," said Balin; "this is not the first despite that thou hast done me, and therefore I will doe that I came for;" and rose up fiersly, and clave his head to the shoulders. "Give me the troncheon," said Balin to his lady, "wherewith he slew your knight." Anone she gave it him, for alway she bare that troncheon with her; and therewith Balin smote him through the body, and said openly, "With that troncheon thou hast slaine a good knight, and now it sticketh in thy body." And then Balin called to him his hoast, saying, "Now may yee fetch blood inough to heale your sonne withall." Anone all the knights arose from the table for to set on Balin. And king Pellam himself arose up fiersly, and said, "Knight, why hast thou slaine my brother? thou shalt dye therefor, or thou depart." "Wel," said Balin, "then doe it your selfe." "Yes," said king Pellam, "there shall no man have adoe with thee but my selfe for the love of my brother." Then king Pellam caught in his hand a grim weapon, and smote egerly at Balin, but Balin put the sword betweene his head and the stroke, and therewith his sword burst in sunder; and when Balin was weponlesse he ranne into a chamber for to seeke some weapon, and so from chamber to chamber, and no weapon could he find, and alway king Pellam followed him; and at the last he entred into a chamber that was marvelously well dight and richly, and a bed arayed with cloth of gold, the richest that might be thought, and one lying therein; and thereby stood a table of cleane gold, with foure pillars of silver that bare up the table, and upon the table stood a marvailous speare strangely wrought. And when Balin saw the speare, hee gat it in his hand and turned him to king Pellam, and smote him passingly sore with that speare that king Pellam fell downe in a swowne, and therewith the castle rove and the walls brake and fell to the earth, and Balin fel downe so that he might not stir hand nor foot. And so the most part of the castle that was fallen downe through that dolorous stroke lay upon king Pellam and Balin three dayes . . . And that was the same speare that Longius smot our Lord to the heart. And king Pellam was nigh of Josephs kinne, and that was the most worshipfull man that lived in those dayes, and great pittie it was of his hurt.'

354. *besotted*: having the affections foolishly or dotingly engaged.

357–62. 'The goblet is embossed with scenes from the story of Joseph of Arimathea, his voyage, and the wattle-built church he raised at Glastonbury. King Pellam represents the type of asceticism and superstition' (H.T.).

359. *massiest*: heaviest, most solid.

372. *scantly*: scarcely, hardly.

380–420. Picked out by Tennyson as 'a passage of rapid blank verse (where the pauses are light, and the accentuated syllables under the average – some being short in quantity, and the narrative brief and animated)'.

392. *banneret*: crest, badge.

396. *pummel*: the knob terminating the hilt of a sword.

410. *rummage*: bustle, commotion, turmoil.

411. *counter*: opposite.

431–3. In Malory Vivien has no connection with Mark.

435. *wold*: elevated tract of open country or moorland.

438. *quire*: archaic form of choir.

467. *A lustful King*: Mark.

480. *maws*: throats, gullets.

ensepulchre: entomb.

493. *full loth*: very reluctant.

496–514. A deliberate fabrication of Vivien's; see l. 517.

504. *mumbled*: both spoken indistinctly and fondled with the lips.

507. *great tower*: see note to MG 826–7 (p. 328).

513. *The deathless mother-maidenhood of Heaven*: The Virgin Mary.

545. *buckler*: a small round shield.

547. Not so in Malory.

551. *hauberk*: long coat of mail or military tunic.

551. *and Balin's horse/Was wearied to the death, and, when they clash'd,/Rolling back upon Balin, crush'd the man/Inward, and either fell, and swoon'd away*: Malory ii 18: 'but their speares and their course was so big that it bare downe horse and man, so that they lay both in a swowne; but Balin was sore brused with the fall of his horse, for he was weary of travaile.'

560. *down*: first feathering of young birds.

563. *See what I see, be thou where I have been*: connive with me in the whole deception.

564. *casques*: helmets.

573–4. *I better prize/The living dog than the dead lion*: Ecclesiastes ix 4: for a living dog is better than a dead lion'.

578–620. Malory ii 18. 'Then said Balin le Savage, "What knight art thou? for or now I found never no knight that matched me." "My name is," said he, "Balan, brother to the good knight Balin." "Alas!" said Balin, "that ever I should see this day." And therewith he fel backward in a swowne. Then Balan went on all four feete and hands, and put off the helme of his brother, and might not know him by the visage it was so full hewen and bebled (be-bled); but when he awok he said, "O Balan, my brother, thou hast slaine me, and I thee, wherefore all the wide world shall speake of us both." "Alas!" said Balan, "that ever I saw this day, that through mishap I might not know you, for I espied well your two swords, but because yee had another shield, I deemed you had beene another knight." "Alas!" said Balin, 'al that made an unhappy knight in the castle, for he caused me to leave mine own shield to the destruction of us both; and if I might live I would destroy that castle for the ill customes" ... "We came both out of one wombe, that is to say, mothers belly, and so shall we lye both in one pit" ... "Now," said Balin, "when we are buried in one tombe, and the mention made over us how two brethren slew each other, there will never good knight nor good man see our tombe but they will pray for our soules."'

590–606. Not in Malory. Necessitated by Tennyson's completion of his plot.

Merlin and Vivien

Published 1859 as 'Vivien', with final title in 1870. Begun in February and finished on 31 March 1856. Lines 6–146 and 188–94 added in 1875 and 1873 respectively. The story of the poem is essentially original, though founded on the episode of Merlin's seduction by Vivien, Malory iv 1.

2. *Broceliande*: 'The forest of Broceliand in Brittany near St Malo' (T.). In one source Tennyson used, the Vulgate *Merlin*, the site of the mage's seduction.

5, 147. *the wily Vivien*: cf. Satan as 'wily snake', full of 'subtle wiles' and 'wily Adder', *Paradise Lost* ix 91, 184, 625.

10. *Tintagil*: Mark's court, as well as being the site of the supposed coming of Arthur.

14–16. Matthew xxii 30.

33. *Here are snakes within the grass*: Virgil, *Eclogues* ii 93: '*frigidus, O pueri, fugite hinc, latet anguis in herba*' ('O boys, flee from hence, a clammy snake lurks in the grass').

40. *As Love, if Love be perfect, casts out fear*: 1 John iv 18: 'perfect love casteth out fear'.

41. *So Hate, if Hate be perfect, casts out fear*: Psalm cxxxix 21–2: 'Do not I hate them, O Lord, that hate thee? Yea, I hate them with perfect hatred.'

45. *sown upon the wind*: Hoseah vii 8: 'for they have sown the wind, and they shall reap the whirlwind: it hath no stalk: the bud shall yield no meal'.

46. *betimes*: at an early time, period, season.

47–8. *That old true filth, and bottom of the well,/Where Truth is hidden*: Sir Thomas Browne: 'Truth, which wise men say doth lye in a well' (Tilley's *Proverbs*, T582).

51–2. *There is no being pure,/My cherub; saith not Holy Writ the same?*: Proverbs xx 9: 'Who can say, I have made my heart clean, I am pure from my sin?'

86–7. *All glittering like May sunshine on May leaves/In green and gold, and plumed with green*: a recollection of Guinevere going a-maying, Malory xix 1.

98. *askance*: obliquely, askew.

broken-wise: disconnectedly, incoherently.

108. *that gray cricket*: the minstrel, l. 9 ff.

115. *The mortal dream that never yet was mine*: 'The only real bit of feeling, and the only pathetic line which Vivien speaks' (T.).

117. *lubber*: clumsy, stupid.

123. *seeling*: 'sewing up eyes of hawk' (H. T.).

jesses: 'straps of leather fastened to legs' (H. T.).

124. *to check at pies*: 'fly at magpies' (H.T.).

125. *Nor will she rake*: 'nor will she fly at other game' (H. T.).

129. *tower'd*: to mount up, as a hawk, so as to be able to swoop down on the quarry.

134. *As once – of old – among the flowers – they rode*: see CA 449, BB 267, G 386–7.

139. *Leaven'd*: permeated with a transforming influence as leaven does. See Matthew xiii 33.

145–6. *Thereafter as an enemy that has left/Death in the living waters*: 'Poisoned the wells' (T.).

149. *lavish*: loose, wild, licentious.

150–62. Tennyson's invention. Possibly suggested by the fact that in Malory ix 15 another enchantress attempts to seduce Arthur.

165. *Merlin, who knew the range of all their arts,/Had built the King his havens, ships, and halls,/Was also Bard, and knew the starry heavens*: Geoffrey of Monmouth credits Merlin with the building of Stonehenge.

178. *sports*: amorous dalliance.

188. *He walk'd with dreams and darkness*: Proverbs ii 13: 'who leave the paths of uprightness to walk in the ways of darkness'.

190. *An ever-moaning battle in the mist*: 'The vision of the battle at the end' (T.).

199. *Drave*: drove.

203–12. Cf. Vulgate *Merlin*: 'Sir, said Viviane, I would have you teach and show me how to inclose and imprison a man without a tower, without walls, without chains, and by enchantments alone, in such manner that he may never be able to go out, except by me . . . Then the damsel rose and made a ring with her wimple round the bush and round Merlin, and began her enchantments such as he himself had taught her; and nine times she made the ring, and nine times she made the enchantment . . . and when he awoke and looked round him, it seemed to him that he was inclosed in the strongest tower in the world.'

216. *quench'd*: destroyed.

223. *sallows*: willows.

229–31. *As on a dull day in an Ocean cave/The blind wave feeling round his long sea-hall/In silence*: 'This simile is taken from what I saw in the Caves of Ballybunion' (T.). This was in 1842.

236–40. Cf. Vulgate *Merlin*: 'When Vivien heard this, for her great treason, and the better to delude and deceive him, she put her arms round his neck, and began to kiss him, saying, that he might well be hers, seeing that she was his.'

247. *the little elf-god eyeless*: blind Cupid.

248. *arras*: covered with tapestry.

315. *The people call you prophet*: see GL 491.

316. *expound*: to be one's own expositor.

347. *Nadir hell*: very bottom of hell.

365. *spell*: interpret.

403. *Far other was the song that once I heard*: 'The song about the clang of battle-axes, etc., in the *Coming of Arthur*' (T.).

406. *current*: running about.

424. *roundel*: short simple song with refrain.

426–30. *Until they vanish'd by the fairy well/That laughs at iron – as our warriors did – where children cast their pins and nails, and cry,/ "Laugh, little well!" but touch it with a sword,/It buzzes fiercely round the point*: Mabinogion 'The Fountain of Baranton is supplied by a mineral spring, and it bubbles up on a piece of iron or copper being thrown into it. "Les enfants s'amusent à y jeter des épingles, et disent par commun proverbe: 'Ris donc, fontaine de Berendon, et je te donnerai une épingle.'"*

464. *counterchanged*: to change to the opposite.

473–4. *Azure, an Eagle rising or, the Sun/In dexter chief*: these fancied arms are heraldically correct, comprising an azure or sky-blue background, with a golden eagle in flight, and the sun in the top left corner of the shield.

477. *graff*: a graft, shoot inserted in another stock.

485. *prurient*: having an itching desire or curiosity.

489. *But work as vassal to the larger love*: In Memoriam xlviii 8: 'and makes it vassal unto love'.

506–8. *a single misty star,/Which is the second in a line of stars/That seem a sword beneath a belt of three*: 'θ Orionis – the nebula in which is embedded the great multiple star. When this was written some astronomers fancied that this nebula in Orion was the vastest object in the Universe – a firmament of suns too far away to be resolved into stars by the telescope, and yet so huge as to be seen by the naked eye' (T.).

515. *pupilage*: condition of being a minor or ward.

530. *misfaith*: disbelief, mistrust.

540. *buxom*: plump and comely.

550. *unmortised*: unjointed.

553–97. 'People have tried to discover this legend, but there is no legend of the kind that I know of' (T.).

571–2. *for magnet-like she drew/The rustiest iron of old fighters' hearts*: Paradise Regained ii 167–8: 'lead/At will the manliest, resolutest brest,/As the Magnetic hardest Iron draws.'

576. *serpent hands*: Lucretius v 1303, *anguimanus*.

616–48. 'Nor is this legend to be found' (T.).

633. *lash'd*: 'like an eyelash' (T.).

636. *cairn'd*: furnished with or surmounted by a cairn. Tennyson's coinage.

654. *whelm*: cover over.

655. *turfs*: buries, covers with turf.

691. They *ride abroad redressing human wrongs*: one of Arthur's precepts: see Dedication 8, G 468.

697. *drove*: herd of beasts, cattle.

703–17. *Sir Valence*: presumably to be taken in the spirit of Tennyson's notes to 553–97 and 616–48. Not in Malory.

707. *reckling*: youngest or smallest child in a family.

712. *outland*: foreign, alien.

719–43. *Sir Sagramore*: an actual knight in Malory, but no equivalent episode there.

720. *that ardent man*: play upon Sagramore's chivalric designation, 'le desirous', originally meaning eager or ardent in deeds of arms.

732. *darkling*: in the dark, in darkness.

741. *blazed*: published, divulged.

745–65. *Sir Percivale*: approximating an experience of his in Malory xiv 9.

748. *wether*: ram.

768. *commerce*: intercourse of the sexes, especially in a bad sense.

792. *leal*: loyal, faithful.

796. *poach'd*: trampled into mire.

799. *By instance*: by fact or example brought forward in support of a general assertion.

808. *rail*: utter abusive language.

821. *nine tithes of times*: nine times out of ten.

838. *fell*: beard.

842. *session*: the state or posture of being seated.

847. *fairy*: Vivien (Nimue) in Malory had magical powers.

867. *Seethed like a kid in its own mother's milk*: Exodus xxiii 19: 'Thou shalt not seethe a kid in his mother's milk.'

899. *cageling*: a bird kept in a cage. Tennyson's coinage.

911. *passages of love*: amorous relations.

937. *white-listed*: 'striped with white' (T.).

951. *petulancy*: wantonness, immodesty.

963. *overtalk'd*: overcome by talking.

overworn: worn out, exhausted, spent with age, toil.

967. *hollow oak*: in the Vulgate *Merlin* it is a bush of white thorn, and in Malory within a rock or cave.

969. *I have made his glory mine*: reversing Isaiah xlii 8: 'My glory I will not give to another.'

Lancelot and Elaine

Published 1859 as 'Elaine', with final title in 1870. Begun July 1858, virtually complete 8 February 1859. Its origin is in Malory xviii 9–20.

7. *soilure*: soiling, staining.
9. *devices*: emblematic figures or designs.
   blazon'd: painted or depicted according to the rules of heraldry.
10. *tinct*: colour, hue, tint.
30–31 *tilt/For the great diamond in the diamond jousts*: suggested by jousting for a diamond just after this in Malory xviii 21.
34–55. This episode is not in Malory.
35. *Lyonnesse*: 'A land that is said to have stretched between Land's End and Scilly, and to have contained some of Cornwall as well' (T.).
44. *lichen'd*: to cover with lichens. Tennyson's coinage.
53. *scaur*: a precipitous bank.
61. *Once every year*: in Malory the jousts for a diamond are daily till Christmas.
65–6. *The heathen, who, some say, shall rule the land/Hereafter*: historically correct.
75–6. *Hard on the river nigh the place which now/Is this world's hugest*: the river Thames and London.
78–83. Malory xviii 8: 'So king Arthur made him ready to depart to these justs, and would have had the queene with him, but at that time shee would not goe, shee said, for shee was sicke and might not ride at that time. "Then me repenteth," said the king, "for these seven yeares yee saw not such a fellowship together, except at Whisontide (Whitsuntide) when sir Galahad departed from the court." "Truely," said the queene unto the king, "yee must hold me excused, I may not be there, and that me repenteth." And many deemed that the queen would not be there because of sir Launcelot du Lake, for sir Launcelot would not ride with the king; for hee said that hee was not hole of the wound the which sir Mador had given him."'
89. *Love-loyal to the least wish of the Queen*: the line is repeated at G125.
91. *tale*: whole amount.
94. *lets*: hinders.
97–101. Malory xviii 8: '"Sir Launcelot, yee are greatly to blame thus to hold you behind my lord; what trow yee what your enemies and mine will say and deeme? nought else but see how sir Launcelot holdeth him ever behind the king and so doth the queene, for that they would have

their pleasure together; and thus will they say," said the queene unto sir Launcelot.'

101. *pastime*: recreation, amusement, sport (but Tennyson gives the word a sexual innuendo).

103–4. *'Are ye so wise? ye were not once so wise,/My Queen, that summer, when ye loved me first'*: Malory xviii 9: '"Madame," said sir Launcelot to the queene, "I alow your wit, it is of late come sith yee were wise."'

118. *devoir*: duty, business, appointed task.

126–7. *only here to-day/There gleam'd a vague suspicion in his eyes*: cf. Malory xx 2: 'for king Arthur was loth thereto, that any noise should bee upon sir Launcelot and his queene; for the king had a deeming, but he would not here of it'.

134. *The low sun makes the colour*: the colours of sunrise and sunset.

139. *buzz*: *OED* 5, 'to spread as a rumour, with whispering or busy talk'.

140–57. Malory xviii 9: '"But wit yee well," said sir Launcelot unto queene Guenever, "that at those jousts I will be against the king and all his fellowship." "Yee may there doe as yee list," said queene Guenever; "but by my counsaile ye shall not be against your king and your fellowship for therein are many hardy knights of your blood."'

143–4. *Before a King who honours his own word,/As if it were his God's*: see G 470: 'To honour his own word as if his God's.'

147. *wit*: perceptive.

180–81. *'Whence comest thou, my guest, and by what name/Livest between the lips?'*: an epic formula, as in *Aeneid* xii 235.

186. Identical with l. 140.

192. The borrowing of the shield is in Malory.

202. *lustihood*: vigour of body, robustness.

210–13. 'A vision prophetic of Guinevere hurling the diamonds into the Thames' (T.).

214. *belike*: as likely as not.

248. *The flower of all the west and all the world*: Guinevere.

249–52: *but in him/His mood was often like a fiend, and rose/And drove him into wastes and solitudes/For agony, who was yet a living soul*: Luke viii 29: 'For he had commanded the unclean spirit to come out of the man. For oftentimes it had caught him: and he was kept bound with chains and in fetters; and he brake the bands, and was driven of the devil into the wilderness.' Lancelot's madness is in Malory xi 8, xii 5.

259. *And loved him, with that love which was her doom*: reflecting Malory xviii 9: 'and ever shee beheld sir Launcelot wonderfully; and she cast such a love unto sir Launcelot that shee could not withdraw her love, wherefore she died; and her name was Elaine la Blaunche.'

269. *glanced*: referred to obliquely in passing.

272. *reft*: robbed.

279. *Badon hill*: see 302 and note.

286–302. Arthur's twelve battles against the Saxons, as listed in the ninth-century chronicle of Nennius, with modifications of Tennyson's own. For the most important, see below.

287. *Glem*: small river in the north of Tennyson's own county, Lincolnshire.

289. *that on Bassa*: the island called the Bass Rock.

291. *Celidon the forest*: the Caledonian forest, in Scotland.

293. In Nennius Arthur bore the image of the Virgin Mary upon his shoulders. For the cuirass or breastplate cf. *Faerie Queene* I vii 29–30: 'Athwart his brest a bauldrick brave he ware,/That shynd, like twinkling stars, with stons most pretious rare.//And in the midst thereof one pretious stone/Of wondrous worth, and eke of wondrous mights,/Shapt like a Ladies head, exceeding shone.'

296. *Caerleon*: one of Arthur's two capitals.

297. *the wild white Horse*: the emblem of the Saxons was a white horse (not to be confused with the white horse emblem mentioned in GE 935, which is prehistoric).

298. *parapet*: defence of earth or stone to cover troops from the enemy's observation or fire.

299. *Agned-Cathregonion*: the footnote alternative being preferred to the 'Cat Bregion' of the text, as more sonorous.

302. *Badon*: the last and most decisive battle.

312. *For if his own knight cast him down*: as in Malory x 73, xviii 23.

314. *Yet in this heathen war the fire of God/Fills him*: cf. CA 127–8: '"Sir and my liege," he cried, "the fire of God/Descends upon thee in the battle-field."'

338. *rathe*: 'early' (T.).

341. *Down the long tower-stairs, hesitating*: '"Stairs" is to be read as a monosyllable, with a pause after it' (T.).

355–82. Malory xviii 9: 'So thus as shee came too and fro, shee was so hoot in her love that shee besought sir Launcelot to weare upon him at the justs a token of hers. "Faire damosell," said sir Launcelot, "and if I graunt you that, yee may say I doe more for your love then ever I did for lady or damosell." Then hee remembred him that hee would ride unto the justs disguised, and for because he had never before that time borne no manner of token of no damosell, then he bethought him that he would beare on of hers, that none of his blood thereby might know him. And then hee said, "faire damosell, I will graunt you to weare a token of yours upon my helmet, and therefore what it is shew me." "Sir," said shee, "it is a red sleeve of mine of scarlet, well embroadered with great pearles." And so she brought it him. So sir Launcelot received it, and

343

said, "Never or this time did I so much for no damosell." And then sir
Launcelot betooke the faire damosell his shield in keeping, and prayed
her to keepe it until he came againe. And so that night hee had merry
rest and great cheere; for ever the faire damosell Elaine was about sir
Launcelot all the while that she might be suffered.'

360. *favour*: in medieval chivalry something given by a lady to her knight to
be worn conspicuously as a token of affection.

398. *bushless*: devoid of bushes. Tennyson's coinage.

432. *Since to his crown the golden dragon clung*: the dragon is Arthur's symbol
from the first; see note to C A 373 (p. 309).

444. *seat*: seat in the saddle.

446. *crescent*: growing, developing.

447–9. *and in me there dwells/No greatness, save it be some far-off touch/Of great-
ness to know well I am not great*: 'When I wrote that, I was thinking of
Wordsworth and myself' (T.).

459. *bode*: waited. In Malory xv 5 Lancelot waits to see which side is the
weaker, and then joins it.

468–74. Malory xviii 11: '"O mercy, Jesu," said sir Gawaine, "what
knight is that I see yonder that doth so mervailous deedes of armes in the
fields?" "I wote well who is that," said king Arthur, "but at this time I
will not name him." "Sir," said sir Gawaine, "I would say it were sir
Launcelot by the riding, and by his buffets that I see him deale; but
alway me seemeth it should not bee hee, because he beareth the red
sleeve upon the helme, for I wist him never yet beare token at no justs of
lady nor gentlewoman." "Let him be," said king Arthur, "for he will be
better known and doe more or he depart."'

475. *a fiery family passion for the name/Of Lancelot*: as in Malory.

480–84. *as a wild wave in the wide North-sea,/Green-glimmering toward the summit,
bears, with all/Its stormy crests that smoke against the skies,/Down on a bark, and
overbears the bark,/And him that helms it*: 'Seen on a voyage to Norway' (T.).

484. *helms*: steers.

494. *holpen*: assisted, helped.

502–5. Malory xviii 12, after Lancelot has been offered the prize: '"If I
have deserved thankes, I have sore bought it, and that me repenteth, for
I am like never to escape with my life; therefore, faire lords, I pray you
that yee will suffer mee to depart where me liketh, for I am sore hurt; I
take no force of none honour, for I had lever to rest me then to be lord of
all the world."'

509–16. Malory xviii 12: '"O gentle knight sir Lavaine, helpe me that this
trunchion were out of my side, for it sticheth so sore that it almost
sleyeth mee." "O mine owne lord," said sir Lavaine, "I would faine
helpe you, but it dreads me sore and I draw out the trunchion that yee

shall bee in perill of death." "I charge you," said sir Launcelot, "as yee love mee, draw it out," And therewith he discended from his horse, and so did sir Lavaine, and foorthwith sir Lavaine drew the trunchion out of his side; and sir Launcelot gave a great shrieke and a mervailous ghastly grone, and his blood brast out nigh a pinte at once, that at the last hee sanke downe upon his buttocks and sowned paile and deadly.'

554–5. *And after Lancelot, Tristram, and Geraint/And Gareth, a good knight*: As in Malory, with the exception of Geraint, who occurs only in *Mabinogion*.

567. *tarriance*: delay, procrastination.

591. *fantastical*: full of absurd notions.

606. *and writhed upon it*: in different circumstances, Malory xi 8: 'then she writhed and weltered as a mad woman'.

635ff. *Courtesy with a touch of traitor in it*: not in Malory, where Gawain is loyal to Lancelot at this time.

639. *turn'd*: shaped, formed.

657. *but an*: but if.

660. *ramp in the field*: heraldic lions rampant or erect on their hindfeet on the surface or 'field' of the shield.

724. *predoom'd*: precondemned.

739. *wormwood*: emblem or type of what is bitter or grievous to the soul.

786–92. Malory xviii 15: 'By fortune sir Lavaine was riden to play him and to enchafe (heat) his horse. And anone as faire Elaine saw him she knew him, and then she cried aloude unto him; and when hee heard her anon hee came unto her. And then she asked her brother, "How fareth my lord sir Launcelot?" "Who told you, sister, that my lords name was sir Launcelot?"'

787. *caper*: prance.

curvet: leap of the horse in which the fore-legs are raised together and equally advanced, and the hind-legs raised with a spring before the fore-legs reach the ground.

798. *his own far blood*: distant relatives.

807. *battle-writhen*: twisted out of regular shape or form by incessant combat.

810. *unsleek*: unkempt. Tennyson's coinage.

843–56. Malory xviii 15: 'So this maide Elaine never went from sir Launcelot, but watched him daie and night, and gave such attendance upon him, there was never woman did more kindlyer for man then shee did.'

851. *forbore*: tolerated.

857. *simples*: things medicinally pure.

877. *the bright image of one face*: 'Vision of Guinevere' (T.).

904. *festal*: keeping holiday.

922–42. Malory xviii 19: '"Have mercy upon me, and suffer mee not to die for your love." "What would yee that I did?" said sir Launcelot. "I would have you unto my husband," said the maide Elaine. "Faire damosell, I thanke you," said sir Lancelot: "but certainely." said hee, "I cast mee never to bee married." "Then, faire knight," said shee, "will yee bee my paramour?" "Jesu defend mee!" said sir Launcelot, "for then should I reward your father and your brother full evil for their great goodnesse." "Alas!" said she, "then must I needes die for your love . . . for but if ye wil wed mee, or else be my paramour at the least, wit ye well, sir Launcelot, my good daies are done." '

934. *To serve you, and to follow you thro' the world*: cf. *Romeo and Juliet* II ii 148: 'And follow thee my lord throughout the world.'

936. *All ear and eye*: modelled on Adam's being 'all ear', *Paradise Lost* iv 410.

951–2. Malory xviii 19: ' "that wheresoever yee will set your heart upon some good knight that will wed you, I shall give you together a thousand pound yearely to you and to your heires." '

954. *So*: if.

955. *blood*: kin.

966–9. Added to Malory.

998. The song takes the place of Elaine's religious meditation, Malory xviii 19.

1012–19. The Banshee, as described in J. Brand's *Popular Antiquities*.

1065. *discomfort*: desolation, grief, sorrow.

1092. *ghostly man*: priest. Malory has 'ghostly father'.

1096–129. Malory xviii 19: 'And then shee called her father sir Bernard, and her brother sir Tirre, and heartely shee praied her father that her brother might write a letter like as she would endite it. And so his father graunted her. And when the letter was written word by word like as shee had devised, then she prayed her father that shee might bee watched untill she were dead, "And while my body is whole, let this letter be put into my right hand, and my hand bound fast with the letter untill that I bee cold, and let me be put in a faire bed with all the richest clothes that I have about me, and so let my bed and all my rich clothes be laide with me in a chariot to the next place where as the Thamse is, and there let me bee put in a barge, and but one man with me, such as yee trust, to stere me thither, and that my barge be covered with blacke samite over and over. Thus, father, I beseech you let me be done." So her father graunted her faithfully that all this thing should bee done like as shee had devised. Then her father and her brother made great dole, for, when this was done, anon shee died.'

1125. *Was rather in the fantasy than the blood*: imagined rather than real.

1129. *dole*: mourning.

1130–54. Malory xviii 19: 'And so when shee was dead, the corps and the bed and all was led the next way unto the Thamse, and there a man and

the corps and all were put in a barge on the Thamse, and so the man
steered the barge to Westminster, and there hee rowed a great while too
and fro or any man espied it.'

1150. *coverlid*: coverlet, uppermost covering of a bed.

1170–235. Malory xviii 20: 'So by fortune king Arthur and queene Guenev-
er were speaking together at a window; and so as they looked into the
Thamse, they espied the blacke barge, and had mervaile what it might
meane ... and shee lay as though she had smiled.'

1170. *oriel*: large recess with a window.

1179. *Your beauty is your beauty*: cf. LT 556.

1197. *quicker of belief*: more rapid understanding.

1202. *despite*: contempt, scorn, disdain.

1210. *joys*: sexual pleasures.

1253. *girt with*: encircled by.

1256–7. Sir Percivale and Sir Galahad as pallbearers are Tennyson's addi-
tion.

1262. Malory xviii 20: 'Then the queene espied the letter in the right hand,
and told the king thereof. Then the king tooke it in his hand.'

1264–74. Malory xviii 20: '"Most noble knight, my lord sir Launcelot du
Lake, now hath death made us two at debate for your love; I was your
lover, that men call the faire maiden of Astolat; therefore unto all ladies
I make my moone; yet for my soule that yee pray, and bury me at the
least, and offer ye my masse peny. This is my last request; and a cleane
maide I died, I take God to my witnesse. Pray for my soule, sir Launce-
lot, as thou art a knight pearles."'

1275–9. Malory xviii 20: 'And when it was red, the queene and all the
knights wept for pittie of the dolefull complaints.'

1281–98. Malory xviii 20: '"My lord king Arthur, wit you well that I am
right heavy of the death of this faire damosell; God knoweth I was never
causer of her death by my will, and that I will report mee unto her owne
brother, here hee is, sir Lavaine. I will not say nay," said sir Launcelot,
"but that shee was both faire and good, and much I was beholden unto
her, but shee loved me out of measure."'

1298–301. Malory xviii 20: '"Yee might have shewed her," said the
queene, "some bountie and gentlenesse, that ye might have preserved
her life."'

1303–14. Malory xviii 20: '"Madame," said sir Launcelot, "shee would
none other way bee answered but that shee would bee my wife, or else
my paramour, and of these two I would not graunt her; but I proffered
her, for her good love which shee shewed me, a thousand pound yearely
to her and her heires, and to wed any manner of knight that she could
find best to love in her heart; for, madame," said sir Launcelot, "I love

347

not to bee constrained to love, for love must arise of the heart, and not by constraint."

1311. *Estate*: endow with.

1315–18. Malory xviii 20: 'Then said the king unto sir Launcelot, "It will be your worship that ye oversee that shee bee buried worshipfully."'

1319–35. Malory xviii 20: 'And so many knights went thether to behold the faire dead maide. And on the morrow shee was richly buried; and sir Launcelot offered her masse peny, and all the knights of the round table that were there at that time offered with sir Launcelot.' Tennyson says of ll. 1319–27: 'This passage and the "tower-stair" passage (l. 341) are among the best blank verse in *Lancelot and Elaine*, I think' (T.).

1322. *sad beyond his wont*: Virgil, *Georgics* i 412: '*praeter solitum*'.

1333. *blazon'd*: painted with a heraldic device.

1337–42. Malory xviii 20: 'Then the queene sent for sir Launcelot, and praied him of mercy, for because she had been wroth with him causeles. "This is not the first time," said sir Launcelot, "that yee have beene displeased with me causeles; but, madame, ever I must suffer you, but what sorrow that I endure yee take no force."'

1346. *affiance*: faith, trust.

1369–70. Malory xviii 20: '"That is truth," said king Arthur and many knights; "love is free in himselfe, and never wil be bound, for where hee is bound hee loseth himselfe."'

1377. *inrunning*: inflowing.

1395. *Who passes thro' the vision of the night*: Job iv 14: 'in thoughts from the visions of the night, when deep sleep falleth on men.'

1418. *Not knowing he should die a holy man*: Malory xxi 10: 'I asked my father why he did not write an Idyll "How Sir Lancelot came unto the hermitage, and how he took the habit unto him; and how he sent to Almesbury and found Queen Guinevere dead, whom they brought to Glastonbury; and how Sir Lancelot died a holy man"; and he answered, "Because it could not be done better than by Malory". My father loved his own great imaginative knight, the Lancelot of the *Idylls*' (H. T.).

The Holy Grail

Published December 1869 (dated 1870). Begun 9 September 1868, nearly complete by the 14th, complete on the 23rd. Tennyson's source was Malory xi–xvii, which he modifies very considerably, particularly in the character of Percivale, though the Grail appearances are faithful to Malory.

2. *Sir Percivale*: the original hero of the Grail legend, and always a most important person in it, though his place was in the later form of the story (especially Malory) taken by Galahad. Tennyson follows the later legend, but by making Percivale the narrator he gives to him and to his adventures the chief degree of prominence. Percivale as a framing character occurs in Malory however; see xi 14 and xvii 23.

3. *Whom Arthur and his knighthood call'd the Pure*: not in Malory. Tennyson's addition.

5–7. *and leaving for the cowl/The helmet in an abbey far away/From Camelot, there, and not long after, died*: Malory xvii 23.

9. *Ambrosius*: not in Malory.

14. *gustful*: gusty

18. *I have seen this yew-tree smoke*: 'The pollen in Spring, which, blown abroad by the wind, looks like smoke' (T.).

21. *beyond the pale*: beyond the limit or boundary of the monastery.

26–7. *but every one of you/Stamp'd with the image of the King*: cf. CA 269–70.

32. *vainglories*: the only other plural usage is Milton's.

33. *heats*: passions.

40. *one of your own knights*: Bors; see ll. 696–8.

48. *Aromat*: 'Used for Arimathea, the home of Joseph of Arimathea, who, according to the legend, received in the Grail the blood that flowed from our Lord's side' (T.).

49–50. *After the day of darkness, when the dead/Went wandering o'er Moriah*: Matthew xxvii 45 and 52–3: 'Now from the sixth hour there was darkness over all the land unto the ninth hour...And the graves were opened; and many bodies of the saints which slept arose, And came out of the graves after his resurrection, and went into the holy city, and appeared unto many.'
Moriah: 2 Chronicles iii 1.

52–3. *Glastonbury, where the winter thorn/Blossoms at Christmas, mindful of our Lord*: 'It was believed to have been grown from the staff of Joseph of Arimathea' (H. T.).

54. *bode*: remained.

57–8. *the holy cup/Was caught away to Heaven*: see Malory xvii 22.

61. *Arviragus*: king of the Britons.

63. *wattles*: rods or stakes, interlaced with twigs or branches of trees, used to form fences and the walls of buildings.

69–70. *And one no further off in blood from me/Than sister*: Malory xvii 2.

85. *winters*: years.

87. *thro' five or six*: five or six old men.

110. *use*: habit, custom.

136–7. *'God make thee good as thou art beautiful,'/Said Arthur, when he dubb'd him knight*: Malory xiii 1: 'And on the morrow at the houre of prime, at Galahads desire, he (Lancelot) made him knight; and said, "God make him a good man, for beautie faileth him not as any that liveth."'

dubb'd: conferred the rank of knighthood by the ceremony of striking the shoulder with a sword.

143–5. *but some,/Call'd him a son of Lancelot, and some said/Begotten by enchantment*: Malory xi 2 tells of the enchantment by which Lancelot was made to sleep with Elaine (daughter of King Pelles), believing her to be Guinevere: 'and for this entent. The king knew wel that sir Launcelot should get a child upon his daughter, the which should be named sir Galahad the good knight, by whom all the forraine countrey should bee brought out of danger, and by him the holy grale would bee achieved.'

149–60. Malory xvii 7, in which Percivale's sister speaks to Galahad: '"Loe, lords," said the gentlewoman, "here is a girdell that ought to be set about the sword; and wit yee well that the greatest part of this girdell was made of my haire, the which I loved full well while I was a woman of the world; but as soone as I wist that this adventure was ordained mee, I clipped off my haire, and made this girdell . . . Now recke I not though I die, for now I hold mee one of the blessed maidens of the world, which hath made thee the worthiest knight of the world."'

162. *the spiritual city*: in the Grail legends the city of Sarras, where Joseph of Arimathea converted King Evelac.

172. *The Siege perilous*: 'The perilous seat which stands for the spiritual imagination' (T.). See Malory xiii 4 for the empty seat at the Round Table, the letters on which came to read: 'This is the siege of sir Galahad the good knight.'

175. *misadvertence*: absentmindedness, inattention. Tennyson's coinage.

178. *If I lose myself, I save myself*: Matthew x 39: 'He that findeth his life shall lose it: and he that loseth his life for my sake shall find it.'

182–202. Malory xiii 7: 'Then anon they heard cracking and crying of thunder, that hem thought the place should all to-rive; in the midst of the blast entred a sunne beame more clear by seaven times then ever they saw day, and all they were alighted of the grace of the holy Ghost. Then began every knight to behold other, and either saw other by their seeming fairer then ever they saw afore, not for then there was no knight that might speake any word a great while; and so they looked every man on other as they had beene dombe. Then there entred into the hall the holy grale covered with white samite, but there was none that might see it, nor who beare it, and there was all the hall fulfilled with good odours, and every knight had such meate and drinke as hee best loved in this world; and when the holy grale had beene borne through the hall, then the holy vessel departed suddenly, that they wist not where it became.

Then had they breath to speak, and then the king yeelded thanks unto God of his grace that hee had sent them. "Certainely," said king Arthur, "wee ought greatly to thanke our Lord Jesu Christ for that hee hath shewed us this day at the reverence of this high feast of Pentecost." "Now," said sir Gawaine, "we have beene served this day of what meats and drinkes we thought on, but one thing beguiled us, we might not see the holy grale, it was so preciously covered, wherefore I will make heere avow that to morrow, without any longer abiding, I shall labour in quest of the sancgreall, that I shall hold me out a twelve moneths and a day, or more if neede bee, and never shall I returne againe unto the court til I have seene it more openly then it hath beene seene heere; and if I may not speed, I shall returne againe, as hee that may not bee against the will of our Lord Jesu Christ." When they of the round table heard sir Gawaine say so, they arose, the most part of them, and avowed the same. And anon, as king Arthur heard this, he was greatly displeased, for hee wist wel that they might not gainesay their avowes.'

192. *glory*: the circle of light represented as surrounding the head or the whole figure, of the Saviour, the Virgin, or one of the Saints.

202. *And Gawain sware, and louder than the rest*: Tennyson's addition. In Malory above, Gawain is simply the first to swear.

206–21. *for early that same day*: Tennyson's addition. In Malory Arthur is present at the Grail.

228. *dim rich city*: see also LE 842.

232–7. *And four great zones of sculpture*: 'The four zones represent human progress: the savage state of society; the state where man lords it over beast; the full development of man; the progress toward spiritual ideals' (H. T.).

240. *Northern Star*: the pole star, a constant.

248. *twelve great windows blazon Arthur's wars*: the twelve battles against the Saxons: see note to CA 517 (p. 310).

260–61. *wrapt/In unremorseful folds of rolling fire*: 'This line gives onomato-poeically the "unremorseful flames"' (T.).

263. *The golden dragon*: Arthur's emblem or motif; see note to CA 373 (p. 309).

275–6. *Woe is me, my knights . . . Had I been here, ye had not sworn the vow*: Malory xiii 7: 'And anon as king Arthur heard this, he was greatly displeased, for hee wist wel that they might not gainesay their avowes.'

287. *What go ye into the wilderness to see?*: Christ says of John the Baptist: 'What went ye out into the wilderness to see? A reed shaken with the wind?' (Matthew xi 7).

290. *Sir Arthur*: Galahad's addressing Arthur as knight shows him elevated by the Grail vision to spiritual equality with the king.

293–4. *for such/As thou art is the vision, not for these*: 'The king thought that most men ought to do the duty that lies closest to them, and that to few only is given the true spiritual enthusiasm. Those who have it not ought not to affect it' (T.).

300. *Taliessin*: greatest of the ancient Welsh bards.

312. *The strong White Horse*: emblem of the Saxons.

315–27. Malory xiii 7: '"Alas!" said king Arthur unto sir Gawaine, "yee have nigh slaine me with the vow and promise that yee have made; for through you yee have beereft mee of the fairest fellowship and the truest of knighthood that ever were seene together in any realme of the world. For when they shall depart from hence, I am sure that all shall never meete more in this world, for there shall many die in the quest, and so it forethinketh me a little; for I have loved them as well as my life, wherefore it shall grieve me right sore the seperation of this fellowship, for I have had an old custome to have them in my fellowship."'

328–37. As in Malory xiii 6.

343. *totter'd*: OED 2, of a building or a ship: battered and shaken, rendered ruinous and liable to fall.

350. *wyvern*: 'two-legged dragon. Old French *wivre*, viper' (T.).
griffin: imaginary or heraldic animal having head and wings of an eagle and the body and hindquarters of a lion.

353–7. Malory xiii 8: 'Then the queene departed into her chamber so that no man should perceive her great sorrows . . . and there was weeping of the rich and poore, and the king turned away, and might not speak for weeping.'

371–8. *Then every evil word*: suggested by an experience of Percivale's in Malory xiv 7.

387–90. 'The gratification of sensual appetite brings Percivale no content' (T., who comments on the ensuing episodes: 'Nor does wifely love and the love of the family; nor does wealth, which is worshipt by labour; nor does glory; nor does Fame').

427. *clomb*: climbed.

449. *she*: personification of glory.

452–3. *and like a flying star/Led on the gray-hair'd wisdom of the east*: 'The Magi' (T.).

462. *sacring*: 'consecration' (T.).

462–7. Malory xvii 20: 'And then the bishop made semblance as though he would have gone to the sakring of the masse; and then hee tooke a wapher which was made in the likenesse of bread, and at the lifting up there came a figure in the likenesse of a child, and the visage was as red and as bright as any fire, and smote himselfe in to that bread, so that they all saw that the bread was formed of a fleshly man.'

491–2. *Storm at the top, and when we gain'd it, storm/Round us and death*: 'It was a time of storm when men could imagine miracles, and so storm is emphasized' (T.).

493. *gloom'd*: made dark or sombre.

509. *Shoutings of all the sons of God*: Job xxxviii 7: 'When the morning stars sang together, and all the sons of God shouted for joy.'

526–7. *I saw the spiritual city and all her spires/And gateways in a glory like one pearl*: Revelation xxi 21: 'And the twelve gates were twelve pearls; every several gate was of one pearl.'

531–2. *the Holy Grail,/Which never eyes on earth again shall see*: Malory xvii 22: 'Sithen was there never man so hardy to say that he had seen the Sangreal.'

541. *These ancient books*: the Bible and other ancient chronicles.
teem: to be full, and OED 5, 'to cite or call to witness.'

547. *thorpe*: hamlet or village.

548. *martin*: house martin, bird of the swallow family.

554. *lyings-in*: being in childbed.

569. *eft*: newt.

570. *burdock*: coarse weedy plant.

570–71. *I was changed to wan/And meagre*: became pallid, sickly and weak.

575–605. Based on the temptation of Percivale in Malory xiv 9.

628. *earth*: den or burrow.

633. *pelican*: Malory xvi 6 has Bors experience such a bird.

642–3. *I have been the sluggard, and I ride apace,/For now there is a lion in the way*: Proverb xxvi 13: 'The slothful man saith, There is a lion in the way: a lion is in the streets.' Tennyson also makes Lancelot's heraldic device a lion: see GL 571, 1186, LE 659.

645. *Softly*: OED 3, 'with a slow, easy, or gentle pace or motion'.

646. *his former madness*: Malory xii 3–4, on Lancelot's madness and his cure by the Grail.

658. *lonest*: remotest, most lonely.

661–2. *a remnant that were left/Paynim amid their circles, and the stones/They pitch up straight to heaven*: 'The temples and upright stones of the Druidic religion' (T.).
Paynim: pagan.

667. 'The sun-worshippers that were said to dwell on Lyonnesse scoffed at Percivale' (T.).

679. *scud*: clouds in rapid movement.

681. *The seven clear stars of Arthur's Table Round*: 'The Great Bear' (T.).

691–2. 'It might have been a meteor' (T.).

715. *basilisks*: 'the fabulous crowned serpent whose look killed' (T.).
cockatrices: 'in heraldry, winged snakes' (T.). With head, wings and feet

353

of a cock, terminating in a serpent with a barbed tail.

716. *talbots*: 'heraldic dogs' (T.).

717. *raw*: exposed, unprotected by normal finish, figuratively suggesting the living state of Camelot.

720. *tithe*: a tenth; also, for soldiery, the killing of one in ten, decimation.

738–47. Based on Malory xvi 5 and Gawain's exploits elsewhere in Malory.

739. *communed*: held intimate spiritual intercourse with.

759. *like him of Cana in Holy Writ*: John ii 1–10.

784. *My madness came upon me as of old*: Malory xi 8, xii 5.

810. *Carbonek*: the legendary home of the Grail.

810–14. Malory xvii 14: 'So it befell upon a night at midnight hee arived afore a castle on the backe side, which was rich and faire, and there was a posterne that opened toward the sea, and was open without any keeping, save two lions kept the entrie, and the moone shined cleare.'

815–22. Malory xvii 14: 'Then he ranne to his armes, and armed him, and so hee went unto the gate and saw the two lions; then hee sat hands to his sword and drew it; then came there sudainly a dwarfe, that smote him upon the arme so sore that the sword fell out of his hand. Then hee heard a voice that said, "Oh man of evill faith and poore beliefe, wherefore beleevest thou more in thy harneis then in thy maker? for hee might more availe thee then thine armour, in whose service thou art set." Then said sir Launcelot, "Faire Father, Jesu Christ, I thank thee of thy great mercy that thou reprovest mee of my misdeede; now see I well that thou holdest mee for thy servant." Then tooke hee againe his sword, and put it upon his shield, and made a crosse on his forehead, and came to the lions, and they made semblant to doe him harme, notwithstanding he passed by them without hurt, and entred into the castle to the chiefe foretresse.'

827–8. 'My father was fond of quoting these lines for the beauty of the sound' (H. T.).

830–32. *Clear as a lark, high o'er me as a lark,/A sweet voice singing in the topmost tower/To the eastward*: '"The lark" in the tower toward the rising sun symbolizes Hope' (H. T.).

833–6. Malory xvii 15: 'Then he listned, and heard a voice which sung so sweetly, that it seemed none earthly thing, and him thought that the voice said, "Joy and honour be to the Father of heaven."'

838–48. Malory xvii 15: 'And with that he saw the chamber doore open, and there came out a great clearenesse, that the house was as bright as though all the torches of the world had beene there. So came hee to the chamber doore, and would have entred, and anon a voice said unto him, "Flee, sir Launcelot, and enter not, for thou oughtest not to doe it, and if thou enter thou shalt forethinke it." And hee withdrew him backe, and was right heavie in his mind. Then looked hee up in the midest of the chamber, and saw a table of silver, and the holy vessell covered with red samite, and many angels about it, whereof one of them held a candell of waxe burning, and the other held a crosse and the ornaments of the alter … Right so hee entred into the chamber, and came toward the table of silver; and when hee came nigh he felt a breath, that him thought was entermedled with fire, which smote him so sore in the visage, that him thought it all to-brent his visage, and therewith hee fell to the ground, and had no power to arise.'

840. *As from a seventimes-heated furnace*: Daniel iii 19: 'heat the furnace one seven times more than it was wont to be heated' (the story of Shadrach, Meschah and Abednego).

845. *Great angels, awful shapes, and wings and eyes*: Ezekiel x 12: 'And their whole body, and their backs, and their hands, and their wings, and the wheels, were full of eyes round about.'

855. *Hath Gawain fail'd in any quest of thine?*: cf. LE 711–13.

862. *I will be deafer than the blue-eyed cat*: Hallam Tennyson quotes the first chapter of Darwin's *Origin of Species*: 'Thus cats which are entirely white and have blue eyes are generally deaf; but it has lately been pointed out by Mr Tait that this is confined to the males.'

902. *hind*: farm servant, agricultural labourer.

908. *Until this earth he walks on seems not earth*: 'Arthur suggests that all the material universe may be but vision' (T.).

913–14. 'My father said (I think) about this passage: "There is something miraculous in man, and there is more in Christianity than some people think. It is enough to look on Christ as Divine and Ideal without defining more. They will not easily beat the character of Christ, that union of man and woman, strength and sweetness"' (H. T.).

Pelleas and Ettarre

Published December 1869 (dated 1870). Composed the same year. Origin in Malory iv 21–4.

3. *old Caerleon*: Arthur's alternative court to Camelot. Malory's Pelleas episode has no specific setting.

9–11. *the King/Had let proclaim a tournament – the prize/A golden circlet and a knightly sword*: Malory iv 20: 'And who that proved him the best knight should have a passing good sword and a serklet of gold, and the serklet the knight should give it to the fairest lady that was at those justes.'

12. *Full fain*: very eager.

19–20. *Riding at noon, a day or twain before,/Across the forest call'd of Dean, to find/Caerleon*: the setting and time of day are Tennyson's additions.

33–4. *the fern without/Burnt as a living fire of emeralds*: 'Seen as I lay in the New Forest' (T.).

48. *boles*: stems or trunks of trees.

61. *damsels-errant*: female equivalent of the knight-errant.

82–6. Suggested by Malory iv 21: '"My name is sir Pelleas, born in the Isles, and of many isles I am lord, and never have I loved lady nor damosell till now in an unhappie time."'

94. *And she was a great lady in her land*: Malory iv 20: 'He loveth a great lady in this countrey, and her name is Ettarde.'

144. *make*: build.

150–63. Malory iv 20: 'And this knight sir Pelleas was the best knight that was there, and there were five hundred knights, but there was never man that ever sir Pelleas met withal, but that he strooke him downe, or else from his horse. And every day of the three dayes he strooke down twentie knights, therfore they gave him the price.'

169–78. The episode with Guinevere is Tennyson's addition.

182–3. Malory iv 21: 'But she was so proud that she had scorn of him, and said that she would never love him, though he would die for her.'

186. *grizzlier than a bear*: more ferocious than a (grizzly) bear (*Ursus horribilis*, peculiar to the mountainous districts of western North America).

188. *papmeat*: soft or semi-liquid food for infants.

196. *hest*: bidding, command.

202–10. Malory iv 21: 'And so this knight promised the lady Ettarde to follow her into this countrey, and never to leave her till she loved him. And thus he is here the most part nigh her, and lodgeth by a priorie.'

211–28. Malory iv 21: 'And every weeke she sendeth knights to fight with him; and when he hath put them to the worst, then will he suffer them wilfully to take him prisoner, because he would have a sight of this lady.'

218. *A week beyond*: a week later.

227. *minion-knights*: knights behaving in a servile or slavish manner.

234. *donjon*: castle.

266. In Malory, Gawain is told of Pelleas and seeks him out; Pelleas is not being attacked, and simply tells Gawain of Ettarde's treatment. The details are Tennyson's; in Malory Pelleas says: 'When I am brought before her she rebuketh me in the foulest manner.'

290. *marr'd*: disfigured.

309. *lazar's rag*: rags of someone poor and afflicted with leprosy.

332–53. Malory iv 21–2: '"Well," said sir Gawaine, "all this shall I amend, and ye will doe as I shall devise. I wil have your horse and your armour, and so will I ride to her castle, and tell her that I have slaine you, and so shal I come within to her to cause her to cherish me, and then I shall doe my true part, that yee shall not faile to have her love." And therewithall sir Gawaine plight his troth unto sir Pelleas to be true and faithfull unto him. When they had plight their troth the one to the other, they changed horses and harneis.'

335. *leal*: loyal.

341. *From prime to vespers*: from sunrise to sunset.

342. *prowest*: 'noblest' (T.).

344. *lusty*: healthy.

355–81. Malory iv 22: 'And sir Gawaine departed, and came to the castle where as stood the pavilions of this lady without the gate; and so soone as Ettarde had espied sir Gawaine, she fled toward the castle. Then sir Gawaine spoke on high, and bad her abide, for he was not sir Pelleas. "I am another knight that hath slaine sir Pelleas." "Doe off your helme," said the lady Ettarde, "that I may behold your visage." And when she saw it was not sir Pelleas, she made him to alight, and led him unto her castle, and asked him faithfully whether he had slaine sir Pelleas. And he said, yea. And then sir Gawaine told her that his name was sir Gawaine, and of the court of king Arthur, and his sisters sonne. "Truely," said she, "that is great pittie, for hee was a passing good knight of his body, but of all men on live I hated him most, for I could never be quiet for him. And for that yee have slaine him, I shall bee your woman, and doe any thing that may please you." So shee made sir Gawaine good cheere.'

361. *Avaunt*: the order to be off.

362. *vizor*: upper portion of the front part of the helmet.

387. *lay*: short lyric or narrative poem intended to be sung.

411. *postern portal*: gate at the back.

419–26. Malory iv 22: 'And then it was in the moneth of May, that she and sir Gawaine went out of the castle and supped in a pavilion, and there was a bed made, and there sir Gawaine and the lady Ettard went to bed together, and in another pavilion she layed her damosels, and in the third pavilion shee laid part of her knights; for then she had no dread nor feare of sir Pelleas. And there sir Gawaine lay with her, doing his pleasure in that pavilion two daies and two nights, against the faithfull promise that he made to sir Pelleas. And on the third day in the morning early sir Pelleas armed him, for he had not slept sith that sir Gawaine departed from him; for sir Gawaine had promised him by the faith of his body to come unto him to his pavilion by the priory within the space of a day and a night. Then sir Pelleas mounted on horsebacke, and came to the pavilions that stood without the castle, and found in the first pavilion three knights in their beds, and three squires lying at their feete. Then went he to the second pavilion, and found foure gentlewomen lying in foure beds. And then hee went to the third pavilion, and found sir Gawaine lying in a bed with his lady Ettard, and either clipping other in armes.'

421. *lurdane*: 'from Old French *lourdin*, heavy' (T.). Worthless, ill-bred, lazy.

427–46. Malory iv 22: 'And when he saw that, his heart almost brast for sorrow, and said, "Alas! that ever a knight should bee found so false." And then he tooke his horse, and might no longer abide for sorrow. And when he had ridden nigh halfe a mile, he turned againe and thought to sley them both, and when he saw them both lye so fast sleeping, unneth hee might hold him on horsebacke for sorrow, and said thus to himselfe, "Though this knight be never so false, I will not sley him sleeping, for I will never destroy the high order of knighthood." And therewith hee departed againe, and left them sleeping. And or hee had ridden halfe a mile he returned againe, and thought then to sley them both, making the greatest sorrow that any man might make. And when he cam to the pavilions he tied his horse to a tree, and pulled out his sword naked in his hand, and went straight to them wher as they lay together, and yet he thought that it were great shame for him to sley them sleeping, and laid the naked sword overthwart both their throates, and then hee tooke his horse, and rod foorth his way.'

446. *And the sword of the tourney across her throat*: 'The line gives the quiver of the sword across their throats' (T.).

tourney: tournament.

476. *rowel*: wheel or disk at the end of a spur.

478–82. Malory iv 22: 'And then sir Gawaine and the lady Ettard wakned out of their sleepe, and found the naked sword overthwart both their throates. Then she knew well that it was sir Pelleas sword. "Alas!" said she to sir Gawaine, "ye have betraied me and sir Pelleas also, for yee told me that yee have slaine him, and now I know well it is not so, he is on live. And if sir Pelleas had beene as uncourteous to you as you have beene to him, ye had beene a dead knight, but ye have deceived me and betraied me falsly, that all ladies and damosels may beware by you and me."'

482. *he that tells the tale*: Malory.

482–6. Malory iv 22, where the Lady of the Lake 'cast such an enchantment upon her (Ettarre), that shee loved him out of measure, that well nigh shee was out of her mind. "Oh, Lord Jesus," said the lady Ettard, "how is it befallen me that I now love him which I before most hated of all men living?" "This is the rightwise (righteous) judgement of God," said the damosell of the lake.' Pelleas then spurns Ettarre: 'So the lady Ettard died for sorrow, and the damosell of the lake rejoyced sir Pelleas, and loved together during their lives.' Tennyson completely changes this ending, and continues the tale of the bitter and violent Sir Pelleas in 'The Last Tournament'.

491–527. The episode concerning Percivale is Tennyson's addition.

508. *the morning star/Reel'd in the smoke, brake into flame, and fell*: Revelation viii 10: 'and there fell a great star from heaven burning as it were a lamp.'

558. *blaze*: publish, make known.

566. *disedge*: to blunt, dull.

585. *unfrowardly*: without perversity. Tennyson's coinage.

The Last Tournament

Published in *Contemporary Review*, December 1871, then 1872. Being written November 1870, completed 21 May 1871. Essentially original, with a few borrowings from Malory.

1–2. *Dagonet, the fool, whom Gawain in his mood/Had made mock-knight of Arthur's Table Round*: No equivalent in Malory. In Malory x 12 Arthur himself knighted Dagonet.

6. *carcanet*: ornamental collar or necklace.

25. *Nestling*: based on the story of Nesting, a legend of King Alfred, told in Sharon Turner's *History*.

37. *Those diamonds that I rescued from the tarn*: see LE 34–55.

43. *Slid from my hands*: cf. LE 1225–7: 'Saying which she seized,/And, thro' the casement standing wide for heat,/Flung them.'

66. *Yet strangers to the tongue*: 'rough' (T.).
blunt stump: 'where the hand had been cut off and the stump had been pitched' (T.). Cf. PE 330–31: 'But I will slice him handless by the wrist,/And let my lady sear the stump for him.'

69. *table-knight*: derogatory for knight of the Round Table, suggesting membership only for bed and board.

70. *the Red Knight*: 'Pelleas' (T.).

89. *seneschal*: steward.

90. *curiously*: carefully.

98. *Make their last head like Satan in the North*: Isaiah xiv 13.

115–16. *oft I seem as he/Of whom was written, 'A sound is in his ears'*: Job xv 20–21: 'The wicked man travaileth with pain all his days, and the number of years is hidden to the oppressor. A dreadful sound is in his ears: in prosperity the destroyer shall come upon him.'

125. *Reel back into the beast*: cf. PA 25–6: 'and all my realm/Reels back into the beast'.

132–3. *'Where is he who knows?/From the great deep to the great deep he goes'*: quotation of the last two lines of Merlin's song, CA 409–10. The last line of it is repeated, PA 445.

143. *lists*: place or scene of combat or contest.

144. *double-dragon'd chair*: described LE 435–6.

150. *vail'd*: 'drooped' (T.). Hallam Tennyson compares *Hamlet* I ii 70–71: 'Do not ever with thy vailèd lids/Seek for thy noble father in the dust.'

153. 'The autumn of the Round Table' (T.).

166. *Modred, a narrow face*: cf. G 62: 'Modred's narrow foxy face'.

173–4. *and on shield/A spear, a harp, a bugle*: 'He was a harper and hunter' (T.). Malory viii 3: Tristram 'learned to be an harper passing all other, that there was none such called in no countrey. And so in harping and on instruments of musike'hee applied him in his youth for to learne, and after as hee growed in his might and strength, he laboured ever in hunting and hawking.'

177. *of the Woods*: the title is Tennyson's addition.

178–9. *Whom Lancelot knew, had held sometime with pain/His own against him*: the incident occurs in Malory ix 33.

182. *dinted*: impressed or driven in with force.

192. *Art thou the purest, brother?*: referring to ll. 49–50: 'Perchance – who knows? – the purest of thy knights/May win them for the purest of my maids.'

200. *belike*: probably, perhaps.

201. *trow*: trust, have confidence in.

202. *Right arm of Arthur in the battlefield*: cf. G 426 where Arthur himself speaks of Lancelot as 'my right arm'.

205–12. 'It was the law to give the prize to some lady on the field, but the laws are broken, and Tristram the courteous has lost his courtesy, for the great sin of Lancelot was sapping the Round Table' (T.).

206. *Caracole*: horseman's execution of a half-turn or wheel to right or left.

214. *pettish*: peevish, petulant.

220. *The snowdrop only*: 'Because they were dressed in white' (T.).

226. *for he that tells the tale*: Tennyson, because of the following simile.

227–31. 'Seen by me at Mürren in Switzerland' (T.).

234. *kingcup*: buttercup.

250. *catch*: a round.

257. *liefer*: rather.

265. *Her daintier namesake down in Brittany*: 'Isolt of the white hands' (T.).

270. *shell*: 'husk' (T.).

305. *smuttier than blasted grain*: blacker than blighted or diseased grain. Smut is a blackening disease of cereals.

309. *A naked aught*: naught, a worthless thing.

322. *a Paynim harper*: 'Orpheus' (T.).

332–3. *Dost thou know the star/We call the harp of Arthur up in heaven?* 'Lyra' (T.). See GL 1281.

343. *The black king's highway*: Pluto's, the god of the nether world.

345. *the great lake of fire*: Revelation xix 20.

355–6. *Conceits himself as God that he can make/Figs out of thistles*: Matthew vii 16: 'Do men gather grapes of thorns, or figs of thistles?'

357. *burning spurge*: 'The juice of the common spurge' (T.). The acrid juice of this plant is purgative.

366. *outer eye*: 'the hunter's eye' (T.).

371. *slot*: 'trail' (T.).
    fewmets: 'droppings' (T.).

375. *lodge*: hunter's lodge.

385. *bode*: waited.

392. *tonguesters*: Tennyson's coinage for talkative persons, gossips.

399. *Who served him well with those white hands of hers*: nursed him back to health.

421. *plash*: splash.
    sallowy: having willows.

423. *machicolated*: machicolation: an opening between the corbels which support a projecting parapet, or in the vault of a portal, through which combustibles, molten lead, stones. etc., were dropped on the heads of the assailants.

431. *and on the boughs a shield/Showing a shower of blood in a field noir*: to have a shield hung up is a knightly disgrace.
    field noir: black background.

428–35. Malory vii 15: 'And when they came neare the siege, sir Beaumains espied upon great trees, as hee rode, how there hung goodly armed knights by the neckes, and their shields about their neckes with their swords, and gilted spurres upon their heeles, and so there hung shamefully nigh forty knights with rich armes.' Later in the chapter is the horn and a knight in blood red armour.

443–53. Modelled on a speech of the Red Knight to Gareth, Malory vii 17: '"Sir, I loved once a lady, a faire damosell, and shee had her brother slaine, and shee said it was sir Launcelot du Lake, or sir Gawaine, and shee prayed mee that, as I loved her heartily, that I would make her a promise by the faith of my knighthood, for to labour dayly in armes unto the time that I had met with one of them, and all that I might overcome, that I should put them to a villainous death; and this is the cause that I have put all these good knights to death, and so I ensured her to doe all this villanie unto king Arthurs knights, and that I should take vengance upon al his knights." '

445. *clipt*: eradicated.

455. *the name*: 'Pelleas' (T.).

456. *darkling*: obscurely.

461–6. 'As I have heard and seen the sea on the shore of Mablethorpe' (T.).

479. *Alioth and Alcor*: 'two stars in the Great Bear' (T.).

479–81. *Red-pulsing up . . . as the water Moab saw*: 2 Kings iii 22: 'And the sun shone upon the water, and the Moabites saw the water on the other side as red as blood.'

485. *pain was lord*: cf. l. 239.

495. *she*: 'his wife' (T.).

501. *roky*: 'misty' (T.).
belling: bellowing.

509. *the spiring stone that scaled about her tower*: 'Winding stone staircase' (T.).

553. *Sailing from Ireland*: 'Tristram had told his uncle Mark of the beauty of Isolt, when he saw her in Ireland, so Mark demanded her hand in marriage, which he obtained. Then Mark sent Tristram to fetch her as in my *Idylls* Arthur sent Lancelot for Guinevere' (T.).

555. *dole*: allotment, portion.

570. *leading-strings*: strings with which children used to be guided and supported when learning to walk, hence 'to sin in leading strings' means sin as an infant.

590. *unguent*: ointment.

611. *levin-brand*: lightning bolt, from *Faerie Queene* VII vi 30.

620. *leman*: paramour, unlawful lover or mistress.

627. *swineherd's malkin in the mast*: 'Slut among the beech nuts' (T.).
malkin: an untidy female, especially a servant or country wench.

658. *Man, is he man at all?*: cf. Vivien's words, MV 779: 'Man! is he man at all'.

664. *that weird legend of his birth*: see CA 359–410, GL 487–96.

665. *Merlin's mystic babble about his end*: see CA 410, PA 445.

668. *Michaël trampling Satan*: Revelation xii 7.

672. *Believed himself a greater than himself*: 'When the man had an ideal before him' (T.).

692–3. *The ptarmigan that whitens ere his hour/Woos his own end*: 'Seen by me in the Museum at Christiania in Norway' (T.).
ptarmigan: bird of the grouse family inhabiting high altitudes.

695. *yaffingale*: 'old word, and still provincial for the green wood-pecker (so called from its laughter). In Sussex "yaffel" ' (T.).

696. *we love but while we may*: echoing ll. 275, 281.

703. *closes*: encloses, contains.

707. *saw*: wise saying.

711. *apple*: Adam's apple.

723. *craven shifts*: cowardly tricks.

725–32. 'Like an old Gaelic song – the two stars symbolic of the two Isolts' (T.).

738–9. *but the red fruit/Grown on a magic oak-tree in mid-heaven*: see ll. 10–28.

748. *'Mark's way,' said Mark, and clove him thro' the brain*: Malory xx 6: '"That is hard to doe," said sir Launcelot, "for by sir Tristram I may have a warning; for when, by meanes of the treatise, sir Tristram brought againe La beale Isoud unto king Marke from Joyous-gard, looke what fell on the end, how shamefully that false traitour king Marke slew that noble knight as he sat harping before his lady La beale Isoud, with a sharpe grounded glaive thrust him behind to the heart."'

Guinevere

Published 1859. Begun 9 July, 1857 and completed by 15 March 1858. Largely original, with setting only from Malory xxi 7.

1–2 *Queen Guinevere had fled the court, and sat/There in the holy house at Almesbury*: Malory xxi 7: 'And when queene Guenever understood that her lord king Arthur was slaine, and all the noble knights, sir Modred and all the remnant, then shee stole away and five ladies with her; and so shee went to Almesbury, and there shee let make her selfe a nunne and ware white cloathes and blacke. And great pennance shee tooke as ever did sinfull lady in this land; and never creature could make her merry, but lived in fastings, prayers, and almes deedes, that all manner of people mervailed how vertuously shee was changed. Now leave wee queene Guenever in Almesbury, that was a nunne in white cloathes and blacke; and there shee was abbesse and ruler, as reason would.'

10. *subtle beast*: Genesis iii 1: 'Now the serpent was more subtil than any beast of the field which the Lord God had made.'

11. *couchant*: heraldic term for lying with the body resting on the legs and with head lifted up.

15. *Lords of the White Horse*: the Saxons.

16. *Hengist*: Saxon leader.

20. *Were sharpen'd by strong hate for Lancelot*: as in Malory.

21–52. Tennyson's addition. There is no such incident in Malory or elsewhere.

23. *a-maying*: celebrating May Day.

27–28. *who sat betwixt her best/Enid, and lissome Vivien*: Tennyson runs together previously separate Arthurian traditions in juxtaposing Enid (from the Welsh *Mabinogion*) and Vivien (who as Nimue stems from Malory).

32. *colewort*: cabbage.

41. *halt*: lame.

45. *holp*: helped.

55–6. *Then shudder'd, as the village wife who cries/'I shudder, some one steps across my grave'*: based on an item in Francis Grose's *A Provincial Glossary*: 'A person being suddenly taken with a shivering, is a sign that someone has just then walked over the spot of their future grave.'

61. *front*: face.

62. *Modred's narrow foxy face*: cf. LT 166: 'Modred, a narrow face'.

91–3. As in Malory.

97–8. *Vivien, lurking, heard./She told Sir Modred*: line inserted in 1890 as Tennyson's last link in his pattern.

102–24. Based on Malory xx 1–4.

125. *Love-loyal to the least wish of the Queen*: see LE 89 for the identical formula.

127. *weald*: wooded district or open country.

132. *the Raven*: emblem of the Saxons, and a symbol of destruction.

134. *Heathen of the Northern Sea*: Saxons.

147. *housel*: 'Anglo-Saxon *husel*, the Eucharist' (T.).

157. *brook'd*: tolerated.

163. *list*: desire.

166–77. Based on Matthew xxv 1–13, the parable of the virgins.

223. *prate*: profitless or irrelevant talk.

262–4. *for every knight/Had whatsoever meat he longed for served/By hands unseen*: compare the appearance of the Grail in Camelot, Malory xiii 7: 'and there was all the hall fulfilled with great odours, and every knight had such meat and drink as he best loved in this world'.

265–7. *Down in the cellars merry bloated things/Shoulder'd the spigot, straddling on the butts/While the wine ran*: suggested by a detail in T. Crofton Croker's *Fairy Legends*: 'and on advancing perceived a little figure, about six inches in height, seated astride upon the pipe of the oldest port in the place, and bearing a spigot upon his shoulder'.

spigot: 'bung' (T.).

270. *ill*: evil.

277. *Ev'n in the presence of an enemy's fleet*: one of a bard's responsibilities.

286. *Gorloïs*: see CA 72 and note (p. 307).

289. *Bude and Bos*: 'north of Tintagil' (T.).

295–6. *And that his grave should be a mystery/From all men, like his birth*: ambiguity about Arthur's precise burial occurs in Malory xxi 6.

311. *gadding*: wandering.

319. *come next*: by next year.

395. *The Dragon of the great Pendragonship*: 'The headship of the tribes who had confederated against the Lords of the White Horse. "Pendragon" not a dactyl as some make it, but Pén-drágon' (T.).

419–20. *one/I honour'd*: Leodogran, Guinevere's father.

424. *craft*: cunning.

429. *twelve great battles*: see especially LE 284–307 and note (p. 343).

431. *From waging bitter war with him*: as in Malory.

437. *Clave*: clung to.

446. *Howbeit I know, if ancient prophecies/Have err'd not, that I march to meet my doom*: the ancient prophecies are Merlin's, CA 306, 410.

487. *ensample*: pattern or model of conduct.

491. *scathe*: hurt, harm.

495. *wonted*: accustomed.

500. *Usk*: Caerleon upon Usk.

534–5. *that fierce law,/The doom of treason and the flaming death*: In Malory, Arthur condemned Guinevere to be burnt to death, and she was rescued by Lancelot.

568. *that great battle in the west*: the battle of Camlan.

569–70. *the man they call//My sister's son – no kin of mine*: Modred, who indeed in Malory is Arthur's own son.

591–2. *so she did not see the face,/Which then was as an angel's*: Acts vi 15, of Stephen: 'And all that sat in the council, looking stedfastly on him, saw his face as it had been the face of an angel.'

628. *fume*: a fit of anger.

657. *vail*: lower.

670–80. Expansion of Malory: see opening note to this idyll.

679. *haler*: more wholesome.

The Passing of Arthur

Published December 1869 (dated 1870). Tennyson created it around his *Morte d'Arthur* (1842), which forms ll. 170–440 of this later poem. Based on Malory xxi 4–5.

1−3. *That story which the bold Sir Bedivere . . . Told*: Malory xxi 6: 'For this tale sir Bedivere, knight of the round table, made it plainly to be written.'

6−28. Tennyson's addition.

14. *As if some lesser god had made the world*: 'Cf. the demiurge of Plato, and the gnostic belief that lesser Powers created the world' (T.).

26. *Reels back into the beast*: cf. LT 125: 'Reel back into the beast.'

27. *My God, thou hast forgotten me in my death*: Matthew xxvii 46: 'My God, my God, why hast thou forsaken me?'

30−31. *There came on Arthur sleeping, Gawain kill'd/In Lancelot's war, the ghost of Gawain blown*: Malory has Gawain's death in the battle between Lancelot and the king. Malory xxi 4 has the ghost of Gawain warn Arthur not to fight that day, but battle commences when a knight treads on an adder.

36. *And I am blown along a wandering wind*: Tennyson compares Aeneid vi 740−41, on the fate of the dead: '*aliae panduntur inanes/suspensae ad ventos*' ('Some are hung stretched out to the empty winds').

52. *Elves, and the harmless glamour of the field*: 'The legends which cluster round the king's name' (T.).

57. *for the ghost is as the man*: 'the spirit' (T.).

67−9. *than when we strove in youth,/And brake the petty kings, and fought with Rome,/Or thrust the heathen from the Roman wall*: referring to CA 95−120, 503−12.

81. *sunset bound*: due west, where the sun sinks over the horizon.

82−3. *A land of old upheaven from the abyss/By fire, to sink into the abyss again*: both tradition and geology. The rocks of Cornwall are largely igneous.

84. *Where fragments of forgotten peoples dwelt*: 'perhaps old Celts' (T.).

91. *Burn'd at his lowest in the rolling year*: 'The winter solstice' (T.).

93−4. *Nor ever yet had Arthur fought a fight/Like this last, dim, weird battle of the west*: 'A Vision of Death' (T.).

114. *Oaths, insult, filth, and monstrous blasphemies*: Tennyson compares Revelation xvi 21: 'and men blasphemed God', after the battle of Armageddon. 'This grim battle in the mist contrasts with Arthur's glorious battle in *The Coming of Arthur*, fought on a bright day when "he saw the smallest rock far on the faintest hill"' (T.). The landscape and the mist are additions to Malory.

164−9. Malory xxi 4: 'Then king Arthur gate his speare in both his hands, and ranne toward sir Mordred, crying, "Traitour, now is thy death day come!" And when sir Mordred heard king Arthur, hee ran unto him with his sword drawen in his hand, and there king Arthur smote sir Modred under the shield with a foine of his speare throughout the body more than a fadom. And when sir Mordred felt that hee had his death wound, he thrust himselfe with all the might that hee had up to the end of king Arthurs speare, and right so he smote his father Arthur with his sword that hee held in both his hands on the side of the head, that the sword perced the helmet and the brain-pan. And therwith sir Mordred fel downe starke dead to the earth.'

170. *So all day long the noise of battle roll'd*: Where the *Morte d'Arthur* of 1842 takes up, and continues to l. 440. Tennyson's line is one of the 'Homeric echoes' mentioned in the frame to the *Morte* (*The Epic* 39): *Iliad* vi, l, xvii 384. Cf. Tennyson's translation, 'Achilles' 9: 'All day the men contend in grievous war.'

173. *Lyonnesse*: 'the country of legend that lay between Cornwall and the Scilly Islands' (T.).

174–81. Malory xxi 4: 'And the noble king Arthur fell in a sowne to the earth, and there hee sowned oftentimes. And sir Lucan and sir Bedivere oftentimes heaved him up, and so weakly they lad him betweene them both unto a little chappell not farre from the sea side.'

182–5. Malory xx 9: 'For I have now lost the fairest fellowship of noble knights that ever held christian king together.'
unsolders: dissolves.

191. *Tho' Merlin sware that I should come again*: Malory xxi 7: 'Some men yet say in many parts of England that king Arthur is not dead, but had by the will of our Lord Jesu Christ into another place; and men say that hee will come againe.'

195–201. Malory i 25: 'So they rode til they came to a lake, which was a faire water and a broade, and in the middes of the lake king Arthur was ware of an arme clothed in white samite, that held a faire sword in the hand.'

204–12. Malory xxi 5 (subsequent quotations from Malory, unless noted otherwise, run on consecutively without omissions): '"Therefore take thou Excalibur my good sword, and goe with it unto yonder water side, and, when thou commest there, I charge thee throw my sword into that water, and come againe and tell me what thou shalt see there." "My lord," said sir Bedivere, "your commande shall be done, and lightly bring you word againe."'

211. *hest*: command.

213–33. Malory: 'And so sir Bedivere departed; and by the way he beheld that noble sword where the pummell and the haft were all of precious stones, and then hee said to himselfe, "If I throw this rich sword into the water, thereof shall never come good, but harme and losse." And then sir Bedivere hid Excalibur under a tree, and as soone as hee might he came againe unto king Arthur, and said hee had beene at the water, and had throwen the sword into the water.'

218. *juts*: projections.

225. *jacinth-work*: inlaid with blue or reddish gems.

228. *This way and that dividing the swift mind*: Tennyson compares *Aeneid* iv 285: '*atque animum nunc huc celerem, nunc dividit illuc*' ('And now hither, now thither, he swiftly throws his mind').

234-49. Malory: '"What sawest thou there?" said the king. "Sir," said he, "I saw nothing but waves and wind." "That is untruely said of thee," said king Arthur, "therefore goe thou lightly and doe my command, as thou art to mee lefe and deere; spare not, but throw it in."'

250-80. Malory: 'Then sir Bedivere returned againe, and tooke the sword in his hand; and then him thought it sinne and shame to throw away that noble sword. And so eft (again) hee hid the sword, and returned againe and told to the king that hee had beene at the water and done his command.'

254. *chased*: ornamented with embossed work, engraved in relief.

272. *lonely maiden*: the friendly sorceress of Malory i 25 (out of the sequence): '"That is the lady of the lake," said Merlin, "and within that lake is a roch, and therein is as faire a place as any is on earth, and richly beseene."'

273-4. *Nine years she wrought it, sitting in the deeps/Upon the hidden bases of the hills*: Cf. Pope's *Iliad* xviii 468-72, where Vulcan is about to make the shield of Achilles: 'Chains, bracelets, pendants, all their toys I wrought./Nine years kept secret in the dark abode,/Secure I lay concealed from man and God./Deep in a caverned rock my days were led;/The rushing ocean murmured o'er my head.'

278. *conceit*: fancy.

281-300. Malory: '"What saw yee there?" said the king. "Sir," said hee, "I saw nothing but the water wap and waves waune." "Ah, traitour untrue!" said king Arthur, "now hast thou betraied me two times. Who would have wend that thou that hast beene unto me so selfe and deere, and thou art named a noble knight, and wouldest betray mee for the rich sword? But now goe againe lightly, for thy long tarying putteth me in great jeopardie of my life, for I have taken cold; and but if thou doe as I commaund thee, and if ever I may see thee, I shall sley thee with my owne hands, for thou wouldst for my rich sword see me dead."'

296. *Valuing the giddy pleasure of the eyes*: cf. Horace, *Epistles* II i 188: '*oculos et gaudia vana*'.

301-34. Malory: 'Then sir Bedivere departed, and went to the sword, and lightly tooke it up, and went to the waters side; and there hee bound the girdell about the hilts, and then hee threw the sword into the water as farre as hee might; and there came an arme and an hand above the water, and met it and caught it, and so shooke it thrise and brandished. And then the hand vanished away with the sword in the water. So sir

Bedivere came againe to the king, and told him what he had seene. "Alas!" said the king, "helpe me from hence, for I dread me I have taried over long."'

306. *And flashing round and round, and whirl'd in an arch*: 'The extra syllable gives the rush of the sword as it is whirled in a parabolic curve' (T.).

307. *streamer*: the Aurora Borealis.

323. *Not tho' I live three lives of mortal men*: Tennyson compares *Odyssey* iii 245: 'For thrice, men say, has he been King for a generation of men.'

335–71. Malory: 'Then sir Bedivere took king Arthur upon his backe, and so went with him to the waters side. And when they were at the waters side, even fast by the banke hoved a little barge with many faire ladies in it, and among them all was a queene, and all they had blacke hoods, and they wept and shriked when they saw king Arthur.'

351. *Larger than human: humano maior*, like the ghost of Romulus in Ovid, *Fasti* ii 503.

366–7. *and from them rose/A cry that shiver'd to the tingling stars*: cf. *Aeneid* ii 387: '*at domus interior gemitu miseroque tumultu/miscetur penitusque cavae plangoribus aedes/femineis ululant: ferit aurea sidera clamor*' ('The echoing halls resounded through and through with the keening of women, whose wails and shrieks beat at the golden stars').

372–93. Malory: '"Now put mee into the barge," said the king; and so hee did softly; and there received him three queenes with great mourning, and so these three queenes set them downe, and in one of their laps king Arthur laide his head. And then that queene said, "Ah! deer brother, why have ye taried so long from me? Alas! this wound on your head hath taken over much cold."'

373–4. *There those three Queens/Put forth their hands, and took the King, and wept*: Malory xxi 6(out of the sequence): 'But thus was hee led away in a barge, wherein were three queenes; that one was king Arthurs sister Morgan le Fay; the other was the queene of Northgalis; and the third was the queene of the wast lands.'

383. *greaves and cuisses*: armour for shin and thigh.

394–406. Malory: 'And so then they rowed from the land, and sir Bedivere beheld al those ladies goe from him; then sir Bedivere cried, "Ah! my lord Arthur, what shall become of mee now ye goe from me, and leave me here alone among mine enemies?"'

402–3. *But now the whole Round Table is dissolved/Which was an image of the mighty world*: Malory xiv 2 (out of the sequence): 'Also Merlin made the round table in token of the roundnesse of the world; for by the round table is the world signified by right.'

407–32. Malory: '"Comfort thy selfe," said king Arthur, "and do as well as thou maiest, for in mee is no trust for to trust in; for I wil into the vale of

Avilion for to heale me of my greivous wound; and if thou never heere more of mee, pray for my soule."'

410. *Lest one good custom should corrupt the world*: 'e.g. chivalry, by formalism of habit or by any other means' (T.).

423. *Bound by gold chains about the feet of God*: a commonplace found variously in Homer, Plato, Chaucer, Spenser, Milton – though none exactly parallels Tennyson's use.

427. *To the island-valley of Avilion*: 'From which he will some day return – the Isle of the Blest' (T.).

428–31. Tennyson compares *Odyssey* iv 566ff., and Lucretius iii 18ff.

430. *Deep-meadow'd*: Tennyson compares Pindar, *Pythian Odes* x 23, and *Iliad* ix 151.

431. *bowery hollows crown'd with summer sea*: Tennyson compares *Odyssey* x 195: 'the island, about which is set as a crown the boundless deep'.

433–40. Malory: 'But evermore the queenes and the ladies wept and shriked that it was pittie for to heare them. And as soone as sir Bedivere had lost the sight of the barge, hee wept and wailed, and so tooke the forrest; and so he went all the night.'

438. *Revolving*: *Paradise Lost* iv 31: 'much revolving', deriving from *Aeneid* i 305: '*per noctem plurima volvens*'.

445. '*From the great deep to the great deep he goes*': 'Merlin's song when he was born' (T.). See CA 410.

453–6. Referring to CA 275–8.

457. *Then from the dawn*: 'From (the dawn) the East, whence have sprung all the great religions of the world. A triumph of welcome is given to him who has proved himself "more than conqueror"' (T.).

468. *From less to less and vanish into light*: 'The purpose of the individual man may fail for a time, but his work cannot die' (T.). Tennyson compares Malory xxi 7: 'Some men yet say in many parts of England that king Arthur is not dead, but had by the will of our Lord Jesu Christ into another place; and men say that hee will come againe, and hee shall winne the holy crosse.' Tennyson adds: 'And cf. what Arthur says in Layamon's *Brut*, 28619, Madden's edition iii 144: "And seothe ich cumen wulle/to mine kineriche,/and wunien mid Brutten,/mid muchelere wunne." (And afterwards I will come (again) to my kingdom, and dwell with the Britons with much joy.)'

To the Queen

Published 1873. Tennyson had 'just written' it, 25 December 1872.

3. *that rememberable day*: 'When the Queen and the Prince of Wales went to the thanksgiving at St Paul's (after the Prince's dangerous illness) in Feb. 1872' (T.).

12–13. *Thunderless lightnings striking under sea*: communication by submarine cable, telegraph.

14–17. *And that true North, whereof we lately heard/A strain to shame us 'keep you to yourselves;/So loyal is too costly: friends – your love/Is but a burthen: loose the bond, and go.'* 'Canada. A leading London journal had written advocating that Canada should sever her connection with Great Britain, as she was "too costly": hence these lines' (T.). Referring to *The Times*.

20. *Hougoumont*: 'Waterloo' (T.).

35. *For one to whom I made it o'er his grave*: the Prince Consort, see Dedication.

38. *Ideal manhood closed in real man*: '...having this vision of Arthur, my father thought that perhaps he had not made the real humanity of the King sufficiently clear in his epilogue, so he inserted in 1891 (this line) as his last correction' (H. T.).

41. *cairn*: a pyramid of rough stones, raised as a memorial.
   cromlech: prehistoric structure of large flat unhewn stone resting horizontally on three or more stones set upright, usually marking a burial.

41–2. *or him/Of Geoffrey's book*: 'Geoffrey of Monmouth's' (T.).
   Malleor's: 'Malory's name is given as Maleorye, Maleore, and Malleor' (T.).

43–4. *a time/That hover'd between war and wantonness*: When Malory was writing *Morte d'Arthur* England was in the throes of the Wars of the Roses and the final break-up of medieval chivalry.

56. *Or Art with poisonous honey stol'n from France*: art for art's sake.

65. *that battle in the West*: Arthur's last.